Work in Non-Market and Transitional Societies

SUNY SERIES IN THE ANTHROPOLOGY OF WORK
JUNE NASH, EDITOR

Edited by HERBERT APPLEBAUM

Work in Non-Market and Transitional Societies

State University of New York Press
ALBANY

Dedicated to Hymie and Rose Applebaum,
My father and mother

Published by State University of New York Press, Albany.
© 1984 State University of New York. All rights reserved. Printed in the
United States of America. No part of this book may be used or reproduced
in any manner whatsoever without written permission except in the case of
brief quotations embodied in critical articles and reviews. For information,
address State University of New York Press, State University Plaza, Albany,
N.Y., 12246.

Library of Congress Cataloging in Publication Data

Main entry under title:
Work in non-market and transitional societies.
   (SUNY series in the anthropology of work)
   Bibliography: p.
   1. Work—Social aspects—Addresses, essays, lectures. 2. Ethnology—Ad-
dresses, essays, lectures. I. Applebaum, Herbert A. II. Series.
HD6955.W666   1984   306'.36   83–4970
ISBN 0–87395–774–1
ISBN 0–87395–775–X (pbk.)
10 9 8 7 6 5 4 3 2 1

Contents

v

Preface

When I was a youth growing up in a Jewish neighborhood in Brooklyn, my father constantly told me, "Get a trade, then you'll always be able to make a living." My father was a man for whom work was the source of all valued things in life. To him it was like a religion. It gave moral value to one's life. Through work one became involved with the gifts of nature, transforming God's offerings into human sustenance and beautiful objects for them to admire and enjoy.

But my father was a topsy-turvy maverick in the Jewish community of Brownsville, Brooklyn, because, while the Jewish ethos stressed business and mental labor, his own prestige system focused on physical and manual labor. He was also out of step with the society in which he lived, the capitalist America where most people worked for wages. My father was a great believer in self-labor, working for oneself and enjoying the fruits of one's own work. He never quite achieved this but he came close. He was a milkman, with control over his own time, and independence and autonomy in the way he served his route and organized his work. He enjoyed the comradeship with fellow milk drivers he saw each day at the "barn."* He took pleasure in the face-to-face contact he had with his customers. He was fond of his horse who pulled his wagon each day and "knew" the houses my father served well enough to move and stop at each house without my father having to re-enter the wagon.

Why am I introducing a book on anthropology with this brief autobiographical note? This background reveals my orientation in

* My father drove a horse and wagon between 1920 and 1946. In the early days the horses were kept in a barn and each driver hitched up his own horse. Even after the company switched to trucks in 1946, the men still called the garage, and the factory dock where they loaded the milk, the "barn."

this book. My perspective on the study of work is humanistic and expressive, in the tradition of anthropology, which sees work as an intrinsic aspect of what it means to be human. Through work and language humans became part of larger social groups, conscious of themselves as total beings and a part of nature in a relationship of mutuality and reciprocity. Work and its organization is the principle force in the building of civilizations; without its efficient use no society or culture can have any future. I do not believe in a future society in which we shall all do nothing; rather, I hope for a future in which we shall be busily engaged in work that satisfies and fulfills our human capacities.

This book will present the reader with a view of how work is carried on by men and women in different kinds of societies and cultures. I will provide guidelines for understanding the different value systems that underlie the different ways of working, and I will discuss why each way of working is appropriate for a specific societal structure. I will be using the terms "society" and "culture" interchangeably because social scientists have defined these two terms so that each includes the other. Society can be defined as a set of interlocking institutions that regulate and coordinate behavior according to an established set of norms and values. Culture can be defined as a patterned way of life which is structured by the institutions of society and reinforced with particular norms and values.

The book is divided into seven parts, the first of which deals with theoretical questions. The remaining parts are separated into two sections, one treating non-market cultures and the other, mixed cultures which combine non-market and market elements. The term non-market is not meant to imply an unchanging or static society, nor is it meant to carry such value-laden connotations as "backward" or "primitive." Any classification carries the difficulty that it implies a total category of pure traits, whereas in the real world all societies are complex mixtures in which certain patterns are predominant. Thus, one should be aware that classifications refer to complex types and that the purpose of using categories is to make cross-cultural comparisons possible. Anthropologists do not work with preordained models or expectations. Our holistic approach requires that we seek all factors conditioning the work environment. We would expect to deal with elements of industrial cultures in non-market societies in remote parts of the world just as we will find traces of non-market cultures in industrial nation-states.

This is an attempt to search for an approach to the study of work which encompasses diversity and ranges of cultures. It is part of the anthropological tradition to search for that which is distinctive and that which is similar between various cultures and societies. The book is guided by that tradition.

I want to thank my wife, *Mika*, for her constant encouragement of my efforts; *June Nash*, who thought this project worthwhile and made many valuable recommendations; *Fred Gamst*, whose colleague-ship and scholarship continues to be a source of ideas and stimulation for me; *David Boynton*, who first encouraged me to embark upon the concept of this book; *Bill Eastman*, without whose help and interest this book would have never seen its fruition; and *George and Louise Spindler*, who read the first version and thought it worthy. I also want to extend a special thanks to Malcolm Willison for a brilliant job of editing, for his many useful suggestions and his keen sense of detail.

Acknowledgements

Chapter 1 from: Nash, June 1981 *The Anthropology of Work*, Anthropology of Work Newsletter, Vol. 2, No. 1, Pp. 2–7. Permission granted by June Nash and the AWN.

Chapter 2 from: Gamst, Frederick C. 1981. *Considerations for an Anthropology of Work*, Vol. 2, No. 1, Pp. 7–9. Permission granted by Frederick C. Gamst and the AWN.

Chapter 3 from: Lee, Richard B. 1980 *The !Kung San; Men, Women and Work in a Foraging Society*. London: Cambridge University Press, Pp. 205–23. Permission granted by Cambridge University Press, Cambridge, England.

Chapter 4 from: Hoebel, E. Adamson 1960 *The Cheyennes: Indians of the Great Plains*. New York: Holt, Rinehart and Winston. Permission granted by Holt, Rinehart and Winston and CBS College Publishing Co., Pp. 59–68.

Chapter 5 from: Suttles, Wayne 1968 "Coping with Abundance: Subsistence on the Northwest Coast," In *Man the Hunter*, Edited by Richard B. Lee and Irven DeVore. New York: Aldine Publishing Company, Pp. 56–68. Permission granted by the Aldine Publishing Company.

Chapter 6 from: Evans-Pritchard, E. E. 1940. *The Nuer*. Oxford: Oxford University Press. Pp. 31–40. Permission granted by Oxford University Press.

Chapter 7 from: Misra, P. K. 1975 "The Gadulia Lohars—Nomadism and Economic Activities", In *Pastoralists and Nomads in South Asia*, Edited by Lawrence Saadia Leshnik and Gunther-Dietz Sontheimer. Wiesbaden: Otto Harrassowitz. Pp. 235–46. Permission granted by Dr. Helmut Petzolt, Otto Harrassowitz, Verlag.

Chapter 8 from: Goldschmidt, Walter 1971 *Independence as an Element in Pastoral Social Systems*. Anthropological Quarterly, Vol. 44, No. 3, July, Pp. 132–41. Permission granted by The Catholic University of America Press.

Chapter 9 from: Vincze, Lajos 1974 *Organization of Work in Herding Teams of the Great Hungarian Plain.* Ethnology, Vol. XIII, No. 2, April, Pp. 159–69. Permission granted by Ethnology.

Chapter 10 from: Malinowski, Bronislaw 1965 *Soil-Tilling and Agricultural Rites in the Trobriand Islands.* Bloomington: Indiana University Press. Pp. 61–67. Permission granted by Paul R. Reynolds, Inc., who have copyright to Vol. I, Coral Gardens and Their Magic from which "Soil-Tilling, etc." was taken.

Chapter 11 from: Erasmus, Charles J. 1955 *Work Patterns in a Mayo Village.* American Anthropologist 57 (2, Part 1), Pp. 322–33. Permission granted by the American Anthropological Association.

Chapter 12 from: Pospisil, Leopold 1972 *Kapauku Papuan Economy.* Yale University Publications in Anthropology, No. 67, New Haven: Human Relations Area Files Press. Pp. 144–48. Reprint of 1963 Edition. Permission granted by Human Relations Area Files, Inc., New Haven, Conn.

Chapter 13 from: Firth, Raymond 1972 *The Organization of Work Among the New Zealand Maori.* Wellington, New Zealand: Shearer., Pp. 221–44. Permission granted by the Government Printing Office, Wellington, New Zealand.

Chapter 14 from: Salz, Beate R. 1955 *The Human Element in Industrialization.* American Anthropological Association Memoir 85, American Anthropologist 57 (6, Pt. 2): Pp. 103–14. Permission granted by the American Anthropological Association.

Chapter 15 from: Johnson, Allen 1975 *Time Allocation in a Machiguenga Community.* Ethnology, Vol. XIV, No. 3, July, Pp. 301–10. Permission granted by Ethnology.

Chapter 16 from: Finney, Ben 1967 *Money Work, Fast Money and Prize Money: Aspects of the Tahitian Labor Commitment.* Human Organization, Vol. 26 (4), Pp. 195–99. Permission granted by the Society for Applied Anthropology.

Chapter 17 from: Hobart, Charles W. 1982 *Industrial Employment of Rural Indigenes: The Case of Canada.* Human Organization, Vol. 41 (1), Pp. 54–63. Permission granted by the Society for Applied Anthropology.

Chapter 18 from: Graves, Theodore D. 1970 *The Personal Adjustment of Navajo Indian Migrants to Denver, Colorado.* American Anthropologist, Vol. 72 (1), Pp. 44–54. Permission granted by the American Anthropological Association.

Chapter 19 from: Waddell, Jack O. 1969 *Papago Indians at Work.* Tucson: University of Arizona Press. Pp. 134–50. Permission granted by the University of Arizona Press.

Chapter 20 from: Kruse, John A., Judith Kleinfeld and Robert Travis 1982 *Energy Development of Alaska's North Slope: Effects on the Inupiat Population.* Human Organization, Vol. 41 (2), Pp. 97–106. Permission granted by the Society for Applied Anthropology.

Chapter 21 from: Willner, Ann Ruth 1963 *Problems of Management and Authority in a Transitional Society: A Case Study of a Javanese Factory.* Human Organization, Vol. 22 (2), Pp. 133–41. Permission granted by the Society for Applied Anthropology.

Chapter 22 from: Minge-Kalman, Wanda 1978 *Household Economy During the Peasant-to-Worker Transition in the Swiss Alps.* Ethnology, Vol. XVII, Pp. 183–96. Permission granted by Ethnology.

Theoretical Introduction

HERBERT APPLEBAUM

This book deals with two main categories, non-market and mixed societies. Non-market societies are non-industrial cultures where work and all other institutions are embedded in kinship relations. Mixed societies are those which retain a large measure of the characteristics of non-market societies but are in the process of change and modernization, i.e., a growing influence of industrialization and market relations.

All societies have work and production and systems of exchange and distribution, but the way these relate to the social fabric differ. Work exists everywhere because people must solve the problems of subsistence in order to meet their human needs. The way in which work integrates with other aspects of culture is highly variable. The notion of a societal category like market, non-market or mixed society refers to a generalized type during a historical period, within and between which there are untold possibilities.

In non-market societies work is directed mainly to meet subsistence needs. Work performed for other than subsistence is usually channeled into religious or political relationships. Work relations are based on kinship, and exchanges of work or goods are based on reciprocity. The tools needed for work are owned by individuals or the kinship group. People generally work for themselves or their kinship group and the time allocation and work rhythms are based on the needs of those who participate directly in the performance of work. Wherever markets do exist within the framework of non-market societies, they are convenient places for exchanging goods and are not the dominant institutions where all goods and labor must be exchanged for people to exist.

In mixed societies, we find resistance to changes affecting the social relations described for non-market societies and at the same time change, modernization and industrialization being introduced and affecting the attitudes, beliefs and behavior appropriate to the tra-

1

ditional, non-market culture. In the mixed society, the profit motive appears and work is increasingly based on working for money, i.e., wages. The exchange system is increasingly based on the market and people go to the marketplace not only for the exchange of goods but to realize profits. Those who work find that they no longer own or control the tools and technology needed to perform work and they must sell their ability to work to others who own the wherewithal to engage in production. The time orientation is no longer determined by those who work but by those who own enterprises where work takes place and they, under the constraints of marketplace competition, must stress speed, strict time allocation and discipline in their workplaces. Reciprocity, which is the hallmark of non-market societies, slowly gives way in mixed cultures to the notion of an individual or group trying to gain the upper hand at the expense of others.

The process of change from non-market to mixed societies is an uneven and often a discontinuous process, with advances and retreats, personal achievements and individual dislocations and in general, a difficult and often painful adjustment and adaptation to a new way of life. It can be exciting because new challenges and promises of improvements are on the horizon and it can be disturbing because comfortable and familiar patterns of behavior are no longer effective or appropriate.

SECTION 1. WORK IN NON-MARKET SOCIETIES

One of the most difficult tasks facing the social scientist is to draw meaningful generalizations from the unlimited data about human behavior. Even when the focus is limited to work, finding patterns or central threads that sum up data remains difficult. Notwithstanding these obstacles, one finds three main concepts that explain and sum up the nature of work in non-market cultures. These three ideas are the following:

(1) *Work in non-market societies is embedded* in the total cultural fabric and is intimately linked to all other institutions in those societies. Within this general proposition, non-market societies exhibit strong ties between: (a) *work and kinship* structures; (b) *work and religion;* (c) *work and taboos;* (d) work and political leadership.

(2) *Communal aspects of work in non-market societies is* a *predominant* force. People in non-market societies have a sense of mutuality and utilize reciprocal exchange in the performance of work. Thus, within the general heading of the communal aspects of work we can single out three specific attributes of work in non-market societies:

(a) *work and reciprocity;* (b) the *mutual interdependence of women's work and men's work;* (c) the influence of *communality in work incentives.*

(3) *Work in non-market societies tends to be task-oriented* rather than time-oriented. The discussion will deal with three aspects of this: (a) *work and the attitudes toward time;* (b) *subsistence work;* (c) *the limited use of specialization.*

The discussion in the theoretical introduction will deal in turn with each of the themes and concepts outlined above.

To be added to the themes is one additional item that fits into any of the three main characteristics of non-market societies, namely "energy." Energy is involved in all aspects and all kinds of work. Some investigators have used it as an independent variable to compare and analyze different societies and cultures and to evaluate the evolution of cultures (Harris 1975; White 1959). Energy will be treated independently in the text.

One should remember that abstractions of the sort contained in the list of characteristics inevitably are distortions of a reality that is more complicated and less categorical than the ideas we use to describe it. Nor can the observer ever be exhaustive about the concepts and data used to explain or describe any kind of human behavior. Yet it is possible to isolate certain concepts which are useful to illuminate, explain, and analyze social phenomena.

A. Work Embedded in Society

In industrialized cultures what one does to earn a living is usually divorced from what one does the rest of the time. This contrasts with non-market cultures, where work is a part of life and not a separate sphere. In such cultures there is a unity between hunting and raising a family, between making pots and training children, between the building of houses and the practice of religion. Often there is no separate word for work, because work is a natural part of life. An anthropologist will find that he or she cannot understand work unless data is collected on kinship, religion, taboos, political leadership, and all other aspects of the social structure.

People who live in non-market cultures do not live apart from the social environment; thus activity in any single social field is influenced by that person's position in all of them. On Mount Hagen, New Guinea, for example, the term "kongon" is not only associated with work but also with the preparations for the Female Spirit cult (Strathern 1982:308–9). Gardening work among the Trobriand Islanders is a part of a social system in which they have obligations to kinship groups. A man must turn over fifty percent of his harvest to his sister's husband and he in turn receives half the harvest of his wife's brother's gardens (Malinowski 1922). Cheyenne women must build shelters as part of social and kinship obligations; they would lose prestige if they failed to do so (Hoebel 1960). Nuer women milk dairy cows as one of their duties toward their family and community, and a woman without a cow to milk has no standing in the kinship group (Evans-Pritchard 1940).

The work performed by people who live in non-market societies is part of the natural order of their world, part of the swirling relationships and counterrelationships that hold them fast to a past that established the time-honored rhythms of their lives. A boy growing up among the !Kung Bushmen is socialized into his role as a hunter and does not question whether this is something he wishes or does not wish to do. It is a way of life accepted as being as inevitable as the cycle of days and nights, as inevitable as the fact that his father and uncles and their fathers and uncles before them were hunters (Lee 1980).

1. *Work and Kinship* In many if not most small-scale, non-market societies, the main integrating institution is the kinship group. Thus, work is intimately related to family and kinship obligations. One central feature of this relationship between work and kinship is that the family is the producing unit. Work is carried on as a family, with the division of labor based on sex and age. There are tasks on which a single family works as a collective unit. Other work, such as clearing a field, raising the roof of a house, or harvesting a large crop, are undertaken through the collaboration of several families. This kind of work arrangement is found in industrial societies on small farms or in small business enterprises. In such situations all members of the family share and divide the work and constitute the producing and managing unit. In industrial societies the products are made and sold for the market, while in the non-market societies the crops or goods are consumed by the producing group.

In industrial societies the division of labor is based on the breakdown of tasks and functions needed by industrial corporations and firms, offices and service establishments. The number of jobs and occupations in industrial cultures is part of a myriad of complex work organizations involving the cooperation and interdependence of millions. In non-market cultures the jobs and occupations are based on a simplified division of labor involving the cooperation and obligations of family units united by lineage, marriage, and territory. Among hunting and gathering societies the kinship group is recognized as the unit which maintains and wields control over a common hunting territory (Herskovits 1952:335). These hunting territories are comprised of stretches of land with natural boundaries marked off by rivers, lakes, swamps, forests, hills, and other landmarks. It is forbidden for anyone outside the kinship group to hunt in the territory, and trespassers are often punished with death. Permission might be granted to outsiders to hunt in a particular territory if there is a reciprocal arrangement. Through control over territory kinship groups control the basic precondition for work.

Among non-market horticultural and agricultural people, land is allotted and distributed also through the kinship group. In many cases, as in Africa, land is occupied by the tribe and administered by the chief. Among the Tiv every man or woman has the right to work a farm through their membership in a clan (Bohannan 1963:224-26). This does not mean that the person owns the land. Each person's right is to use the land. Variations of this system are found in Polynesia, Melanesia, and North and South America. In principle, kinship property is administered by the head of the kinship group and no sale of land is permitted. Land use is assured to every member of the kinship group as an inherited right, and so the right to work is supported by the entire community. This applies to both men and women.

Another aspect of the integration of work within the kinship group in non-market cultures is that training and preparation for acquiring skills takes place within the family. In return the person who receives the training gives back to his kinship group his participation in the family's work. The chapter here on the Gadulia Lohars and the training for blacksmithing is a good illustration of this training and participation of all members of a family unit in a joint enterprise.

2. *Work and Religion* Non-market societies, like all others, possess a body of knowledge and skills relied upon for subsistence and survival. Non-market communities believe that they depend upon the natural world for survival. In addition to applying their own efforts to their work, they appeal to their gods and spirits for good fortune—fishermen propitiate the gods with ceremonies before embarking on long voyages; gardeners appeal to earth spirits to be bountiful; hunters use magic to capture the desired qualities possessed by the animals they hunt.

In small-scale, non-market cultures the function of the shaman is to learn the chants and rituals appropriate for success in the hunt, the tilling of the soil, and the capture of fish. The shaman must seek the right magic for success and he must root out the reasons for lack of success—hence the search for sorcery and witchcraft if the community is experiencing difficult times. Religion, magic, and witchcraft in non-market cultures all serve to reinforce the norms of the culture, especially those related to community cooperation. The self-centered loner is a threat to such community and is apt to be accused of sorcery.

In non-market societies human beings are viewed as having a kinship relation with the natural world. Nature is seen as a living spirit which must be appealed to in the quest for food and for all other essentials for life. Kinship, the basic institution, is also the basis for the relationship with the world of nature. Appeals to nature's spirits and magic is a community endeavor. Hoebel describes the antelope hunt as a total Cheyenne village effort led by shamans. Malinowski (1965:52–68) points to the magicians and magic unique to each Trobriand village. Raymond Firth (1981:587) states that Tikopia chiefs are credited with mystic power. When they speak ritually, their words are believed to secure crops, fish, and the health of their people.

In non-market cultures magic and religion serves as the main expression of village, band, and community unity in the face of the natural world, of which they are a part and from which subsistence must be wrested and survival guaranteed through individual and communal work.

3. *Work and Taboos* Work in most non-market societies is affected by religious and magical taboos which dictate what kind of subsistence activities may be pursued and by which sex, what materials may be utilized for tools, and on which days work may or may not be undertaken. Many societies do not utilize resources that they have the technology to exploit because they are forbidden by taboo. These taboos often lower the efficiency with which certain socities deal with their natural environment. In East Africa, although they have had long contact with agriculturalists, the Masai refuse to grasp the opportunity to learn agriculture because of their taboos against the products of the soil. For the Masai, agriculture represents a sacrilege of the earth because it entails penetrating the soil. Agriculturalists are viewed as destructrive beings, attenuated shadows of hunters who produce from the soil food that is less worthy than the products of the cow produced by the Masai (Galaty 1982:7).

Non-market societies have certain days when it is forbidden to work. This prohibition can have substantial repercusions. In his ethnography of Malay fishermen, Firth (1966:94) points to a loss of 562 man-days in fishing due to the Muslim sabbath, Muslim holidays, and a preoccupation with funerals and marriages. Both Lee (1980) and Hoebel (1960) point to days when hunting is not undertaken because the signs are unfavorable. Taboos against work on certain days are also present in industrial societies, such as not working on the Sabbath.

In non-market societies taboos exist against the killing of certain animals or the eating of certain food, which often represent the group's totem. Among the Australian aborigines, various groups profess kinship not only to one another but also to one or more vegetable or animal species, such as the kangaroo, emu or witchety grub. A patrilineal or matrilineal group's totem is regarded as its own flesh or meat, as well as its guardian, friend, or kinsperson. When the aborigine states that the wooley-butt tree, his totem, is his uncle, he ignores a distinction between man and nature. An aborigine must not kill or eat his group's totem, since all who share the same totem share the same flesh, and union through eating the flesh is considered incest (Peacock and Kirsch 1970:89).

Taboos are also associated with the performance of work. For example, in return for help that an Eskimo hunter seeks from his Spirit Helper, he must observe certain taboos and refrain from hunting or occupying a particular area. Hunters must also observe the taboo of not sleeping on the ice-edge because the Sea Spirit does not like her creatures to smell human beings while they are not hunting (Rasmussen 1929:76). Other examples of taboos against work: Boro women in the western Amazon forest are forbidden to plant cocoa; in the Solomons women are not allowed to fish; among the Masai the building of huts and kraals is forbidden to men and only performed by women (Forde 1963: 137, 96, 294).

One of the most famous taboos associated with work and subsistence is the taboo against the slaughter of cows in India. The subject has been the center of a theoretical controversy as to whether religious or economic factors are the underlying cause of the taboo (Simoons 1979; Harris 1966, 1977; Freed and Freed 1981).

4. Work and Political Leadership In non-market societies leadership in work can come from various sources—family, religious leaders, political leaders, or skilled practitioners of a craft. Leadership in work stems from performance, and there is no predetermined hierarchy. Most work can be started without the need for formal organization. Leaders work alongside those they lead. Among the Maori, (Firth 1972b:221–24) political chieftians are also the leaders in communal work. With a culture like the !Kung San, a group of hunters will gather around a certain leader who has proven himself by his skill and ability as evidenced by the number of animals he has slain (Lee 1980: chapter 12). Among northern nomadic hunters—Chukchi, Lapps, Naskapi, Greenlanders, Waswanipi, Montegnais, and the Beaver— according to Robert Paine (1971b:165–66), a hunter's expertise and personal prowess leads to certain hunters becoming leaders in the community. Paine states that hunting leaders, upon the successful completion of the hunt, continue to exercise leadership in the camp. He plays the role of host during the distribution of the meat, with the families who are the recipients of food playing the role of guests. The leader's reward is not only in the kills made but also in the prestige gained in proportion to the number of families to which he can distribute meat and gain an audience (Paine 1971b:165).

Julian Steward describes leadership in work among the Great Basin Shoshonean Indians of North America (1967:249–50). The Shoshoneans do not undertake communal hunts until an appropriate leader is available. The principal communal hunt among the Shoshoneans is the rabbit drive. Nets are used, about the height and mesh of a tennis net and several hundred feet long. The nets are placed end to end to form a huge semicircle. Men, women, and children, accompanied by dogs, beat the brush over a wide area, gradually closing in so that the rabbits that are not clubbed or shot become entangled in the nets, where they are killed. Experienced men called "rabbit bosses" are given supreme authority to coordinate all acitivities in this operation. They choose the locality of the drive, direct the disposition of the nets, regulate the drivers and divide the game according to kinship and custom. The families with nets receive a somewhat greater portion of the rabbits caught in the nets. Unlike the northern nomadic hunters, the Shoshonean leaders only hold authority during the drives. A given family is under no obligation to follow any leader on a permanent basis. Communal antelope hunts among the Shoshoneans, like those among the Cheyennes, were led by shamans (Steward 1967:250).

In non-market, preindustrial societies a person exercises leadership in work because the person has knowledge or is thought to possess power over the natural environment (Malinowski 1965: 52–68; Steward 1967:250). Such a person might be a chief, a shaman, or a magician. They exercise leadership not because they have inherited positions but because of deeds they can perform. In Maori society an individual who is a work leader is not only versed in magic but has technical skills (Firth 1972b:221–24). A Maori chief posseses three elements of leadership—family, religion, and knowledge.

In summary, in non-market societies leadership in work is exercised by individuals through example, performance, knowledge, and skill.

B. The Communal Aspect of Work

The communal aspects of work in non-market, non-industrial cultures constitute one of their major distinctive features. Communal and cooperative work is performed by all groups of both sexes and all ages, and involves all kinds of work tasks. The family, which is the primary social as well as work organization, is a cooperative group. Communality is also expressed through the involvement of the community as a whole in work. Evans-Pritchard describes the Nuer (1940:92):

> The members of various segments of a village have common economic interests, forming a corporation which owns its particular gardens, water-supplies, fishing-pools and grazing grounds; which herds its cattle in a compact camp in the drought, and operates jointly in defense, in herding, and in other activities; and in which, especially in the smaller villages, there is much cooperation in labour and sharing of food.

Communal work organizations, free or compulsory, temporary or permanent, organized or unorganized, are part of the cultures of non-market societies throughout the world.

From the Americas, Haiti may be cited as an example (Herskovits (1937:70–76). When a field has to be cleared, the farmer passes the word that he wishes to have a work group formed to do the work. If he tries to do the work himself, the planting season would be gone before he could clear the field. With the help of the cooperative group, he can get his fields cleared in a day or two and go on to the next phase of work.

As workers gather, their work is supervised by one individual who sees that the pace is adequate. The workers, each with a hoe in hand, form a line while drums mark the rhythm for the songs and set the beat for the hoes. The stimulus of group effort on the workers is such that in a single afternoon a field of several acres can be cleared of the dry season growth by a work force of sixty to sixty-five men. At the end of the work day, when darkness falls, there is a feast. The one who supervised the work gets the choice portions. If a wealthy man's fields are involved, the best workers may find a few coins at the bottom of their dish.

In Dahomey, West Africa, communal work is used in the building of walls for large houses, the thatching of roofs, and the hoeing of large fields. This communal pattern is also found in Dahomean crafts. Among the ironworkers, each forge is worked by a cooperative group. At any one time all members of a forge will be working on the iron of one man. The product of their work will belong to the one whose iron is forged. He will later sell it for personal gain. He, in turn, will work the iron of each of his fellow iron workers until the cycle swings around to him again (Herskovits 1938:75). Communal labor among the Dahomeans is further fostered by the custom which requires every son-in-law to perform a task of some magnitude for the father of each of his wives. A man with many daughters will have a number of men working for him on large projects.

In East Africa, the Kikuyu employ two types of communal work when they are weeding gardens. One is where four or five men, working together, care for the fields of each other. The other is the working-bee, where the task is performed in a festive spirit of communal work, and food and beer are given to make the occasion even more enjoyable. Kenyatta describes the scene (1938:59–60):

> If a stranger happens to pass by at this time of enjoyment after labour he will have no idea that these people who are now singing, dancing and laughing merrily, have completed their day's work. For after they have cleaned off the dust which they got from the fields, they look, in all respects as though they have been enjoying themselves the whole day. This is why most Europeans have erred by not realizing that the African in his own environment does not count hours of work by the movement of the clock, but works with good spirit and enthusiasm to complete the tasks before him.

Communal labor and work was prevalent throughout the Indian cultures of North America. Among the Cheyennes there was the communal buffalo hunt and the communal antelope drive (Hoebel 1960). Kroeber listed among the characteristics of Eskimo society communal houses and cooperative gathering and communal sharing of animals hunted (Owen et al. 1967: 134, 136). The Ojibwa had communal hunting and eating of bear meat, sharing the work of making sugar, and communal harvesting of rice in the late summer (Jenness 1967:195). In an article on "The Social Aspects of Huron Property" (1956:1044–58), Mary Herman states that the feeling of communal responsibility among the Huron rests on the belief that all members of the community have a right to the basic necessities of life.

Data from the Pacific is no less rich with regard to communal work. On Melville Island, the Tiwi have a communal kangaroo hunt. At an appointed time the hunters gather, perhaps ten or fifteen adult men, with younger ones doing the actual hunting and the older ones supervising. The women and children act as beaters; the grass is set on fire over a large area and the kangaroos are rounded up and killed while dazed by the smoke and noise. The bag of animals killed in such communal hunts runs higher than one kangaroo per participant, so that every man, woman and child present is able to gorge themselves on kangaroo meat for a day or two (Hart and

Pilling 1960:42). On Tongo Island in the Pacific an instance is cited of communal fishing where 40 specialists directed the efforts of more than a thousand people in a communal work effort (Herskovits 1952:104).

In analyzing communal work it would be a mistake to think that only altruism prevails and that self-interest is lacking. In many instances men and women work for each other with the expectation of a return when the work of others is needed. Competition is not absent from communal work. Within any given work group there is competition for the prestige of being the best worker. During the communal feasts of the Ponapeans, there is competition among the farmers over who has produced the largest yam (Bascom 1948). The Kula trade of the Trobriands (Malinowski 1922) and the potlatch of the Kwakiutl (Boas 1921) were communal enterprises that involved group (clans or tribes) and individual (chiefs) competition.

Finally, it should be kept in mind that communal and group work is not always voluntary. Group work performed for chiefs, headmen, and priests in the Pacific (Sahlins 1970) and in Africa (Kuper 1963) is an obligation owed to these political and religious leaders, and anyone who refuses might suffer the sanctions of ostracism or accusations of sorcery. Every society has its shirkers and individuals who abstain from communal effort and go their own way. In non-market societies such people are controlled through religion and accusations of witchcraft or sorcery, if they defy the communal interests of their community (Harris 1975:363–65).

1. Work and Reciprocity An essential part of the communal aspect of work in non-market societies is the system of reciprocity in which goods, services, work, and symbolic objects are exchanged and given as gifts. In these reciprocal exchanges the offering of work or goods is not based on the desire to gain an advantage over the next party. Individuals and families receive in accordance with their needs and offer labor for work according to their kinship and their community obligations (Mauss 1967).

What is distinctive about reciprocity in non-market cultures is that no system exists for making the exchanges exactly balance. A person will gain prestige if, in returning a gift, he or she renders more to others than what was recieved. In Polynesia, reciprocal feasts and presents are part of wedding ceremonies. On Tonga Island, the father of the bridegroom keeps track of the gifts contributed by his relatives toward the bride wealth. It is a matter of pride for him to see that everyone who has contributed receives twice what he donated. Sometimes a man will strip his house of all its possessions, counting the social prestige of his family of greater value than his material property (Herskovits (1952:163).

Another example of communal reciprocity comes from the Pacific, on the island of Maola, where approximately twelve hundred Fijians live (Sahlins 1970). Among the Maolans, the institution of *kerekere* is practiced. To kerekere is to solicit work or goods from one's relatives. One may ask for their help in gardening or the services of several types of part-time specialists. One may also ask for the use of land or of goods such as food, mats, tools, clothes, tobacco, and canoes. Two conditions must pertain—that the person making the request and the donor be part of the same kinship group, and that the one soliciting a service or a good have a genuine need. One should not kerekere for greed. On the other hand, the only legitimate reason for refusing a kerekere is that giving what is requested would place the donor in a condition of need. In kerekere, one party receives work or goods and the other party receives prestige. There is a balancing of prestige. The person who kerekere's shows weakness and loses prestige and the person who donates shows strength and gains prestige.

Many non-market societies desire products that are controlled by people with whom they have no kinship relationship. This kind of demand is satisfied through trade. Since trade is between people who are non-kin, those engaged in it might be tempted to gain undue advantage. this can lead to anger and hostility between neighboring communities. One answer is to have a silent trade, where one party places its goods at a particular site and leaves. When the other trading partner comes to the site, if he believes the exchange is fair he will leave his own goods and take what is offered. If not, he will leave without taking anything. In this fashion the Pygmies of the Ituri forest trade meat for bananas with the Bantu agriculturalists; and the Vedda of Ceylon trade honey for iron tools with the Sinhalese. Herodotus reported that this was the manner in which the Carthaginians obtained gold from African tribes living south of the Straits of Gibraltar. (Harris 1975:286).

Another element in the exchange of gifts and work in non-market societies is that non-economic as well as economic components are involved in the process. Ritual and community prestige are considered along with the goods and services rendered. In non-market cultures everyone has the same scale of comforts or lack of them. Everyone spends about the same amount of time working and enjoys similar diets and housing accomodations. Accumulating wealth for one's own benefit might not only be senseless but also dangerous. Anyone who is overly selfish and hoarding might be accused of sorcery. Prestige is gained through the giving of gifts or feasts or the sharing of work and food from a successful hunting or fishing trip or a good harvest. These non-economic elements of work are the basis for the communality of work and the reciprocity of relationships in non-market cultures.

2. *Women's Work and Men's Work* The communality of work in non-market societies is related to the family as the productive unit. Since the family is the productive unit, the cooperation and reciprocal exchange between men and women is decisive for the functioning of the family as the work organization. The division of work in non-market cultures is mainly based on sex. Unless there is fulfillment of roles by each member of the kinship group, the family cannot provide the necessry work to provide subsistence for its members, care and nurture for the young, and emotional stability for all members. The sexual divison of work has received much attention and many theories have been advanced to explain the origins of this basic principle. These theories are speculative and not subject to verification. Given the complexity of the forms of sexual division of labor throughout the world, it is unlikely that any single generalization will suffice to cover all cases.

Certain factors about the sexual division of work can be taken into account, however. Being childbearers, women are at times prevented from doing heavy work. Having the task of caring for children confines women and prevents them from embarking upon long hunting or fishing trips. Still, Kaberry (1939) and Goodale (1971) show that Australian aboriginal women did sometimes go on hunting and fishing excursions with the men. Ethnographers have also shown that women work as hard as men and contribute as significantly as men to the necessary labor and food supply required in all cultures (Lee 1980; Gale 1974; Gough 1970; A. Johnson 1975; Leacock 1978; Reiter 1975).

In discussing the sexual division of work it is difficult to make any statement for which there are no exceptions. In general among herders women do not care for the animals, but they do among the Tungus and other reindeer herders (Forde 1963:360–61). In Africa, among the Bantu tribes in the east, apart from clearing heavy brush, agriculture is almost entirely in the hands of women. But among the Yoruba and other west African peoples, agricultural work is in the hands of men (Forde (1963:153). Murdock has correlated the existence of certain factors associated with the sexual division of work in various societies (Murdock and Provost 1973:203–25). However, he presents the correlations without offering explanations why work is drawn along the particular sexual lines in the various cultures surveyed.

The only hard and fast rule about the sexual division of work is that there are no hard and fast rules. Women usually cook, but if a wife is sick or absent the man can, and often will, prepare the meals. Men usually work with the hoe and digging stick, but in an emergency women can continue the work started by the men. Among the Kota, women are not blacksmiths, but if someone is needed to operate the bellows there is no taboo against a woman doing it (Herskovits 1965:132).

The emotional attitudes associated with what is considered women's work or men's work is what solidifies the division of labor according to sex. The reason for this is that socialization into accepted rules for the sexual division of labor occurs early in life and the rules become powerful emotional values. In our own industrial society, youngsters think about careers in emotionally-laden choices based on what they consider appropriate for males and females.

If women's work can be viewed within the context of the communal aspect of work, women's work might receive more recognition for its importance and necessity. In industrial cultures where only productive work outside the home is rewarded by wages, and monetary payment for work is the basis for the definition of work, work within the home is thus afforded less prestige and social standing. Yet, without this work by women, workers within the family as a co-operative unit could not survive. In viewing non-market culture we have many examples of societies where women enjoy prestige and standing because all work is embedded in the culture and the communal aspect of work brings recognition to women's work as well as men's work.

3. *Work Incentives* Among all societies one incentive for work is the necessity to provide subsistence for survival. But the totality of incentives for work also includes the force of tradition, the desire for appreciation and the securing of community approval for work well done. Herskovits comments on this idea (1965:123):

> The prestige that accrues to the hard worker, the fast worker, the careful worker, the competent worker is thus a significant factor in motivating labor in most societies.

One illustration of prestige as a motive for work comes from the island of Ponape, second largest of the Caroline Islands in Micronesia (Bascom 1948:211–21). In this society one of the strongest motives for work is to gain prestige through the display of large yams and breadfruit at yearly festivals (Bascom 1948:212):

> His (Ponapean) motivations and attitudes toward work cannot be explained simply in terms of a desire to earn enough

money to purchase necessary imports and to produce enough
food to keep himself and his family from hunger. Not
infrequently families go hungry at home when they have large
yams in their farms ready for harvest.
Only small yams are used at home for subsistence purposes;
prize yams are saved for feasts. Each family is said to grow
about fifty yams each year solely for the purpose of feasting.

Some of the prize yams weigh more than two hundred pounds and
must be carried between poles by a half dozen men. Bascom says
that Ponapean yam growers are willing to work long, arduous hours,
even for years, to produce something they will give away at feasts
and which will attest to their skills as farmers. They wish to be
admired for their skills and generosity, not for their accumulation of
wealth—this is one of their motivations for work.

Raymond Firth (1972a:8–16) talks about fishermen in Tikopia who
when they make a large catch of bonito fish are known as "men of
bonito," a label of high prestige. As Firth says (1972a:10), "In such
societies work is not just an economic service, it is a social service."
Motivations for work, reciprocity, and the division of work according
to sex are all involved with the communal aspect of work in non-
market societies. People do not choose their work according to
idiosyncratic preferences. They are born into a social system that
requires them to be part of a larger structure of relationships. Their
work is not just one facet of their lives; it is an entire way of looking
at the world. They play a role which gives them a place in that
world and they strive for goals which make their work and all other
activities part of a whole fabric of living.

C. Task-Oriented Work in Non-Market Societies

Associated with the other two major elements of work in non-
market societies—the communal aspect of work and the embedded
nature of work in the total culture—is the task-oriented nature of
work. Work being task-oriented rather than time-oriented, the motivations for work take on a social significance beyond the needs of
individuals. They acquire a community orientation. The task orientation provides wider perspectives on work for the individual at the
same time that it directs work toward clearly focused tasks. In non-
market societies people do not work, as they do for the most part
in industrial societies, on the basis of "putting in time." In explaining
Tahitian attitudes toward work, Finney states that "this is a classic
case of the conflict between the European idea of looking at work
in terms of time, and the probably more widespread idea or regarding
work in terms of tasks to be completed" (1967a:195).

Work is a continuous process that leads eventually to the output of some good or service. This is true in both market and non-market cultures. But there is a large difference in the way work is related to time. In industrialized factories, a worker will work for eight hours and then break off what he or she is doing and go home. The worker may continue the process the next day or some other worker may take up the task and continue it. People who work in non-market cultures usually keep at a task and complete it themselves. If it takes more than a day or a week they do not time themselves but break off their work at convenient intervals. They may suspend work when it gets dark or when it is time to attend a funeral, a festival, or a marriage. Eventually the task to be performed is worked through by the person who started it. This attitude is also true of people in industrialized cultures who do work for themselves in their leisure hours away from their place of employment. The task, not the time it takes, is what is important when one is making a product for his own use.

E. P. Thompson sums up task-oriented work with the following (1967:60):

(1) Task-oriented work is more humanly comprehensible than time-oriented work, the worker, peasant, or hunter doing what appears to be an observed necessity.

(2) A community which is task-oriented maintains the least demarcation between work and life, with social intercourse and work intermingled. The workday lengthens or contracts according to the work at hand and there is no sense of a conflict between work and passing time.

(3) To those who live in societies where work is time-oriented rather than task-oriented, the attitudes described in paragraphs (1) and (2) above appear to be "wasteful."

1. Work and the Concept of Time If task-oriented work is a major aspect of non-market societies, the notion of time becomes a crucial variable within the concept of task-oriented work. Time is one of the dramatic features of society. Like other cultural phenomena, temporal frames of references vary profoundly from one type of culture to another. People regulate their daily, weekly, monthly, and yearly activities according to the customary time cycles prevalent in their social environment, their institutions, and their value system.

That work is not time-oriented in non-market societies means that people are not heavily bound by time as set by work organizations. Work is an integral part of the family and kinship organization. The pattern of work activities follow the rhythms of the sun and the seasons. The changes in the length of dawn-to-dusk workdays vary with the length of the day as the earth revolves about the sun. People work when the land needs to be tilled, when crops must be harvested, when animals have to be milked, and when the time of day or the coming of a new season makes it opportune to hunt, trap, or fish. Discipline is not absent from work in non-market societies. A !Kung San hunter might have to be on the trail of a giraffe for two weeks, tracking from early morning to dark; during harvest time, peasants work from dawn to dusk, fourteen hours a day; village blacksmiths, once they place their iron in the fire must work at it so it will not fail. The main distinction between task-oriented work and time-oriented work is that the former is flexible and varied while the latter is rigid and strictly regulated.

Time is an integrating concept, and as such is a crucial denominator in differentiating types of cultures and societies. The attitude toward time among present day non-market peoples is similar to that of people in pre-industrial medieval Europe. LeGoff states (1980:43–44) that the change in the view of time from medieval to modern times entailed a change in the definition of the working day as from sunrise to sunset to a notion of the unit of labor-time, divided into various hours of the working day (1980:43–44).

Temporal frames of reference vary according to the cultural features of a society. In medieval Europe, the church was the dominant institution and thus defined the attitudes toward time. The church rejected the notion of earnings from the mere passage of time, a notion that ruled out interest and credit. Merchants who made profits through purchase at one time and sale at another had to overcome the church view of time in order to capitalize on their knowledge of the market. Another aspect of church attitude toward time was the notion of eternity as uncalculable and unlimited. Once commercial networks were organized, time became an object of calculable and limited measurement. The duration of a sea voyage, a journey on land, or the length of the workday were all measured in units of time that could be converted into profit for merchants and businessmen.

During the middle ages in Europe, peasants were subject to the dominion of meteorological time, to the cycle of seasons, and the unpredictability of natural phenomena, in the same way as are those who live in small-scale, non-market cultures today. Human beings had no choice but to submit to the natural order of events which they hoped to influence with prayer and magic; this too is what people do today in pre-industrial, non-market cultures. For the rising merchant class it was necessary to impose a new, measurable time on the world of commerce, requiring predictable time measurements. The medieval view of the natural world was predicated on a time both eternally renewed and perpetually unpredictable. Merchants and businessmen needed to replace this view with a notion of time that could be divided, counted, and controlled. They needed factory clocks to measure the workday rather than use church and country bells. The clock was the symbol of change. When the power of the state developed, the nobility were seen posing in painted pictures standing next to clocks, the symbol of modernity (LeGoff 1980:35).

A clear idea of the way time and work are seen in non-market cultures can be viewed from this quote in Audrey Richards' classic study of the Bemba of Northern Rhodesia (1939:392–94):

> We, after all can hardly conceive of time except in terms of energy expenditure and, to many of us, a fixed money value as well. But the Bemba, in his unspecialized society, does different tasks daily and a different amount of work each day . . . . The working hours also change in what seems to us a most erratic manner. In fact I do not think the [Bemba] people ever conceive of such periods as the month, week or day in relation to regular work at all. The major agricultural tasks have to coincide with certain seasons and moons and that is all. A man says he has to cut trees between such-and-such climatic changes, but not that he has so many hours of work to get through, and daily work, which has become from habit almost a physiological necessity to many Europeans, only occurs at certain times of the year.

Among the Nuer, Evans-Pritchard says, "the daily timepiece is the cattle clock, the round of pastoral tasks; and the time of day and the passage of time through a day are to a Nuer primarily the succession of those tasks and their relation to one another" (1940:100). Among the Nandi, an occupational time-clock associates each half hour with particular tasks involving the grazing of animals. In Madagascar, time is measured by "rice cooking" (about half an hour) or the frying of a locust (a moment). In Chile, the cooking time of an egg is judged by the saying aloud of an Ave Maria. Among the Kabyle in Algeria, haste is seen as a lack of decorum combined with diabolical ambition, and the clock is sometimes known as the "devil's mill." (Thompson 1967:58–9)

Another characteristic of work in non-market societies is the seeming lack of division of time between work and leisure activities. A good deal of time in non-market cultures is taken up with ceremonies, feasting, drinking, visiting, and celebrations. Feasts are approached with the same seriousness as clearing a field, and in some respects it is just as important since it is part of one's obligations to the community. Salz (1955:99) points out that festivals and holidays constitute almost one third of all working days among the Ecuadorian Indians she studied. There are also fairs, weekly markets, house building, harvest celebrations, and collective work parties *(mingas)* that constitute part of one's work activities among the Ecuadorean Indians.

Hallowell (1937:669) describes the temporal orientation of the Salteau Indians as based on the recurrence and succession of concrete events in their qualitative aspects. The Salteau temporal orientation is local, limited in application to the immediate future and recent past, and related to activities within the tribe's own environment. Beyond that, all is vague and loosely conceived. Hallowell compares this with the industrial-scientific orientation of time in which time is detached from phenomena and thought of as a month or a day made up of discrete, measurable units. Time conceived in this abstract fashion is continuous and quantitatively defined, and as such it is the concept of an intellectual order that makes time available for use as a standard of reference and a measure for classes of events. Time in the industrial context assumes an autonomous character to be manipulated without reference to specific events. Thus, we can think of it as infinitely divisible, a means for coordinating activities of all sorts with great precision. It also makes possible the measurement of exact temporal intervals and the rate of speed of movable objects (Hallowell 1937:670).

In summary, among people in non-market societies, where life is of one piece with no separation of one social sphere from another, there is no conception of carefully rationed time. In these cultures where roles are clearly assigned and there is no competition for rank or occupation, there is no differentiation between work and nonwork, between work and leisure. For people in these societies, time is not economically valued, and thus they steadily pursue their tasks or set of tasks until the work is completed. They do not conceive of themselves as "wasting" or "marking" time but suit their lives and their activities to the course of natural events. They believe and adhere to their community's values just as they adhere to the natural ordering of diurnal and seasonal time.

In the arrangement of readings in this volume, the section on the attitude toward time (Part 5) is placed between the two main bodies of readings, those which deal with non-market societies and those which deal with mixed and traditional societies. The section on time has been placed there because attitudes toward time are bridges which signify differences between cultures. Changes in time orientations also indicate when changes are taking place within cultures moving from purely subsistence societies to mixed societies engaging in both subsistence work and wage work.

2. *Work and Subsistence* The overwhelming majority of people who work in non-market societies are involved directly in subsistence activities. Estellie Smith has defined subsistence work as one which "consists of the work which humans perform in order to provide the wherewithal to survive" (1977:18). Most people in industrialized countries are not directly engaged in subsistence work. Instead, they work for money wages which they exchange for the goods and services they require for survival.

The natural environment is a silent partner in subsistence work and may be a benefactor one year and a hard taskmaster the next. Subsistence cultures are restricted in population since the technology can support no more than the number of people who can be maintained with enough food for energy to furnish the necessary labor to perform the work required for survival. Single subsistence strategies are rare; people do not confine their efforts to just one main form of work. Where agriculture is the dominant means of livelihood, fishing and hunting may also be carried on. The people of New Guinea and the gardeners in South America, like the Yanomamo, combine gardening with hunting. People will utilize whatever is given them by their natural environment so long as their technology permits them to use the resources, and their customs do not prohibit such use.

Many non-market societies are not in climates which permit food storage beyond a few days. Thus, food is produced for immediate consumption. Most of these cultures depend on daily gathering, hunting or harvesting. These cultures produce mainly for use rather than exchange, and do not have monetary units that express fixed exchange values between goods. Exchange of food and goods among kin involves personal exchanges expressing social obligations and family affection. Food sharing is the clearest expression of communal solidarity.

In the informal and voluntary nature of sharing among close relatives and associates in non-market cultures, there is no attempt to quantify values of goods so as to facilitate repayment. Obligation is not based on a fixed value expressed in monetary terms but on a subjective scale of need and desire. Cooperation in subsistence activities goes along with sharing work, materials, and tools according to the interests, desires, and good will of one's kinship group, neighbors, and community associates.

The subsistence basis for exchange works well among close associates but it is hard to extend to outsiders because of the need for personal contact in order to work out obligations. To exchange subsistence products with outsiders the feast is used as a gesture of good will and a means of political alliance. Not only is food exchanged at these feasts but other gifts are passed from hand to hand. Food, the basis for survival, the ultimate subsistence product, seems to be used throughout the world as an object of sharing as a means of establishing friendship within and without one's community. "Breaking bread together" or exchanging drink is a give and take of the means for survival, and as such is both the foundation for physical continuity and the means for social integration. Each society has its own particular goods or crops or animals that are the basis for its survival and either the same product or a different one is used for getting along with its neighbors or strangers.

In industrial cultures people do not directly share or exchange their products of work; perhaps this is one of the reasons for the lessened solidarity among them. The sharing that does occur takes place outside the marketplace, in the drinking taverns, the home, and places of leisure. But the exchanges are not in "survival" goods and the act of exchange is often one of giving up superfluities, not essentials. Sometimes, we learn of the person who sacrificed all worldly possessions for another and most of us, having been socialized in a selfish, self-centered value system, find such a happening hard, if not impossible, to understand.

3. Limited Use of Specialization With task orientation toward work predominant and little concern with efficient production based on time, there is less stress in non-market cultures on intensified subdivision of work and specialization. It is rare in non-market cultures to find work so subdivided that a person becomes a specialist in just part of a product. Only in the production of very large items such as houses or canoes does specialization occur. In any case, even where specialization does occur, the worker devoting himself or herself to part of a product is often competent to perform all other phases of the work as well.

The degree of specialization in non-market societies varies from society to society. Where the primary division of work is along sex lines every man and woman knows how to do all those things at which their own sex habitually work. In societies where technologies are more developed certain men spend a larger proportion of their time doing wood carving or ironworking and certain women spend much of their time making pots or weaving cloth. In some cases, people devote themselves to a particular technique or a particular type of product. One woman may make pots for everyday use and another woman those for religious purposes. However, it is rare for specialization to develop where one woman gathers clay, another moulds it, and a third fire the pots; or where one man gathers wood, another shapes it, and a third finishes it. Given the limited use of specialization in non-market cultures, whatever specialization does exist is craft specialization; that is, specialists turn out an entire product and not a part of one.

The variety of cases regarding specialization is so vast only a few examples can be cited. First, it should be noted that some non-market cultures have a virtual absence of craft specialization. Examples are the Andaman Islanders (Radcliffe-Brown 1933:40–43) or the Yanomano (Chagnon 1977:33–9). In both these cultures each man makes his own bow and arrow while the women make their own baskets. Chagnon remarks (1977:33):

> Techniques of manufacturing are so simple and direct that each individual can produce any item he needs from the resources immediately around him.

Africa has a long history of craft specialization in ironmaking. Ironworkers have a high degree of technical skills which require long apprenticeship in the craft. They are true specialists. Craft specialization is also well developed in West Africa in pottery, baskets, weaving, and wood carving. Craftspeople who produce these commodities are recognized as specialists in their communities and are supported by an extensive system of markets (Bohannan and Dalton 1962). In some cases an entire village is made up of specialists. In Ghana, the village of Akuraa houses wood-carvers who have produced regalia for Ashanti royalty for two hundred and fifty years (Silver 1981:42). Today, wood-carvers in the village produce wood-carved objects which are sold in national and international markets. The training of the wood-carvers is based on an apprenticeship system that has been in operation since precolonial times (Silver 1981:43–9). Malinowski also found village specialization in the Trobriand Islands for the making of kula gifts (1935:21–3). Examples of specialization can be found in all continents—South America (G. Foster 1948), North America (Boas 1921), The Pacific (Rappaport 1968), and the Far East (Herskovits 1952:149).

Specialization has been studied by economists, social scientists, and anthropologists, who perceive a relationship between specialization, population growth, and creation of an economic surplus (A. Smith 1937; Marx 1933; Childe 1946; Durkheim 1947; Harris 1975). Other investigators of work have pointed to specialization as necessary for the creation of market societies (Braverman 1974; Forde 1963). While it may be necessary to demonstrate the specific relationship in each case, growth of markets has generally been accompanied by increased specialization and the division of labor (M. Nash 1956).

D. Energy

Just as time has become an important clue to understanding the nature of work in various societies, the type and level of energy available to a society or culture is another indicator about the organization of work in a given social environment. Most non-market societies rely on human energy for their work. Peasant cultures supplement human energy with animal power. With human energy as the predominant form of power, hand tools are dominant—hoes, knives, axes, bows, arrows, choppers, grinders, digging sticks, throwing spears. With reliance on human energy large-scale tasks can only be undertaken with communal labor—projects such as clearing of land, house building, canoe building, trench digging. This reinforces mutual dependence among members of the community.

Marvin Harris has presented the proposition that a crucial aspect of work in pre-industrial, non-market societies is the relation between human energy and food production (1975:233). He formulates an equation based on five variables:

E — the number of calories a system produces annually.

m — the number of food producers.

t — time in hours of work per food producer.

r — calories expended per food producer per hour.

e — the ratio of the average calories of food produced for each calorie expended.

Harris' equation is E equals $m \times t \times r \times e$

If a society is to survive, that is, if it is to produce on a consistent basis what it needs to survive, the last term in Harris' equation, e, must have a value greater than 1. This would mean that more energy is produced by those who work than they expend in performing the work. This factor, e, reflects the technological capability and the material and food inventory possessed by a society. The larger the value of e, the greater the labor productivity of the food producers. With this equation as a guide Harris compares non-market with market cultures and sets forth the range of values for mixed societies.

Based on the notion of e, Harris found that a hunting and gathering society like the !Kung San, relying on human energy exclusively, had an average e value of 9.6. An agricultural society such as the Genieri Village in Gambia, West Africa, also relying mainly on human energy but using the hand hoe, had an e value of 11.2. The Tsembaga Maring in New Guinea, a slash-and-burn agricultural society which keeps pigs, had an e value of 18 (Rappaport 1968). In the village of Luts'un, in the Yunnan Province of pre-Communist China, which practiced agriculture with draft animals, the estimated value of e was 53.5 (Fei Hsiao-t'ung and Chang Chih-i 1947).

In order to validate the usefulness of Harris' equation more studies will be needed. However, conceptually it provides a useful way of thinking about measurement of work and provides a means for quantifying comparisons between various cultures and societies regarding the efficiency of work.

SECTION 2. TRANSITIONAL AND MIXED SOCIETIES

Transitional and mixed societies are those which combine both market and non-market features. They are drawn into local, national and world markets through the introduction of cash crops and the spread of work for wages. There are many mixes of market and non-market cultures and thus many variations in the paths of transition from non-market to market cultures. A country like India is so large and diverse that it contains village cultures, nomads, herders, and itinerant craftsmen along with highly developed industrial organizations, a sophisticated bourgeois class, and an advanced high technology sector in the economy. Mexico has a backward peasantry along with an advanced oil and steel industry. China is mainly agricultural but has a nuclear industry. Even a highly industrialized society such as the United States contains within its borders Indian cultures on reservations, the Amish who live in communities that reject the materialism of the dominant culture, migrant agricultural workers who live in squalid conditions, and urban slums which rival those in less developed nations as far as depressed and deteriorating housing conditions.

In studying mixed societies it is useful to examine a model presented by Prattis which outlines the character and basis for the relationship between cultures that are on the margins of industrialized nations and the highly developed industrial centers (1979:361–75). Prattis' model applies to sectors within nations and to the global differentiation between developed and underdeveloped nations and regions. Prattis' model is as follows:

Regional variation in natural endowment, accessibility of markets, labor pools, etc., encourages a concentration of productivity in some regions and not in others. Once initiated, economic growth in a region continues long after its advantages have ceased to be relevant.

Entrepreneurs focus on opportunities available in advanced regions and neglect potential opportunities elsewhere. This sets in motion a concentration of interests which give a competitive advantage to the expanding area. Capital, trade, and investment cluster in such an area because the return is greater than in regions which have not experienced growth.

Once economic growth begins in a region, it becomes highly diversified and denudes marginal regions of investment capital and entrepreneurial talent. Marginal regions develop as specialized appendages of developed ones. Whatever capital is expended in the marginal regions is concentrated in the extractive sector—mining, agriculture, oil. Peripheral areas become dependent upon their raw material outputs that fuel industrial expansion at the center.

One consequence of this relationship between the center and the periphery is that the population on the periphery tends to form into a large "underclass" of poor farmers and peasants, marginal fishermen, and self-employed artisans on the fringe of the capitalist market society. The existence of this semi-proletariat is satisfactory for the industrial center, since it constitutes a pool of surplus labor kept on the land or otherwise involved in community solidarities and non-market work relations that can be mobilized in the event of capitalist expansion on the periphery. A considerable proportion of the productive members of peripheral populations exchange their labor power for a wage on either a seasonal or temporary basis which permits them to spend only part of every year in their home community. Migrant labor and occupational pluralism constitute familiar structural ties with the wider economic system, a functional integration that serves the interests of the market economy if and when it should expand (Prattis 1979; see also Hobart 1982; Murray 1979; Frantz 1981).[1]

In Section 1 of this introduction, dealing with non-market cultures, three main themes were developed to describe the various aspects of work in those cultures. With regard to mixed non-market and market cultures, there are two main themes that can be used to encompass their characteristics of work. One theme is the clash of old and new values. The other is the adjustment patterns and adaptations that occur when traditional values are forced into competition with new values and new work patterns. These themes can be summarized as follows:

A. Clash of New Work Patterns and Old Values	B. Adjustment and Change to New Work Patterns
1. New time orientation.	1. New work patterns within the household.
2. Traditional values and work for wages.	2. New management work roles.
3. Problems of identification.	
4. Non-market enclaves in market society.	

A. Clash between New Work Patterns and Old Values.

Enough experience has now been gathered on the contact between technologically advanced societies and non-market societies to confirm that the clash between existing values and new work patterns is a basic problem facing cultures at a transitional stage.

It used to be thought that technological advances were signs of "progress" and that less advanced societies technologically were "backward." Without questioning the objective fact that industrial societies produce more and support larger populations with more material goods, there has been increasing concern with preserving traditional ways of life because there was much that was valued and valuable in them. We now realize in the industrially advanced nations that the price we have paid for our technological progress has been a decline in community, an increase in the alienation of work from self, and a way of life that is fractured rather than of a total piece in rhythm with the natural world. Not only do we not feel "sorry" for people in non-market cultures but we often admire them for the strength of their kinship relations, the mutuality that marks their personal relationships, and their unhurried and natural approach to their work. This is not to say that industrial societies can or would want to exchange their own cultural patterns for those of non-market societies. This is neither possible nor warranted. Further, no value judgment is implied by the caution that changes in work that result from technological changes also contain consequences that are socially undesirable.

In mixed or transitional cultures it is one thing to introduce factories and offices with machines and efficient methods of work, but quite another to find the work force that will adjust to the discipline of factory and office life. A non-market society that achieves its national independence and then tries to industrialize, as in Indonesia, may find old values clashing with new requirements for rationalized production. In industrial societies jobs are supposed to be dispensed on the basis of qualifications. In non-market societies, work is distributed on the basis of kinship. If this latter principle is applied in industrial society it is considered nepotism; but in a non-market society it is considered a discharge of one's responsibilities to one's family. In Willner's chapter in this volume, the author describes what happens when these two values collide.

In a non-market society in the process of change, it may be considered a good idea to pipe water from a central supply source to various homesteads so women and children do not have to carry the water from the well to their homes. This would be a lightening of the work load. But the daily work of going to the well and carrying water is part of a social occasion which women and children enjoy and to which they look forward. Thus, for the convenience of having piped water they may be paying a social price. Again, no argument is being made that such women do not want the convenience of piped water but what is pointed out is that here again is an example of the clash between old values and new work patterns.

In mixed cultures incentives to work are a mixture of old and new values. This is the case among American Indians who leave the reservation or their Indian communities to seek employment in urban centers (Honigmann 1949; Graves 1970; Waddell 1969; Useem et al. 1943). Work managers in industrialized cultures are usually neither aware of nor sensitive to the value system of non-white migrants. Honigmann (1949) points out that Attawapiskat Indians in James Bay, Canada, were not prepared for wage labor because they were not trained for the daily routine and discipline that employment for wages required. Attawapiskat Indians felt that whites who were trying to get them to accept wage labor did not understand Indian ways. Thus, when traditional alternatives were present—going goose hunting—Attawapiskats spurned wage labor. Whites, for their part, believed that economic necessity was the only factor determining work incentives. They ridiculed the Attawapiskats for going goose hunting when wage labor employment was available. The Attawapiskats did not value material goods or money as much as engaging in such a prestigeful activity as hunting.

Other aspects of the conflict of values between market and non-market cultures involve communication. Methods of communication that may be adaptive in non-market cultures may be maladaptive in wage labor settings. Politeness among the Rosebud Sioux dictates that one should refrain from directly and abruptly getting to the main point in a conversation (Useem et al. 1943). Among the Sioux, good taste stresses silence when there is nothing important to say. One can see how the traditional value would get in the way of work in a factory. White employers who ask direct questions expect direct answers and are frustrated and angry by rambling stories or conversations that seem irrelevant to them. At work, when people are in a group, everyone is expected to participate in a conversation and those who are continually silent, for whatever reason, are looked upon as unsociable; so a Sioux who follows the precepts of his upbringing by remaining silent if he has nothing to say courts the disapproval of the work group of which he is a part.

This conflict of work patterns and values exists in industrial market societies among those who come from non-market cultures. The history and literature of all industrial nations is replete with tales of people whose heads and hearts were torn between two cultures— one industrial and the other village-oriented.

1. A New Time Orientation One of the most painful adjustments for persons involved in the transition from a non-market to a market environment is the adaptation to a new time orientation. It is difficult because attitudes toward time are so fundamental to one's world view. Allen Johnson comments on this idea (1975:301):

> The manner in which individuals spend their time is a basic dimension of ethnographic description. Under such headings as "the daily round," "the annual cycle," or "the division of labor by sex," most ethnographers eventually describe the broad outlines of time allocation in the community. This information is then used by theorists to construct comparative generalizations.

The time orientation of people in non-market societies is concrete and unhurried. The time orientation in market societies is abstract and based on speed. People are evaluated by how fast they work, and those who do not value speed in industrial societies are considered out of step with society. Intelligence tests, output per hour, being "on time" for work and appointments, calendars and clocks are all part of the industrial culture which stresses speed. Mumford summed up the time orientation of industrial society (1934:42).

> Those masters of regimentation [the new bourgeosie] reduced life to a careful, uninterrupted routine: so long for business; so long for dinner; so long for pleasure—all carefully measured out . . . . Timed payments; timed contracts; timed work; timed meals; from this period on nothing was quite free from the stamp of the calendar or the clock.

In the non-market cultures, the rhythm of life is based on cycles of seasons. Work, although it may be long, hard, and intensive, is not based on speed and is not rushed. There is regularity, but it is rhythmically paced, and if work must be broken off to meet kinship or community obligations, there is no sense of "lost time." The orientation toward working time in non-market and market cultures is a clash and contrasts between the unhurried, personalized relations in work and life and the fast-paced, depersonalized relations in the factory, office, and marketplace.

Work in non-market cultures can be pursued with a relaxed attitude toward the quality of the product. Usually there is a positive relationship between high quality and the length of time for crafting. But even if the quality were not high there would be no reason to reject it or not use it, as would be the case in a factory using wage labor and producing for a market. Persons reared in non-market cultures where they control their own work, time, and standards of workmanship, find it difficult to adapt to a factory environment based on strict discipline and rigid standards of quality which cause them to discard perfectly useable objects.

People in mixed societies are regarded by those trying to speed up development in such cultures as lacking initiative and willingness to work hard. The literature of development in third world countries is filled with complaints by engineers of economic growth that people in these cultures are not time-oriented, too interested in activities other than wage labor, and maladapted to regular hours. (Hoselitz 1952)

The question of time and work in mixed and market cultures is not one of which way of life is better or worse. Rather, it is a far-reaching distinction between two sets of values—one in which "time is money" and the other in which time is related to human and natural events.

2. *Traditional Values and Work for Wages* One of the characteristics of people in non-market cultures is that their roles and status is based on custom and kinship. They do not have to "play" a role. Born into a kinship structure, their behavior is governed by a set of rules and their status is established by their place in the kinship structure. However, when they move into the environment of industrialized society they are required to play a large number of roles which require behaviors that are contrasting and at times contradictory.

Persons in non-market cultures are used to their traditional settings where they can be themselves. If they venture outside to find work in a factory or office, they must be capable of "turning on" those behaviors that are appropriate to an industrial work environment and "turning off" those behaviors that are not. A person may be authoritative within their kinship group but must be obedient and compliant at work. He or she may be cheerful and outgoing with family and friends but find work behavior requires that she or he be serious and withdrawn. For persons in mixed cultures these wide shifts in roles and expectations are difficult to attain, and senseless from their perspective. People in non-market cultures may find they cannot or will not play the expected role in industrialized society effectively, and they resort to a number of responses that break the norm in industrial society, indicating their dissatisfaction with wage work.

There are other reasons why wage work causes discontent among people in non-market cultures. It imposes upon them a new discipline. Work starts and stops with the clock instead of workers' own inclinations; work is based on the persistence of the machine instead of rhythm of morning and evening. This to them unnatural way of working has to be done under orders. They are no longer masters of their work and product but carry out tasks whose purpose they may not know and which is at the command of persons they may never see. Thus, they feel the goals of their work are others', not their own. They look for support from kinsmen and kinswomen but the old ties of blood and village have often been severed by their own migration to the urban centers to find work.

Anthropological literature contains many studies of individuals in non-market cultures or mixed cultures trying to adapt with difficulty to wage work (Finney 1967a; Honigmann 1949; Graves 1970; Waddell 1969; Useem et al. 1943; Hobart 1982; Kruse et al. 1982). These studies reveal patterns of personal and group dislocation, and interruption of or inability to practice traditional activities such as hunting that are important for self-esteem. In many cases there is resort to escape mechanisms, like alcohol. In her study of Ecuadorean Indians, Salz (1955:94–114) relates how managers complained about Indian drinking habits interfering with their work. Salz points out that communal drinking was part of a communal social function and that an Indian would lose prestige if he did not participate in it. Waddell (1969:86–98) discusses the same phenomena among Papago Indians in industrial work, as does Graves (1970) regarding Navajo migrants to Denver. Alcoholism and other forms of escape clash with industrial work values, which stress regularity, sobriety, and discipline in the workplace.

In the preparation for adulthood in a market society, youngsters are trained in schools to be on time and to accept strict work discipline. This training prepares them to enter the world of work (Neff 1977:186–90). For many American Indians living on reservations there is a conflict between the values taught in school and the values taught in their own ethnic communities.

Many American Indians retain a deep emotional attachment to their kinship group and ethnic community for which the city offers few or no alternatives. The Indian migrant who goes to the city to seek wage work has a number of handicaps. They have limited use of the ways of city residents. They are often identifiable as members of a different race or cultural group and are treated with caution and outright suspicion. Under these circumstances they become involved in acts at variance with the very society into which they seek entry.

Contrasting with the experience of American Indians is that of Temne migrants to the city of Freetown in Sierra Leone, West Africa. The Temne set up associations which enabled them to adapt to city life and still preserve their tribal ties and responsibilities (Banton 1970:326–40). The Temne associations took up collections and provided dances, entertainment, and opportunities for social action for their members. The Temne associations, called "companies," become politically significant in Freetown, and their leader, a young schoolmaster, became a political spokesman for all Temne in Sierra Leone.

Banton's study showed that it is possible to provide migrants with means by which to adapt to urban life and wage employment and still retain kinship and tribal values. The Temne companies stressed those values required in the workplaces of market society, while encouraging Temne migrants to maintain their tribal ties and practice their customs. By providing themselves with an organization, they could adapt to market society and still adhere to non-market orientations. They avoided the conflict of values so familiar to mixed societies.

It was not always so for the Temne. They had gone through a period of disintegration, turning their backs on their own culture and facing the conflict between urban society and their tribal responsibilities. However, with the formation and rise to prominence of their companies, the Temne restored their self-respect, the status of their cultural traditions, and their chances for successful adaptation to wage work and the market culture of the city.

3. Problems of Identification In non-market societies a person's place in his community and in the scheme of things in the world is established by membership in a kinship group. They are relatives of an array of people to whom they have obligations and from whom they receive respect, support, and recognition. Within their communities they have social comfort because they have a community of language and custom and are recognized as whole persons.

Once people living within mixed or isolated environments move into the urban, industrialized world and take on the role of wage-worker, problems of identity become manifest. No longer is each one recognized as a whole person to whom others have responsibilities and obligations. Now, as with all wage workers, they are viewed in single dimensions and treated in an impersonal manner. The main requirements of their employers or supervisors is that they show up for work on time and perform their work according to some pre-established standard. Migrants to urban centers have difficulty identifying with those who supervise them as well as with those who work alongside them. The threat to their identity stems from a combination of factors—from contact with different behavior and communication styles, and from entry into a work process in which they are not masters of their own work.

In the United States some of the major ethnic groups that have resisted assimilation and struggled to retain their identity are American Indians. The policy of the federal government has been one of trying to push them down the road to assimilation. The majority of Indian peoples who live on reservations are organized into band or tribal councils operating according to models set down by federal agencies. Band membership and land ownership are legalistically defined. Kinship, marriage, and divorce must conform to white culture and laws. Plant gathering, hunting, trapping, fishing, and farming are restricted to legal areas, legal times, and other legal limitations legislated by the white society. Indians outside the reservation community must conform to the institutions of the white communites. Christian missionary programs attempt to provide religious services to Indian communities which displace Indian religious beliefs and practices. The individual Indian is forced into the role of a consumer of services that emanate from outside his community.

In the face of this situation, American Indians have experienced a devaluation of their cultures and have had to struggle to find the organizational forms and institutions to maintain their identity and traditional values. In the last twenty years there has been a large movement of American and Canadian Indians into cities where they seek work for wages, mostly in blue-collar jobs. Of the roughly 850,000 Indians and Eskimos in the United States, about 350,000 live in towns and cities. Of the 593,000 Indians, Métis, and Eskimos in Canada, 215,000 live in cities (Price 1975:36). In Los Angeles, which has the largest urban Indian population (45,000), Indian institutions date back as far as the 1920s. In many of the other cities of the United States and Canada new associations have been formed in the last decade—kinship and friendship groups, Indian centers, athletic and dancing clubs, cultural groups, Indian publications, employment assistance programs, and occupational groups.

John Price (1975:41–2) has distinguished four stages in the experience of Indian migrants. During the initial stage, there is the setting up of Indian bars where migrants go to drink and socialize. This exists in urban centers. The bar culture tends to be dysfunctional and often leads to behavior that breaks white societal norms. During this stage there is much commuting between the city and the reservation.

In the second stage, kinship-friendship and occupational networks are established. Now it is easier for Indians to find employment. In Albuquerque these networks were responsible for many of the Navajos going into the manufacture of silver jewelry. In Brooklyn and Niagara Falls, New York, occupational networks helped American Indians gain entry into the construction industry.

The third stage brings the formation of common interest associations such as Indian athletic leagues, Indian churches, pow-wow clubs, and political organizations. During this stage, which is going on at present, there is a drive to foster Indian staffing of their own associations. Up to ten years ago most Indian associations were staffed by whites. During the present stage Indians are seeking a reinterpretation of every aspect of their life and history and are seeking new ways of looking at their religion and politics. Price predicts that the fourth stage will come with the setting up of professional, academic, and entrepreneurial associations.

If we compare the experience of American Indians and West Africans, it becomes manifest that to the extent that migrants have banded together and established associations it has aided the adaptation to urban life and wage employment while at the same time helping them to maintain their identity with their ethnic community. In spite of the help given by associations and organizations, migrants still live with the conflict of values. This is true especially for the first generation. It remains to be seen what will happen by the time the third generation grows up. American Indians hope they will still be able to maintain their identity. Industrialized societies tend to bureaucratize the work place, reduce work to a common denominator, and force assimilation upon diverse ethnic groups.

4. Non-Market Enclaves in Market Society There are many examples of traditional, basically non-market cultures within the borders of predominantly market societies. Some of the most prevalent types are nomadic cultures which maintain their traditional customs and practices. They subsist by herding and pastoralism, and trade with markets in the dominant society for goods and services only obtainable in urban centers or villages. Nomadic societies can be found throughout the Middle East, Turkey, Iran, North Africa, India, and Asia. There are also nomads and transhumans in Northern Europe, Northern Canada, and Siberia. The governments of nation-states that contain nomads have difficulty placing these people under the same controls applied to the rest of their populations. Nomads have historically resisted such controls and have maintained their independence and distinctive way of life in the face of many efforts to modernize them.

Nomadic people have not been indifferent to changes in the dominant culture, particularly technological ones. One example comes from Saudi Arabia (Cole 1973:632–638). The Bedouin Arabs of Saudi Arabia have successfully adapted to the ecology of arid and semiarid lands for thousands of years. Moving with their entire families, nomads leave their summer camps located around permanent water sources and take herds of sheep, goats, and camels wherever the desert blooms. Animals are the basis of their livelihood. They are the source of milk and milk products that are the staples of their diet. Sheep and camels provide wool for sale in the markets and for weaving carpets. From the hair of goats nomads weave the black tents in which they live. They also raise surplus animals which they sell.

The Bedouins are deeply attached to their animals and their way of life. They feel that their long-time survival will depend on their not abandoning the desert and their herds. They view oil exploitation as a passing thing that will eventually run out. Still, they do not isolate themselves from the changes taking place around them. In the early days of oil exploration in the late 1930s, Bedouins worked as guides for American oil companies and later as unskilled laborers. Because of the lack of skilled laborers, Aramco set up special schools to train their laborers, most of whom are young Bedouins who were trained to drive and maintain trucks. Later, in central and western Saudi Arabia, the government distributed pickup trucks to the Bedouins. In time, the Bedouins sold their baggage camels and used pick-up trucks for transporting goods. The pickup trucks also enabled the Bedouins to herd with these trucks and to transport water to their herds. Oil companies made their deep water wells available to the nomads.

With increased ease of travel by trucks many Bedouin males were able to combine herding with military service and part-time employment for wages. Today, there is much coming and going between the desert and the city. The Bedouins are prospering and are still in control of their major resources—the pasture lands of the desert and their herds. But Bedouin life has not changed that much. They still work and live as pastoralists and their society and culture promises to remain intact for a long time.

B. Adaptation and Change

The last section of this book and this introduction deal with just two aspects of a broad subject—change. The two aspects are changes in the work of the household and the emergence of new roles in work management.

Changes within household work is an important subject since it affects the nature of the family and the status of women. What affects household labor during the transition from a non-market to a market culture is the shift of work from within the family as the productive unit to the factory and office. Once work is transferred outside the household, work within the household falls increasingly upon women. They must not only fill in for the labor of the husband who works for wages in the factory or office, but they must also take up the slack for the children who now go to school rather than stay at home to work.

The other aspect of change that takes place as non-market societies take on the characteristics of market cultures is that new work roles appear on the occupational landscape. One of these roles is that of management and supervision. This is a new role for people who are used to non-market societies where work relationships are without intermediaries. In industrial work organizations there is often an elaborate system of intermediate management jobs. Their roles are based on impersonal evaluation of those they supervise. They straddle the interests of those above and below them and try to effectively satisfy both.

1. Changes in Work within the Household As non-market cultures are drawn into market systems and wage work beckons to those on the farm seeking higher living standards, the division of work within the family must be readjusted. If the male member of the household seeks wage labor as the main form of income, then women are left to perform most of the work on the farm or in the village. As children are attracted to education as a mean for upward mobility, they stay in school during those years when they formerly were working within the household unit. The reallocation of work results in women having to work longer hours and both parents having to perform work on the farm or in the household that was previously done in part by their children (A. Johnson 1975; Minge-Kalman 1978a; Minge-Klevana 1980; Pellow 1978; Kelly 1981).

During the transitional stage from non-market to market society, women who are excluded from the world of wage work are confined to the household, where they must carry a heavy load of work without remuneration. In North Yemen, it is estimated that the average household of six to eight persons requires the labor of two women to carry out the minimum chores necessary for subsistence— fetching water, caring for livestock, gathering fuel, preparing meals, and caring for children. The sexual division of labor within the household effectively bars women from access to wage employment.

In examining mixed societies, it is important to recognize the role of the household, which influences and significantly affects the supply of labor in the market. By studying household strategies it is possible to appreciate the ways in which individuals and families deal with the pressure of larger socioeconomic forces. It is useful to view the household and the wage-labor market as a continuum, rather than as separate spheres as they are viewed in industrial societies. Seeing the household and the wage-labor market as a continuum is a key to understanding the movement of women into the wage-labor market and children out of the household as part of structurally determined processes which accompany changes from non-market to market societies.

With respect to the reallocation of work in the family as a result of change toward a market society, the question arises as to what degree women's status is improved or worsened. Boserup (1970) has argued that in subsistence cultures women had a strong role in the household from which they attained status and prestige. With the rise of industrialization they become a cheap supply of labor and are forced into wage employment at low wages, thus losing their former position which they enjoyed. Others (Kelly 1981) have reasoned that such effects on women could be corrected through the implementation of programs to give women education and training for higher-paying jobs and entry into the professions.

In the study of changes from non-market to market cultures it is important to develop a greater appreciation for the role of the household in the distribution of work during such societal change. Studies that examine the role of the household can heighten our understanding of the dynamics of the supply of labor—male, female, and children—for the work that needs to be performed in a society. The reproductive role is the complement of the productive role; and the family, which has been allotted a subsidiary role in industrial society as compared with non-market society, is still a crucial factor in the supply of labor for work in every kind of society.

2. New Management Roles during the Change from Non-Market to Market Cultures. Many mixed and developing societies seeking to industrialize introduce factories into their economy as part of the process of growth and change. The factory as a work organization utilizes a set of intermediary roles generally unknown to groups organized for work in non-market environments. These roles of supervisor, foreman, or plant manager involves the intervention of people between those who work and those who contract for work.

Those who perform work in a village do so directly for the person who wants the work done. The person wanting the work done either pays for it or exchanges work for work received. The Ilakia Awa of Papua, New Guinea, exchange labor on nearly a daily basis during periods of intensive labor inputs (Boyd 1981:80).

In small industrial establishments in small villages, the proprietor is usually both employer and supervisor. In the case of Ghanian wood-carvers, the master craftsman hires and directly supervises his own apprentices (Silver 1981:41–52). In most craft enterprises the employer works alongside his hired help and supervision is not a discrete function. In non-market societies a person's ownership of land or an enterprise is viewed as their authority to direct and supervise work. People in non-market cultures find it hard to accept non-owners—managers, foremen, and superintendents—as having the legitimacy to direct work and give orders.

With the development of market institutions in non-market societies, and the rise of large-scale enterprises, a new management role appears, that of the supervisor. In place of the direct, face-to-face contact with the employer there now appears a person who is neither owner nor one engaged in work, but rather one who passes on orders from owners to those who are working. In the past, with face-to-face relationships, there was the possibility of adjustment in the status of the parties; with the interposing of the non-working supervisor who has no power to negotiate a change in the status of the worker, work is now subject to a set of rules from which there is to be no deviation or appeal.

A variation of the intermediary role comes from Zulu migrants on farms in Natal's sugar belt in South Africa (Loudon 1979:122–23). Employers of blacks on these farms become involved in the personal affairs of their workers. Blacks view the relationship in the following way (Loudon 1979:127):

> They balance the regular involvement of their employers in almost any aspect of their personal lives against the uncaring unpredictability of remote white supervisors in industry who do not know if you are married or not nor how many children or other dependents you have to support.

This paternalistic structure is linked to a system which employs intermediaries who are called "monitors." The monitors serve as communication links and as mediators in disputes. Often they are older men who are trusted by both workers and employers. They also have links with clan chiefs in the district or region. To run a large farm, white employers need a system of communication. They need intermediaries who are trusted by the workers. The monitors have ties with tribal networks and are effective in settling disputes. The role of "monitor" is a variation on the role of foreman and goes beyond the work relationship, reaching into involvement in the personal affairs of the workers they are involved with.

Summary

If we examine societies from a comparative viewpoint, it is apparent that human beings have entered into immensely varied forms of social organization. Human societies differ greatly in the content of their institutions—legal, religious, economic, kinship and political. They also differ tremendously in the ways that they make their living, the tools and technologies employed and the meanings they attach to work. If we attempt to order societies on the basis of their organizations of work and means of gaining their livelihood we find hunting and gathering societies at one extreme, societies based on kinship, small bands and hand technology. At the other extreme are industrialized societies, such as those in North America and Europe, which are urbanized and based on machine technology. The hunting and gathering societies are very ancient and the industrialized societies very recent. Between these two forms there have existed a wide variety of non-market and mixed societies based on peasant agriculture, pastoralism and the domestication of animals. These societies vary enormously in development, complexity and unique historical and social characteristics.

In the sections which follow an attempt will be made to characterize the work performed in various types of non-market and mixed societies. The objective will be to relate the attitudes toward work and the organization of work to the characteristics of various types of cultures. We can then begin to see the many possibilities and the many meanings given to work which differ and contrast with those that we have been familiar with in industrial society. A comparative view of how other societies view the nature of work can serve to sharply outline our own attitudes and patterns of work behavior.

I

Introduction
Theory and the Anthropology of Work

Work is such a pervasive activity that it influences and affects all individuals and all social phenomena. Until recently most people had to work most of their waking hours to earn their livelihood. Even today, in industrial societies with high productivity and an eight-hour workday, people must still work half their waking hours. Thus, work is a significant part of the human condition, both as regards the amount of time humans must devote to it and the fact that it relates to all social phenomena.

Work has always been one of the main determinants in the way people in societies organize and function. It is not an accident that the main ways people make a living has a large influence on kinship and family structure, on a society's political and legal system, including property and human rights, and on moral and religious teachings prevalent in a society. Work has been and still is a crucial factor in a person's self-esteem and in the way people are viewed by others. Control over other people's work has been a strong motive in war and revolution, political upheaval and social conflict. Work has also been the focal point for the cooperative efforts of human beings, from simple reciprocity in helping each other build a house to the grandest achievements of monuments, science, engineering, and art. Through work, human beings express their physical capacities, manual dexterity and their mental faculties.

Despite the importance and centrality of work as a human activity, it is only during the last thirty or forty years that it has engaged the attention of social scientists. With few exceptions, such as Malinowski, Firth, Forde, and Herskovits, and the researchers of economic anthropologists, most anthropologists have concentrated on kinship organization, marital patterns, religion and myth, ecology and evolution, political structure and tribal affiliation. Applied anthropologists were involved in the human relations movement in industry during the 'thirties but today the study of work is not central to their interests. The sociologists developed a subfield, the sociology of work, in the 'forties and 'fifties, but their interests are not global and they have largely confined their research to industrial societies. In history, most traditional studies deal with nations and classes, monarchs and armies, and broad social trends. It is only recently that there have been significant historical studies of labor movements and people who work. Particularly noteworthy are the researchers of Eric Wolf, Herbert Gutman, David Montgomery, and Tamara Harevan. The archaeologist touches on the subject of work because their findings include tools but they cannot tell us what people who worked thought or felt or how they behaved, except for speculative deductions from their material remains. Since World War II, the physiologist and physical anthropologist have done good work in the study of hand, eye, and body coordination associated with various types of work and with people who must use military equipment. And finally, industrial psychologists have studied work and have much to offer on the subject, but that too has been only a recent trend.

The study of work did not begin to take place until work became a "problem." In the past the study of work was undertaken by industrial engineers and psychologists concerned with the goals of management who wished to create a work force which would submit to corporate objectives. Despite all the years of scientific management, human relations and job redesign, however, worker dissatisfaction and alienation persisted; thus there continued a strong interest in research on work. The fall in productivity, the rise in absenteeism, and the growing use of drugs in the workplace were all signs that something had gone wrong with the world of work. Consequently, corporations and governments sponsored new studies. The United States Department of Health, Education and Welfare produced the study, "Work in America"; (1975) in England, the Tavistock Institute was established to study and recommend new forms of work organization; worldwide, the "Quality of Working Life" movement was launched. All of this signalled that work, which had been taken for granted in the past, was an important aspect of human life that needed greater attention and looking into.

What was different from the past? One profound change was that people worked less and had more leisure time. Accordingly, various proponents asserted that work need no longer be as important as it once was in society. They said that with increased industrial productivity, the aim of society should be to reduce working to a bare minimum. Never mind the billions of person-years that are needed to build roads and bridges, to provide health and social services and to feed and clothe the majority of the world's people. Social scientists like David Macarov (1980) said we were now on the verge of a "leisure society," in which leisure time was to be so pervasive that people would now measure their self-esteem by their leisure activities rather than by their work and occupation. Work was to be an interruption of leisure rather than the other way around. And everyone could be as creative as they wished during their leisure hours since society would be productive enough to satisfy the material needs of its inhabitants with a minimum of work.

Such an ideal is certainly attractive. But aside from the practical consideration that nature does not give up her bounty without humans performing work, there are social scientists and philosophers who believe that work is a fundamental condition of human existence (Heilbroner 1970; Thompson 1978; Udy 1970; Harris 1975; Arendt 1959; Heidegger 1971). Indeed, as work has been a creative force in the past, so it is today and can become even more so in the future. It is not necessary to have a split between work and leisure. In fact, those who lack satisfaction in their work often lack the resources to be creative in their leisure.

Another change that occurred which made work a "problem" was that certain aspects of work associated with non-market cultures were lost as societies industrialized. What were some of these aspects of work? First, with the mechanization of work we have reduced creative and manual dexterity in work. Work performed in non-market societies, although often arduous, calls upon a person's total faculties. The !Kung San hunter must become totally involved in the enterprise of gaining his livelihood. He must cooperate with others. He must care for and prepare his tools. During the hunt he uses all his physical and mental faculties. The same is true for the herder and the farmer, the blacksmith and the potter, the fisherman and the gardener, the weaver and the shoemaker. They control their work and its product. With industrialism, total involvement and control is relinquished. Work is now a "problem" and it is necessary to search for ways to bring the workers' mental and manual faculties once more to bear in the work process. There is also a search for means to offer autonomy and control to those who do industrialized work. This is the challenge of the future, not seeing work as a necessary evil to be dispensed with as quickly as possible so human beings can devote themselves solely to leisure. There are many human beings who seek a unity between work and all other spheres of their social being, including leisure activities.

A second aspect of work relinquished by industrial societies and prevalent in non-industrial cultures is the requirement in work for physical strength and manual dexterity. Machine power has replaced human power. It can lift greater weights and work faster and more accurately than human beings. Machine technology has left humans to wait passively before the machines, watching their dials or making repetitive hand and arm motions which hardly test their mental and physical abilities. Those who sit before computers, punching in raw data which they hardly understand, are also using a fraction of their capacities. Physical exertion can be exhilirating and healthy for human beings; studies have shown that those most vulnerable to cardiovascular troubles very often have sedentary occupations. Pitting one's strength against the natural elements is a source of satisfaction for many occupations—construction, logging, longshore work, seafaring, mining, pipe laying, ranching, farming, fishing, trucking, and many others. People who work in these occupations know from their sweat that they have done a good day's work, and they are proud of it. Similarly, the worker who can display manual dexterity using tools and instruments has the same satisfaction from marrying his mind with his hand. Antique shops are full of objects that bear testimony to the creative work of anonymous craftspeople. It is a sad fact that the so-called simple hunter in the Kalihari Desert in Southwest Africa uses more of his mental and physical capacities in his work than the factory worker living in a sophisticated, urban environment in Detroit, Michigan.

A third attribute of work that is a problem in industrial societies is the need to strengthen the social environment of the workplace. Industrial technology has so tied many workers to the machine and has so isolated office and factory workers, that many find it unnecessary to engage in social cooperation or reciprocity in order to carry out their work. In addition, bureaucratization has made work so impersonal that social relations on the job are superficial and without affect, leaving the emotional resources of individuals at work largely dormant. Work in the past and today in non-market cultures features comradeship and community; social scientists are now seeking ways to rekindle such features in the workplace. The Japanese have achieved much in this respect; all industrial societies are studying their success, but a good deal of their community in the workplace stems from their unique cultural traditions which western societies do not share.

A fourth attribute of work relinquished with the transition from non-market to market society was the informal nature of work. In its place there is a hierarchical system which develops levels of authority and supervision, and a vast bureaucracy of clerks, office and white-collar workers who do not turn out products but are instructed instead to keep track of those who do. The personalized, face-to-face character of work, in which there is a direct exchange of services and a cooperative effort to achieve mutually agreed upon goals, fosters satisfaction in work as well as solidarity with the work group. When it is replaced with an impersonal hierarchy, a person who works no longer has an interest in the goals of the organization because they are not of one's own making. Unlike machines, humans have wills and when they are not motivated they do not work well.

These four factors, and no doubt others, have contributed to the sense of insecurity about work and a feeling that there are social, organizational, and environmental factors over which people who work no longer have control: consequently, the sense of malaise about work and the desire for change. Just as the science of thermodynamics filled the need for more non-human forms of energy in developing industrial societies, so the research on work and the various proposals for the redesign of work is a response to a need to make work once again satisfying, a source of self-esteem, and a means for mental and manual creativity.

The first two selections which follow will delineate a number of theoretical and methodological issues which touch on the questions raised above, as well as others that should concern all investigators in the subject of work.

NOTES

1. While relations between the core economic centers and the periphery are unequal, it does not mean that the periphery area will not receive benefits. There are cases where a relationship between two countries or between capital and labor, while remaining unequal, contributes to the welfare of both parties. The mutually beneficial results does not make the relationship less equal or less distorted. It only implies that it does not always lead to absolute deprivation of the dependent country or sector, even though the relative distribution of benefits may remain the same or may even grow in favor of the more advanced nation or sector. A good example is Spain. Since the 1950's, it has become a modern, industrial nation, with dramatic shifts from agriculture, which was the main sector of the economy, to manufacturing and services, which now account for 37% and 40% of the labor force in Spain. Spain is now part of the world industrial and financial system, exporting maching tools, autos, electrical equipment, machinery and ships. This growth was the result of external capital investment from advanced industrial nations. While Spain is more dependent on the international financial and industrial market and less autonomous than previously, she has benefited with regard to a rising standard of living and the creation of an industrial base in the country. For a long time Spain was content to forego industrialization because it meant dependency upon foreign capital. Other developing nations

face a similar decision—whether to sacrifice a measure of its independence and allow foreign capital investment or try to develop an industrial base on the basis of its own resources, which are often inadequate for any rapid advance. For a discussion of Spain and this issue see Casanova, José (1980).

CHAPTER ONE

The Anthropology of Work

JUNE NASH

If we take as the definition of work purposive activity directed towad meeting physical and social needs satisfying to those who either produce or consume goods and services, we can encompass the broad range of human activities in time and space that anthropologists study.[1] Because of the discipline's holistic approach, anthropologists have richly documented the proposition that work is both the realization of human capacity and the basis for reproducing that capacity. Some have gone on to show that, in the process of working, human beings not only recognize their functions in society, but transform it. I shall review some of the contributions anthropologists and others have made that shed light on work processes that have transformed society.

The evolution of humanity can be marked in the archaeological record of tools, seeds, structures and art. The ability to apply intelligence in this productive activity became a selective factor for genetic advances (Oakley 1972, Washburn 1975). The dialectical reinforcement of genetic and cultural advance is of less significance once culture is the conditioning factor. With the advance of civilization, people learn more than they invent; they know less about more of their culture in an increasingly complex society. Whereas most members of the human species shared the ability to make and use tools during the Paleolithic and early Neolithic, as stratified societies developed, elites emerged who planned and organized the work of others. The trend is toward a narrowing scope for the application of the intelligence humans share as members of the same species.

This trend has become acute with industrialization in the particular historical form in which it has developed. The debasement of most jobs to repetitive, short-cycle operations requiring little training and subject to managerial control eliminates the creative interaction that was the basis for human transformation. The concentration of decision-making and control is eliminating the variability and adaptability that were the principle advantages of the human species in evolution. Indeed, the capital intensive high-energy conversion industrialization characteristic of monopoly capitalism may even eliminate the human input in production. The central problem for an applied anthropology of work is to find ways of improving the relationship between human potential and the productive process.

The increasing specialization in the division of labor and the growing hierarchy of skills and managerial levels were developments associated with the rise of civilization. I shall briefly review some of the developments that led to the present crisis.

The Division of Labor and Stratification

The earliest specialization in the division of labor was probably based on sex and age. Extrapolating from historical and contemporary evidence on hunting and gathering people, Slocum (1975) speculates on the contribution women's gathering activities made in the transition to agricultural societies. MacNeish (1964) demonstrates the gradual increase in wild plant foods and the acquisition of cultivated plants throughout the ten millenia of occupation in the Tamaulipas caves in Mexico. The knowledge of the micro-environment gained by women as they maximized their harvesting of tubers, pods, fruits and berries each season enabled this Middle American hunting group to survive the extinction of the great mammals in the climatological shift from 10,000 B.C. to 6,700 B.C. MacNeish (1964) relates these patterns to similar developments in the Zagros mountains of Iraq. Flannery (1969) and Flannery and Coe (1968) corroborate the importance of the exploitation of these microenvironments as a precondition for the introduction of agriculture. The development of alternative sources of food and regional specialization reinforced neolithic adaptations. Shellfish collectors on the Gulf of Mexico and coastal Peru maintained high density, fairly permanent settlements without an agricultural base, but they supplemented their diet with exchanges with inland horticultural villages. (Patterson 1971).

Self-sufficient villages with limited regional specialization were probably organized by egalitarian institutions (Fried 1967; Leacock 1978). Even in ranked societies few individuals were removed from the productive labor force. It is not until stratified societies emerge that the division of labor between manual and what is often called "mental"—but often boils down to relatively simple administrative tasks—becomes crystallized. As the division of labor exceeded the simple specialization by sex, sanctions commanding power beyond the resources of a kinship system are needed (Fried 1967:286). Leacock (1978) points to the two conditions that accelerated the trend toward stratification: (1) production of goods for exchange and (2) separation of individual families from the larger collectivity and their emergence as the basic economic unity. In this process, female labor became a private, unrecompensed service.

Ideological control through a supernatural or religious sanctioning system was one of the early techniques developed for the maintenance of order and the expropriation of the labor power of others. The widespread evidence for religious cults with standardized deity images and established shrine sites in the Far East, Middle East, northern Africa, Middle America, and in the Andes attest to the importance of religious techniques of control (Bellah 1964).

Ideologies justifying the domination by an elite are concurrent with expressions of rebellion and dissent on the part of the subordinated. Class consciousness developed in the early theocracies despite the divine claims of the kings. In the year 29 of Rameses III, the craftsmen who worked on the tombs in the Valley of the Dead at Thebes stopped work in protest of short rations. It was apparently an organized strike action, involving the stewards as intermediaries negotiating with the vizier.[2] Çerný (1973:131) records the episode:

> The foremen had a difficult time when the gang went on hunger strike in the 29th year of Rameses III. They left the work in the tomb. The scribe of the tomb, . . . The two foremen, the (two) deputies and two district officers came and called to them: "Come home." They also tried to soothe them with promises. Some time later, however, after the gang had been given two khar of wheat as the ration for the month (clearly not enough) the foreman Kohns said to the gang: "Look, I am telling you: Accept the ration and go down to the port to the gate. Let the minions of the vizier tell him; and when the scribe Amennakhte finished giving them the ration they started toward the port as he (Kohns) had told them.

Çerný goes on to note that the scribe had to resort to threats, since the foreman supported the workers. The grievance workers expressed was limited to dissatisfaction with the rewards for their labor. So far as we can infer, they accepted the role structure and their place in it. The craftsmen who painted, sculpted and engineered the tombs for the royalty designed similar tombs for themselves. Though they were of a more modest scale, and rabbits rather than serpents were the totemic representations, the workmanship was as good or better than that performed for their rulers.

Ideological support for social systems based on a division of labor with increasing disparities in the rewards and satisfaction in work responded to differences in the composition of the work force and in turn reinforced those differences. When the division of labor accorded superior prestige and rewards to some members of the same population, an ideology related to divine inheritance often developed, as in the Middle East. When it involved exchanges between ethnically differentiated groups, an ideology focusing on the traditional transmission of skills might result. When the task specialization is coterminous with community, the social integration is reinforced, as in the hereditary castes of India, tribal specialization of African blacksmiths, and in early Mediterranean cities where Jews were tanners and weavers, Mohammedans were armorers and Greeks and Copts were goldsmiths (Durkheim 1964). The ideology of racism supported slavery but came after the segregation of the labor force in the international division of labor brought about by the expansion of the world capitalist system (Cox 1948).

Education as validation for superior social and occupational status had an ancient history. An early Egyptian text used to train scribes urges the students to apply themselves diligently to learning their trade so that they might escape a life of endless drudgery (Childe 1951). Recognizing the limitation of most occupational roles even in his ideal Republic, Plato proposed different educational tracts for "iron", "silver", and "gold" people to narrow the horizons for those in the baser categories. However, it was not until the industrial era that education became the principle means of allocating people to narrowly defined occupational roles.

The Division of Labor in Industry

The transformation from specialization of tasks characteristic of preindustrial production to atomization of tasks in industrial enterprises is supported by two basic premises. The first is technological determinism justifying the organization of work; the second is education validating the prerogatives of management. At surface level, technological innovation seems to be self-evident: "The hand mill gives you a society with a feudal lord, the steam mill a society with the industrial capitalist," Bottomore (1971:51) quotes Marx, but we cannot go on, as Bottomore does, to ask what kind of a mill would give rise to a classless society. The hand mill and the steam mill are metaphors for the material base of feudalism and capitalism that might have supported other kinds of power relations. Although the marxist rhetoric stimulates material determinism, the dialectical view of mode of production can be understood only as they interact upon each other. This is congenial with the holistic approach cultivated in anthropology (Udy 1970).

Rereading the history of the rise of capitalism from this holistic view, the mill is not so important in the changes the organization of production brought about in capitalism as is windpower captured by the sails of eighteenth century vessels that extended markets from Europe to overseas trade (Cottrell 1955: li, 50). This overseas trade had far-reaching consequences on the social relations in industry, since, heretofore, production for the internal market had been controlled by guilds. The guilds had been able to limit the volume of output as well as entry into production through their monopoly of retail trade within a country. These restrictions had the side effect of limiting the degree of specialization within the trade throughout the seventeenth and into the eighteenth century (Smith 1909:126-7). But as manufacturers began to produce for a world market, they were able to bypass guild restrictions on entry into production (Hobsbawn 1964). Industrialization was promoted by an international market and in turn brought about an international division of labor.

The changing organization of production from household production for home use to retail handicraft and itinerant crafts production, and finally to the location of production in centralized factories was not, in any of these transformations, technologically predetermined. The centralization of the labor force in factories preceded the application of water power or steam (Gras 1930) and set the stage for the efficient use of power beyond that of human labor, while the shift from domestic to retail handicrafts rarely involved any technological change. Adam Smith (1909) described the division of labor in a nail factory in the mid-eighteenth century in which nine men were involved in the production of nails without the use of any energy other than human labor power.

This kind of specialization marks a new step in the organization of production. Whereas in craft production the only division of labor was in the kind of article produced—bootmakers might be specialists in men's or women's shoes or in fine or cheap quality merchandise with each journeyman making the whole shoe—in the factory, management increasingly took over control of the organization of work.

In addition to strengthening the managerial control over production, industrialization brought about another significant change in the relations in production by separating production for exchange from the domestic setting. The consequence of this was to sharpen the difference between a primary and secondary labor force. In the early years of industrial capitalism, accumulation was made possible by the extreme exploitation of women and children. Until 1838, they constituted 62 per cent of the labor force in England (Hobsbawm 1968). As the population of England increased and alternative employment for men decreased, men became the principle source of labor for the factories. The demand by men for a "family wage" and the elimination of competitive female labor in preferred factory employment resulted in a segregated labor force. The result, as Jane Humphries (1977:247) points out, is that the domestic labor process, separated from the dominant mode of production and from the means of exchange, renders it "invaluable" but, ironically, valueless. Sexist ideologies legitimated this separation of women and their children from the productive roles they had filled throughout human history as a "result" of physiology.

Despite the wealth of ethnographic data contradicting such an ideology, some anthropologists have supported this position. Murdock (1937) hypothesizes that males, being stronger, can undertake more strenuous economic tasks while females being handicapped by burdens of pregnancy and nursing must undertake simpler tasks. Aronoff and Crano (1975) show how data contained in the Human Relations Area File set up by Murdock disprove his thesis. Women actually provide nearly half, or 44 per cent of the total subsistence products in all of the 862 societies included in the Human Relations Area Files.

The step from a division of labor in specialized work—butcher, baker, candlestick-maker—to a dividing up of the productive process marks the major change in industrialization. The transformation from worker control over the job to subordination of the worker to industrial managers threatens the adaptive capability of the system. Marx said of it (1971:73):

> This step into industrial forms of labor required coercion since it was so alien to human existence. In the early times of industrialization, factories were connected to prisons, workhouses and orphanages—the subdivision of the task, when carried on without regard to human capabilities and needs is a crime against the person and against humanity.

Braverman (1975) documents the debasement of labor resulting from the shattering of the work process showing how the quality of work as "purposive action guided by intelligence as the special product of humankind" was distorted in industrialization under monopoly capitalism. At the turn of the century, the control over the work process was given a "scientific" base with the work of Frederick Winslow Taylor (Braverman 1975:90). His techniques of job control succeeded in breaking whatever remaining craft hold there was in the early decades of the twentieth century at the same time that he provided an ideology for technocratic control. Lenin introduced the Taylor system of job atomization and assembly line operation into the factories of the Union of Soviet Socialist Republics and thereby created the basis for the managerial elite in the new Communist state. The ongoing process of work debasement in industry is amply documented in anthropology for railroad workers (Kemnitzer 1975), mines (Nash 1979; Orlove 1975), the shoe industry (Warner and Low 1947), automobile production (Gartman 1979), and printing (Zimbalist 1979). The proletarianization of the white collar work force documented by Mills (1956) proceeds along with the technological revolution in computerized data processing (Glenn and Feldberg 1979; Kraft 1979).

Worker resistance to managerial control takes many forms. Mothe (1959), a worker in a French Renault plant, describes the contradictions in the machine shop where the specialization of tasks eliminates the self-correcting processes when a worker carries out an entire sequence of operations. He points out (Mothe 1959:20) that the worker "who has an idea of the finished object in his head" makes fewer errors than when there are many people carrying out the same operation "none of whom have the ideal machine in their heads". As Mothe shows in his remarkable autobiography, the organization of work in the modern automobile factory denies the possibility for workers to use their intelligence since any decisions, innovations, or cooperation among the so-called manual workers would threaten the very structure of the worker-management hierarchy.

The opposition of manual and technical workers is found in varying degrees in all industries. Kusterer (1976) records the survival techniques developed by workers and their transmission of this knowledge to other workers. Balzer (1976:131) describes the socialization of new workers to the work norms in an electrical plant. Electrical machinery workers I interviewed in a Massachusetts plant said that operators who revealed workers know-how by submitting suggestions to management that shortened work cycles were subject to sabotage of their automobiles or homes by their co-workers. During a long term strike in a large plant in western Massachusetts in 1969, one of the greatest fears of the striking workers was that the managers who took over on the assembly line would learn some of the shortcuts they had already mastered and would cut down the piece rates (Nash 1978).

One of the greatest sources of complaints in a modern factory is the failure of management to compensate workers for their ideas, submitted either as suggestions or in competitions. Many workers complain that when they asked their supervisors what they thought of a proposed change in the work process, the supervisors rejected it as unfeasible and then submitted the suggestion themselves. Because this compensation is not part of their formal contract, there is no discussion of the terms in union negotiation. As a result, the workers' knowledge gained in experience on the job is not fed back into improvements in the work process.

As a basis for developing the field of applied anthropology of work, we must take into consideration the effect of the present organization of production on the work force. We need to develop measures of comparative advantage of work systems and measures of productivity that will include the effect on human physical, psychological and intellectual health. As a step in that direction, I shall summarize material from an interview with Richard Brown, an assembly worker in the former Mahwah, New Jersey Ford plant, conducted in a seminar on systems of production at City College. Richard was fired for his activities in organizing a slowdown in 1973. He described the dissatisfaction of the men when the line was speeded from 54 to 62 cars an hour:

> My job cycle took 1.2 minutes and was repeated 389 times a day. I had to move the axle from the rear line, push it ahead on a double hook, turn it, tighten the control knobs and undo the brake cable. I hated that line—I was on the "heavy" line. My body couldn't stand it. I used the same muscles over and over, not my whole body. At the end of the day, I was worn out and in pain. I didn't even want any overtime. If you get a little ahead, say 1.1 minutes on a 1.2 cycle, and try to light a cigarette, these efficiency guys would give you more work.
> You are a slave to the line—if you "go in the hole," you are subject to discipline.

When the line was speeded up, he and some of the other men planned to sabotage the work by "going into the hole," that is, by failing to keep up with the line. With a half-hour slowdown, they could make the company lose over $60,000.

The problem for the workers was to gain the cooperation of the line. This was difficult because of what appeared to be a deliberate policy on the part of management to atomize the work force as well as the work process. The plant was built at the intersection of four major highways and the workers were drawn from the industrial cities of New Jersey, New York and Pennsylvania with a trilingual population of Hispanic, French-speaking Haitians, blacks and whites. The line is segregated, with young black workers on the night shift, older whites on the truck line—called the "gravy line" because of the overtime—and new workers like Richard on the "heavy" line. Men were pitted against women when anti-discrimination laws were enforced. Women would be put on a light job a man would work ten years to ease into, and all the workers would turn against them and make it hard for them to work.

Added to the problem of creating solidarity in the heterogeneous labor force divided by preferential system based on race and sex, the workers had neither the time nor the ability to discuss their problems during work time. The din in the assembly room on the mile-long line was enough to cause 12 per cent loss of Richard's hearing after one year of work. During an eight hour day in the plant, the workers have 42 minutes to take care of natural functions. The dining room was a mile away in the same building, and in order to get down there and have some time to eat, they had to run. But then, there was a rule against running. One man fell and ruptured a hernia while running to the lunchroom. He was not given compensation for on-the-job accident because he broke the rule against running.

I asked Richard how, given these conditions, the workers found the basis for social solidarity in the slow-down. His answer was revealing: since the workers do not have the money to buy the cars they make and since all live in a far-flung radius of up to two hours of commuting time each way, they form car pools of up to five men. It is in the commuting time that they worked out the basic strategy. They distributed leaflets in Spanish and English, and later even in French when Haitian workers were hired.

The slow-down was brought about without the help of the union. Richard was contemptuous of many of the shop stewards. Health safety and job conditions were, according to Richard, largely ignored. In addition to the din, workers were expected to adjust to air pollution from propane gas and the exhaust fumes of the vehicles driven around inside the plant.

The upshot of the slowdown was that 38 men were fired. They supported the movement until their unemployment compensation stopped coming in and then drifted into other jobs. Richard took up work in construction. He did not want to work at a job where he had no control over his time and his movements.

The Mahwah plant incorporated all of the features in the organization of work that social scientists had criticized in the decades following World War II. Walker and Guest (1951) analyzed worker discontent in automobile factories in the forties where the pace of repetitious, short-cycle jobs was set by the line. They presented worker suggestions for alleviating the deadening routine: more opportunities for workers to set their own pace, including "bank stocking", subassembly work, rotating jobs in teams, and job enlargement. Their major advice was to have workers enter into decision-making in the organization of production. Blauner (1964) anticipated a solution in continuous-process production, with increased leisure time a trade-off for routine assembly line jobs that persisted. This has failed to materialize since the forty-hour week is still standard and workers feel compelled to accept overtime even when they don't want it.

The failure to take into account the advice of social science findings and the experience in factory production resulted in the replication of past errors in plants such as Mahwah and Vega in Youngstown. When the Mahwah plant was closed in April, 1980, Ford directors blamed poor workmanship and low productivity as the reason (*New York Times*, April, 1980). At the root of the problem were managerial decisions that failed to take into account the workers' revolt against speedup and job exploitation.

Anthropologists are in a good position to analyze the potential for changing the organization of production to meet human needs. Because of our holistic approach to the study of human groups, we can question the biological, environmental and social effects of a task structure that encourages the atrophy of the mind and the wasteful expenditure of human physical resources as Richard describes for his work. Our accumulated knowledge of non-industrialized societies provides us with some basis for determining alternative ways of organizing production. This knowledge must be brought into comparative perspective with industrial societies in raising questions about the rationality and efficiency of a productive system that relegates an increasing number of productive workers to welfare dependence because of high energy converters and automation at the same time that it debases the jobs of the employed work force. We must question the efficiency of a factory system that fails to integrate the work process with the planning process, that pits the floor workers who implement plans against those who formulate plans. And furthermore we must question a productive system that puts succeeding generations in conflict with each other, as young workers are seen as a competitive threat to senior employees.

The evolutionary perspective of the field enables us to analyze these problems in a cultural system that contradicts the selective advantages of the human species: the plasticity and adaptability to change and the ability to transmit knowledge from one generation to the next. Large scale enterprise with heavy capital inputs and highly concentrated decision-making is seemingly incapable of making the kind of adjustments to energy shortages and economic slowdown. Given our holistic approach to analyzing problems, we could work out a cost accounting system to assess the psychological, social and health effects of modern industry on the work force along with the increasing hazards of environmental and occupational diseases caused by industrial pollutants.

Elliot Chappel (1981) has called for a reinvigoration of the applied industrial anthropology he helped to pioneer. For the most part, the advice of social scientists calling attention to the problems of alienation in the work place have been rejected (Carr and Sterner 1952; Walker and Guest 1952; Blauner 1964). Richardson and Walker (1957) demonstrated the advantages of IBM corporation in its resistance to the centralization of responsibility and to extending the lines of communication and greater job specialization in its period of expansion. These lessons have been ignored by Ford Management in the Mahwah plant and other classic cases of companies that have persisted in earlier trends toward increasing specialization that have proven disastrous such as the Vega Chevrolet plant.

Possibly we would find a readier audience in labor unions, who may soon demand a larger role in management decision-making as the government is called upon to rescue ailing companies such as Chrysler. Whatever our point of entry, the insights gained in the four sub-disciplines must be brought to bear in the policy-making arenas where they can assist in transforming productive processes.

NOTES

I am indebted to Eleanor Leacock for many helpful suggestions as well as to Miriam Kaprow who succeeded in clarifying some of the ideas presented in this version of a paper presented at the 1976 meeting of the American Anthropological Association in Washington, D.C.

1. Udy (1970) defines work as "purposive human efforts to modify man's environment." While I have tried to retain his goal of seeking a culture-free definition, I prefer to emphasize the goal of satisfying human needs, since I feel that environmental modification is an inadvertant (and increasingly more disastrous) consequence of the work we do.

2. The term for work gang in Egypt was the same as that used for a crew of a ship. The Latin term for class was, likewise, derived from a boat's crew. This suggests the basis in solidarity that results in class consciousness.

CHAPTER TWO

Considerations for an Anthropology of Work

FREDERICK C. GAMST

I

Presented in this paper are a number of considerations for understanding the nature of the now burgeoning *anthropology of work*. Almost all ethnologists (that is, social and cultural anthropologists) in their study of primitive/tribal societies for over a century and of agrarian and industrial civilization one-half of a century have been concerned with the study of work. Such study was ordinarily a byproduct of producing a wholistic ethnography, but was a central part of the case study. Reflecting this central concern, ethnologists have customarily classified societies in an evolutionary taxonomy according to the predominant work of these. Work, then, is regarded by ethnologists as the very basis of human society. Ethnologists find that as mankind moves along the technologic continuum of efficiency in harnessing and using energy, less of a societal time budget is devoted to food-getting work and more to other kinds of work.

During the 1930s through 1960s, especially in North America, a handful of pioneering ethnologists studied work self-consciously, not as a part of a larger emphasis, but as an end in itself. Although having wider application, much of such study of work was oriented toward Western society. (For review statements on the pioneering scholarship see Chapple 1953; Harding 1955; Richardson 1955; Arensberg et al. 1957; Keesing et al. 1957; Gardner and Moore 1964; Goldschmidt 1968; Gamst 1977; Burawoy 1979; Richardson 1979).

II

The 1970s saw the florescence of the anthropology of work as a self-conscious study and especially of recognized, or formal, occupations. The greater acceptability of such study in the 1970s by our discipline is an important difference between research of the current wave and the pioneering studies of earlier decades. This paper gives some considerations for the new wave. We examine first *anthropology* and, then, *work* as concepts.

In North America, four-field *anthropology* is truly interdisciplinary, a much sought after but often illusive scholarly goal. However, we often lapse into use of the generic interfield term, anthropology, to mean only one of the four component fields: ethnology, archeology, physical anthropology, and linguistics. For example, the anthroplogy of education and applied anthropology (Gamst 1975a:37–39) are usually only ethnology. Is the anthropology of work to follow this frequently trodden path of narrow definition of the term for the science of man? That is, will it be developed as a sociocultural anthropology of work or as a true (integrated) anthropology of work? Unbeknown to many ethnologists, a large body of scholarship for a physical anthroplogy and for an archeology of work exists, especially in the industrial and occupational aspects of work. (For reviews of industrial physical anthropology see Morant 1948; Hertzberg 1958; Damon et al. 1963, 1966; Gamst 1975:37–39; Damon 1975; Robbins 1976; Hertzberg 1979. And for discussion of industrial archeology see Taylor 1958; Vogel 1969; Buchanan 1972; Schuyler 1974; Atkinson 1974; Buchanan 1976; Sande 1976; Hudson 1976, 1979.)

In all, ethnologists would profit by an inclusion of the scholarship of other anthropologists in their study of work. Because one dimension of work is physical exertion, the physiological ecology of work (Thomas 1975) should be a necessary part of many sociocultural studies on the subject. Human factors research into the interface of man, machine, and spatial and temporal social organization can be fruitfully conducted by a blending of ethnology and physical anthroplogy (cf. Gamst 1975a, 1975b, 1975c). Historical development of particular kinds of work ethnologically studied can often be understood better by means of historical archeology.

III

Little consensus exists in the various disciplines about what is researched under the term *work* (cf. Tilgher 1931; Weiss and Kahn 1960; Friedman, et al. 1961; Thorns 1971; Wolfbein 1971). Speaking generally, through work man transforms nature and human society into culturally organized ends by use of appropriate cognitive maps. Because most work is not just physical and mental, but also social, it includes not only techniques and tools, but, usually, also patterns of interpersonal relations and spatial and temporal dimensions of social organization. The social relations and organization concern division and political control of labor. Especially significant for the student of work is the allocation and consumption of the product of toil and the decision making conditions for labor and for the nature of the good or service produced.

Broadly considered, human work is the purposeful exertion of physical and mental faculties to accomplish something, usually a change in the geographic or social environment. More narrowly considered, work refers to being engaged in a *gainful* occupation such as being a cultivator, craftsman, or administrator. Gainful refers to an occupation in which a livelihood is earned in money, kind, or labor. Livelihood may be earned in a market economy or in a largely subsistence one. Gainful work is paid in money in industrial societies, but less or not so in preindustrial groups. Even where work is gainful the occupational emphasis of its value varies greatly. Automobile assemblers work so that they can eat and poets eat so that they can work. As with the broader definition of anthropology, the broader one for work would be more useful and fitting for our interdiscipline (cf. O'Toole et al. 1973; O'Toole 1974). This broad use would not preclude specifically narrowed research, for example, an ethnology of occupation in one industry (Gamst 1980a, 1980b) or a study of an industry in its wider community context (Nash 1979). Broad usage would permit us to comprehend work without inadvertently delimiting our analytic focus.

To a large extent we are trapped by our own cultural heritage when attempting to reflect upon the nature of work. Accordingly, we must examine our folk and scholarly ideas of work, if we are to understand what it is we study. Anglo-Saxons have an ambivalent view of work. It is both a moral necessity ("Satan finds work for idle hands") and a curse visited by the deity from generation to generation as punishment for the original sin ("in the sweat of thy face shalt thou eat bread"). In our society, the "freedom" of free time (leisure) is a relative one. After a person gives time to gainful work, he/she is *said* to be off duty. However, our Satan-thwarting values concerning work and use of time prescribe the ways in which free time may be used (cf. De Grazia 1963; Alasdair 1974).

Considered diachronically, Anglo-Saxon folk concepts of work have been in flux and will so continue (cf. Wadel 1979). Our folk, and scholarly, distinctions between work and nonwork are in part a concomitant of the industrial market dominating our society. Apparently, Regency England produced the first marked conceptual differentiation between gainful work and leisure activity (Bailey 1978:1–2). However, as early as 1670 we find recorded the familiar saying, "All work and no play, makes Jack a dull boy" (OED 1971,

2:3818). With industrialization, our ideas of work and leisure evolved from an intertwined to a more dichotomous state. Because of our present strict folk demarcation of work from nonwork activity, as scholars we often have a problem with readily recognizing the almost boundless range of variation of work, intra- and cross-culturally. (For classic and recent ethnological treatment of this problem see Richards 1932, 1939; Udy 1959, 1970; Sahlins 1972; Arensberg 1978; Searle-Chattergee 1979; Parkin 1979.) What is and is not work, then, is culturally defined. Our own native view of work is that it must be gainful for economic maintenance of self and family, and work-like activity should be performed during leisure time.

Importantly, work is thought to be segregated from other activity. To Anglo folk and scholars, not only must "work" be gainful, it must also be a specialized activity rigidly separated in time and space from other social acts; for example, "I work at the factory from four until midnight." Ethnologists should broaden the folk and formal economic view of work to allow for other forms of production. The narrow folk-formal conception of work is not fully informative in understanding work in our own society and is not heuristic in comprehending work cross-culturally.

IV

Certainly, for certain analytic purposes investigation of work may be limited to gainful toil. However, under the customary in-depth and long-term research of ethnology, our folk-formal distinctions should dissolve between: time of gainful work and of other similar activity, monetarily paid work and unpaid work-like activity, workplace and nonworkplace. For our society, all manner of what could be called *volitional work*, uncompensated by wages, salaries, fees or in goods, is not only widespread but is essential to societal wellbeing and preservation. Men do not live by bread alone and thus work is not just economically instrumental (for example, one of the major factors in production). Work gradates into activities marginal to or of no direct relation to earning a living. Work satisfies not just material need, but social aspiration for status and organization of community. It satisfies psychological maintenance of self-image and provides a label for easing interpersonal relations. Thus, even members of the unemployed underclass and of the elite leisure class have purposeful volitional work, albeit not necessarily gainful. The particular social forms of such work might be street "rumbles" or yachting regattas.

Volitional work may be considered in a number of nonexhaustive, partially overlapping categories. Each category is a suitable subject of research for the anthropology of work in addition to gainful work. *Do-it-yourself work* comprises all manner of uncompensated productivity for one's self and family usually in and around one's domicile. Such work includes repairing one's auto, painting the house, growing vegetables, photographing the children, and housework. All of these forms of work could easily be gainful, that is, done in the market place in return for paid compensation. As do-it-yourself work, the forms diminish cash outflow rather than increase cash income, but consequently have the same net affect upon the familial economy. At times, in accord with a largely unverbalized cognitive map of generalized, long-term reciprocity, such forms may be rendered to kin, friends, or neighbors for an immediate or eventual return of the same or other service and thereby become *reciprocal work*. Our market economy probably has several tens of billions of dollars annually of reciprocal exchange of work of this kind.

Community-service work is given the common term of "volunteer work" and the bulk of it is performed in our society for civic organizations by women whose husbands are gainfully employed. The range of this work not only includes unskilled worktasks such as door-to-door solicitation, chauffeuring, and babysitting, but also highly skilled functions such as business administration in its various forms. *Expressive work* has a very great range including the creation of music, fine arts, many crafts, and literature as a nonprofessional (amateur). *Athletic work* has a similar nonprofessional dimension. Both kinds of individually creative amateur work may have as great a display of ability as demonstrated by professionals. The distinction between professional and amateur creator of art or athletics is often lost in the murkiness of clouded definitions, usually related to amounts of pay.

Volitional *work pro bono publico*, nominally for the public good, comprises political service to various levels of government and to charitable agencies. Such work may be overt or covert to the public but is known to the recipient agency or person, or it may be clandestine, unbeknown to the recipient body. All three exist, for example, in the government of New England towns.

Informally organized work at a worksite is usually not recognized as work, but, instead, often branded as "goofing off." At times, after formally discussing how a procedure of work will be done "by the book" while under the scrutiny of a supervisor, workers, while leaning against their work materials, will later chat about how they will actually perform the task. This informal discussion can be a vital part of the work process on the job. Such communication contributes to maintenance of shared expectations of work practice and thus to appropriate cognitive maps for work.

V

In summation, the anthroplogy of work should construe *anthroplogy* and *work* broadly. This approach will facilitate the understanding of work in our own society and in others. The approach will foster a multifaceted, true anthropological investigation of work. Investigation of this kind has a potential for a conceptualization of work not present in the customary disciplinary concerns outside of anthropology regarding the study of work. Such broad focus upon anthropology and work does present the danger of too much diversity. This could justifiably open the anthropology of work to the kind of criticism leveled by Anthony Leeds at urban anthropology, which he describes, as constituting through the mid-1970s, "a non-field" which "has no future" (Leeds 1980:6). The difference between a disjointed nonfield and a broad useful field lies in part in the quality of our developing and communicating about the anthropology of work.

Section 1

Non-Market Cultures

II

Introduction
Non-Market Cultures: Work among Hunters and Gatherers

For most of human beings' existence on earth they have been hunters and gatherers. The paleoarchaeologists have found some of the tools they made and the animals they hunted. Cave paintings and inscriptions provide a brief but animated view of the hunt. Burial sites provide some clues to the existence of religious beliefs. We can infer that Paleolithic hunters and gatherers lived in small bands and were migratory. Our evidence from the past is too fragmentary to give us a picture of those societies and how they relate to present-day hunters and gatherers.

Contemporary hunting and gathering societies occupy areas of the world in which it is difficult for the more developed societies to use their technologies—the deserts of Southwest Africa and Central Australia, the thick rain forests of Asia, Africa, and South America, and the barren, frozen lands of the Arctic. Surviving hunting and gathering societies include the !Kung, Mbuti, and Hadza in Africa; the aboriginal cultures of Central Australia; the Paiute Indians of the Great Basin in North America; and some tribal cultures in the rain forests of the Malayan Peninsula. Most Eskimo groups are traditionally included, but most are undergoing such rapid cultural change that they are no longer hunting and gathering societies. A striking illustration of this is the current TV ad which shows an Eskimo family sitting in front of a Sony television set with the voice in the background saying, "the nearest TV repair man is 200 miles away." From Greenland to Canada and Alaska, many Eskimos have moved into settlements and villages, seeking work for wages. In Siberia, hunting is done by collectives using mechanized transport.

What is common to hunting and gathering cultures of the present is that, given the meager resources available in their environment, everyone in the society is expected to work, including children. Under these circumstances, the concept of work as a separate social sphere has no meaning; there is no distinction between work and non-work, between work and leisure. Herskovits (1940) pointed out that work among hunters and gatherers is continuous. Even when people are sitting around talking or visiting they are working—making an arrowhead, shaping a tool, or constructing a carrying device. While the languages of hunting and gathering societies are unusually rich in different words for the animals or plants they depend on for life or the features of their natural environment they must learn about to survive, they have no separate word for work, which is as natural to them as living and breathing.

What is the organization of work among hunting and gathering cultures? The discussion which follows is based on Lee (1980).

Hunting and gathering subsistence work is based on the hunting of wild game animals, the gathering of wild plant food, and the catching of fish and gathering shellfish. The basic attributes of work in these societies are: (1) a division of labor based on sex; (2) a technology based on human energy; (3) a communal ownership of land and its resources; and (4) widespread food sharing and the application of the principles of reciprocity.

While hunting and gathering cultures make their own tools and utensils, which was also true of the early gardeners and agriculturalists, what is different between growing crops and hunting and gathering is the fact that hunters and gatherers live on what nature has to offer, while farmers and gardeners induce nature to give them what it can. Hunters and gatherers must suit their work and its organization to the environment as they find it. Consequently, their organization of work follows specific patterns. First, they must cover a wide area and be highly mobile to find the food necessary for their survival. Lee estimates that the !Kung San cover between 1500 to 2000 miles per year (1979:118). Second, the environment and its relatively limited resources set upper limits on the size of the group, which affects the number of people available for work, as well as the amount of food necessary for their survival. Third, because they are dependent upon what the natural environment affords them, hunters and gatherers must be flexible in their work habits to adjust to the regional and seasonal variations in resources available. Their work organization must adapt to changing opportunities not only during the course of a year but from year to year, as the climate varies. Fourth, the need for constant mobility sets limits to the amount of material wealth that can be accumulated and transported. Fifth, because of the limited resources available on the land, hunting and gathering groups develop elaborate rules for cooperative and reciprocal access to resources.

Unlike agricultural or pastoral societies, hunting and gathering cultures do not have the luxury of saving consumption resources from one season or year to the next. Hunting and gathering groups must immediately consume what they catch or find. Among tropical foragers most food is distributed and consumed within forty-eight hours of its collection. There are no peak periods similar to the harvesting time for farmers. Hunters and gatherers have a life of steady work and leisure throughout the year. Coupled with this kind of work rhythm there is an extensive, wide-ranging use of land, rather than an intensive, concentrated utilization of resources in the environment.

The division of labor is by sex. The men hunt and gather. Women mostly gather but do occasionally hunt. Both men and women fish and gather shellfish. People work either alone or collectively. The communal or collective nature of the society is most apparent in the distribution and consumption of resources that result from the input of work. Food is never consumed alone by a family and is shared with members of a group or band comprising up to thirty members or more. Even if only a portion of the band work, the day's return of meat and gathered foods are shared with all members of the band, with each member getting an equitable share. This principle of reciprocity and sharing has been reported for hunters and gatherers throughout the world and for every kind of environment (Sahlins 1965).

Land is usually utilized on the basis of control by a group or a band. In Australia it is controlled by a patrilineage. (Bohannan 1963:134–35.) In a few cases, as with the Hadza of Tanzania there is unrestricted use of the land. (Woodburn: 1964; Ember & Ember 1973:112.) Usually there is a group of leaders from whom one must get permission to use the land. Both men and women are members of the landowning collective. All hunting and gathering groups regularly permit visits by other groups and in turn they are given reciprocal rights to use the land controlled by these others.

Land and its resources are collectively owned and utilized. Tools and other personal belongings are the private property of individuals. Meat from a slain animal is distributed to all members of a band, but the bow and arrow, the spear, or the club used to kill the animal belongs to the hunter. Material goods are also used for trade and to establish networks and social relations within the group and with neighbors. But the tools, the means of production, belong to the people who perform the work.

In the selections on hunting and gathering societies which follow, the !Kung San and the classic Cheyennes of the North American Great Plains both illustrate most of the features outlined in this introduction. On the other hand, the Indians of the Pacific Northwest are an exception to the generalized case of hunting and gathering cultures. The Indians of the Pacific Northwest had an abundance of resources rather than scarcity, a stratified society rather than an egalitarian one, and an ability to accumulate wealth and store goods rather than having to consume immediately what they had hunted or gathered. Contrasts and exceptions are often telling in pointing to the generalized concepts that prevail in a majority of cases, and the selection from Suttles provides such an example.

Chapter Three

Hunting among the !Kung San

Richard B. Lee

!Kung men are excellent hunters, and they devote a great deal of time and effort to the pursuit of game. In energy returns hunting is a less rewarding activity than gathering, and vegetable foods provide the major part of the diet. On the other hand, the hunt and its products hold a central place in the life of the camp and in the community. The formalized distribution of meat is always an eagerly anticipated occasion. Graphic descriptions of hunts, both recent and distant, constitute an almost nightly activity of the men around the campfire. In storytelling, men can portray a hunt, step-by-step, in microscopic and baroque detail. And the food returns of hunting are far from negligible. Throughout the year the proportion of meat in the diet rarely falls below 20 percent, and during peak periods when the hunting is good may reach 90 percent, with a per capita consumption of meat of over 2 kg per day! Furthermore, animal products may provide essential nutrients that are lacking or scarce in the vegetable diet. Overall the hunt provides around 40 percent of the calories of the !Kung.

In this account we consider the basic techniques of hunting (tracking, stalking, shooting, killing, and butchery) as well as some specialized techniques (snaring, underground work, and capture of small game). Then we present an inventory of all the 55 species of mammals, birds, reptiles, and insects eaten by the !Kung, with more detailed discussion of species of big game hunted and not hunted by the !Kung. The chapter concludes with a discussion of hunting as a career and a life's work, including socialization as a hunter, hunting magic and ritual, initiation, and data on hunting success. The material covered here forms only a bare introduction to the subject. More extensive research on hunting has been conducted by Edwin Wilmsen, from whom a more substantial account can be expected in the future. The chapter also touches on the excellent work of S. A. Marks on hunting among the agricultural Valley Bisa

(Marks 1976), though it should be noted that the Bisa hunt almost entirely with guns.

THE WORLD OF THE HUNTER

It is useful to introduce the subject with a glossary of some of the terms used in hunting. To hunt is *!gai,* and a hunter is a *!gaik"au* ("hunt owner"). Game animals, large and small, are called generically *!ha* ("meat") and distinguished from the *zhum* or *!hohm* ("clawed or predatory animals"). All the species are individually named as well, and each has, in addition to its everyday name, a secret name that is used under special circumstances (as when an animal is wounded but not yet dead). The small antelopes, steenbok and duiker, are known collectively as *≠da≠hxaisi* ("daughters of the plains") because they prefer the open habitat of the plains; they are hunted interchangeably.

The basic toolkit consists of the bow *(n!au)*, arrows *(chisi)*, and a quiver *(!kuru).* The last epitomizes the hunter and hunting more than any of the weapons. When a man is actively hunting, he //*kama!uru* ("shoulders his quiver"); when he is not hunting, he is *kwara!uru* ("without a quiver"). The bow, on the other hand, is a bawdy metaphor for the penis. When a man jokingly says *mi kwara n!au* ("I have no bow"), he implies he is at a loss sexually.

A hunting trip of several days' duration is *guni.* Hunting without a strong lead is *!gai n//o* ("hunting around"). Stalking an animal is */o* ("to follow"). A very close stalk is *sum.* Shooting an arrow is *chi//a;* to miss your shot is *chi//a da-ma* ("shoot failing"); and to strike home is //*'xopo or tah.*

A struck animal *!gaa u¯* ("take off like a shot") or *kxokxoni* ("staggers") or *!gow a /te* ("falls down"). To finish off a wounded animal with a club, you *n≠em!ku a* ("strike-kill it"); with a spear or knife, you *!n !ku a* ("stab-kill it"). Then the hunter *cho ka !ha (Butchers the meat")*, //*gau// hwanasi* ("loads it on carrying yokes"), and // *kama//hwanasi* ("shoulders the yokes") for the trip back to camp. There the meat is *n/wa* ("boiled") or *sau* ("roasted"); the members of the camp are //*kai/kaikwe* ("assembled"), and the *!ha* ("meat") is *≠twi n//o* or *hxaba* ("distributed"). Afterward, *n//ae* ("men") gather at a fire to *du n≠wao !gai ga* ("tell the story of the hunt") until *n!a //gai* ("dawn breaks," literally "sky rips open").

There are many dozens of synonyms, metaphors, and euphemisms for the words and phrases listed above; hunting vocabularly has undergone a fantastic elaboration in !Kung speech. These terms, nevertheless, give some sense of the hunter's world.

The Hunting Process

The goal of hunting is to kill game to provide food. Killing for sport is unknown. All !Kung hunting techniques have three basic steps: the preparations for the hunt, the act of hunting itself, and the killing and butchering (see Marks 1976:114ff.). The first and third steps are common to all hunting. The act of hunting may take many forms. A distinction is made between snaring, which requires fixed facilities, and all other techniques, which depend on mobile searching for game. The latter method provides most of the meat. The search for game may focus on above-ground or below-ground animals. Underground work involves blocking an animal in the burrow and digging it out. Four important species are taken this way. Above-ground work includes knocking down and snaring very small game, chasing small- to medium-sized game with dogs, and the classic hunt for the large mammals in which poisoned arrows are used. This last technique is the one popularly associated with !Kung Bushmen hunting and made famous by the giraffe hunt in John Marshall's film, *The Hunters* (1956). The following discussion considers each of the steps and techniques in turn, starting with snaring and concluding with big game hunting.

Snaring

Snaring is a modest technique used largely by older men and young boys whose mobility is limited. It is time-consuming and provides little meat per man-hour, but it is a particularly good technique for the older hunter because it maximizes know-how and experience while making minimum demands on eyesight, endurance, speed, and energy reserves. Young boys set snares for rather different reasons: to gain experience in their craft through the study of animal behavior and through the feedback from successful and unsuccessful snaring.

Winter is the snareline season. Each hunter who is wintering at his home water hole starts to build his snareline in May and continues to refine and improve the lines until October, when they are abandoned, impromptu snares may also be set up at temporary winter camps where the hunters are spending a few days. Snaring is rare during the rainy season because the rains ruin the delicate trigger mechanisms. The hunters of the camp agree before the snares are built where each man will set up his lines. A man surveys his snaring area for fresh tracks of steenbok, the major animal snared. The steenbok is a nonmigratory small antelope with a restricted home range—a characteristic that makes it eminently suitable for snaring. The hunter gradually lays down an unobtrusive line of brush, 200 to 300 meters long, that zigzags from bush to bush until by degrees he closes off a tract of ground with a brush barrier. The object of this operation is to habituate the animals to crossing his line at a limited number of gaps. Each day he inspects his line for fresh tracks. If the animals are breaching his line regularly at one gap, he then sets a rope snare in the gap.

The snare . . . consists of a length of rope with a noose and trigger on the ground at one end and a springy sapling bent over at the other. When the forefoot of the animal falls within the noose, the trigger is released and the animal is caught. Its struggles serve to tighten the noose more securely around its foot. Birds caught pecking at the baited noose are strangled, but the antelopes are not injured and must be dispatched with a club by the hunter making his daily rounds of the snarelines. On his round the hunter also repairs the brush fence and resets the snares. Often a man checks the lines of his brother, father, or son, as well as his own, so that it is not necessary for each man to go out every day.

At the height of the snaring season each hunter has one to three lines in operation, and each line has seven to nine gaps set with snares. At the Dobe camp in 1964 hunters who had set 20 to 25 separate snares averaged one small animal per hunter per week through the winter. A hunter's success in snaring seems to depend on his interpretation of game tracks and the patience with which he habituates the animals to crossing his lines where he wants them to. At the Dobe camp during the 4-week period from July 7 to August 2, 1964, 18 animals were killed, 11 of them in snares. The snared animals included five steenbok, two hare, one honey badger, and three game birds (two korhaan and one kori bustard). Although snared animals constituted 61 percent of the kills during the period, they accounted for only 20 percent of the meat; 40.8 kg out of a total of 205.9 kg.

The Bisa, by contrast, used a much wider variety of snares than the !Kung and these were of many different types. Trapping and snaring for the Bisa has fallen largely into disuse (Marks 1976:80–5).

Mobile Hunting

Preparations for the hunt. In the mobile hunt (!gai) the hunter carries with him the equipment necessary to kill over 40 different species of animals, from the smallest mongoose up to a giraffe. The hunter may have a single species as his objective, but he does not neglect the possibility that other game may come along. Therefore, the preparations for the hunt are standard and generalized, with attention to both technical and informational aspects. The first ensures that the toolkit is assembled and all the components are in working order; the second provides the best information available on where the best hunting is to be found.

The evening before the hunt, the hunter sits by his fire checking his kit. First he empties his quiver, lays the arrows carefully on the ground, and examines each arrow in turn, testing the link shaft and binding for a tight fit and sighting down the length of the arrow to check for straightness. If the arrow is out of true, he straightens it by twirling it lightly over a small fire and bending it gently in his hands. If he is not satisfied, he returns the arrow to his quiver making a mental note not to use it. After checking his arrows, he selects the three or four he will shoot and puts the rest back in the quiver. Then he may apply touch-up posion directly on the foreshaft to provide a little added killing power.

Next he examines his bow, pulling the bowstring a few times to check whether the tension is correct. He may oil the bow itself to condition the wood against cracking. Then he checks his spear and springhare hook to ensure that all the hafts are tight and that the wood is both straight and supple. In this extremely dry climate wood becomes brittle and often cracks or breaks in the hunt.

The technical preparations conclude with the assembly of the kit. The quiver is capped and its handle intertwined with the spear, bow, and digging stick to make a neat bundle. The springhare hook is carefully hung in the branches of a tree, out of reach of children. Into the shoulder bag go the following items:

1. Knife, for butcherey and a variety of other tasks, such as cutting branches or twine and making quick repairs in the field

2. A whetstone (optional)

3. A flint-and steel fire-making kit (if none is available, the traditional fire drill is stowed in the quiver)

4. Lengths of sinew, for making instant repairs on link-shaft bindings

5. Snares, to set for birds if a nest is encountered; also doubles as binding to tie up small game for carrying home

6. A net bag (optional) if gathering is planned as an alternative or for carrying filleted meat

7. Iron adze/ax, for butchery, opening beehives, or cutting carrying yokes

8. Smoking pipe and tobacco (if available)

The whole kit is hung from a customary branch near the man's hut or inside the hut if rain is threatening. In the morning there is little more for a man to do than shoulder his kit and move out.

In deciding *where* and *what* to hunt, the hunter seeks both empirical and magical forms of data. In the actual choice of routes and tactics, the empirical data play an important role. The magical data from divination and dreams are more important in telling a man whether to hunt and giving him a feeling of confidence, and are particularly sought after by hunters who feel they are down on their luck. Dreams and omens are widely used by the Bisa hunters as well (Marks 1976:102). First the hunter consults with the men and women of the camp to get reports on game sighting, game tracks, and weather conditions. Some of the questions he asks, depending on season, include these:

Spring: If rain clouds are sighted, on what localities did the rain actually fall?
Late summer: Which of the seasonal water points still hold water?
Late winter, early spring: What is the state of the grazing in different localities? Is there any new growth on bum patches?
Midsummer: If an animal has been killed in an area, how many others were there? Were any wounded but not pursued? Have the females dropped their young?
Anytime of year: Are there signs of occupied burrows?

Discussion of these questions may occupy several hundred hours a year of a man's time. Yet this is not considered by the !Kung as work. It is both part of a hunter's job and a pleasure to sit with a group of four or five men discussing the current situation, the habits of game, and the hunts of the recent and distant past. Even men who are not hunting contribute their experiences. Women participate in these discussions too. They cover much ground on their gathering trips and because they are keen observers of the environment as are the men, their observations are sought and taken seriously.

Based on the information and opinion of others, on the oracle disks, and on his own observations of the environment, the hunter decides on a rough strategy for the day's hunt. This includes a direction to set out in, a set of working leads based on recent tracks, and perhaps backup alternatives like digging out a springhare or gathering nuts if nothing else turns up. With this plan in mind, the hunter turns in for the night.

The search for game. In the morning the hunters, single or in twos or threes, shoulder their weapons and set out. They move in the direction determined the day before at a brisk pace, scanning the ground a meter or two ahead of them for signs of game. As fresh spoor is sighted there is a great deal of discussion about what the animal is doing, where it is going, and whether it is worth following. If the trail becomes very fresh, the men fall silent and communicate with each other by sign language as they move quickly but quietly through the bush (see Howell 1965:184–5); Marshall 1976:136). When hunters lose sight of one another, they signal each other by prearranged birdlike calls that act as homing signals but do not alarm the animals.

The man in the lead, if two or more are hunting, follows the spoor and stops only when the track divides or seems to disappear; then the hunters fan out to search for the correct spoor and resume tracking. This can be a laborious process, and if fresher spoor crosses the one they are following, the hunters may instantly switch to the more promising lead. So a day's hunting is made up of a series of spatially connected pathways; each point of intersection represents a decision by the hunters to follow the pathway that offers the better chance of success.

Hunting from a blind does not require initial tracking; the hunter waits for the prey to come to him. This method is infrequently used among the Dobe area !Kung. There are six stone blinds at ≠Gi water hole near !Kubi that have a considerable antiquity, according to John Yellen. They are very occasionally used for night hunting by !Kung men from !Kubi. I was also shown two small pit blinds dug at the edge of ≠Ta flats near N!um!koma, 35 km south of /Xai/xai. Fairly large herds of kudu, wildebeest, and gemsbok congregate on these flats, attracted by the salt licks (*hwanasi*). A hunter approaches the flats cautiously at dawn, and if he finds animals present crawls carefully out to his pit to wait there in absolute stillness for the animals to approach the ring of licking places that lie within a 20-meter radius of the blind. If he is lucky and the wind is right, he may get a chance at a shot. But it is not a particularly successful spot. ≠Toma !kom!gowsi, who dug the blinds and who is an excellent hunter, claims to have killed only a few kudu here over a period of years. ≠Toma, along with all the other !Kung hunters, has found the great majority of his kills through mobile hunting and tracking.

How to track. This section discusses some of the basics of tracking and how the variables in a situation are weighed in arriving at a decision about which lead to follow (see also Marks 1976:117ff.).

The !Kung are such superb trackers and make such accurate deductions from the faintest marks in the sand that at first their skill seems uncanny. For example, both men and women are able to identify an individual person merely by the sight of his or her footprint in the sand. There is nothing mysterious about this. Their tracking is a skill, cultivated over a lifetime, that builds on literally tens of thousands of observations. The !Kung hunter can deduce the following kinds of information about the animal he is tracking; its species and sex, its age, how fast it is traveling, whether it is alone or with other animals, its physical condition (healthy or ill), whether and on what it is feeding, and the time of day the animal passed this way.

The species, of course, is identified by the shape of the hoofprint and by the dung or scat; that is the simplest information to be deduced, and any 12-year-old boy can accurately reproduce in the sand the prints of a dozen species. The sex of the animal is identified in some species by the print's shape, in others by the print's size and the length of the stride. A set of adult hoofprints and a set of immature prints moving together signify, of course, a mother and her young. Similarly, the !Kung use their knowledge of the seasonal social organization of different species to determine the age-sex composition of a group of animals. The size or age of an animal correlates directly with the size of its prints. The depth of the print indicates the weight of the animals. An old or infirm animal may be distinguished by a halting gait or uneven stride length. Evidence of crippling is eagerly sought and is discerned when one hoofprint is deepr than the others.

The number of animals in a herd is difficult to determine, especially if they are many and their tracks crisscross, but given the relatively small herd size of the current ungulate populations, it is usually easy to distinguish three from four, or four from five, animals if the herd is followed for a kilometer or two. Feeding animals stop every 10 meters to browse or graze; animals that are not feeding move in a relatively straight course. Their speed is shown by the depth of the print, the amount of sand kicked up, and the distance between footfalls. A galloping animal leaves clusters of very deep prints spaced far apart, sharp at the leading edge and blurred at the following edge, with a considerable scatter of sand behind. What the animal is feeding on can be observed in several ways. Examining the dung is perhaps the least useful technique because it indicates the diet for hours or days previously. More helpful is observing the scatter of fresh forage that has fallen from the lips of the animal as it moves along feeding or examining which plants have their tips missing in the vicinity of the animal's milling prints.

Knowledge of the animal's habits aids in determining the time of day it passed by. Some of the signs are surprisingly simple. If the tracks zigzag from shade tree to tree, the animal went through in the heat of the day. If the tracks go under the west side of the trees, the animal was catching the morning shade; if under the east side, the afternoon shade; and if under either side, the animal passed at midday. Milling tracks within a small radius out in the open suggest the animal was there at night and was sleeping. Tracks leading into a dense thicket indicate the animal rested up during midday.

The number of minutes or hours elapsed since the animal went through can be determined from changes in the spoor. This is crucial information; to obtain it, the !Kung have developed their discriminating powers to the highest degree. After a print has been made, it provides a miniature physiographic feature that is acted upon by natural processes. Consider a simple example. When fresh, the print is clean-cut, but after an hour (or less if the day is windy) a fine covering of windblown sand collects in the depression. Later twigs and grass fall in, and then insect and other animal tracks are superimposed. The moisture content of the soil 1, 2, 3, or 4 cm below the surface and the rate at which soil dries out after being exposed by a footfall are two variables that are exceedingly well studied by the !Kung. When an animal is being closely followed, the present position of the shade in relation to the animal's footprint plus these other signs can indicate within 15 minutes the time the animal passed by.

All these kinds of information are interpreted and processed by the hunters and are weighed in deciding whether a spoor is worthy following. Distance ahead is the most important variable. Fresh spoor of an animal only a few hundred meters ahead is a first-rate lead. If the animal is more than 2 km ahead, pursuit is not considered feasible. Next in importance come factors of wind direction and vegetation cover. If the wind is blowing the hunters' scent *toward* the animal, the chances of success are small, unless the men circle to downwind. Thick vegetation covers is preferred to open plains. In deep bush the hunter can creep forward well concealed. In the open it is harder to move in close without startling the prey. In a bare molapo it is almost imposible to get close. Next in importance come the factors of the animal's speed and behavior as it moves. A fast-moving animal, even if it is unaware of the hunter's presence, is poor quarry. It will quickly widen the distance between the hunters and itself. An animal that is feeding and resting, moving slowly from bush to bush, is a promising target. The hunter by a series of deft moves can take advantage of the cover to get close enough for a shot. Thus the ideal lead for a hunter is a slowly moving animal, upwind, 500 meters ahead or less, resting and feeding in deep bush, and with a marked limp for good measure.

If none of these conditions is present, any signs of small or underground game is sufficient to turn a hunter aside. We now consider small game and underground game before going on to discuss the killing of the major larger antelopes.

Small game killing. The weights and edible yields of some small and underground game species are listed in Table 3.1. In mobile hunting, small game is knocked down with a throwing club, shot with an arrow, or chased with dogs. Club, dogs, and/or spear are used to finish off the animal at close quarters. The ≠da≠hxaisi (steenbok and duiker) are the most common small game animals killed. Rarely tracked for any distance, they are usually sighted frozen in the shadows or they may break cover immediately in front of the hunting party. Dogs are most effective in this situation: They chase the prey, wound or kill it, and wait over the kill for the hunter to arrive at the kill site. If there are no dogs, the hunter throws his club or walking stick at the prey; the men are surprisingly accurate with these unpromising instruments. if the animal is stunned and takes off, a merry chase follows: The hunter retrieves his club and goes crashing through the bush striking at the prey until it is beaten insensible. Usually the animal is clubbed rather than stabbed to death to ensure that the valuable hide is undamaged.

Poisoned arrows are also used for small game, though my impression is the !Kung regard this as a form of overkill. A full dose of poison, well placed, can kill an animal as small as a steenbok or duiker in half an hour or less. Even the iron-tipped arrow itself has considerable knock-down power for these small animals. Yet we know of cases where a duiker has been tracked for 2 days in the same way as a large antelope.

The ≠da≠hxaisi are systematically hunted, but other small game are not neglected. Next in importance is the common hare, followed by the bat-eared fox, genet, and the several species of mongoose. The meat of this last group of animals may be fed to the dogs if other meat is available back at the camp, but people do eat this meat on occasion.

Game birds—mainly guinea fowl, francolin, and korhaan—are hunted with snares on an ad hoc basis. The snare is baited with a pea-sized edible bulb. During the breeding season, the hunter often finds a nest of eggs with the mother hen absent; he then sets a snare baited with one of the eggs to trap the hen on her return. Other game birds are knocked down with throwing clubs, then retrieved by dogs.

The young of all small game species are frequently run down on foot and captured in the hand. For the ≠da≠hxaisi, immatures may constitute a third to a half of the animals killed.

Table 3.1 Weights of Some Small and Underground Game Species and Their Edible Yield

Animal	Male: gross weight (kg)	Male: edible yield		Female: gross weight (kg)	Female: edible yield		Immature: gross weight (kg)	Immature: edible yield	
		kg	c_K		kg	c_K		kg	c_K
Small game									
Duiker	18.5	9.3	50	20.2	11.1	50	13.6	6.8	50
Steenbok	11.1	5.6	50	11.2	5.6	50	8.2	4.1	50
Hare	2.4	1.4	60	2.3	1.4	60	1.8	1.0	60
Honey badger	9.8	4.9	50						
Wild cat	5.5	2.8	50	4.6	2.3	50			
Underground game									
Springhare	3.5	2.5	70	3.2	2.2	70			
Ant bear	63.5	38.1	60	41.0	24.6	60			
Porcupine	17.2	8.6	50	19.1	9.6	50			

Source: Reay Smithers (personal communication).

Underground game killing. Four important species are hunted below the ground: springhare, ant bear, porcupine, and warthog. The last two are hunted above ground as well. The aardwolf *(Proteles cristatus)* and the pangolin or scaly anteater *(Manis temmincki)* may also be taken underground.

Chapter 5 describes how the springhare is relatively easily captured by means of the 4-meter-long springhare probe. The other underground species are much more formidable: they live in large burrows; they readily attack a man, if cornered; and each is armed with a respectible means of defense: quills for the porcupine, claws for the ant bear, and tusks and hooves for the warthog. For all three, the basic hunting process is similar. The hunter examines a series of recent burrows to see if they are occupied. Most of the burrows are dug originally by ant bears, often but not always in the base of an anthill. The other two species occupy burrows abandoned by ant bears.

The porcupine and the ant bear are nocturnal animals. The hunter's task is to find one living up in a burrow during the day. If he finds a porcupine-occupied burrow, he can go into the burrow himself with his spear and try to kill the animal underground, or he can block off the entrance and start digging down to the animal just as he would for a springhare. If the larger ant bear or a warthog is found, the hunter may build a fire at the mouth of the burrow, hoping to stupefy the prey with smoke and goad it to break out into the open. Then the hunter and, if available, his dogs, can wound and kill the prey at close quarters. If the animal fails to break out and dies of asphyxiation in the burrow, the hunter has to drag or dig it out. Which technique is used depends on the terrain. If the ground is hard, as it is around an anthill, and/or if the burrow is deep, digging out becomes unprofitable. Similarly, an ant bear that dies in its burrow may be wedged in so tightly that hauling it out is extremely difficult. Trying to goad the animal to the surface is the tactic of choice for these species.

This is dangerous work and demands personal bravery on the part of the hunters. A man enters a burrow only if he is hunting with a partner, who kneels poised at the mouth ready to haul out the hunter by the ankles. If the burrow is in soft sand, there is the danger of cave-in if the ant bear thrases about. Several men bear the scars of ant bear claws on their faces and shoulders, and our records show that at least one man died from injuries and another from being smothered in a cave-in. The theme of a dangerous underworld inhabited by a society of ant bears exists in the mythology of the !Kung (Biesele, in press).

Porcupines are frequently killed above ground. If a sleeping porcupine is encountered on the trail, it is immediately set upon with whatever weapons are available—clubs, spears, digging sticks, or any piece of dead wood that is ready to hand. A merry chase follows, with shouting, crashing through the bush, and confusion, but the porcupine is usually killed. Such an episode is shown in Marshall's film, *The Hunter* (1956).

The ant bear (along with the pangolin) is the most subterranean of all the larger game species; it is rarely observed in daylight above ground. Only after heavy rains, when its burrow is temporarily flooded, is an ant bear found in the morning curled up at the mouth of its burrow. Then it may be shot with a poison arrow.

The warthog is basically an above-ground species that goes to ground in certain circumstances—the sow when she is dropping a litter and either sex when it is under attack. Many warthogs are killed on the surface, expecially with the aid of dogs. When they do go to ground, they must be smoked out into the open. As the cornered warthog breaks out of its burrow, there are moments of high drama. The hog may be slashing out at the dogs, and the hunter must dodge around to spear the prey while avoiding hitting the dogs or being himself attacked by the hog. Warthog hunting often maims and occasionally kills dogs. When a sow and a litter of piglets break out, the confusion and excitement are compounded. In spite of these difficulties warthog is the most frequently killed of the larger game animals.

Big game hunting. By *big game* is meant the six large antelope species whose adult forms weigh over 100 kg: kudu, gemsbok, wildebeest, eland, hartebeest, and roan. All these, plus the giraffe, are hunted in the classic manner with bow and arrows. The killing of the adults of any of these seven species is a major event, and though few hunters kill as many as five big game animals a year, the meat from these seven species probably provides over 50 percent of the annual wild game supply of a camp. Easier to kill are the young of these species, especialy the first three. These can be run down and clubbed as are steenbok and duiker. The returns in meat from the young are much smaller. Several other species usually classified as big game by white hunters are not hunted systematically by the !Kung; these include zebra, elephant, ostrich, lion, leopard, and cheetah.

There are five elements in the successful killing of big game. We have already considered the preparation for the hunt and the tracking of game; here we dicuss the stalking, wounding, and killing of the animal.

When a very fresh lead is being followed, the hunters move extremely carefully, without a sound, taking pains to see that the animal is always upwind, even if this means leaving the actual spoor of the animal. As the hunters close the distance to a few hundred meters, it is often possible to catch glimpses of the prey through the underbrush. Now comes the final stalk: One man moves forward, crouching at first, then crawling, then inching forward on his belly to get in as close as possible for a shot. The upper limit for reasonable accuracy seems to be 25 meters, and 10 meters is considered the optimum distance for a shot. It may take the hunter 20, 30 or even 40 minutes to cover the distance. Beforehand, the hunter has chosen two or three arrows to carry forward with his bow, leaving the rest of his kit behind. As he moves forward, he watches the animal closely, especially its ears, for any signs of alarm. When it raises its head or turns in his direction, the hunter freezes, holding still several minutes at a time if necessary; then when the animal's head turns or drops, the stalker moves forward again. If the animal is skittish and keeps moving away, the hunter may have to risk a less than ideal shot before the prey moves out of range. Usually the hunter does not have a clear view of the prey; only the outline of the back or the legs may be visible through the bush. Before shooting, the hunter may have to figure out what trajectory his arrow should follow to avoid branches and trees in its path.

Reaching his optimum range, the hunter tries a shot: He draws the bow, takes careful aim, and silently lets fly. After this first shot, he holds stock-still; if he has missed completely, there is a chance the animal has noticed nothing and the hunter gets a second shot. If the animal bolts, the hunter may still hold his position because sometimes the prey moves only a few steps and stands still again, allowing the hunter a second shot from a standing position.

If the arrow strikes home, clearly wounding the animal, the next phase of the hunt begins. The hunter breaks cover and runs forward on a diagonal path trying to intercept and get another shot at the now-alarmed animal as it runs by. He may shoot all his arrows hoping to put more poison into the prey and thereby hasten its collapse. The hunter tries to hit a spot that will lame or hobble the animal.

In the meantime, the second hunter has moved in the direction of the animal's probable escape route, positioning himself for one or more shots as the animal runs by. The first hunter may help the second by chasing the prey in the latter's direction.

Ordinarily the hunters are fortunate to wound one animal a day. When two or more animals are being stalked, each hunter may choose an animal to creep up on. Hunters shoot as many animals as possible, even if not all can be followed. This increases chances of getting at least one and allows hunters to choose the most promising spoor. If their final approach is exceptionally good, it is not unknown for two hunters to shoot at and wound four or even five different animals in a single flurry. It is hunts like these, when five buck are killed in one day, the men discuss around the campfire for years and generations afterwards.

In a few seconds the animal runs out of range. It is not pursued, for there is far more important work to be done. The first task is to retrieve and account for all the arrows shot. By this means the hunter can quickly confirm whether his animal is well wounded or even wounded at all. If he finds all his arrows, he is out of luck. If one is missing, this supports his visual impression that the animal is wounded. Next he begins to track the fleeing animal. If necessary, he must sort out his tracks from those of other animals in the herd. He looks for various signs. Blood on the ground indicates a good wound, but not an ideal one because the bleeding may flush much of the poison out of the animal's system. Finding a main shaft alone is an excellent sign, indicating a deeper wound with little bleeding and the detachable arrowhead inside the prey. Finding the whole arrow intact suggests it has been worked out of the wound by muscular contraction. In this event, the hunter examines the foreshaft carefully; if little poison remains, it indicates that most of the poison has already been absorbed and the animal may still die. I think another reason the hunters try to account for and retrieve all the arrows is to prevent someone's accidentally stepping on a stray arrow and poisoning himself at a later date.

Having made the initial diagnosis and retrieved their arrows, the hunters break off to get their full kits and to discuss the situation. They must consider many possibilities. How seriously is the animal wounded? Will it die or will it recover and keep going? Even if it is fatally wounded, how far can it travel before it collapses? Will that be too far away for the meat to be carried back? They also take into account the presence of large carnivores in the vicinity. Will the lions scavenge most of the kill before the hunters can reach it? To answer these questions, the hunters pick up the wounded animal's trail and follow it for several kilometers, observing carefully. They assess the animal's speed-how fast it is increasing the distance between them; its direction-whether it is moving away from or toward their base camp; and its strength-whether it shows signs of weakening.

The last is an indication of how rapidly the poison is taking effect, and this is the crucial factor. The hunters look for a number of signs. Zigzagging, milling, and stamping tracks indicate the prey is agitated, an early symptom of the poison. Bursts of running in panic tire the prey and hasten the working of the poison through the system. Signs of black blood or blood in the feces shows the poisoning is well advanced. The dung of a fatally wounded animal has a peculiar smell, and this is a most hopeful sign. If the wound is well placed, an hour of tracking enables the hunters to estimate the probable time and location of the animal's death. More often only an approximate idea of the animal's condition and direction is gained because the poison works slowly at first. In either case, after an hour or two of tracking the men break of the trail and go home to the camp.

The poison takes an average of six to twenty-four hours or more to work, and once the nature of the wound is established there is no point in tracking the animal to its deathplace. If pursued too closely, the prey may be spurred to run much further before dying. The !Kung prefer to let the poison do the work for them. Only on rare occasions when hunters find themselves tracking as night falls do they stay out overnight, and as they never carry blankets, they have only their fire to keep them warm. Sometimes if the animal is lightly wounded, the hunters go home with the intention of resuming tracking the next day. However, the major reason the hunters leave the wounded animal before it is killed is to organize a party at camp to carry the meat back the following day.

CHAPTER FOUR

Women's and Men's Work among the Cheyennes

E. ADAMSON HOEBEL

WOMEN'S ACTIVITIES

Men and women cooperate to supply the food, but the division of labor is strict. Women are the vegetable gatherers. The dibble, or digging stick, is their basic tool. It was given by the Great Medicine Spirit and it figures in the ritual paraphernalia of the Sun Dance, for it has its sacred aspects. Cheyenne dibbles are of two types. The short kind has a knob at one end and is pushed under the desired root by pressure against the stomach when the digger is down on both knees. The other kind is long, and used as a crowbar. The sharp ends are fire hardened.

Some eight or ten different wild roots are gathered, including the bulbs of several varieties of lilies. Most conspicuous of the tubers used is the well-known Indian turnip (*Psoralea lanceolaia*), also known by the French name, *pomme blanche*. It is dug in the spring when still edible, and is sometimes eaten raw, but more commonly boiled. After cutting it into slices, the Cheyenne women dehydrate it by sun drying for year-long preservation. Dried slices are pulverized and used as a thickening for soup. It is a major source of starch. The "red turnip" (*Psoralea hypogeoe*) is smaller and more tasty, and a great favorite of the Cheyenne palate.

The fruit of the prickly pear cactus (*Opiurc polyacantha*) is collected in parfleche bags, worked over with twig brooms to remove the spines, and finally picked clean by the women, who wear deerskin thimbles especially made for the purpose. The fruit is then split, the seeds removed, and the remainder sun dried. The product is added to meat stew and is also used as a soup thickener.

84

Milkweed buds, collected just before the flower opens, are boiled in soup or stew. The "milk" of the plant is evaporated to make a favorite chewing gum.

Thistle *(Arsium edule)* stalks are peeled and eaten with great pleasure. Cheyennes compare it with the banana as a delicacy.

Many varieties of berries are collected by the women, but most common is the chokecherry *(Prunus melanocarpa)*. The whole berry, including the pit, is pulped on stone mortars and made into sundried cakes. Mixed with dried, pounded meats, it produces the best pemmican.

Of the wild plants gathered by the women for their family larder, some sixteen varieties are fruits, eight or ten are roots, and a dozen to fifteen are vegetable stalks or buds. Many of them add variety to boiled meat dishes or nourishing quality to soups. The Cheyennes do not bake or fry breads made of plant flour.

Although root digging is a tiresome chore, the girls and women do not treat it as such. They leave the camp in the morning in small work parties without a male guard against enemy marauders. Their spirits are usually gay, for they look on the day's activity as an outing. Far out on the prairie they scatter to their individual tasks, for the actual gathering requires no cooperative effort. When they come together in the late afternoon, they often react to the monotony of their work by gambling their roots against each other in a game of seeing who can throw her digging stick the farthest, or by throwing "dice" of buffalo metacarpals.

If it is *pomme blanche* they have been gathering, they excitedly anticipate the sport with the men that awaits them at the camp. The sport consists of the women making believe they are a war party and the men are their enemies. When not far from the camp, they arrange their roots in a row of piles and take their positions behind them, sitting down. Now one woman rises and signals with her blanket, letting out a great war whoop. In the camp the men start up, and other women rush out to see the fun. The young men grab scrubby old horses and lazy nags. Some snatch women's rawhides from under the pounding stones. Others already have imitation shields of willow twigs. Pounding away on their burlesque war steeds, whooping and hollering like mad, they charge down on the line of root diggers. These await them with ammunition of sticks and chips of dry buffalo manure which they let fly when the men are within range. The men dodge and twist; one who is hit is "wounded" and out of the game. Only one who has had a horse shot under him or has himself been wounded in war may dismount to snatch some roots, if he gets through the barrage unscathed. Others just mill around making a great to-do. When a few roots have at last been captured, the men withdraw to a hill to eat them and joke about their exploits and casualties while the women pick up their burdens and go on into the camp.

Sometimes the men plan a surprise attack during which, after counting a coup, they may make off with some roots. But if the women see them coming, they gather together behind a circle drawn in the ground with a digging stick. This represents a fortified camp, and no man may cross the line unless he has killed an enemy or counted coup within enemy breastworks. He who has done so dismounts after entering the circle, recites his coup, and exercises his privilege of helping himself to as many roots as he wishes to carry away. If there is no man in the party who qualifies for this deed, the women hoot and insult the men who presumed to attack them.

This horseplay reveals several things. In the first place, of course, it provides fun and sport after a day of monotonous work. But its special form is significant. It is clearly a vicarious release of suppressed sex antagonisms: the men attack the women, and the women dare them to do it. Yet the men are at the same time satirically burlesqueing the pretensions of their own superiority to women—save for those few men who are sterling examples of Cheyenne success in warfare. The others are targets of ridicule and hurled refuse from the hands of the uncowed women.

Women also go out in foraging groups to gather wood for their fires. Except for collecting expeditions, however, most of a woman's work when the camp is not moving is in and about the lodge preparing food, dressing hides, sewing and decorating clothing, robes, and lodges. A good woman is cheerful, busy, and skillful. The raising and lowering of tipis is solely the job of women, and they do it with skill and speed. In the more permanent camps they excavate the floor of the tipi four or five inches, leaving a sod bench around the outer part to serve as a foundation for the beds. The bare floor is wetted and packed down. A lodge lining is tied part way up the poles and folded inward over the bench so that no draft blows under the tipi cover on the sleepers. With the help of her children, the lodge mistress gathers bundles of grass to lay on the bench as padding. Mats made of horizontal willow withes which are attached to tripods are raised between the ends of each sleeping place and covered with buffalo robes to form backrests. In well-provided lodges each person therefore has a comfortable chaise lounge as well as a private bed. A couple of buffalo robes are enough to keep the sleepers warm and comfortable within the tipi no matter how cold it may be outside. The area under the backrest tripods form cupboards for the storage of gear and the parfleches of dried food.

The basic household item of the woman is her stone maul—an oval river stone with pecked-out grooves on the short sides around which is fixed a supple willow withe firmly fastened with green rawhide. When dried out, the rawhide shrinks and holds the maul within the handle with the grip of a vise. With the maul she breaks up fuel, drives tipi pegs, and crushes large bones to be cooked in soup. With smaller handstones the housewife crushes her choke-cherries and pulverizes her dried meat. The Cheyennes are essentially a Stone Age people.

Every household has its complement of horn spoons. These are made by steaming or boiling the horns of buffalo or mountain sheep until pliable. Tortoise shell and wood are also sometimes used.

Prior to contact with white traders, the Cheyenne women produced a variety of pottery dishes for cooking and serving. By the time covered by this study, however, these had been supplanted by trade goods. Crude wooden bowls and dishes continue to be used. For the carrying and storage of water, "Western" water bags are conveniently fashioned from buffalo pouches, bladders, or pericardia. The general name for water bags, *histaiwitsts* ("heart covering"), suggests the most ancient form.

Each woman has a tanning kit of four tools: a scraper, flesher, drawblade, and softening rope or buffalo scapula (shoulder blade). The scraper is a prepared flat, oval stone held in both hands and used to remove extraneous meat and fat from the inner surface of the hide. Metal scrapers supplied by traders are also used.

The flesher is a more delicate instrument. Shaped like an adze, it is made of an elkhorn handle bent at right angle, with a sharp chipped flint lashed across the short end. It is used to hack down the inner surface of the skin to get it to the right degree of thinness. Its proper use is a high skill, and a good fleshing tool is a cherished family heirloom. Grinnell acquired a flesher that had passed through the hands of five mothers and daughters (all known) and had been in continuous use for about a hundred and fifty years when he received it.

The drawblade is a slightly curved willow stick, into the concave side of which is glued a sharpened bone splinter. With the hide draped over an inclined pole, the woman worker shaves off the hair from the outer side of the skin.

Tanning calls for chemical applications; otherwise, the result is rawhide. Brains, liver, and soapweed provide the essentials of the working compound, which is mixed with grease to provide body. The stuff is well rubbed into both sides of the hide, which is then put to soak overnight. After drying in the sun, it is laboriously softened by being worked back and forth over a rawhide rope or

88   E. ADAMSON HOEBEL

by being pulled through a hole in a buffalo shoulder blade fastened to a tree.

A small lodge requires eleven buffalo cowhides, thinned and tanned. A big lodge takes as many as twenty-one. A woman does all the work on her lodge skins up to the point of the rope- or blade-softening process. For this last step she invites in her friends and relatives—one for each hide—and gives them a big feast. Each one is then given a hide to take home to finish, with a rawhide rope to use for the work. Meanwhile, she has to split and make quantities of thread from the buffalo sinews she has been hoarding. Her next chore is the preparation of another great feast, for the process of cutting and sewing the lodge is an all-day sewing-bee to which all her friends will bring the hides she has parceled out to them. At daybreak she must first seek out a woman known as an expert lodge maker, to whom she supplies paint and a cutting knife. Before the guests arrive, the lodge maker fits the pieces and marks them for cutting. The sewers subsequently arrive for breakfast and work all day long, with a meal in the afternoon and a supper at night—this last after the lodge has been raised and stretched on its foundation. For her pains, the expert lodge maker receives a small present.

A new home is a great thing for all the tribe, and it is so recognized in a ritual of dedication. Except for the women working on it, no one may enter a new lodge until the bravest man available has counted coup on it and has entered, followed by other outstanding warriors. The women have completed a hard and great piece of work, and in this way the men give recognition to their achievement.

All clothing is also made by the women. Unfamiliar with the art of weaving, they tan the necessary skins and loosely tailor the garments for themselves, their men and children. Awls are made of ground-down bones (animal or fish), or thorns. These, with thread and decorative materials, are kept by each woman in a hair-covered leather bag worn at her belt. Dresses are tubular sacks sewn together down the sides and reaching well below the knees. Short sleeves hang down from the shoulders.

Old-type moccasins are made of one piece, with the insole as a flap which is folded under and sewed along the outer edge. A durable rawhide sole is sewed on to this. The result is tough and comfortable footgear. Later types are constructed with a separate upper sewed onto a rawhide sole. They are adorned with porcupine-quill or trade-bead embroidery done in geometric patterns, or with little cone-shaped tinklers of tin, obtained from the white traders.

The essential garment of the male is the breechclout. Without it a man believes he will become unsexed, and so regards it as the magical protector of his virility. It is no more than a soft, square skin worn in front and suspended from a cord around the waist. In ceremony and many dances it is the sole garb. In summer, or on a raid, it may be all that is worn; there may be more, but never less.

In inclement weather, the men add leggings which cover the leg from moccasin top outside to the hip and inside to the crotch. Most of them have long fingers or a flap of deer skin on the outside below the knee; either way, walking makes quite a stir. Men's shirts are fashioned much like women's dresses, except that they reach no more than half-way to the knee and have full sleeves. A fully dressed man looks as though he is wearing trousers with a tunic, although the leggings do not, of course, make real pants. Shirts are highly decorated with quill embroidery, trade beads, or, in special cases, the scalps of enemies sewed along the seams of the sleeves. Buffalo robes round out the cold-weather garb of both sexes.

The quilling of robes is an extra, decorative flourish done as a vowed deed. It is a sacred occupation controlled by the Quillers' Society, mentioned earlier as an honored and exclusive group of selected women. A woman or girl not a member of the society has to obtain the help and direction of one member as well as the assistance of the other members. The whole procedure of instruction is highly ritualistic and sacred. The neophyte must provide food and materials. Before the work begins, all the women recite the making of their best pieces—just as a warrior counts coup. An old male crier announces to the whole camp what is being done and publicly invites some poor person to come to see the girl who is going to decorate her first robe. For coming, the visitor recieves the gift of a horse, and if he is a man, he rides it around the camp singing a song of praise extolling the giver. Two to four brave warriors are invited to the women's "coup counting," and when the women have told their quilling exploits, the men tell their great war deeds and dedicate the kettle of meat, which is offered to the spirits and divided among the women.

The sewing is done later. If a mistake is made, a warrior who has scalped an enemy must be sent for. He tells his coup and says, "And when I scalped him, this is how I did it," so cutting the misplaced quills loose.

When the Quillers are sewing the lodge decorations, the warriors may "attack" them in a very formal way. They choose a scout who at some time has been the first to spot the enemy, and he goes into the Quillers' lodge to see what they have to eat. He is followed by the bravest of all the men, who counts coup on the pot and is privileged to carry away the food without objection from the women.

MEN'S ACTIVITIES

While women gather vegetable foods and make the home and its accoutrements, men bring home the meat, make weapons, wage war, and perform the major part of the necessary rituals.

The Cheyenne men are almost exclusively big-game hunters, even as the postglacial paleo-Indians of the Plains. Bison stand out as their basic staple, with antelope next, then deer, elk, and wild sheep. Smaller game, such as wolves and foxes, are taken occasionally for their furs. Of their domesticated animals, the dog is a favorite delicacy reserved for feasts. "With us, a nice fat, boiled puppy dog is just like a turkey at Thanksgiving with you," High Forehead used to say to me. Horsemeat is eaten, but not preferred. As a heritage from their days in the Woodlands, the Cheyennes (unlike most Plains tribes) also take fish.

A superficial paradox governs buffalo hunting. When buffalo are scarce, anyone may hunt when and as he pleases. When they are plentiful, the restrictions of the communal hunt come into force. The reasons for this are clear and simple: while scattered buffalo in small herds cannot be efficiently hunted by large groups, the massive early-summer herds, as already indicated, are best attacked by a closely working, cooperative group.

The communal buffalo hunt is a development stemming from the old-time antelope drive, which was a mystic procedure. Antelopes, as is well known, are the fleetest of animals, adapted to survival by speed of flight. They are at the same time, however, endowed with an odd sense of curiosity. They want to observe any unusual object and will, for instance, move toward a gently moving flag. It is this trait that the Cheyennes seized upon, magically elaborating their exploitation of it. In the nineteenth century, magical antelope surrounds (hunts) have become infrequent, but every now and then some medicine man puts one on. The basic pattern is not confined to the Cheyennes, but is widespread among Indians of the Plains, Great Basin, and Southwest (Underhill 1948:28–34).

The antelope shaman receives his power from Maiyun in a series of dreams. When he feels ready to put on a hunt, the news is passed by word of mouth rather than through a crier. This, and the fact that the shaman also lets it be known that no guns or ordinary weapons are to be used in the hunt, indicates that the pattern was set before the tribe established itself in the Plains, for the crier and gun are both culture traits acquired after the Cheyennes had migrated into the Plains.

As a first step, the shaman raises a small medicine tipi within which he performs an all-night ritual, the details of which are not known. At certain stages, the members of a military society beat on the lodge covering over four of the lodge poles which are mystically endowed. If the hunt is going to be successful, large quantities of antelope hair fall off the lodge covering.

The next morning, the shaman leads the people out toward where his power has told him the antelope will be. The hunters are on their fastest horses, but he is afoot. At the chosen spot, he selects two exemplary virgin girls. They must be good-tempered, or the antelope will be fractious and hard to control. They should also be plump, or the antelope will be skinny and stringy. Each is given a so-called antelope arrow: a wand with a medicine wheel at one end. The shaman has already used these to draw the antelope toward the spot. Each girl begins running outward on diverging, diagonal courses so that their paths begin to describe a wide V. Two young men, supposed to be their suitors, chase after them on the fastest and longest-winded horses available. The hunters on their horses tail out after them in two long lines.

As soon as the hunters are on their way, the remaining women and children form a circle at the foot of the V, with the shaman in the center. As the two leading young men pass the pair of girls, each takes one of the wands the girls have been carrying. They continue on the diverging line for a couple of miles, riding at a fast pace. Soon they are on both sides of an antelope herd, which, instead of running away, turns toward the shaman. The men with the wands then turn in and cross behind the herd, continuing to ride back outside the lines of hunters, who have followed them and entirely surrounded the herd. When the two reach the shaman, they return the wands. Down the V the antelope are driven at a fast pace, pell-mell into the circle of old men, women, and children, who with waving blankets close around them to form a human corral. Using his two wands as directional signals, the shaman makes the antelope rush around and around until they are utterly confused and exhausted. This is the drama that is reenacted in the Crazy Animal Dance. Then the people set upon the befuddled beasts and kill them with clubs. For his pains and skill the shaman receives all the tongues (a choice delicacy) and his choice of two antelope. The two girls and two young men make their choice next. After that, an even distribution is made among all the families.

William Bent, the trader, was with the Sourthern Cheyenne in 1858 when such a hunt was held under the direction of White Faced Bull. It was so successful that every one of six hundred Cheyenne lodges had an antelope, and Bent's wagon train had all it could use (Grinnell 1923:1, 288).

Other times, antelope are led and driven into a pit or over a bluff in the same way. Occasionally, the V is formed of brush piles behind which people hide until the antelope are between them.

The same technique is also applied to buffalo hunts. On one such occasion some enemy Shoshones turned up just after the hunt was completed. The Cheyennes attacked them in the ordinary battle manner, but afterwards thought it a shame that the Shoshones had not arrived a bit earlier. "We could then have sent those two girls around them and killed them all off just as we had the buffalo." (Hoebel n.d.).

For general purposes, the nonmagical hunt suffices in taking bison. They are not so skittish as the antelope, and the soldier-policed secular hunt is more usable as an everyday affair. In such hunts, when the charge is made, the hunter rides his horse up along the right side of a running beast and sends an arrow down and between its ribs. The horses are trained to follow tight beside the animal so that both the rider's hands are free to use the bow. Strong men sometimes shoot an arrow right through one bison and into another. If a spear is being used, it is driven down with the full force of both arms, between the ribs and into the heart. If a man is not good enough to do this, or conditions are not right, he thrusts for the kidneys, which are easier to reach. This does not bring such a quick kill, but it is a fatal wound with which a buffalo cannot run far. Lances and bows are preferred for large hunts even by those Cheyennes who possess guns, for many more animals can be killed this way; guns are too slow to reload for a man on horseback.

When the hunt is done, the men skin and butcher the take, loading it all on pack horses for the trip back to the camp where it is turned over to the women for cooking or cutting into thin slices which are hung on racks to sun dry. Later, the dried meat is shredded by pounding with the stone mauls and packed away as pemmican.

Deer and elk are taken by individual hunters who stalk them with bow and arrow, or ambush them from hiding places along their trails.

The large gray wolf is taken in pitfalls—deep holes dug wider at the bottom than at the top so that the wolf cannot jump out. A pole with bait at the center is staked across the hole, which is roofed over with split reeds covered with earth and grass. As the wolf moves out on the mat to seize the bait, the whole covering gives way beneath him. He may then be shot in his prison.

Since foxes are too light to be taken this way, they are caught in deadfalls. In this type of trap two logs are arranged, one on the ground and another supported by a trigger above it. A little willow twig house, open at the deadfall end, is built over the baited trigger.

Thus, the fox is forced to put his head under the fall-log if he is to get at the bait. A tug on the lure springs the trap; the log falls on his neck or back, killing or paralyzing him.

Eagles are not eaten but are highly prized for their feathers. They are caught by human hand and strangled. This is a crafty, ticklish undertaking, and one for specialists only—men who have eagle-catching power and knowledge of its associated rituals. Eagles have a wingspread up to seven feet and a beak as long as their heads. The trick is done from a pit-blind, which must be painstakingly prepared. The pit can be dug only when there are no eagles in the sky, and the dirt must be scattered a long way off, because eagles are farsighted and cautious. Before digging the pit, the eagle catcher must sing his sacred eagle songs alone in his lodge all night long. His pit, which is just large enough for him to sit in, is roofed over with long grass through which are left a few spy holes. He deodorizes himself in a sweat bath and greases himself all over with eagle-grease paint. He enters the hole before daybreak, when the eagles cannot see him. Over his head a piece of fresh bait is tied firmly down. When an eagle settles down to tear at the bait, the hunter slowly slips his hands through the grass, grabs its legs and pulls it into the hole. The hunter is then in a 3-by-5 hole with a fighting, clawing eagle that he must strangle with a noose! The reward is considerable prestige and a good return in trade value: a horse for twenty or thirty feathers, for example. Eagle catching must be done in four-day stints (a ritual requirement). At the end, a ceremonial offering and apology are made to the dead eagles, followed by the hunter's taking four sweat baths to neutralize the sacred power worked up for use in the enterprise.

Turtles are taken from ponds and roasted or boiled in the shell for food.

When still in the lake country, the Cheyennes used to seine for fish, setting willow nets into which they drove the fish. Now they construct a fish weir in rivers under the supervision of a medicine man. The weir is a circle made of willow poles driven closely together into the bottom and lashed with rawhide. The weir is left alone at night for the fish to enter, while the medicine man in his lodge tries to draw them into the pen. During the next day, one man works with a long, narrow basket which is placed against an opening made in the downstream side of the weir. As the fish enter his basket, he removes them and tosses them up on the shore for the waiting people.

In summing up, we see that the Cheyennes provision themselves with a fair variety of food that gives a reasonably balanced diet in good times. Their techniques and skills are of a high order; they work together in smoothly cooperative teams for the common weal. Still, they live under feast-or-famine conditions, and famine is never forgotten. So uncertain is their food situation that, except for root and berry-gathering activities, and the policed, secular buffalo hunts, ritual and supernatural power suffuse their undertakings. They are anything but improvident, and the drying power of the High Plains sun is constantly used to preserve meat and vegetables for leaner times. That the Cheyennes go to such lengths to preserve their food supply, despite the fact that it must all be packed along whenever they move, is indicative of their efforts to maintain their larder.

CHAPTER FIVE

Coping with Abundance: Subsistence on the Northwest Coast

WAYNE SUTTLES

Although the aboriginal peoples of the Northwest coast of North America were not hunters so much as fishermen, they seem especially worth including in a survey of Man the Hunter for two reasons: First, their rich, maritime, temperate-zone habitat is a type in which few food-gathering peoples survived until historic times, partly because this very type of habitat elsewhere saw the growth of more advanced forms of subsistence.[1] Second, the Northwest coast peoples seem to have attained the highest known levels of cultural complexity achieved on a food-gathering base and among the highest known levels of population density. The Northwest coast refutes many seemingly easy generalizations about people without horticulture or herds. Here were people with permanent houses in villages of more than a thousand; social stratification, including a hereditary caste of slaves and ranked nobility; specialization in several kinds of hunting and fishing, crafts, and curing; social units larger than villages; elaborate ceremonies; and one of the world's great art styles. The area appears to have been matched in population density, among food-gathering areas, by only two or three areas adjacent to it— California and parts of the Arctic and Plateau culture areas. (Kroeber, 1939; but it would be good to have comparable data for the Ainu and the Lower Amur peoples.) These features of Northwest coast culture and demography are generally thought to have been made possible, or even inevitably produced, by the richness of the habitat of the area and the efficiency of the subsistence techniques of its peoples. Perhaps, then, the study of Northwest coast subsistence can offer some guidance in estimating the possibilities of cultural development under comparable conditions in prehistoric times.

In a short paper I cannot hope to do justice to the variety and complexity of Northwest coast culture and its historic relations (for a general survey, see Drucker, 1955, 1965),[2] nor to go into the problem of aboriginal population sizes and densities except to comment that Mooney's and Kroeber's figures (Kroeber, 1939, pp. 131 ff.) have generally been revised upwards (Baumhoff, 1963, pp. 157–61; Duff, 1964, pp. 38–46; H. Taylor, 1963). I shall simply take the cultural complexity and population density as proven, and discuss our knowledge of subsistence and its relationship to them. But as you will see, I do not consider the relationship a simple one and so I must range through several sorts of phenomena. In general, my thesis is that while the habitat was undeniably rich, abundance did not exist the year round but only here and there and now and then and that such temporary abundances—though they may well be a necessary condition for population density and cultural development of the sort seen on the Northwest coast—are not sufficient to create them. Equally necessary conditions were the presence of good though limited food-getting techniques, food-storing techniques, a social system providing the organization for subsistence activities and permitting exchanges, and a value system that provided the motivation for getting food, storing food, and participating fully in the social system. I shall deal with each of these conditions in succession.

HABITAT

The Northwest coast was an area where one could find, on a single occasion, quite literally tons of food. Salmon ran into the smaller streams by the thousands and into larger streams by the tens and hundreds of thousands. Waterfowl came to the marshes by the tens and hundreds of thousands. A single sturgeon can weigh nearly a ton, a bull sea lion more than a ton, a whale up to thirty tons. But this aspect of the Northwest coast habitat is only too well known. It has been so emphasized that the implications of the phrase used above, "on a single occasion," have been ignored and the habitat has been presented as a constant source of plenty. But as I have said elsewhere (Suttles, 1960, 1962), it was not constant. It did not provide an ever-reliable abundance of natural resources simply there for the taking. Abundance there consisted only of certain things at certain places at certain times and always with some possibility of failure. Describing the central coast Salish[3] habitat, I wrote:

> The environmental setting of native culture was characterized by four significant features: 1) *variety of types of food*, including sprouts, roots, berries, shellfish, fishes,

waterfowl, land and sea mammals; 2) *local variation* in the occurrence of these types, due to irregular shorelines, broken topography, differences between fresh and salt water, local differences in temperature and precipitation; 3) *seasonal variation*, especially in vegetable foods and in anadromous fishes; 4) *fluctuation from year to year*, in part due to the regular cycles of the different populations of fish, in part to less predictable changes, as in weather (1960, p. 302; see also Suttles, 1962, pp. 527–29).

In their subsistence activities, the central coast Salish had to cope with these variable features of the habitat. It seems likely that farther north on the coast there were fewer types of resources but greater concentrations and thus possibly greater dangers in failure, through human error or natural calamity, of resources to appear at the right place at the right time (1962, pp. 530–33). Farther south I would expect the opposite to hold. But these subareal differences have yet to be worked out.

One cause of unexpected hardship was purely climatic. Because of the Japan Current and prevailingly westerly winds from the ocean, the weather is usually mild and damp. Summers are cool and during many winters the temperature only now and again drops below the freezing point. In the central coast Salish area, winters without frost are not unknown. But occasionally masses of extremely cold continental air break out through the coast mountains to bring periods of as much as ten days of near-zero (Fahrenheit) weather to the outer coast. In British Columbia such severe outbreaks have been recorded at twelve- to eighteen-year intervals (Young, 1943, pp. xli–xlii).

From a number of places along the coast we have indications that there were times when food was scarce. For groups dependent upon the open ocean, the cause was usually a stretch of bad weather; for groups on rivers, it was tardiness or failure in a fish run. In both situations it was of course also a matter of human failure to have accumulated enough food for the emergency.

For the Haida of the Queen Charlotte islands we have a statement by an early observer, Poole, quoted by Niblack, who writes:

> Some of these berries are collected and dried for winter's use, forming, with dried fish, the principal winter's supply. Poole, (1863) says of the Haida, that they often, through feasting or improvidence, eat up all the dried berries before spring, and "were it not for a few bulbs which they dig out of the soil in the early spring-time, while awaiting the halibut

season, numbers of Indians really would starve to death"
(Niblack, 1890, pp. 276–77).

For the Tsimshian of the Nass and Skeena rivers we have Boas's
statement, derived from his analysis of Tsimshian mythology, that
"sometimes when the olachen were late in coming, there would be
a famine on Nass River" (Boas, 1916). In his comparison of Tsimshian
data with Kwakiutl data in *Kwakiutl Culture as Reflected in Mythology*,
Boas writes:

> The difficulties of obtaining an adequate food supply must
> have been much more serious among the Tsimshian than
> among the Kwakiutl, for starvation and the rescue of the tribe
> by the deeds of a great hunter or by supernatural help are an
> ever-recurring theme which, among the Kwakiutl, is rather
> rare. One story of this type is clearly a Tsimshian story retold.
> . . . Starvation stories of the Kwakiutl occur particularly
> among the tribes living at the heads of the inlets of the
> mainland, not among those who dwell near the open sea,
> where seals, sealions, salmon and halibut are plentiful (Boas,
> 1935, p. 171; see other references in Piddocke, 1965, p. 247).

For the Nootka, who occupy the west coast of Vancouver Island
in less sheltered waters than the Kwakiutl, we have Drucker's statement that a poor dog salmon or herring run followed by weather
bad enough to prevent people from going out for cod or halibut
"quickly brought privation" when people sought foods they ordinarily
disdained. He cites Father Brabant's report of "two successive springs
at Hesquiat when pickings were lean and children cried out with
hunger, until the weather abated enough for the fishermen to go
out." He also cites family traditions of the hardships of winters on
the outer coast before alliances had been made with groups with
salmon streams (Drucker, 1951, pp. 36–37).

Swan says of the Makah at Cape Flattery:

> The ease with which these Indians can obtain their
> subsistence from the ocean makes them improvident in laying
> in supplies for winter use, except of halibut; for, on any day
> in the year when the weather will permit, they can procure,
> in a few hours, provisions enough to last them for several
> days (1870, p. 30).

Yet he later (p. 76) describes a period in April of 1864 when the
weather did not permit going out fishing or whaling and how the
Ozette were concerned enough about this to accuse an old man of
sorcery and threaten to kill him if he didn't stop his incantations

and make fair weather. The Quileute, Swan was told, had killed an alleged sorcerer for bringing bad weather during the halibut season only a few summers earlier.

Discussing relations between the upper and lower classes among the Chinook of the mouth of the Columbia River, Ray (1938, p. 56) says that his principal informant "declared that the upper class could infringe as much as it pleased upon the lower classes and added that famine was unknown to the former since the food of the latter was appropriated in such a circumstance." Ray adds that the informant's specific examples were the acts of chiefs. In the context of Ray's other statements, it appears that the Chinook village chief received, or seized, tribute and redistributed food to his people, favoring the upper class. My point in citing this is simply to indicate that shortages were conceivable.

Finally, we have Gould's (1966) recent reanalysis of the wealth quest among the Tolowa, an Athapaskan-speaking people on the Oregon-California border. This is the group described by DuBois (1936) as having distinctly separate "subsistence" and "prestige" economies in the paper that first introduced these terms into the study of primitive economies. According to DuBois, subsistence was not a problem; scarcity existed only in "treasures" (dentalia shells, obsidian blades, and woodpecker scalps); food circulated freely in a "subsistence economy," while men bent their efforts in gaining prestige through amassing wealth in the "prestige economy." But Gould has found no separate "subsistence economy" in that there is no evidence for specialization in subsistence or the exchange of foods. There do appear, however, to have been differences in the productivity of households due in part to differences in the number of women available to process foods in season. It is true that "treasure" items were not constantly used to buy food, nor ideally nor publicly so used, but they were commonly used to buy food during periods of shortage. In fact, storing food to sell to others was recognized as an important method of acquiring wealth; hence, the interest the Tolowa show in acquiring women, the processors of food. Wealth is converted into prestige by its use in ceremonial displays and in payment of bride price, which establishes the social status of children to the marriage (Gould, 1966, pp. 70, 77, 86). Thus recognition of the existence of periods of shortage and problems in subsistence has made possible a reinterpretation of the data that give them a greater coherence than in the earlier analysis.[4] There is really only one Tolowa economy; in it food is converted into wealth and wealth is converted into prestige. Occasional shortages of food provided the occasions for converting wealth into food. Hungry people wanted food; greedy people wanted wealth. Why did the greedy want wealth? Because wealth brought prestige. Gould does not ask why the Tolowa sought prestige. But it seems likely that it was because indirectly prestige-seeking enabled hungry people to obtain food. Or, if this seems to imply conscious purposiveness, we may say it is because populations that have unconsciously stumbled on ways of feeding hungry members survive better than those who let them starve.

I have dwelt at length on the existence of times of scarcity on the Northwest coast-precisely because recognizing their existence may be essential to our understanding of the complexities of Northwest coast culture. Some years ago Bartholomew and Birdsell pointed out that it is a firmly established ecological generalization, known as "Liebig's law of the minimum," that the size of a population is determined not by the mean condition but by the extremes. "A semi-arid area may have many fruitful years in succession, but a single drought year occurring once in a human generation may restrict the population to an otherwise inexplicably low density" (Bartholomew and Birdsell, 1953, pp. 487–88; see also comment by Sherwood L. Washburn and June Helm, Chapter 9a, this volume). Perhaps, also, a single, once-a-generation failure of a major fish run or prolonged period of severe weather may explain an otherwise inexplicable practice such as the Northwest coast search for prestige.

What we need to know for the whole coast is not merely what resources were present and when and where they were found under ordinary conditions, but also the *minimal* occurrences in space, time, and quantity. This means we should pay special attention to what foods are, or were, available in winter, even though winter was culturally defined by most peoples of the area as the ceremonial season during which people lived on stored food. As we have seen from the quotations given, stored food was not always available. It also appears that there were differences between inland river environments, sheltered saltwater bays, and the open ocean shores. There were probably also differences from south to north. None of these has been worked out in detail, but I am confident, that, with the growing body of biological and climatological data on the area, we shall one day be able to state fairly accurately what the resource base of each people's territory were.

Of course it is necessary to distinguish between what foods *could* have been hunted, fished, and gathered, and those foods actually obtained in practice. The difference between potential and actual is in part a function of the efficiency of food-getting methods.

FOOD-GETTING METHODS

The state of our knowledge in this respect, too, is certainly not as good as we would want it. We do not have and probably shall never have any figures on the quantities of food actually collected and consumed per capita, on the ratio of meat, fish, and vegetable food in the diet,[5] on the number of man-hours spent in the food quest, and on percent of the population supported in leisure or other non-subsistence activities. Moreover, for much of the area we do not even have the facts in the form of good ethnographic accounts of just how food was obtained. This is not to say there are no good works at all. Boas's material on Kwakiutl subsistence activities, mainly in the form of native texts with translations (Boas, 1909, pp. 461–516; 1921, part I), gives the native view of a number of food-getting and food-storing techniques and a great many recipes. In these texts we see what was important to the informant, but do not always find the answers to questions the ethnographer would ask. From some, however, we can make inferences about quantities of food taken and consumed. Among the ethnographies of the area, Drucker's (1951) on the Nootka (see also Drucker, 1965, chap. 7, for a dramatic account of Nootka whaling) and Elmendorf's (1960) on the Twana (a coast Salish group) are outstanding. The only specialized monograph is Kroeber and Barrett (1960) on fishing in northwestern California. But for much of the area between the Klamath and the Columbia and north of the Kwakiutl, we have only very sketchy accounts.

The reason for the deficiency in figures on subsistence is not hard to find. The purely aboriginal way of life had been greatly altered in most parts of the Northwest coast by the end of the last century and quantitative data are, as Kroeber pointed out (1939, p. 3), not ordinary recoverable by the method of ethnographic reconstruction we must use in western North America. The reasons for the scant attention often paid to subsistence techniques are also easy to find. Some of the techniques had disappeared by the beginning of this century or had survived in forms altered by the introduction of European goods. But, also, the very complexity of social forms and richness of art and ceremony that draw attention to the area are likely to draw attention away from mere subsistence. Thus when McIlwraith (1948) had the opportunity to play a part himself in the Bella Coola winter ceremonies, he did so and the results form a good part of his two-volume work on that people. I find this quite understandable, but still wish we had more on Bella Coola salmon fishing than the pluses and minuses in Drucker's (1950) element list. Another reason for the neglect of subsistence probably lies in the assumption that the habitat was so rich that subsistence simply was not a problem. Finally, an understanding of just how any given subsistence technique works requires moving outside of culture and seeing the technique as part of an ecosystem; this is not easily done if one is unfamiliar with the natural history of the area and has only a few summer months to spend in it.

But the situation is by no means hopeless. In spite of the fact that year by year the purely aboriginal way of life recedes into the past, I fully expect that a few years hence we shall know much more about Northwest coast subsistence than we know today. I have several reasons for this optimism. First, contrary to gloomy predictions by colleagues that I'd find all was lost, when I began working with the coast Salish I discovered that it was still possible to do ethnography and to get much new data on subsistence. I am sure that my experience could still be duplicated in other areas, if for no other reason than that some activities survive yet in modified form. Second, data from the related fields of linguistics, archeology, and ethnohistory and from the ethnography of other areas can be increasingly used in interpreting the ethnography of one's own area. For example, some of my informants and the informants of others have believed that the gill net is not aboriginal in the Salish area. However, a comparison of native terms for the gill net and the record of an earlier observer suggest that it probably was, in fact, aboriginal. I expect that further probing will settle the matter. Third, the growing body of biological and climatological knowledge can be used to interpret the ethnographic data. For example, the testimony of informants that their ancestors fished by trolling in winter as well as spring is supported by the work of researchers in fisheries (for example, Rounsefell and Kelez, 1938, pp. 749–50). Their work indicates not only that spring salmon are present in winter but that Indians did troll for them. Also, other biological work shows that herring spawn in this area in winter and early spring (Clemens and Wilby, 1946, pp. 79–80) and would therefore be available during times of the month when tides are low. Finally, meteorological data could undoubtedly be obtained indicating average number of days during winter months when weather would permit trolling in each of several areas.

When I express this optimism about the possibility of increasing our knowledge of Northwest coast subsistence, I do not mean to imply that we shall surely be able to reconstruct the quantitative data. But what we surely can do is define more narrowly the requisites and limits of each technique so that we can make some estimates of the relative effectiveness of the different techniques under similar conditions and the same technique under different conditions.

FOOD-STORING METHODS

The techniques for preserving food are certainly as important as those for getting food. Thousands of salmon swimming upstream in September would not make winter a time of ceremonial activity if people lacked the means of preserving them, nor would several tons of blubber on the beach. No doubt some people would not have survived some winters without storage methods.

A few foods do not keep well at all. Mussels and salmonberries, for example, seem to be too soft and watery. But most fishes and meats, some shellfishes, and some berries can be preserved by drying, either with or without smoke. Clams and some meats were steamed and *salal* berries were sometimes cooked before drying.

Whether fish or meat can be dried outside in the sun or must be smoked indoors depends of course upon the season of the catch and the climate of the area. In the central coast Salish area, where summers are relatively dry and sunny, summer catches of sockeye and humpback salmon, as well as halibut, lingcod, and other fish, were generally dried on outdoor racks at summer fishing camps, where the fishermen could live in mat shelters. Fall runs of springs, cohoes, and dog salmon, however, usually had to be smoked indoors because of the danger of rain. Occasionally separate structures may have been built for smoking fish, but evidently the usual "smokehouse" was the ordinary winter plank house and in local English usage this is what it is still called. The importance of this difference in preserving methods for social relations is easily seen. In the drier season a nuclear family, on its own, could store up a considerable amount of food with a minimum of shelter, but in the wetter season it would be bound to the plank house of its extended family. Because of its use as a smokehouse, the plank house is thus an important instrument of production, and the ownership or control of a house at the stie of a fish weir used in the fall may have had as important social and economic consequences as ownership or control of the weir itself. In the Salish area, weirs were in fact usually public property but houses were not.

In many other parts of the coast, climatic conditions probably did not permit as much preserving of food outside as in the Salish area. During the three months of summer, Victoria (in the Salish area) gets an average of 14 days of rain (out of an annual total of 133) while Port Hardy (in Kwakiutl country) gets 38 (out of a total of 204), Masset (Haida) 41 (out of 210), and Prince Rupert (Tsimshian) 46 (out of 215). During an average year Victoria gets a total of 2,092 hours of sunshine while Prince Rupert gets 1,019, or roughly half (figures from Kendrew and Kerr, 1955). Precipitation is also greater on the outer coast to the south than in the central coast Salish area. These differences certainly have implications for food preserving and possibly for social relations.

It should be noted that not all species of salmon, perhaps not even all populations of the same species, keep equally well. My Salish informants say that fatter fish last longer and thus sockeye and dog salmon are their favorites. Other species may not last through the winter months.

Another very important method of storage is the rendering of fat into oil, which can then be kept in such containers as seal bladders (in the Salish area), kelp bulbs (Kwakiutl), or wooden boxes (Chinook). Throughout most of the coast, dried fish or meat was eaten after being dipped in oil; sea-mammal oil was used from the Salish and Nootka southward, and eulachon oil was used from the Kwakiutl northward. On the Fraser, where seal oil was less plentiful, salmon oil was also used (Duff, 1952, p. 66). This constant use of oil seemed excessive to Europeans but it may have compensated for the scarcity of carbohydrates (Drucker, 1951, p. 62; Rivera 1949, p. 34; see also note 5 of the present paper).

In the north, oil was also used for preserving some kinds of berries. From the Chinook southward, meat was preserved by pulverizing it and mixing it with grease. Salmon eggs were first allowed to get "high" and to form a kind of cheese-like substance, and eulachon were also allowed to decay before rendering; however there was evidently no general practice of allowing fish to decay. Storage pits are reported for a few areas and so are raised caches, but probably throughout most of the area preserved food was stored in boxes, baskets, and bags placed on racks inside the dwelling house.

A number of foods, such as dog salmon, must have required far more effort in the storing than in the taking. Thus limits in the exploitation of times of abundance may have been set less by people's capacity to *get* food than by their capacity to *store* it. How much of a very heavy fall run of dog salmon could be stored must have depended on the number of hands available for the work of cutting and skewering, the drying-rack capacity of the houses at the site, fuel for smoke, and finally the number of containers available. As Gould has stressed, preserving food was largely the work of women and for this reason rights over women and bride prices were so important in the economy of the Tolowa. The role of women in subsistence no doubt deserves reappraisal elsewhere on the Northwest coast. But it must be remembered that women need not be wives; they may also be slaves.

VALUES AND SOCIAL ORGANIZATION

Of course the possibilities offered by the environment and the techniques of food-getting and food-storing could be realized only through the work of people, organized by their social systems and motivated by their value system. To survive that occasional period of scarcity, people had to have not only the earlier periods of abundance; the weirs, nets, etc., to take the food with; and the drying racks, houses, etc., to preserve and store it with; but they also had to have a reason for doing it and the ability to mobilize the labor for it.

Probably the knowledge that there is an occasional period of scarcity is not reason enough to make most people store up food for every winter. But the Northwest coast peoples had "better" reasons. From the Yurok and Tolowa northward there was the ultimate goal of prestige, into which food was eventually converted. From the Chinook northward there was also the cultural definition of winter as a ceremonial season, when people should not have to seek food. (This last reason for storing food was also found through much of the Plateau as well.) Swan's account for sorcery among the Makah (1870) suggests that some people did not expect random variation in their environment anyway; they attributed bad weather to human malice and coped with it by threatening the supposed sorcerer. If people stored food for "cultural" reasons rather than rational recognition of possible failure in the environment, this may explain why they sometimes did improvidently eat up all their stores in feasting, as Poole reported for the Haida. Nevertheless, the "cultural" reasons may have enabled larger populations to survive in this habitat than rational planning alone would have done.

In social organization, there seems to have been a rough sort of south-to-north gradient of increasing tightness of structure and size of social unit. Kroeber found the Yurok so individualistic that he declared:

> Property and rights pertain to the realm of the individual, and the Yurok recognizes no public claim and the existence of no community. His world is wholly an aggregation of individuals. There being no society as such, there is no social organization. Clans, exogamic groups, chiefs or governors, political units are unrepresented even by traces in northwestern California (1952, p. 3).

Nevertheless, Kroeber's data suggest possibly three kinds of social groups engaging in subsistence activities: the members of the household, the joint owners of a fishing place, and the large group from several villages that built the *Kepel* weir. This last group is an example of what Anastasio (1955) has called a "task grouping," in which members of social units defined by other criteria come together for a particular purpose at a particular time and place. These task groupings are generally under the leadership of a person who has the requisite technical and/or ritual knowledge. Treide (1965) has recently analyzed the function of such "salmon chiefs" as the ritual director of the Kepel weir for much of western North America.

Northward, on the Oregon coast the village seems to have consisted of an unnamed patrilineal kin group formed by patrilocal residence and to have functioned as a unit under some circumstances (Barnett, 1937, elements 1345, 1400). Among the Chinook at the mouth of the Columbia, there was a village chief (who may have been simply the head of a patrilocal kin group) who evidently exacted tribute from his villagers and redistributed it (Ray, 1938, p. 56).

The central coast Salish social organization was seemingly looser than that of the Chinook. Village exogamy was preferred but residence was ambilocal so neither the household nor the village formed any kind of definable kin group. There were, however, cognatic kin groups perhaps best understood as "stem kindreds," that is, the personal kindreds of successive generations of "owners" of certain ceremonial rights and one or more of the more productive natural resources. One of these men might tend to dominate a village but there was no village chief as such. The village was recognized as a unit when it came to certain types of sharing and certain ceremonial activities, but in general the household was autonomous. Task groups were directed by the "owners" of resources, such as fishing sites and clam beds; by owners of special gear, as the net for a deer drive; or simply by skilled specialists in the activity. Such subsistence activities and also ceremonial activities often brought together people from several villages over areas which crossed dialect and even language boundaries, but there were no structural principles that allowed for the definition of discrete social units.

Wakashan (Nootka and Kwakiutl) social structure seems to have been similar to that of the Salish in that both lacked rules of unilocal residence and unilinear descent. The Nootka and Kwakiutl, however, were much more structured through the principle of ranking of titles in series. Within the cognatic kin group, individuals, at least the more important ones, held positions ranked in relation to one another. Within the village (or "tribe"), kin groups were so ranked. In a few areas "tribes" formed confederacies through the same principle. Among the Wakashans, as among the Chinook, "chiefs" (in fact, kin group heads) evidently received tribute and acted as redistributers. (For the Nootka, see Drucker, 1951, especially pp. 220–21, 251–57).

The highest development of formal organization with permanent discrete social units was that found among the northern peoples. The Tsimshian, Tlingit, Haida, together with the Haisla (the northernmost Kwakiutl), had a system of matrilineages, sibs, and phratries or moieties. The largest of these kin groups were the phratries of the Haisla and Tsimshian and the moieties of the Tlingit and Haida. These were simply exogamous units and served to classify every person in the whole northern area for marriageability. Except for the Tsimshian, the largest unit with economic and political functions was the lineage. But the Tsimshian of the lower Skeena and Nass rivers went farther and acknowledged the chief of the leading lineage of a village as the village chief. Garfield believes that this probably occurred early in the eighteenth century. Then, early in the nineteenth century, villages up the Skeena established colonies near its mouth and these each remained under the authority of the chief of the mother village, who in some cases also moved to the colony. "At this stage," writes Garfield, "tribal chieftainship emerged and the tribal chief was regarded as the active leader of his tribesmen regardless of where they lived." The village chief and the tribal chief, like the earlier lineage chief, received tribute and made decisions regarding moves to fishing sites and other subsistence activities (Garfield, 1951, pp. 34–35).

The greater development of formal organization in the north was probably accompanied by more effective control of larger labor forces. This difference in turn may account for the remarkably different views we find on the economic importance of slavery on the Northwest coast.

Barnett, writing primarily of the Kwakiutl and coast Salish, suggests that slaves were "in bondage . . . as much a liability as an asset and . . . useful primarily as overt demonstration of the ability to possess them" (1938, p. 352). Drucker writing about the area in general says:

> It is difficult to estimate the slave population of the area, but it was certainly never very large, for slave mortality was high. Slaves' economic utility was negligible. They gathered firewood, dug clams, and fished, but so did their masters (1965, p. 52).

Kroeber, listing exchange values among the Yurok, expressed mainly in strings of dentalia, writes:

> A slave was rated at only one or two strings. Evidently the Yurok did not know how to exact full value from the labor of their bondsmen, not because the latter could not be held to

work, but because industry was too little organized (1925, p. 27).

The Yurok did not take slaves in war nor buy them from other peoples; all Yurok slaves were fellow Yurok enslaved by debt. The greatest number of slaves held by one man did not exceed three (p. 32).

On the other hand, Garfield (1945, p. 628; 1951, p. 30) has strongly opposed the view that slaves were kept merely for prestige value and argued that their contribution must have increased the productivity of their owners' households. A potlatching Tsimshian chief was not expected to mention what his slaves contributed in labor, but if he gave them away he boasted of what he had paid for them. During the nineteenth century a slave was worth from two hundred to a thousand dollars. They were mainly war captives and their descendants. The numbers held were much higher than among the southern tribes.

> Ten to twenty slaves are reported as belonging to each of the nine tribal chiefs of Port Simpson in the middle nineteenth century. Each of approximately fifty Port Simpson lineage heads is also reported to have owned from two to as many as ten slaves (Garfield, 1951, p. 30).

It does seem that the mere fact that slaves performed the same task as their masters does not rule out their being of economic importance. If adding a wife or daughter-in-law can increase the productivity of a Tolowa household and give additional economic advantage, as Gould reports, why not adding a slave to a Tsimshian household? Kroeber may have been correct regarding the organization of labor among the Yurok, but can't we expect more from the Tsimshian? Driver (1961, pp.245–46, 387–38) has pointed out that at the southern end of the Northwest coast a master could not kill a slave nor did he have sexual rights over a female slave, while in the north he held both these rights. This too suggests the possibility of greater control over their labor in the north.

Slavery may also be seen as one of several possible ways of making the human population fit the resources. The most drastic of these is infanticide in times of scarcity. As far as we know this was not practiced on the Northwest coast. The least drastic is fluidity of social groupings, allowing "surplus" people at a place with poor resources to move in with those at more favored places. This fluidity was a prominent feature of the coast Salish social system. With local exogamy, a man's four grandparents were likely to have been from four different villages; at each of these he had residence rights and he also had the option of living with his wife's people. For men of property it was certainly preferable to stay in one's father's village, but no rule required it. The Wakashans also seem to have been flexible in the residence of lower-ranking people. For the northerners, the sib system may have facilitated the mobility of sib-identified groups. But for northwestern California and the Oregon coast we get consistent reports of patrilocal residence and also of impoverished parents selling their children into slavery. Perhaps if residence rules are rigid, selling "surplus" children is the only peaceful alternative to infanticide.

Finally, in looking at social organization in relation to subsistence we should note that the local group was not simply a task force for the exploitation of resources. In one season it could function as a producer and distributor of surplus *and* in another season as an absorber of surplus produced by other groups. Elsewhere (Suttles, 1960, 1962) in discussing the central coast Salish socioeconomic system, I have pointed out how the preference for local exogamy and the exchanges that occurred between affines in different villages may have been adaptive under conditions of variable occurrence of natural resources. A man with a temporary abundance of any food had three choices: (1) he could share it with his fellow villagers, if they could consume it (which they could not if they too had the same abundance); (2) he could preserve it, if it were preservable and he had the labor force and time before the next harvest of fish, berries, etc., was due; or (3) he could take it to his in-laws in another village (where this particular food might be scarce) and receive in return a gift of wealth, which he might give later to in-laws bringing food to him. If he got more wealth than he gave, he could always potlatch and convert the wealth into glory, which of course might attract more prosperous in-laws. Thus, exchange between affines made it possible for a household *not* to store food and still take advantage of times of abundance.[6]

Vayda (1961a) and Piddocke (1965) have suggested that the Kwakiutl potlach system may also be seen as an adaptation to a fluctuating environment rather than the "absurdly wasteful" epiphenomenon it had sometimes been labeled. From Piddocke's review of the data, it appears that the Kwakiutl converted food into wealth by selling it to those in need (somewhat as Gould reports the Tolowa having done) and then (unlike the Tolowa) converted the wealth into prestige through competitive potlatching. Piddocke argues that the entry of new wealth into the system and the reduction of the population through disease increased the size and frequency of potlatches to the "fantastic" level of the classic descriptions.

Weinberg (1965) has criticized and expanded on Vayda's suggestion and worked out a model of Kwakiutl culture as a self-regulating adaptive system in which the stability of culture is dependent on fluctuation in the environment within certain limits. When, in the nineteenth century, the limits were exceeded in the direction of surplus, the spectacular growth of the potlatch that followed was essentially an effort to maintain the stability of the culture (cf. "Romer's Rule" of Hockett and Ascher, 1964).

It has been implicit in the previous discussion of the coast Salish that items of "wealth" (blankets, canoes, hide shirts, etc.) did not constitute all-purpose money. As in several other parts of the world, there were restrictions on the occasions when wealth items could properly change hands. These restrictions seem to have been less severe among the Tolowa, but still present in that only exchanges that related to marriage and litigation were publicized, while those that were purely commercial were not, hence the appearance of a separate "prestige economy." Among the Kwakiutl, too, giving was certainly more honorable than selling. The areas where commercial transactions were most open and honorable seem to have been the north and, most especially, the lower Columbia. But even here commerce was not wholly free for it is reported that chiefs (lineage heads?) held monopolies over trade in their territories. It seems possible that such monopolies may have had their origins in exchanges between affines in areas of different resources. In both cases the most important trade was between the coast and interior—the Tlingit with the Athapaskan hinterland and the Chinookans with the Plateau Sahaptins. Perhaps the most important question, at present unanswerable, is: *Why didn't* a market economy develop and spread out from these areas? Or were these commercial developments so recent that there was no time left for further growth? This may be, yet archeological evidence suggests that some form of trade goes back to the early occupation of the area.

CONCLUSIONS

I am afraid I have raised more questions about the Northwest coast than I have been able to answer. If I can offer any conclusion it can only be this: The Northwest coast material suggests that where people are faced with great seasonal and local variations in the amount of food offered by their habitat, their success in exploiting the abundance depends on more than technology alone. They must also have: (1) the organization of labor for getting and storing food (marital rights? kin obligations? property rights? monopoly of technical and/or ritual knowledge?); (2) some means of redistributing population on the habitat (wide kin ties and fluidity of residence? slavery?) and/or of redistributing the bounty of the habitat among the population (barter in food? exchange of food for durable goods? markets?); and (3) some motivating value (prestige?). It seems to me that these factors together with an adequate technology, are necessary conditions for coping with abundance, regardless of whether it appears in the form of fish, sea mammals, land game, or even vegetable food.

From the data presented on the "simpler" hunters by other members of the symposium, it appears that those hunters often are capable of organizing drives and other activities that would take quantities of animals if available. They also seem to have, and necessarily so, a fluidity of organization that permits redistribution of population and at least rudimentary trade. Perhaps the greatest point of contrast is that the simpler hunters lacked the characteristic Northwest coast feature of motivation to achieve and maintain superior status through production of surplus. For this reason it seems to me that the "hunting ideology" or nomadic style (Lee and DeVore, 1968) may turn out to be well worth the attention it seems to have attracted. Finally, I would ask, when we find archeological evidence of unexpected cultural complexity and population density, is it altogether hopeless to seek ethnographic parallels from the Northwest coast? This is not to say that I believe the Upper Paleolithic Europeans held slaves and gave potlatches. But I expect that some day we will be in a position to say whether they possessed the functional equivalents.

NOTES

1. The Ainu, described in this volume by Watanabe, Chap. 7, are perhaps the food-gathering people in the most similar habitat, but northwestern North America is climatically more like northwestern Europe than like northeastern Asia.

2. A complete bibliography of the area may be found in Murdock, 1960.

3. The coast Salish groups with whom I have worked on and off for a number of years are the speakers of the Halkomelem and Straits languages, whose territory includes the lower Fraser valley, the southern end of Georgia Strait, and the northern shores of the Strait of Juan de Fuca. Since they are roughly at the center of the total coast Salish area, I call them the central coast Salish.

4. The fact of shortages in the Tolowa area was not just recently discovered. Driver, in his element list for northwestern California, under "Slaves," shows that "Starving person gives self for keep" was affirmed by his Tolowa informant, one of his two Karok informants, and both Yurok, while "Girls traded for food in time of famine" was affirmed by the Tolowa and both Yurok (Driver, 1939, p. 357). But Gould (1966) has indicated the relevance of the fact to the Tolowa socioeconomic system. For a suggestion regarding the relevance of the exchange of girls for food to residence rules, see the last section of this paper.

5. While going through central coast Salish material for the symposium, I guessed that in the diet of adults, vegetable foods would have amounted to less than 10 per cent of volume but might have been higher for children, who probably foraged for

such things as cattail roots and thimble berries that adults would be less likely to bother with. I assume that in the diet of all, even small amounts of certain vegetable foods may have been very important to health. I was surprised then to note, in Murdock's *Ethnographic Atlas*, estimates of 20 per cent dependence on gathering for the Nootka and 30 per cent for the Kwakiutl (cf. Lee, chap. 4, this volume). As Lee notes, the *Atlas* defines "gathering" as the "gathering of wild plants and small land fauna," while "shellfishing" is included with "fishing" as is sea mammal hunting. Since small land fauna were almost wholly ignored on the Northwest coast, the figures must refer to vegetable foods alone.

I am willing to admit that my guess of 10 per cent dependence on vegetable foods for the central coast Salish may be too low, but the Kwakiutl figure given in the *Atlas* is surely too high. The *Atlas* gives estimates for twenty Northwest coast "societies." In the extreme south, the Yurok and the Tolowa proportions of gathering/hunting/fishing are 40/10/50 per cent and 40/20/40 per cent, respectively. This is an area where acorns were used and naturally the proportion for gathering is greater. From here northward the most common figure for gathering is 20 per cent; only the Puyallup and Kwakiutl have 30 per cent, while the Coos, Quileute, Twana, and Klallam have 10 per cent. The Puyallup are a coast Salish group living inland from Puget Sound who quite likely did depend more on roots and bulbs than did their salt-water neighbors, though with the complex exchange systems of the area we cannot be sure. But there seems no reason at all to give the Kwakiutl a higher figure than the Nootka, Bella Coola, and coast Salish of northern Georgia Strait, all of them adjacent to Kwakiutl and all given 20 per cent. It is true that George Hunt recorded 44 recipes for preparing vegetable foods and instructions for preserving some fifteen of them (Boas, 1921, part I). But the texts indicate that some of these foods were quite restricted in where they grew and the small quantities served to feast a village. Some too were described as emergency foods and evidently dangerous if eaten in quantity. Most of the roots were in fact so small that it is hard to imagine gathering large amounts of them. Altogether it does not seem to me that the Kwakiutl would have been very different from the Nootka, of whom Drucker writes:

> There was a tremendous emphasis on fats—oils and grease—in the dietary pattern. Probably the fats made up for the virtual lack of starch and sugar forms of carbohydrates. Prior to the introduction of potatoes, flour, and pilot bread in historic times, starch foods were limited to the very occasional meals of clover and fern roots, and the few other roots. It is obviously impossible to judge at this late date, but one receives the impression from informants that if the average person ate a dozen or two meals of roots in the course of a year, it was a lot. Berries provided the only sugar prior to the introduction of molasses, and were highly prized. But the berry season was rather short, except for that of *salal* berries, and the few baskets of them women picked seem to have adorned rather than materially augmented the diet. Instead of these things, one hears constantly of fats and oils (1952, pp. 62–63).

To me this statement hardly implies the 20 per cent gathering given the Nootka by the *Atlas*. On the other hand, some of the coast Salish groups probably did have more vegetable food in their diet than the Nootka and Kwakiutl, yet 10 per cent— my original guess for those I am calling the "central" groups, which include the Lummi, who are given 20 per cent by the *Atlas*. I can only conclude that the question should be left open.

I agree with Lee that shellfish gathering has more in common with the gathering of plant foods than with fishing. Both plants and shellfish are immobile and were collected (on the Northwest coast) mainly by women using digging sticks and baskets.

They differ only in food value. But sea-mammal hunting and fishing can present a similar case. The difference between catching a 5-pound salmon in a net and harpooning a 20-ton whale seems clear enough, but what do we do when we find the same coast Salish "sea-food producer" (a native category) harpooning at one time a 200-pound seal and at another a 1,000-pound sturgeon? The difference, as it was with roots and shellfish, is simply a matter of food value, and not a very great one at that. The coast Salish also harpooned salmon and netted seals, ducks, and deer. If we base our taxonomy on implements and activities, we have to ignore the taxonomy of biology, and vice versa. If we set up a category of activity based on either type of implement (as "net") or biological taxon (as "fish"), we will still be ignoring two other variables, specialization and cooperation, which may be more pertinent to the questions we are asking than are types of implements or animals.

6. Exchange between affines may also have served simply to keep more people busy. Woodburn states (Chapter 17c, this volume) that a skilled Hadza hunter could not control the number of his hangers-on. I suspect that a good provider among the coast Salish had the same problem, an increased number of less productive resident kin. But this was offset by his obligation to take food to his in-laws, who were honor-bound to repay him with wealth, which he did not have to redistribute. A man's affines in other villages may have been his covert allies against potential spongers at home.

III

Introduction
Non-Market Cultures:
Work in Pastoralist Societies

Pastoralist and herding societies exist through the keeping and managing of animals which provide meat, blood, and hides. The hair and wool of the animals can be used as a textile or felting material. The milking of females is also a source of food that does not necessitate the slaughter of animals. Furthermore, milk can be converted into dairy products which can be conserved and stored for considerable periods of time. Pastoralists use some animals to ride, some as carrying animals and some as draught animals. It is important to note that most pastoralists use animals for only a few of the uses listed. The use of animals for meat is the most widespread practice.

Animals kept by herders depend for their nourishment on natural vegetation. Thus, the movements of pastoralists, who are basically a mobile and migratory culture, are related to the needs of their animals for food, water, salt, and protection. Gardening, trading, and raiding for booty are also carried on by pastoralists but these are subordinate to the basic subsistence strategy which is the keeping of animals.

As compared with agriculture, pastoralism does not pre-suppose an intensive level of land use. It is practiced in areas of the world where there is sufficient rainfall to sustain grass and brush but which is not sufficient for agriculture. Some pastoralist societies are partial cultivators, but in the main they make use of an arid environment not suitable for crop cultivation.

Goldschmidt (1971:134) sums up the pastoralists as follows:

Thus, permanently or seasonally the pastoralist must live in an environment of physical hardships and danger from predatory animals. Furthermore, he must constantly or seasonally spread out thinly over the land. Finally, as the pastoralists' capital is of a kind that is easily stolen, he lives under a constant danger of raids and warfare. These are the essential ecological features to which pastoral institutions must adjust.

Pastoralism as a dominant way of life can be found in areas of the Middle East, Africa, Asia, and Europe. The only truly pastoral people in the Americas are the Navajo in the Southwest region of the United States. The Navajo are an example of a people who were once a hunting and gathering society and who changed their culture and way of making a living to that of horsemen herding sheep, a change which probably occurred many times in history with other societies.

The pastoralist's habitat range from tundra to arid deserts, from tropical savannas to cool highlands. It is almost totally absent from forest country, which is difficult to traverse. Some pastoralist groups divide their work between cultivation along the margins of streams and springs and the herding of livestock in the surrounding pastureland. Other pastoralists spend the winter in the lowlands where they sow crops and there is grass for their livestock to feed upon; when the grasses dry up in the summer they move their stock to the mountains where the grass is still green. This seasonal migration, called transhumance, from winter to summer pasture for the benefit of livestock was widespread in the past in southern Europe and is still the pattern in central Asia and northern Europe.

One of the characteristics of nomadic pastoralists has been their aggressiveness and military prowess. Living in a culture subject to raids upon their primary source of subsistence, they have developed traditions that encourage fighting ability. Their mobility, their use of riding animals, and their decentralized organization, along with their ability to cooperate within the tribal structure, have all combined to make pastoral nomads into formidable military organizations. In addition, their way of life, in which raiding and conflict with both sedentary and nomadic neighbors can be a major activity, has trained them in the arts of warfare. Their social systems give high prestige to fighting men. Each day when they must move their animals they simulate military campaigns in the way they have to mobilize and organize for movement. Pastoralists are usually organized as tribal units based on segmentary lineages, which permits them to split up easily and still retain their independent groups, each of which can act as a unit. How effective this organization is in resisting dominance from others has been proven in Afghanistan, where tribal groups have fought the Russians to a standstill. It was also demonstrated in the United States in the nineteenth century by the Indians of the Great Plains who were able to withstand the United States army for a long period.

Pastoralists have a reputation for hostility towards cultivators. It stems in part from their contempt for a people with a different way of life. It is also based on the fact that sedentary cultivators have accumulated wealth which can be stolen. Pastoralists have very little wealth besides their herds. They are thus wont to attack sedentary villages. They also raid and carry off the herds of other pastoralist groups. In many instances they live in a state of perpetual readiness to fend off attacks from others and carry out their own raids.

Historically, the Mongols of Central Asia and the nomadic Arabs who conquered all of North Africa are testimony to the military aspect of pastoralist cultures. In central Africa there is the case of the Watutsi (Maquet 1961), a pastoral people who had conquered and subjugated the sedentary agriculturalists, the Bahutu. The cattle-breeding Watutsi imposed a feudal regime upon the Bahutu, who cultivated food and provided all the necessities for the Watutsi. The latter spent their time on the arts of war and government and remained passionately devoted to their cattle. Pastoralists have often subjugated cultivators and at the same time fostered the belief that agriculture and working the land was to be scorned. In many cases they have driven out cultivators from an area, as the Masai did (Forde 1963:Chapter 14) in highland Kenya, and then, by religious myth and taboo, maintained the purity of their own pastoralist way of life. Where they have permitted cultivation, it has been made the work of women,

> In Eastern Africa from the Equator to the eastern half of Cape Province, pastoralism exists in a hybrid culture as a male economy in juxtaposition with female tillage. (Forde 1963:398)

Another characteristic of pastoralists is their close, symbiotic relationship with their animals. Evans-Pritchard (1940) observed that among the Nuer their entire conversation, their thoughts, and the preoccupation during their idle hours was infused with the lifeways of their animals. Even their manner of keeping time was based on the habits of their cattle. No matter what subject Evans-Pritchard brought up when he conversed with the Nuer, they would always turn it around so that they talked about their animals. This close relationship of pastoralists with their animals is based in part on their dependence upon their animals for food, clothing, and shelter.

It is also based on the fact that animals are used to cement social relationships through exchanges of gifts and the use of cattle as bride price during marriages. Cattle are a sign of wealth and prestige in pastoralist communities. Many pastoralists never kill their animals. Like the Masai, they use them for milking or for drinking blood and keep them until they are old and debilitated. Caring for animals among herders extends to feelings of emotion and an expressiveness toward them which approach love and tenderness. Often, animals are permitted within the household areas; when the animals are very young they are given to children who care for them and love them as pets.

Pastoralists are not as completely dependent upon the natural environment in the way hunters and gatherers are, because by keeping animals they have a daily, stable source of food. But they are still highly dependent upon their habitat since their animals require grazing land and water. Pastoralists do practice cultivation that supplements their food supply, but generally such cultivation as they do practice only constitutes about 15 per cent of their diet (Cohen 1968:236). As far as dependence upon the environment is concerned, pastoralists are less dependent than hunters and gatherers but more dependent than agriculturalists.

Pastoralism is not any more or less stable than any other type of society. Pastoralists, like agriculturalists, often resist change because of the tendency for all social systems to sustain their own way of life and disdain that of others. Nomadic herders still constitute a considerable number of people in Asia, the Middle East, Africa, and Europe. Modern nation-states which have nomadic pastoralists within their borders attempt to induce them to adopt a sedentary way of life. The transition from a nomadic to a sedentary existence is a complex phenomenon involving transformations that include adjustments in values, a new perception and knowledge of ways to work, and changes in kinship, political, and religious institutions. This is not an easy task. Countries such as Syria, Iran, India, Turkey, Kenya, and the Soviet Union, which have significant nomadic populations, continue to experience great difficulty in bringing these populations under complete control. For this reason, nomadic cultures are likely to persist for a long time and will continue to be a source of unrest and disturbance within the national borders of their host country.

CHAPTER SIX

The Nuer: Interest in Cattle

E. E. EVANS-PRITCHARD

Although cattle have many uses they are chiefly useful for the milk they provide. Milk and millet (sorghum) are the staple foods of the Nuer. In some parts of their country, especially among the Lou, the millet supply seldom lasts the whole year, and when it is exhausted people are dependent on milk and fish. At such times a family may be sustained by the milk of a single cow. In all parts the millet crop is uncertain and more or less severe famines are frequent, during which people rely on fish, wild roots, fruits, and seeds, but mainly on the milk of their herds. Even when millet is plentiful it is seldom eaten alone, for without milk, whey, or liquid cheese, Nuer find it stodgy, unpalatable, and, especially for children, indigestible. They regard milk as essential for children, believing that they cannot be well and happy without it, and the needs of children are always the first to be satisfied even if, as happens in times of privation, their elders have to deny themselves. In Nuer eyes the happiest state is that in which a family possesses several lactating cows, for then the children are well-nourished and there is a surplus that can be devoted to cheese-making and to assisting kinsmen and entertaining guests. A household can generally obtain milk for its little children because a kinsman will lend them a lactating cow, or give them part of its milk, if they do not possess one. This kinship obligation is acknowledged by all and is generously fulfilled, because it is recognized that the needs of children are the concern of neighbours and relatives, and not of the parents alone. Occasionally, however, after an epidemic or, to a lesser degree, after two or three youths of the group have married, an entire hamlet, or even a whole village may experience scarcity. Sometimes, also, shortage is caused by a tendency for the cows of a village to cease lactating at about the same time.

Nuer value their cows according to the amount of milk they give and they know the merits of each in this respect. The calves of a good milch cow are more highly prized than the calves of a cow that gives little milk. A cow is never to them just a cow, but is always a good cow or a bad cow and a Nuer who is owed a cow will not accept in payment of his debt one that does not meet with his approval. If you ask a Nuer in a cattle camp which are the best and worst cows in the herd he can tell you at once. In judging their points he pays little attention to those aesthetic qualities which please him in an ox, especially fatness, colour, and shape of horns, but he selects those which indicate a good milch cow: a broad loose back, prominent haunch bones, large milk-veins, and a much-wrinkled milk-bag. In judging the age of a cow he notes the depth of the trenches which run on either side of its rump towards the tail, the number and sharpness of its teeth, the firmness of its gait, and the number of rings on its horns. Nuer cows have the familiar angular and thin-fleshed characteristics of dairy stock.

Milking is performed twice daily by women, girls, and uninitiated boys. Men are forbidden to milk cows unless, as on journeys or war expeditions, there are no women or boys present. The milker squats by the cow and milks a single teat at a time into the narrow mouth of a bottle-necked gourd balanced on her thighs. She milks with thumb and first finger but, the other fingers being closed, the teat is to some extent pressed against the whole hand. It is both a squeezing and a pulling motion. The gourd is kept in position by the downward stroke of the hands which press it against the thighs. When a pot, or a gourd with a wider mouth, is used it is held between the knees and the milker squeezes two teats at a time. Occasionally one sees two girls milking a cow, one at either side. If a cow is restless a man may hold it still by putting his hand in its mouth and gripping its muzzle, and if it kicks, a noose is placed round its hind legs and they are pulled together. I was told that sometimes they ring the nose of a cow that is habitually restless during milking.

The process of milking is as follows. The calf is loosened and with its tethering-cord round its neck runs at once to its dam and begins violently butting her udder. This starts the flow of milk, and Nuer hold that if the calf were not first to suck the cow would hold up its milk. They do not pat the udder with the hand unless the calf is dead, for this is considered bad for the cow. When the calf has sucked a little it is dragged away, resisting stubbornly, and tethered to its dam's peg, where it rubs against her forelegs and she licks it. The girl now milks the first milking, known as the *wic*. When the teats become soft and empty the calf is again loosened and the process is repeated. The second milking is called *tip indit*, the greater *tip*. As a rule there are only two milkings, but if it is a very good milch cow at the height of her lactation period the calf may once more be loosened and a third milking, called *tip intot*, the lesser *tip*, be taken. When the girl has finished milking she wipes her thighs and the milk-gourd with the cow's tail and loosens the calf to finish off what milk is left. The first milking takes longer time and produces more milk than the second, and the second more than the third. The morning yield is greater than the evening yield.

A series of measurements suggest that four to five pints a day may be regarded as a general average for Nuer cows during their lactation period, which lasts, on an average, about seven months. It must be remembered, however, that this is an estimate of the yield for human consumption. The calf gets its share before, during, and after the milking. It is possible, moreover, that, as Nuer declare, some cows hold up their milk for their calves, since the calves often suck for several minutes after milking before their dams refuse them by kicking them or moving so that they cannot reach their udders. Sometimes a small boy drags the calf away and milks the udders himself, licking the milk off his hands, or shares the teats with the calf, but as a rule the calf gets the remainder of the milk. The total yield may, therefore, be as high as seven to nine pints a day and it appears to be far richer than milk given by English cows. It is not suprising that the yield is small, because Nuer cows receive no artificial feeding, succulent pasturage is often difficult to obtain, and they have to endure great hardship. It must, moreover, be emphasized that whereas English dairy farmers require only milk, Nuer herdsmen require milk and also wish to preserve every calf. Human needs have to be subordinated to the needs of the calves, which are the first consideration if the herd is to be perpetuated.

Milk is consumed in various ways. Fresh milk is drunk, especially by children, and is also consumed with millet-porridge. Fresh milk is chiefly drunk by adults in the heat of the dry season when a refreshing draught is most appreciated and food is scarce. Some milk is put aside, where it soon, very rapidly in hot weather, sours and thickens, in which condition it is relished. Nuer like to have a gourd of sour milk always at hand in case visitors come. Part of the daily yield is kept for making cheese, and if there are several cows in lactation one may be reserved for this purpose. Milk for churning is drawn into a different gourd to that used for drinking milk. It is then transferred to a churning gourd, in which it stands for several hours, and as churning gourds are not cleaned, unless they smell bad, the acids which remain from the previous churning curdle the milk. After standing it is churned by a woman, or girl, who sits on the ground with her legs stretched in front of her, and, raising the gourd, brings it down with a jerk on her thighs where she rocks it

a few times before repeating her actions: a simple but lengthy way
of churning. A small quantity of water is poured into the gourd
when the curds are beginning to form to make them set well and
to increase the quantity of whey, and some ox's urine may be added
to give them consistency. When they have formed, the woman pours
the milk into a cup-shaped gourd and scoops them out with a mussel
shell into another gourd vessel which is hung up in a hut. The
whey, mixed with fresh milk, is mainly drunk by women and boys.
Every day they add to the supply of curds and now and again stir
some ox's urine with them to prevent them from going bad. They
may add to the supply for several weeks before the final boiling
over a quick fire, which turns the curds, *lieth in bor*, into solid deep
yellow cheese, *lieth in car*. After boiling for a time the liquid is
poured into a gourd and the oil on top is removed, to be used as
a flavouring for porridge. The cheese is suspended in a net from the
roof of a hut in a round gourd, a piece of the shell of which has
been cut out so that cords run through it and it acts as a sliding lid
and, if air is excluded by a coating of cattle dung, it will keep in
good condition for months. Milk may thus be stored in the form of
cheese. It is eaten with porridge and is also used for anointing the
body.

Sheep and goats are also milked in the mornings, but little importance is attached to their yield, which is drunk by small children
and not used for dairy work. The woman milks and the kids and
lambs finish what is left in the udders. As they run with their dams
at pasture an evening milking is not taken; but during the day hungry
herdboys often squeeze the udders and lick the milk off their hands.

Some points that arise from an account of milking and dairy-work
deserve emphasis. (1) The present number and distribution of cattle
do not permit the Nuer to lead an entirely pastoral life as they would
like to do, and possibly did at one time. On a generous estimate
the average daily yield to the byre is probably no more than twelve
pints, or one and a half pints per person. A mixed economy is,
therefore, necessary. (2) Furthermore the fluctuation in household
resources, due to epidemics and transmission of bride-wealth, is
further accentuated by the organic character of the staple diet, for
cows only produce milk for a certain period after calving and the
yield is not constant. It follows that a single family is not a self-
sufficient unit, as far as milk is concerned, for it cannot always ensure
an adequate supply. Therefore, since milk is considered essential,
the economic unit must be larger than the simple family group. (3)
Environmental conditions, as well as need for cereal food to supplement their milk diet, prevent Nuer from being entirely nomadic,
but milk food enables them to lead a roving life for part of the year

and gives them mobility and elusiveness, as their history shows and as has been recently demonstrated in the Government campaign against them. Milk requires neither storage nor transport, being daily renewed, but, on the other hand, involves a straight dependence on water and vegetation which not only permits, but compels, a wandering life. Such a life nurtures the qualities of the shepherd— courage, love of fighting, and contempt of hunger and hardship— rather than shapes the industrious character of the peasant. . . .

It has been remarked that the Nuer might be called parasites of the cow, but it might be said with equal force that the cow is a parasite of the Nuer, whose lives are spent in ensuring its welfare. They build byres, kindle fires, and clean kraals for its comfort; move from villages to camps, from camp to camp, and from camps back to villages, for its health; defy wild beasts for its protection; and fashion ornaments for its adornment. It lives its gentle, indolent, sluggish life thanks to the Nuer's devotion. In truth the relationship is symbiotic: cattle and men sustain life by their reciprocal services to one another. In this intimate symbiotic relationship men and beasts form a single community of the closest kind. In a few paragraphs I direct attention to this intimacy.

The men wake about dawn at camp in the midst of their cattle and sit contentedly watching them till milking is finished. They then either take them to pasture and spend the day watching them graze, driving them to water, composing songs about them, and bringing them back to camp, or they remain in the kraal to drink their milk, make tethering-cords and ornaments for them, water and in other ways care for their calves, clean their kraal, and dry their dung for fuel. Nuer wash their hands and faces in the urine of the cattle, especially when cows urinate during milking, drink their milk and blood, and sleep on their hides by the side of their smouldering dung. They cover their bodies, dress their hair, and clean their teeth with the ashes of cattle dung, and eat their food with spoons made from their horns. When the cattle return in the evening they tether each beast to its peg with cords made from the skins of their dead companions and sit in the windscreens to contemplate them and to watch them being milked. A man knows each animal of his herd and of the herds of his neighbours and kinsmen: its colour, the shape of its horns, its peculiarities, the number of its teats, the amount of milk it gives, its history, its ancestry and its progeny. Miss Soule tells me that most Nuer know the points of the dam and grand-dam of a beast and that some know the points of its forebears up to five generations of ascent. A Nuer knows the habits of all his oxen, how one bellows in the evenings, how another likes to lead the herd on its return to camp, and how another tosses its head more than the rest are wont to do. He knows which cows are restless during milking, which are troublesome with their calves, which like to drink on the way to pasture, and so forth.

If he is a young man he gets a boy to lead his favourite ox, after which he takes his name, round the camp in the morning and leaps and sings behind it; and often at night he walks among the cattle ringing an ox-bell and singing the praises of his kinsmen, his sweethearts, and his oxen. When his ox comes home in the evening he pets it, rubs ashes on its back, removes ticks from its belly and scrotum, and picks adherent dung from its anus. He tethers it in front of his windscreen so that he can see it if he wakes, for no sight so fills a Nuer with contentment and pride as his oxen. The more he can display the happier he is, and to make them more attractive he decorates their horns with long tassels, which he can admire as they toss their heads and shake them on their return to camp, and their necks with bells, which tinkle in the pastures. Even the bull calves are adorned by their boy-owners with wooden beads and bells. The horns of young bulls, destined to be castrated later, are generally cut so that they will grow in a shape that pleases their masters. The operation, called *ngat*, is probably performed towards the end of their first year and usually takes place in the dry season, as it is said that a steer may die if its horns are cut in the rains. The animal is thrown and held down while its horns are cut through obliquely with a spear. They grow against the cut. The beasts appear to suffer much pain during the operation and I have sometimes heard Nuer compare their ordeal to the initiation of youths into manhood.

When a Nuer mentions an ox his habitual moroseness leaves him and he speaks with enthusiasm, throwing up his arms to show you how its horns are trained. 'I have a fine ox', he says, 'a brindled ox with a large white splash on its back and with one horn trained over its muzzle'—and up go his hands, one above his head and the other bent at the elbow across his face. In singing and dancing they call out the names of their oxen and hold their arms in imitation of their horns.

The attitude towards cattle varies with varying situations in social life and with changes in social development. As soon as children can crawl they are brought into close intimacy with the flocks and herds. The kraal is their playground and they are generally smeared with dung in which they roll and tumble. The calves and sheep and goats are their companions in play and they pull them about and sprawl in the midst of them. Their feelings about the animals are probably dominated by desire for food, for the cows, ewes, and she-goats directly satisfy their hunger, often suckling them. As soon as a baby can drink animal's milk its mother carries it to the sheep and goats and gives it warm milk to drink straight from the udders.

The games of rather older children of both sexes centre round cattle. They build byres of sand in camps and of moistened ashes or mud in villages, and fill the toy kraals with fine mud, cows and oxen with which they play at herding and marriage. The first tasks of childhood concern cattle. Very small children hold the sheep and goats while their mothers milk them, and when their mothers milk the cows they carry the gourds and pull the calves away from the udders and tether them in front of their dams. They collect urine in gourds and wash themselves in it. When they are a little older and stronger they have to clean the byres and kraals, assist in the milking, and herd the small calves and the sheep and goats at pasture. Food and play contacts with the cattle have changed to labour contacts. At this age the interests of the sexes in cattle begin to diverge and the divergence becomes more apparent as they grow up. The labour of girls and women is restricted to the byres and the kraals and is concerned mostly with the cows, while boys herd the calves at pasture, as well as assisting in the kraal, and after initiation they herd the adult cattle and in the kraal give their attention mainly to the oxen. The women are dairy-maids; the men herdsmen. Moreover, to a girl the cows are essentially providers of milk and cheese and they remain such when she grows up and is married and milks and churns for her husband's people, whereas to a boy they are part of the family herd in which he has property rights. They have entered the herd on the marriage of his kinswomen and one day he will marry with them. A girl is separated from the herd on marriage; a boy remains as its owner. When a boy becomes a youth and is initiated into manhood the cattle become something more than food and the cause of labour. They are also a means of display and marriage. It is only when a man marries and has children and an independent household and herd, when he has become an elder and man of position, that he often uses cattle as sacrifices, invests them with a sacred significance, and employs them in ritual.

The Nuer and his herd form a corporate community with solidarity of interests, to serve which the lives of both are adjusted, and their symbiotic relationship is one of close physical contact. The cattle are docile and readily respond to human care and guidance. No high barriers of culture divide men from beasts in their common home, but the stark nakedness of Nuer amid their cattle and the intimacy of their contact with them present a classic picture of savagery. . . .

Cattle are not only an object of absorbing interest to Nuer, having great economic utility and social value, but they live in the closest possible association with them. Moreover, irrespective of use, they are in themselves a cultural end, and the mere possession of, and proximity to, them gives a man his heart's desire. On them are concentrated his immediate interests and his farthest ambitions. More than anything else they determine his daily actions and dominate his attention. . . .

CHAPTER SEVEN

The Gadulia Lohars: Nomadism and Blacksmithy

P. K. MISRA

The Gadulia Lohars are one of the major nomadic communities found in northern India. Although mostly seen in eastern Rajasthan, they are also encountered in the neighboring States of Punjab, Haryana, Uttar Pradesh, Madhya Pradesh, Maharashtra and Gujarat. In these regions they are known under various names and in Rajasthan alone they may be called Gadi Lohars, Gadoli Lohars or Gadulia Lohars. All these forms relate to the bullock carts in which these people live and to their occupation as blacksmiths. (In the dialects of Rajasthan *gadi* or *gadulia* means "bullock cart" and *lohar* means "blacksmith".) To outsiders they are Gadulia Lohars but among themselves they are just Lohars; iron-workers. In this paper I shall present a descriptive analysis of their nomadism and economic activities emphasizing particularly the integration of both.

The data here refers to the Gadulia Lohars of eastern Rajasthan in the period between 1961 and 1964. It derives from field-work done in three phases, in which major emphasis was placed on the Gadulia Lohars of Chittorgarh but other bands of eastern Rajasthan were also studied. I also conducted field-work among the settled Gadulia Lohars of Beawar (90 households). The population in a camp or in transit is continually changing, but from three to 150 households came under my observation at different periods of my work among them.

The Gadulia Lohars claim Chittorgarh[1] as their ancestral home. Tradition has it that they left this fortress along with other Hindu inhabitants after having fought honorably alongside them when it fell to the Moghul army in 1568 A.D. At the entrance gate of the fortress there is a tablet[2] bearing an inscription in Hindi which proclaims that when defeat came the great warriors and the Gadi Lohars vowed upon their departure neither to return to the fortress of Chittor nor to live in houses, sleep on cots or to light lamps or use ropes for drawing water from a well until its liberation. The inscription further reads that since then these lovers of freedom live in their bullock carts and move from place to place. On 6th April, 1955, Jawaharlal Nehru, the then Prime Minister of India led them in a procession into this fortress and thus fulfilled their age old vows. But the Gadulia Lohars, even after being absolved of their vows, continue to move in their bullock carts from place to place, making and repairing iron implements, leading a life which their fathers and theirs before them had led for centuries.

The documented histories of the area do not mention the Gadulia Lohars or the circumstances under which they left Chittorgarh. Nor is the ordinary Gadulia Lohar conversant with the story of what actually happened to his community during those momentous days, some 400 years ago. With the passage of time and changes in the social, political and historical circumstances, the vows have largely lost any significance, such as they may once have had. None is observed now except that of not living in houses. Even before 1955, the Gadulia Lohars used to go up to the fortress of Chittor whenever there was an occasion to do so. They sleep on cots and have been doing so for a long time. It is true that generally the Gadulia Lohars do not use lamps. Their camps usually remain dark at night except for the glow of their hearths, but on certain occasions, such as childbirth, or when a person is possessed by spirits, they do use oil lamps. Some people also possess hurricane or modern Petromax lanterns which are used on ceremonial occasions, (e.g., marriage, recitation of devotional songs etc.). The Gadulia Lohars do not often need artificial light but do not hesitate to ignore their ancestral vow as the occasion arises. However, ropes for drawing water from wells are still not generally kept, and therefore they depend upon others either to draw water for them or to lend them ropes. This inconvenience is causing more and more Gadulia Lohars to acquire ropes and buckets. Thus these people do not observe their traditional vows, except that of not living in houses. Of course there is no need for pious observance now. Perhaps it may not have been different formerly, but the story regarding their vows persists. At the time of the Gadulia Lohar Convention in 1955 it gained official recognition and all-India popularity. According to another story current among them, Kalka Mata (a powerful female deity capable of irreparable destruction) on some occasion had cursed the Gadulia Lohars, thus condemning them to lead a nomadic life.

The nature of nomadic life and the circumstances arising out of it have to be kept in mind in understanding what a band is in the case of the Gadulia Lohars. On the one hand a band has a fluid character; it lacks apparent and professed aims and it hardly acts as a group except under certain situations of "crisis" (e.g. a feud between a band-member and a member of another community, involvement with the police etc.). On the other hand, the society of the Gadulia Lohars is visible only through these aggregates which have been called "bands" here. The whole gamut of social control becomes effectively operative at the band level. An emotional aspect is also involved for the people who live and camp together share the stresses and strains of the nomadic way of life, resulting in a "we" feeling among them. From the point of view of the observer, the band concept is useful in the sense that it is a focal point for the study of these nomads, as is a village for rural studies.

ECONOMIC ACTIVITIES

Blacksmithy

A Gadulia Lohar household is the basic unit of production and consumption. All the members of a household participate in the blacksmithing. The male head of the household usually is the principal artisan, with assistance being given him by his wife and children. Any major blacksmithy task requires the cooperation of at least four persons, although five is considered best. One person is required to manipulate the bellows. This job is usually done by an old man, an old woman or a child. One man is required for *garahi* (Hindi: *garhana*, to make) i.e. to direct the process of hammering, the operation of the bellows and heating of the iron. The worker holds the piece to be forged on an anvil with a pair of long tongs and directs others to hammer strongly or lightly, in quick or slow succession, raise the rate of air flow or lowering it and so on. This requires the specialized knowledge of the experienced master artisan. Two to three adults do the hammering, a task which all Gadulia Lohars learn in childhood.

In the absence of enough hands in a household, two or more similar households may pool their labor resources for a job, and at times this collaboration may continue for an entire season. There is, however, no permanency for such work-units, which usually are formed with close kin and friends. The income is equally shared according to the number of households in the work unit rather than the number of individuals participating in a job. Sometimes there are disputes on the sharing of income which ultimately may result in the breaking up of the association. Such disputes are generally settled on the spot with the intervention of the respected and responsible elders of the camp.

Usually, the Gadulia Lohars camp at places which are known through previous experiences to be convenient. After setting up camp, they either go around the village asking for work or the villagers themselves bring it to them. Certain of the village tasks can only be done by the Gadulia Lohars and the peasants eagerly await their arrival. All kinds of scrap iron collected here and there are given to the iron-workers for making the required things. The customers also provide fuel for the fire, that is, logs of wood. The Gadulia Lohars thus use their skill and labor only in preparing objects upon demand, or in making needed repairs. Tools, the capital investment, are of course their own.

Details of the technique employed in making various iron objects are many, but generally speaking, the blacksmith operations of the Gadulia Lohars fall into two stages. First is the task of refining and improving the quality of the iron and second is the forging of the metal to the desired shape. These two operational stages essentially involve repeated heating and hammering. In the first stage, the use of scrap iron necessitates much hammering until the rough block has the desired homogenity. Small items such as ladles (used for domestic purposes) pincers and scrapers do not require subsequent heating in their preparation. These can be shaped merely by hammering with varying force at different angles. This kind of work is called *thanda kam* (Hindi: cold work) by the Gadulia Lohars.

All iron tools used in blacksmithy are made by the smiths themselves. These conventional tools of iron-working (sledge hammers, tongs, anvils) are made in the off-season camps, when help can readily be obtained from their fellows. The techniques of iron-working employed by the Gadulia Lohars are those learned from their forefathers with hardly any change. There has been no need for a change in their technology since the tools and implements used by the villagers whom they serve remain unaltered.

It may be argued that the particular kind of blacksmithy done by the Gadulia Lohars insulate them from open competition. Their specialty is reworking discarded pieces of iron, and this the settled blacksmiths of the villages are not prepared to do, because it is uneconomic for them. The women and children of the village smiths do not participate in the blacksmithy since it is considered beneath their dignity. Instead the womenfolk are often involved in other tasks such as land cultivation, tending cattle or doing labor. Among the Gadulia Lohars, on the contrary, all available persons in a household share in the work. The actual number of persons employed is never included in assessing the costs of the items made. This is also indicated in the way earnings are shared between partners of a work-unit.

Besides specializing in the re-use of scrap iron, the Gadulia Lohars have techniques for the repair of agricultural tools. For example only the Gadulia Lohars undertake the resetting of axe blades. The worn edge of the axe is cut away after which the new end is heated and split up the middle to permit insertion of a piece of steel of the same length as the edge and about half an inch wide. This segment is then heated and hammered until it is firmly set and the joint is smooth. After the edge is set, it is immersed in cold water to harden and toughen it. This technique is locally known as *angrez bandhana* (Hindi: fixing English iron). The steel used for this purpose is cut from a broken automobile spring plate. Fixing a plate like this is a laborious job as steel requires lengthy heating and heavy hammering. There is much demand for this kind of work for it produces an efficient implement which does not require frequent sharpening and is therefore comparatively inexpensive. Such work is not profitable for the settled blacksmiths and indeed they and the village carpenters as well as the peasants have their axes repaired by the Gadulia Lohars. Thus it is seen that the social system of the Gadulia Lohars which utilizes all the labor resources of the household in blacksmithy enables them to monopolize the work they do. Despite the economic development of rural areas and likely introduction of a new variety of tools one might expect that the need for repairs will continue and so too then, the Gadulia Lohars blacksmithy.

Trade in Bullocks

The other principal economic activity of the Gadulia Lohars is their trade in bullocks. How long they have been engaged in buying and selling these animals is not known, but evidently the scale of these operations is today greater than formerly. It is generally the head of the household who transacts all business concerning bullock trading. The knowledge of animals, cleverness at bargaining and willingness to accept a risk which make a successful trader are all founded in long experience. Hence even after the partition of a household, a son continues to associate himself with his father in bullock trading and only gradually starts trading independently.

Although trading goes on throughout the year, the intensity fluctuates seasonally. The farmers need for bullocks is associated with agricultural operations, more particularly at the time of field preparation for the sowing of the winter crops and at the time of harvesting and threshing. Bullocks are also used for a shorter duration in the preparation of the fields for rainy season crops.

At such occasions the bullock trade is brisk, cattle markets become alive and there are quick transactions. Then the Gadulia Lohars generally camp near the weekly cattle markets or travel in its vicinity. Trading is done there but also in the villages themselves during the travelling season. Unlike their blacksmithy, the Gadulia Lohars face stiff competition from other traders in this business. In fact, compared to the others, the investment of the Gadulia Lohars is small.

Bullock trading is complex and is full of uncertainties, be it at the weekly markets or at the villages. A bullock which would easily bring in a profit of rupees twenty in one market, might not be able to fetch even half of that profit at another or it might even be sold at a loss. Much depends upon the skill of the trader, but market forces or other unforeseen circumstances such as injury to or illness of the animal determine success. An additional factor is the availability of capital. The economy of a people is closely related to their social and cultural practices and among the Gadulia Lohars the payment of large bride-prices augments the trading capital of the receiver but weakens the position of the giver. It may decline to such an extent that a household remains incapable of trading for several years. The margin of profit acceptable to a Gadulia Lohars varies with the actual or anticipated financial position. Thus predictable events, such as marriage or division of a household affect trading decisions. The Gadulia Lohars may have taken to nomadism on account of some historical incident but that is a minor point now for understanding their nomadism, social life or economy. The important point is their persistence as nomads over years. This has led to the development of a social system which sustains their nomadic life.

The nomadism of the Gadulia Lohars cannot be understood in isolation. This is true for all India's nomadic communities, for they function as a part of the social, ritual and economic network of the region they inhabit. The Gadulia Lohars claim Kahatriya status in the Hindu caste system. They try to observe all the appropriate customs and practices, but they are also aware that their nomadism and blacksmithing are not considered Kahatriya traits. Some abstain from eating meat or drinking alcohol and they participate in *bhajan* sessions and attend religious discourses. Such persons are not only respected in their own community but by others also.

For food grains and other items of diet the Gadulia Lohars depend upon the settled people. In return they provide certain services in the course of which their movements are organized to optimally serve their own interests. Relations with the settled population are then characterized by mutual interdependence. So far the Gadulia Lohars have not deviated from their traditional economical activities. One reason is because there has been no radical change in the traditional economic structure of the region they inhabit. Secondly, they do not have any social units exclusively based on productive activities only. The Gadulia Lohar household is the producing unit which is only a part of its total activity. Thirdly, the Gadulia Lohar society, being a closely knit one, restricts any kind of deviant behavior. The development of special techniques of repairs and the way they organize their work gives them edge over others on account of which one may expect that the demands for their goods and services would continue.

NOTES

1. Chittorgarh is the district headquarters of the district of the same name in the Indian State of Rajasthan. Popularly it is also called as Chittor. It was formerly the seat of the kingdom of Mewar of Sisodia Rajputs. Formerly, Chittorgarh was a fort city. The formidable fort at the top of a hill is still intact. Apart from its historical importance it has a number of temples, including that of Kalka Mata.

2. The tablet was fixed in 1955 when an All-India Gadi Lohar Convention was organized.

CHAPTER EIGHT

Independence among Pastoralists

WALTER GOLDSCHMIDT

I

In the first volume of our general studies in Culture and Ecology in East Africa, *The Individual in Ecological Adaptation*, by Robert B. Edgerton (1971), the author[1] concludes that in comparison to the farmers of the same tribes, the pastoralists tend to:

1. Display a more open emotionality and are generally freer in the expression of affect, whether positive or negative

2. Be more given to direct action in interpersonal relationships and less to deviousness and indirection

3. Be more independent-minded in their behavior

4. Display more social cohesiveness despite their greater independence of action

5. Have stronger and more sharply defined social values. Among these values are (a) independence, (b) self-control, and (c) bravery.

In these characteristics, the pastoralists and the farmers behaved in conformity with the models that we had formulated prior to our field work. These models were based on a set of assumptions regarding the effect of economic exploitation on the character of interpersonal relationships. Among the most important of these was seen to be the relative mobility of the pastoral population, an element that is evaluated in the following words: "If I were now to select the one environmental variable that I believe would explain most about the difference between farmers and pastoralists, it would be this one" (Edgerton 1971).

In this essay, I want to show that this independence of action is a characteristic of pastoral peoples (both as an institution and as a personality trait), and that it is structured into the social situation by the requirements of the pastoral economy. That is, I am trying to demonstrate that personality attributes characteristic of a population are in a very large measure to be seen as an aspect of ecological adaptation. I must emphasize, however, that this survey is preliminary and partial, and represents more an exploration of the possibilities of this viewpoint than a demonstration of the conclusions.[2]

II

The rationale of this procedure rests on the establishment of an ideal type of pastoralism, singling out those features which are to be seen as essential to the particular form of economy. It is not a new approach, for it is the essential element in the sociology of urbanism, but it has been little used in anthropology.[3] I assume this procedure to be legitimate and I think my own data indicate that it is a feasible one for pastoralists as a category.

Ideal-typological analysis of this kind makes, implicitly if not explicitly, certain assumptions: (1) The basis for unity is essentially in the economic life modes of the people; (2) There are ecological factors in the productive economy that bring about consistent patterns of noneconomic behavior; and, therefore, (3) Sets of causal chains may be established between these basic elements and other aspects of social life. The procedure is therefore at once functional, ecological, holistic, and causal.

III

Pastoral society may be defined as one in which the people depend for their livelihood on the management of ungulates which obtain their nourishment primarily from natural vegetation, and in so doing the daily and seasonal round of the population is determined by the needs of their animals for food, water, salt and protection. There may be alternate resources, such as agriculture, trade or booty, but these are subordinate to the requirements of the animals if the society is to be counted as pastoral. It is perhaps better to state the relationship the other way around: a society is pastoral to the degree that the needs of the animals set the patterns of activity.

Since pastoralism does not suppose a very high level of land use compared to cultivation, it is limited largely to environments sufficiently endowed with moisture to enable grass and brush to grow, but inadequately endowed with rainfall (or available irrigation water) to enable cultivation to take place. While pastoral peoples may be partially agricultural, the pastoralist must nevertheless make use at least seasonally of an arid environment. Thus permanently or seasonally the pastoralist must live in an environment of physical hardships and danger from predatory animals. Furthermore, he must constantly or seasonally spread out thinly over the land. Finally, as the pastoralist's capital is of a kind that is easily stolen, he lives under a constant danger of raids and warfare. These are the essential ecological features to which pastoral institutions must adjust. Simple as they are to express, they have far-reaching implications for the form and character his society takes on.

IV

Before proceeding to the examination of the independence syndrome, it is necessary to remove one apparent contradiction in our data; namely, the combination of highly independent behavior together with a strong commitment to the social order. This latter was demonstrated in Edgerton's data with the pastoralists' responses (as compared to farmers') that indicate a stronger sense of shame or guilt, a greater respect for authority, more concern with wrongdoing and a higher degree of cooperativeness. The farmers, by contrast, expressed more disrespect for authority, more hatred, more impulsive aggression, were more litigious and displayed more jealously in their neighbors' wealth.

In order to clear away this paradox, it is necessary to take note of the fact that the opposite of independence is dependence (in the sense of subordination); not interdependence. Thus, for instance, the pastoralists showed respect for authority, but not subordination, obedience or other characteristics suggestive of dependency. Paul Spencer was aware of this. After pointing up the independence of the individual Samburu herdsman, he says: "Neighboring families are esentially interdependent, and, as we shall see, this lack of real economic independence within the homestead is concurrent with a lack of social autonomy: to a significant extent each Samburu is answerable to others for his actions and in final resort the running of his homestead is not solely his concern (Spencer 1965:23)." Note that Spencer uses the word "interdependent."

There are two reasons why the pastoralists have a stronger commitment to an orderly community. The very fact that they must operate alone in much of what they do leads them to realize that they are in fact dependent in many ways on their fellow man, and this interdependence is inculcated in them. At the same time, they do not suffer to the same extent the constant abrasions of a closely ordered social life. When conflict arises, they find it possible simply to move away from it—a fact independently noted by Evans-Pritchard (1940:210), Gulliver (1955:165), Lewis (1961:26) and Spencer

(1965:207). Under such circumstances, the *ideal* of social solidarity can more readily be sustained.

V

This preliminary examination of the problem is based on twelve pastoral peoples: Samburu (Spencer 1965), Masai (Jacobs 1959), Nandi (Huntingford 1950, 1953), Jie, (Gulliver 1955), Turkana (Gulliver 1955), Karimojong (Dyson-Hudson 1966), Nuer (Evans-Pritchard 1940), Rwala Beduoin (Musil 1928), Cyrenaica Bedouin (Evans-Pritchard 1949), Basseri (Barth 1961) and Marri Baluch (Pehrson 1966). I have examined a number of specific propositions and will indicate for each the societies which explicitly support the point.

1. The pastoralists engage in occupations which require that the normal adult man must act as an independent entrepreneur, making decisions which affect his and his family's welfare at least during a significant sector of the year. Thus, for instance: ". . . each family [regulates] its affairs as it pleases and [acts] independently as it chooses" (Jacobs 1959:4). This idea is in one way or another indicated for each of the societies examined except the Nandi.

2. This independence of action is not merely a matter of personal choice, but is necessitated by environmental circumstance—i.e., it is an ecological adjustment. This is discussed at considerable length, for instance by Dyson-Hudson (1966:45–65) regarding the Karimojong. It again appears to be true for all the societies examined except the Nandi, though I found no explicit statement to support the position for the Bedouins of Cyrenaica and the Rwala.

3. Independence of action involves not merely herding on one's own or in small groups, but the repeated necessity to make decisions affecting the welfare of the herd—migratory routes, stopping places, collaboration with others, culling animals, and the like. These decisions involve considerations of environmental and economic factors, and while they may be based on traditional considerations, the choices are not traditionalized. These points are important, because the welfare of the individual herd, and the social and economic status of the herdsman rests on the quality of his decisions. In the appendix to *Kambuya's Cattle* (Goldschmidt 1969) I have shown the economic effects of the decisions made with respect to transactions upon Kambuya's capital value. Spencer notes that: "As compared with other forms of property, cattle herds are subject to unusually high and unpredictable rates of increase and decrease. Even under primitive conditions of management, it is quite possible for a herd to double in size over five years. It is also possible that in the course of a stock epidemic, it will be reduced by more than one-half in a matter

of months. . . . The success or failure of certain men in stock keeping is widely known. . . ." (Spencer 1965:25).

I have found evidence for the importance of good husbandry as an element in personal success and failure to be specifically noted for the Turkana, Basseri, Marri, Karimojong, as well as the Samburu, and I suspect that more information would reveal this to be more widespread if not in fact a universal feature.

4. There are specific elements in the socialization process which foster the spirit of independence that is so necessary to pastoral success. These may be in the form of giving boys responsibility for small stock, or may appear in ritual behavior. This is not an aspect of pastoral life that is given much attention by students of pastoral society; nevertheless, there are explicit indications of such socialization for the Massai, Basseri, Tuareg, Marri and Karimojong. Thus, for instance, Jacobs notes that residential separation "fosters independence and egalitarianism within the family." (Jacobs 1959:52).

5. It is a matter of some significance to this syndrome that the pastoralist must face hardships, difficulties, and dangers in the ordinary course of his economic activities. Many of these hardships and dangers require instant and often individual action. The point is important, because it reinforces the need for the capacity for independent action. I think this situation is operative in each of the 12 tribes, though in one or two instances I have no specific reference in support of the point.

6. Interdependence, as discussed earlier, involves the recognition by individuals that they must maintain collaborative arrangements with their fellows, without coercion or subordination to some superior authority. A sense of such interdependence has been found among all the groups investigated.

Dyson-Hudson has shown how the Karimojong are socialized to such collaboration:

> Initiation ceremonies . . . mark the new age-set relationship about to be created between initiands as future members of a single group of coevals. . . . All initiands work together as a single group in the preparation of the elders' enclosure and fire; and they work together in serving the elders with meat, dividing the task necessary for this purpose. This is the first time this happens for the initiand, but at every future ritual he will again work corporately with his age-mates in serving the elders. . . . If only one initiand is to be inducted, members of the age-set he is to join act as his supporters, sitting with him in the enclosure, being blessed with him, helping him to serve, and joining him in the calf pen at the

final stage of the ceremonies. . . . The emphasis is on comradship that his new age-set membership represents (Dyson-Hudson 1966:171).

There are diverse ways in which such interdependence is institutionalized. Among sub-Saharan pastoralists it is frequently based on age-set organization, as we are all aware. It may be institutionalized through segmentary lineages which articulate men agnatically. It may involve economic transactions which create bonds between those who engage in them, or it may be through small friable collaborative groups under an acknowledged leader. There is no basis in the data for establishing what circumstances favor which particular solution to this recurrent need, and the fact that all may be found in a single society makes it difficult to find a way to reach such a conclusion.

7. Pastoral societies characteristically operate without strong authoritarian systems. Those of us who have worked in Africa take this for granted, perhaps, and certainly pastoral Africans generally belong to the acephalous category of political organization. Exceptions such as those posed by Ruanda and Burundi prove not to be real exceptions, it seems to me. Evans-Pritchard says simply of the leopard-skin chief that "It might be supposed that this functionary has a position of great authority, but this is not so." (Evans-Pritchard 1940:172).

But the pastoralists of Asia not only operate within long-established political states but have themselves been organized into great units for collaborative action. It is therefore necessary to examine them in greater detail. Consider, for instance, Pehrson's analysis of the Marri Baluch. The Marri do have authority roles among the more settled groups, but these nomadizing Marri assiduously avoid them, operating internally without official roles and insofar as possible without the intervention of these sedentary officials. Again, Barth's description of the Basseri should be kept in mind. Though he describes the absolute autocracy of the tribal khans, the following conditions prevail: (a) among the nomadizing pastoralists there is no authority role, but leadership is entirely based on personal qualities, and is very minimal; (b) the Khan's authority is limited largely to those aspects of behavior which establish intertribal relationships, such as tribal migratory routes and relations with the sedentary populations of Iran; (c) the accession to khanship is based upon charisma (and internal politics among the pretenders) so that there must be popular acceptance of his leadership; and (d) the very existence of his role quite clearly derives from the fact that the Khamseh tribes are part of a modern state, which has an interest in the maintenance of peaceful coexistence, the power to enforce it, and the need for the khans as a point of articulation between tribesmen and the settled populations.

Elizabeth Bacon, in writing of the medieval Mongols, says of the khanship: "The tribesmen made the ultimate decision, for a khan held his position of leadership only through his ability to command support" (Bacon 1958:58). And of the Kazaks, she writes:

> The difficulty in obtaining any clear picture of the political structure appears to be related to the Kazak attitude toward chiefs in general. A chief, whether he be khan or *bii*, did not have great authority over his people. He was simply a leader to whom the people were willing to pay occasional taxes and follow in war, so long as he provided the services which were expected of a leader. . . . The extent of chiefly authority was directly proportionate to the willingness of the followers to accept authority. . . . The Russians discovered to their grief that an impressive confirmation ceremony for a khan in no way guaranteed a docile orda (Bacon 1958:71–72).

In the absence of authority roles, social control, decision-making and conflict reduction must be institutionalized otherwise. It appears that there are essentially three ways this is accomplished; by personal charisma (perhaps embellished by ritualized leadership in the form of prophets as among the Massai or the leopard-skin chiefs of the Nuer), by the use of kinship, or by the institutionalization of seniority status through systems of age-grading. The last is elegantly described by Dyson-Hudson as applicable to situations in grazing areas where the people who happen to be together are without ties of kinship or neighborhood. In such situations

> the age-set affiliation has its greatest utility, for it immediately allocates to any individual in any collection of persons, however transient, a niche in a universal ranking system. Every individual has, accordingly, a pattern of response already roughly created, and needing only application to the context in which he finds himself.
>
> Thus quarrels may arise in a temporary camp association composed of men from scattered home areas. The quarrel is brought, as a public dispute, before the hearing of all men of the association, and the senior age-set representatives come to a decision which is binding. That the contestants may be from different sections and the arbitrator different again, is irrelevant (Dyson-Hudson 1966:174).

Such patterns of social control are necessary and effective in maintaining collaborative action and an orderly life, but they do not deny the essentially individualistic and independent behavior of the herdsman, who, as we have seen, must be independent out of economic necessity.

8. Under these circumstances, it is not surprising that wherever any mention of individual personality attributes is made by our authors, a spirit of independence is prominent among them.

VI

This preliminary examination of a handful of pastoral peoples in Africa and southwestern Asia supports the position developed in our Culture and Ecology Project, that independence is a primary feature of pastoral life, expressing itself both institutionally and in terms of personality attributes. Furthermore, it indicates that such independence recurs as a cultural attitude in response to the requirements for animal husbandry under the environmental and technological circumstances in which these societies operate. The approach in this analysis has been based on the ideas developed by me in *Comparative Functionalism*. There I argue, among other things, the interrelated nature of "the worldly tasks of society" and the "psychological needs of the individual," and that any consideration of these must "take place in an environmental context and that, therefore, solutions to social problems are dependent upon matters essentially nonsociological." Recognizing that "institutions beget institutions" and that "secondary, derivative, or contingent functional requisites . . . relate, ultimately and through intervening variables, to the essential and primary requirements" I conclude that "cultural differences, if they are to be explained at all, must be explained in terms of adaptation of human needs and capacities to the diverse ecological circumstances under which societies are to exist and which they must exploit with the techniques available to them" (Goldschmidt 1966:83–85). Indeed, if the data here are substantiated by more detailed investigation, they offer not only an insight into the character of pastoral life, but also a validation of the approach of comparative functionalism.

NOTES

1. The research design and some preliminary conclusions were set forth in a symposium presented at the annual meetings of the American Anthropological Association in in November 1964 (Goldschmidt *et al.*, 1965.

2. Because of the inconsistency with which data is presented in monographic literature and the problems of interpretation, I have prepared a questionnaire on pastoral life, from which I hope to derive a more complete set of information on a

wide range of societies. Readers who have made detailed studies of pastoral tribes are urged to fill out a questionnaire, a copy of which may be had by writing to me.

3. In collaboration with Dr. Evalyn J. Kunkel, I am following a similar approach with respect to peasant societies (Goldschmidt and Kunkel N.D.).

CHAPTER NINE

Organization of Work
in Herding Teams
on the Great Hungarian Plain

LAJOS VINCZE

In the ethnographic literature, herding is characterized as a task that requires diffuse organization of work and loosely defined directive statuses. Among subsistence pastoralists, the family owns the herd and the routine work of pasturing is entrusted to some, generally young, members of the family. Although several family herds pasture together at a given time, the decision with respect to the grazing and direction of movements depends largely on individual family preferences. Family groups aggregated in a herding camp are quite unstable over time (Leeds 1965: 103; Sweet 1965: 137; Dyson-Hudson 1962: 774; Gulliver 1955: 31–37, and others). No strong leadership emerges in the herding camps, and there are no strict rules aimed at assuring the conformity of their members. Barth's (1961: 43–46) description of the erratic and diffuse nature of decision making among the Basseri of Persia aptly illustrates this point, and his findings may be extended to many subsistence pastoralists. It is likely that under these conditions, rules regulating the details of daily work at the herds are likewise imprecise and scarcely enforceable.

In his analysis of the Euro-American ranching complex, which is more akin than tribal pastoralism to the herding on the Hungarian Plain, Strickon (1965: 242–243) similarly points out the diffuse nature of the herdmen's work and their freedom from external controls. Riviére's (1972: 56–59) account of the ranchers of Northern Brazil also shows that there is little carefully organized and co-ordinated labor. On the open ranges of the American West, the need for well-co-ordinated, co-operative work with precise division of tasks and statuses arises only on round-ups and cattle drives (Rollins 1936: 221–224; Ward 1958: 19–35; see also Rivière 1972: 70–71 for similar situations in Brazil). Most of the time, however, the large extension of the pasture and the freedom and mobility of the mounted herdsman call for labor that does not require strict co-ordination and strong leadership.

In this paper an attempt will be made to show that different structural and ecological circumstances may bring about a type of animal herding which unavoidably calls for a rigid system of organization of labor coupled with hierarchically arranged statuses and authoritarian leadership. Without making claim to its uniqueness, the pastoralism of the Great Hungarian Plain will be used as an illustrative case.

In many regions of Hungary, animal raising constituted a form of economic exploitation complementary to the pre-industrial agriculture. Areas which the pre-industrial farm technology was incapable of transforming into arable land provided ecologically advantageous conditions for herding. On the Great Hungarian Plain, broad regions of swampy terrain existed until the end of the nineteenth century, offering grazing grounds for large herds of domestic animals. A portion of the Plain, however, was not covered by the swamps. Elevated grounds and areas bordering on the marshland were occupied by farming towns. Many of these farmers—especially the rich ones—complemented their economy with livestock raising.

Additional factors provided further incentives for animal raising. The growing demand for animal products that came from the increasingly industrializing Western countries stimulated and maintained a profitable animal husbandry since the late Middle Ages (Bökönyi, 1971: 670). The temporary depopulation of the Plain, the deterioration of the agricultural lands caused by the Turkish occupation, and the abortive revolutionary wars against the Hapsburgs in the sixteenth and seventeenth centuries provided further favorable conditions for animal herding. Pastoralism, still using preindustrial methods, attained its highest organizational complexity in the nineteenth century. At that time, however, the rapid growth of the agrarian population, improved farming techniques, and governmental drainage projects presaged its imminent decline. Actually, it ceased to be important at the turn of the century and could survive for a few more decades only in exceptional areas.

There were several types of animal herding in Hungary, but its most developed form existed in the flood plains and swampy lands of the Tisza river and its tributaries on the Great Plain. Pastures in this area were utilized by cattle, horses, sheep, and pigs. Economically, cattle and horses clearly outweighed sheep and pigs. Typically, the herds were owned by a number of associated peasant herd owners who lived in large rural towns. Few of them were financially able to form and provide for their private herds. The association of several owners and the aggregation of the animals into large herds offered indisputable economic advantages (Szilágyi 1968: 361–363). Pasture-land was communal property. Land, grazing permission and oper-ations, and herdsmen were under the control of town government. The owners were not engaged directly in herding operations: they entrusted the herds to specialized herdsmen hired on a contractual basis.

Herdsmen formed a small, although not completely closed, oc-cupational group within the rural population. They assumed a sep-arate social identity, had loose contacts with the rest of the population, and developed a set of distinctive values, life style, and personality traits. In spite of their numerically and economically disadvantageous situation, they claimed social superiority over the peasants (cf. Vincze 1971). Economic conflicts between herd owners and herdsmen existed as the result of the employer-employee relationship, but they were mitigated by the traditional nature of the contracts. Competition between farmers and herders in the style of the American West did not occur, since both lands and animals were in the hands of agriculturalists and herdsmen had no representatives in the town council. Rather, confrontations arose now and then among agricul-turalists, between those who were inclined toward animal husbandry and favored the maintenance of large pastures and those who were eager to put more land under cultivation (Nagy-Czirok 1959: 14–21).

GENERAL CHARACTERISTICS OF THE WORK

In contrast to the American prairies, where the extension of the pastureland permitted the free dispersal of the animals, herding on the Hungarian Plain required constant surveillance. When grazing their animals on the dry edges of the swamp or on fallow lands, herdsmen had to prevent the herd from damaging the cultivated areas. When in the swamp, animals might easily stray and be lost in the dangerous mazeway of the marshland. The relative scarcity of pastures required that individual herds be driven only in designated sections. Predators and outlaws hiding in the swamps also neces-sitated constant vigilance. As the herdsmen directed and followed the movements of the herd, they lived with the animals, sleeping in the open or in improvised huts. Although certain kinds of herds wintered under shelters in or around the towns, most of them spent the winter with their guardians, far from the towns in the midst of the tall vegetation of the marshland.

Animals were divided into herds by species: there were separate herds for cattle, horses, sheep, and pigs, tended by specialized herdsmen. The *gulyás* worked with cattle, the *csikós* with horses, the *juhász* with sheep, and the *kanász* with pigs. Further subdivisions into separate herds existed with respect to the age, sex, mode of grazing, and the way the animals were exploited. A particular herd was kept together all of the time. This made periodical roundups unnecessary, but it required considerably more work, alertness, and careful organization of labor.

Because of open pastures and wide dispersal of the animals, the horse was indispensable on the American continent. Hungarian herdsmen, however, working on more limited pastures, were usually not mounted—even the cattle were cared for by herdsmen working on foot. Only the horse herds were tended by equestrian herdsmen, who were famous for their horsemanship.

THE WORKING TEAM

All the work of herding was accomplished by a small team of herdsmen assigned to each individual herd. The size of the team varied according to the number and kind of the animals. Horses and cattle required more people than did sheep and pigs. A team usually did not comprise more than eight or ten persons, and on the average it was four to six herdsmen strong.

The herding team was established on a contractual basis. The associated owners of the livestock concluded an agreement with an older reputable herdsman (*számadó*) who, according to the stipulation of this agreement, hired a number of helpers (*bojtár*). Contracts were concluded for one year and renewed if the parties were satisfied. Until the end of the nineteenth century, contracts were based on verbal agreement and were subject to the control and regulations of town governments. Wages, which included food, clothing, and some money, were handed over to the *számadó*, who distributed them among his helpers. He was also granted the right to keep a certain number of animals belonging to him and to the *bojtárok* in the herd. The amount of payment and the number of animals in the herd which each team member might keep were in accordance with his rank.

Although kinship might have influenced the composition of the herding teams, contractual relationships appear to be of much more importance.[1] The relationship between the owners and *számadó* tended to be stable over time. The composition of the team, however, showed more fluidity. Although a respected *számadó* could usually retain a number of loyal members who formed the core of his team, many *bojtárok* changed employment frequently (Tálasi 1936: 22). The *számadó* was very rigorous in selecting new members. The aspirant was not admitted if there were any suspicion that he was physically, mentally, or morally weak.[2] There are descriptions of admission trials where physical endurance, mental alertness, and moral qualities were tested (Nagy-Czirok, 1959: 45–48). The *számadó* preferred to select members from herdsman families, but possibilities were open to persons coming from other sectors, if they showed promise of becoming good herdsmen. Many poor peasant lads were tempted by the freedom of life with the herds. For some young men, fallen in disgrace in the opinion of their community or sought by the authorities because of a misdeed, teams working deep in the swamps served as safe refuges (Györffy 1941a: 10–11).

Each team constituted an independent unit submitting to the authority of the *számadó*. The group was highly structured in terms of leadership, rank order, and co-operative effectiveness. Quasi-military discipline and strictly regulated division of labor were maintained at all times.

Supreme authority was invested in the *számadó*. He had to be a married, economically solvent, and morally irreproachable man. He dealt with the employers regarding all aspects of the herd, pastures, grazing, and food supply for the team. He was responsible for loss and injury. The *számadó* selected, hired, payed, and fired the herd boys and was responsible for their moral conduct and general welfare. He taught the younger members the skills of herding and correct behavior in accordance with the herders' unwritten code. His orders had to be obeyed in all circumstances without protest or criticism. His authority was harsh and paternalistically protective at the same time. Acts of disloyalty and disobedience were severely punished.

Administrative responsibilities fell to the lot of the *számadó*. He took over the animals from the owners and rendered account of them when it was required. (The literal translation of the word *számadó* is "he who renders account.") The *számadó* prepared, organized, directed, and supervised the grazing, but he rarely took part in the actual work. His duties included collecting the food supply and supervising the proper cooking and distribution of the meal, as well as inspecting the cleanliness of the camp, the water wells, and troughs. Curing sick animals and performing protective magic were also his responsibility.

At the beginning of the grazing season the *számadó* established the rank order, usually based on seniority, among the herd boys and assigned corresponding duties and responsibilities. Next in rank under the *számadó* was the *öreg-bojtár* (senior herd boy), followed by the *második-bojtár* (second herd boy), *harmadik-bojtár* (third herd boy), etc. down to the *kisbojtár* (little herd boy). The latter was a minor and an apprentice. Every member of the team had to show deference to his superiors and obey orders. Rank order was not restricted to only the work, as the contractual nature of the work organization would suggest, but it was extended also to social activities that had little or no relationship to the work. For instance, the *számadó* had a voice in the marital choice of his herd boys and could punish them for social misconduct. Even such unimportant acts as taking food from the stew pot, entering the door, or feeding the dogs were done in rank order. (Gunda 1970: 177). Rank order was also expressed by differences in their clothing (Törö 1968a: 403).

The actual herding and other work around the camp were carried out by the herd boys. They worked on a strict daily schedule by taking turns at day and night grazing, working in the water wells, and erecting or repairing shelters, wind screens, corrals, etc. The youngest members did the cooking, were responsible for the order and cleanliness in and around the hut, and collected dung for the fire.

The herding teams were not united by an association of herders or by common leadership. The *számadók* were responsible for peaceful relations between their working groups. In spite of the existence of fierce competition for prestige, the occurrence of sporadic hostile acts, and theft of animals (tacitly tolerated by the *számadók*), a general solidarity prevailed among the herdsmen (cf. Vincze 1970).

Ecological Determinants

Until the last decade of the nineteenth century, large extensions of the Great Hungarian Plain were covered by marshland formed by an inundated area of the river Tisza and its tributaries. Grassy portions of these swamps constituted the ecological basis for pastoralism. Because of seasonal variations of climate, the areas and places of available pasturage were exposed to severe fluctuations. The consequences was the development of transhumance within a limited range. During the spring, flood waters covered large areas, and the animals were taken to the higher grounds. During the summer, as the water regressed, the herd followed the watery edges of the shrinking swamp. At the end of fall, certain kinds of herds were taken back to the village, but a considerable number of them crossed the frozen waters to spend the winter in the middle of the marshland, where the dense reeds and other tall marsh plants offered some protection. At the beginning of spring, the herd was taken back to dry land before the ice melted away and flooding occurred.

Under these conditions, herd and herders had to face many dangers. The marshland itself was an almost impenetrable labyrinth, full of hidden perils for all who were not fully acquainted with the terrain.

Moreover, changing water levels, floods, and occasional droughts altered the landscape capriciously. Inclement weather imposed great hardships on people and livestock. Packs of wolves were in ambush to attack the herd. The marshland was the hiding place of many outlaws, who were also eager to pilfer the herd.

In order to cope with all these difficulties, the small work unit of herdsmen had to make a concerted effort to protect the herd and themselves. Strong leadership of the most knowledgeable and experienced person and submission to his orders became essential for the security of the unit. Such a leader needed full knowledge of his area and its grazing possibilities to direct the movement of the livestock, to forestall the harmful effects of incalculable weather and water conditions, and to assume responsibility for the always risky winter grazing. The success of the team depended upon a well coordinated work force, a fact that led to precise assignment of duties and the arrangement of statuses in hierarchical order. Concerned and organized effort was especially in demand in times of crisis, such as windstorms, sudden thawing, or a herd drive across crumbling ice or flooded stream beds. Actions could not be left to chance, since dissenting opinions could lead to disaster.

Growing scarcity of the grazing area gradually imposed the division and systematic allocation of the pastureland, differentiation of the herds, and more rational grazing practices. After the expulsion of the Turks and the suppression of the revolutionary war against the Hapsburgs in 1711, the Great Plain experienced steady growth of the local population augumented by settlers coming from neighboring regions and foreign lands. This was followed by the introduction of improved farming techniques and gradual extension of the agricultural area. Formerly unoccupied lands were distributed among the agrarian population. According to István Szabó (Szabadfalvi 1970: 139), the area of cultivated land increased five- to six-fold in Hungary between 1720 and 1760. Later, central government favored the rearrangement of plots and rights of possession, and, most importantly, initiated a long-range project aimed at the drainage of the marshland. The continuous diminishment of the pastureland required a certain degree of rationalization of pastoral exploitation.

The first step was the differentiation of the herd and pastures. Different kinds of herds were formed according to species, age, sex, and mode of exploitation (Szilágyi 1968: 359). Pastures were delimited, divided into grazing sections (*járás*), and assigned to specific droves following the eating habits, food preferences, and mode of exploitation of the animals (Törö 1968b: 265). Grazing order was also established. For instance, on a particular grazing ground the cattle herd browsed first, because they could eat only the tallest grass; after them came the horse herd; and, finally, came the sheep, because these animals could eat even the smallest grass. In winter, horses went first because they could remove the snow cover with their hooves (Györffy 1941b: 89). Certain areas of the pasture had to be spared for the eventuality of an unusually dry summer or long winter. Organizing the different kinds of herds (Nagy-Czirok [1959: 359–360] enumerates as many as twenty kinds of sheep herds in one region alone), establishing the grazing order, and choosing suitable pastureland were serious matters that required specialized knowledge, circumspection, and judgment (Törö 1968b: 265–266). Delimited areas had to be respected, and surveillance demanded alertness, responsibility, and well defined allocation of duties.

Environmental constraints are expressed also in the number of herdsmen necessary to take care of the animals. On the wide pastures of the United States and Argentina the ratio of herdsmen to cattle is 1:1,000, and in Australia it is 1:2,500 for sheep (Strickon 1965: 245). On the Hungarian Plain it was 1:100 for cattle (Györffy 1941b: 88) and approximately 1:200–250 for sheep (Gunda 1970: 173).

The way the herdsmen acquired their food and its proper allocation also demanded supervision and careful regulations. Because of their occupation, few of the herdsmen were able to grow food. Although some of them had families in the town and could cultivate small plots, the majority of the herdsmen, particularly those who spent the winters with the herds, were bachelors (note the similarity with the American cowboy) [Rollins 1936: 35; Frantz and Choate 1955: 64]). Food was provided by the herd owners as a part of the herdsmen's salary. During winters, when the teams were practically cut off from their suppliers, they relied a great deal on collected wild food. Fishing and the collecting of starchy seeds, tubers, and roots of marsh plants (the root and tuber of *Typha latifolia, Alisma plantago, Butomus umbellatus, Bolboschoenus maritimus, Lathyrus tuberosus*, the seed of *Glyceria fiuitans*, the nut of *Trapa natans*) provided the herdsmen with food in times of isolation (Gunda 1968: 101; also Györffy 1941a: 23–24 and Tálasi 1936: 26–27). For meat, herdsmen sometimes resorted to stealing from other herds, and they made use of many frauds to pilfer the herd they cared for—acts which they did not consider to be immoral (Nagy-Czirok 1959: 258, 319). In collecting and distributing the food from the owners and the wild food, the *számadó* again assumed directive functions. He regulated the amount of food to be consumed and set the mealtime and eating order according to the rank of each of his subordinates.

STRUCTURAL DETERMINANTS

Apart from a few attempts (e.g. Strickon 1965; Szabadfalvi 1970; Vincze 1973), a certain type of pastoralism has escaped the interest of anthropologists. I refer to the form of animal raising adapted to marginal areas—mountains, swamps, open grasslands—which extensive farm technology could not convert into fertile lands, or were left uncultivated for demographic reasons. This pastoralism is market oriented in the main, extensive in technology, and may be regarded as an ecological variant of the pre-industrial agriculture. It is not the purpose of this paper to analyze in detail the structural features of this type of pastoralism, but rather to point out some aspects which generated situations conducive to the form of work organization peculiar to our case—the Hungarian lowland herding. These aspects are the relationship of herding to agriculture and the external market.

Unlike the situation in industrial societies, where farming and stock-raising have achieved a large degree of technological integration, the interdependency between agriculture and animal husbandry in cases of extensive exploitation is minimal or non-existent. Extensive farming cannot provide adequate shelters, grow fodder, replenish overgrazed areas, control breeding, or protect the animals against diseases. Herding, therefore, has to rely on its own, albeit equally extensive, technology. Under these circumstances, herding demands skills which differ from those used in farming; that is, it requires a certain degree of specialization. Actually, in those areas where animal raising achieved economic importance, specialization was so needed that herding became the monopoly of a particular social segment. These herdsmen either tended their own flocks or hired out their skills to livestock owners.

The differentiation between farming and pastoral technology prevailed also on the Hungarian Plain (cf. Szabadfalvi 1970), even if agriculture and livestock were in the hands of the same individuals. Specialized knowledge of herding was alien to the peasant owner, so he was required to hire specialized herdsmen.

In some areas of the world extensive pastoralism achieved a large degree of economic independence and almost complete dissociation from cultivation, e.g., open-range herding of the New World. On the Hungarian Plain, however, the situation was different. Although cultivation and herding were dissociated ecologically and technologically, they complemented each other economically. Both herding and cultivation were exploited by the same individuals and formed an integral part of the same family budget. It is important, however, to point out that the herd owners were, above all, peasant farmers, even if in some areas of the Plain herding overshadowed the economic importance of cultivation. Because of risks involved in herding, the herd owners' security was rooted in cultivation. There is no indication that they ever considered the alternative of giving up cultivation in favor of animal raising, although propitious conditions existed in certain periods of history.[3]

In this condition of divided interest, the peasant herd owner faced problems concerning the organization of both cultivating and herding activities. There were two alternatives: either he divided the family labor between cultivating and herding, or he used it entirely in cultivation, leaving the herding tasks to outsiders. The second alternative had many advantages. Herding operations were largely separated from cultivation; herding work, therefore, would have required complete disengagement from land cultivation for a number of family members. Since pre-industrial farming absorbed large amounts of manual labor, it was advantageous for the peasant herd owner to invest all working potential of his family in cultivation instead of dividing it between cultivation and herding. On the other hand, the fact that the peasant owner divided his capital between the two reduced his economic capability to keep and operate large independent herds. One obvious solution was to combine herds and take turns herding. However, this would have raised serious difficulties concerning the equitable distribution of herding tasks and responsibilities among the associated owners. When we see that the distance of the grazing places varied greatly, and the herds spent several months in remote and hardly accessible areas, it becomes clear why taking turns did not seem practical. In every respect, employing hired, full-time herdsmen offered the most satisfactory solution.

The relationship to the market was also influential in the decision to entrust the animals to a well organized herding team. Although a number of the animals were raised for consumption and to provide draft animals for agricultural labor and transportation, the majority were destined for the market. In spite of the risks involved, livestock raising often turned out to be profitable. The dependence on the external market favored a businesslike management of the herds. Good marketing conditions, due to the demand coming from the Western countries, served as an incentive to maximize gains. Given the technological limitations of the extensive economy, this could be achieved only by augmenting the size of the herds and making full use of the pastures. The tendency to rationalize grazing and exploitation and to organize the work is clearly observable since the eighteenth century (Szilágyi 1968: 359–363) or possibly even earlier (Bencsik 1969: 9). Under these circumstances professional competence at herding become indispensable. Therefore, herd owners, who actually had only loose control over the herds and herdsmen for several months, preferred to entrust their livestock to a well organized, stable, and disciplined team, directed with full authority by a competent and trustworthy leader.

CONCLUSION

In most pastoral economies, either subsistence or market oriented, the work of herding requires minimal organization. In fact the diffuseness of work organization is advantageous in many respects (Strickon 1965: 243; Gulliver 1955: 32–37). If we find strictly regulated patterns of labor and structured work groups in the case of Hungarian lowland herding, the cause of the difference must be sought in its specific circumstances. Pastoralism on the Hungarian Plain showed many basic similarities to the open-range herding of the American continent: both produced for the market, used extensive technology in the management of pastures and herds, and recruited hired labor from a socially distinguishable occupational group. However, there were differences that influenced the structure and organization of work. First, on the Hungarian Plain herding was economically complementary to cultivation. Its exploitation ultimately depended upon the decisions of agriculturally oriented owners, for whom it was economically advantageous to entrust the animals to well organized herding teams. Second, good market possibilities but ever diminishing pastures required differential and specialized exploitation of grazing areas and herds. This work was more efficiently executed by knowledgeable teams of herdsmen than by cultivation-bound owners. Third, because of environmental conditions, the owners and town governments could not exert direct control over the herds for long periods of the year, and thus it was beneficial to delegate managerial power and responsibility to a person in full command of the work group. Fourth, environmental constraints imposed the need for continuous surveillance and expertly directed, concerted effort in assuring the well-being, if not mere survival, of the herd and herdsmen. Discipline and regulated division of labor became essential within the team.

We cannot claim that the organizational form of herding work is unique to the Hungarian Plain. Various arrangements, some of them similar to the Hungarian form, are known, especially in connection with the transhumance and alpine type of sheep raising of the Carpathian area, Central Europe, the Balkans, and the Mediterranean countries (cf. Kopczyńska-Jaworska 1963; Jacobeit 1961; Novak 1960; Dedijer 1916; Fribourg 1910). However, the fact that the *számadó-bojtár* work group became a major, almost exclusive, and consistently uniform organizational arrangement throughout the pastoral areas of the Hungarian Plain indicates its indisputable adaptive advantages for both the environmental conditions and the structural nature of the herding economy.

NOTES

1. Because of lack of data, we cannot ascertain to what extent kinship influenced the recruitment and composition of work groups. It is known that herdsmen had endogamous tendencies (Gunda 1970: 1972). Thus, many herdsmen were related by kinship to some extent, forming a small social group. Gunda (1970: 174) also alludes briefly to the fact that most *bojtárok* chose the *számadó* as godfather for their children. Nevertheless, even the best accounts are silent about the role played by kinship in the recruitment into the teams. Nagy-Czirok (1959: 41) mentions briefly that with smaller sheep droves the *számadó* preferred to take *bojtárok* from among his sons. It is, however, evident from the text that he refers to this as an exception. All in all, one gains the impression that kinship played only a minimal role, and much more importance was given to contractual relationships.

2. Morality here must be understood in terms of the herdsmen's interpretations (cf. Vincze 1972: 173, 177).

3. The fact that ranching-type animal husbandry, so characteristic of the New World, never developed on the Hungarian Plain clearly indicates the preponderance of agricultural preferences. The lowland, especially after the expulsion of the Turks, showed features of a frontier. This frontier, however, was gradually filled with outposts, called *tanya*, which, instead of becoming ranching-type operational centers for livestock grazing, served mainly agricultural purposes. The *tanya*, in fact, became instrumental in the decline of pastoralism by taking away land from the grazing area. The expansion of the *tanya* system and agriculture may be associated with population growth (Györffy 1916: 155). Steadily rising agricultural prices on the European market since 1750 (Clough and Cole 1946: 308, 430) also might have stimulated this trend.

IV

Introduction
Non-Market Cultures: Work among
Cultivators and Gardeners in Villages

A number of anthropologists and archaeologists have asserted that cultivation of land laid the basis for the development of urban civilizations, which rested on food surpluses created by farmers and expropriated by governors, priests, and rulers (Coe and Flannery 1964; Adams 1960; Hole 1966; Carneiro 1970; Wittfogel 1957; Childe 1951). The beginnings of systematic cultivation developed in the southwestern region of Asia, southeastern Asia, southwestern parts of what is now the United States, northern Mexico, sub-Saharan Africa, India and Oceania. These developments took place at different periods in history but they were independent phenomena and involved diverse cultural experiences. The unifying aspect was the fact that human beings through cultivation were able to establish a synthesis with their environment while changing that environment through their own intervention. The wonder of their accomplishment through the combination of their own knowledge and tools and nature's biological transformations caused these societies to attribute to the supernatural the reasons for their successes. Priests, magicians, and shamans became leaders and combined magical ceremony with their own knowledge of plants and soils to instruct people when and how to plant their crops.

Horticulturalists practice a form of cultivation in which the technology involves using a digging stick with which to make holes for their roots and cuttings. The hoe, which is more effective as a tool and can dig a plot more completely although not deeply, is mainly

155

confined to those areas in which there is a knowledge of iron-working—Africa and Asia.

Garden tillage using the digging stick or the hoe is usually associated with a migratory form of cultivation. It is most often found where cultivation depends on direct precipitation alone (Forde 1963:379). Migratory tillage is usually not found in arid regions. There are some instances where, because of favorable physical conditions, such cultures can establish sedentary settlements and villages. Where there are annually flooded river plains, in which the silt from the river is capable of maintaining fertility over long periods, is one such favorable location. The Hopi Pueblos in the southwestern United States are an example of a non-migratory people practicing hoe tillage. Pueblo agriculture is generally non-migratory. The Pueblos utilize natural flood water which they trap and retain through the construction of irrigation channels. Garden tillage survives today mostly in Africa, in the more remote parts of southern Asia, in Indonesia, and in the Pacific.

Hoe and digging stick cultivation is mainly, but not exclusively, involved with the cultivation of roots and fruit trees. Roots and trees are not grown from seed but from eyes and cuttings. Digging stick cultivation is especially suited to tropical forests where there are no prolonged droughts and no sharply concentrated harvest seasons. Yams, taro, and manioc can be dug most of the year, and coconuts, breadfruit, pineapples, and other fruits are continually produced during the entire annual cycle. Thus, in hoe tillage and horticultural societies the storage of food for prolonged periods of time is unnecessary.

Grain growing, by contrast, has a seasonal growing period where there is usually one planting season and a short harvest period. This harvest of a few weeks has to sustain the community for the entire year. This imposes the necessity for storage vessels. Once storage techniques are introduced there is a technology for basketry, pottery, granaries, storage pits, and storage bins. When a society begins to store its material wealth, it must become a sedentary society, because its stored material cannot be transported and it has invested in heavy, non-transportable equipment for food processing and food storage. Testart (1982:523–37) has argued that food storage is the key technology that correlates with sedentarism, a high population density, and socioeconomic inequalities in both cultivating societies and hunting and gathering societies. The necessity for storage facilities and the ability to take control over them is one of the elements in creating centralized political systems in which another group or class can exert control over the class of producers.

Horticulture and tillage based on the hoe or digging stick does not mean that other forms of work are totally ruled out. Cultivators of this kind will often continue to hunt and fish. Where the women do the cultivating, men may be entirely freed for hunting and fishing. In Oceania, although cultivation is shared by men and women, fishing continues to be an important aspect of work pursued by men. Among the ruling classes of central Polynesia, fishing had a higher prestige value than cultivation (Forde 1963:381). The noblest chief in Tahiti would direct and take part in fishing expeditions, but have nothing to do with cultivation.

Where cultivation is more intensive, however, hunting and fishing may decline in importance or be relegated to specialists. Among the Yoruba the intensive cultivation of root crops with its attendant increase in population, led to extensive clearing of the bush so that there was little game left in the region. When men and women are continuously occupied with their fields, there is little time left for hunting and fishing. Agriculture, which is distinguished from horticulture through the use of the plough and draught animals, requires even more concentration and energy than hoe tillage, and hence the time for hunting and fishing declines drastically.

Tillage with the digging stick and hoe has been called a migratory form of cultivation. A main reason for this is that with only a digging stick or a hoe to dig the soil, the soil is not deeply penetrated and its surface fertility is short-lived. This necessitates frequent moving to other sites. One of the more widespread methods in hoe tillage is the slash-and-burn or swidden method of clearing fields. In this method, the undergrowth is first cut away from a given area. Then rings are cut in the bark of the smaller trees so they will weaken and topple. The larger trees are cut by hand, a formidable task given the tools that are used. After the trees and brush have lain for months during the dry season, they are set on fire. There is disagreement as to whether this method has a deleterious effect on the soil (Conklin 1968:126–31). After the fire, the resulting plot is cultivated with digging sticks and used by the community until soil exhaustion requires a move to other sites. In some countries like the Philippines, slash-and-burn cultivation supports up to 10 percent of the population (Conklin 1968:126).

Two environmental limits are pertinent to tropical slash-and-burn systems. First, there is the problem of forest regeneration. Because of leaching by heavy rains and because of invasion by insects and weeds, the productivity of this ecosystem drops rapidly after two or three years of use. Optimum productivity is achieved when there are substantial trees to be burned; otherwise only a small amount of wood-ash fertilizer will be produced by burning. On the other hand, if trees are of large size, they are difficult to cut down. Another problem with slash-and-burn systems is that the main crops—sweet potatoes, yams, manioc, and taro—are protein-deficient, as compared to animals. But the animals that inhabit tropical forests tend to be small, furtive, and arboreal, and are hard to catch. Although plant foods can provide adequate amounts of protein if eaten in variety and abundance, meat is the most effective source of all the amino acids necessary for nutrition. Thus, the availability of animal protein is another limiting factor in slash-and-burn cultivation. (Harris: 1975:241–42)

One of the significant aspects of horticultural work is the role of women. Women are deeply involved in the cultivation of gardens in these societies and, as a result, their status is quite different as compared with hunting and gathering or pastoral societies. In many horticultural societies women's high status is reflected in rules of kinship descent and marital residence, since many of these cultures trace kinship through the female line and base residence after marriage on the female household. This has the effect of raising the status of women in these cultures, as well as affecting the roles of males. Among the Iroquois, who trace kinship through the female line, men must consult women on many important issues, including that of going to war, before they can act. J. Brown (1975) quotes Jenness (1932:137) on this matter:

> If women among the Iroquois enjoyed more privileges and possessed greater freedom than women of other tribes, this was due . . . to the important place that agriculture held in their economic life, and the distribution of labor [which left] the entire cultivation of the fields and the acquisition of the greater part of the food supply to the women.

Land holding among small-scale cultivators ranges from communal ownership similar to that of hunters and food gatherers, to feudal tenures and private property.

With migratory tillage and brush clearing, ownership of land has little value. Control over territory is more important and is in the hands of the community as a whole. Since the cultivating group is forced to move every few years, it makes little sense to have a system of individual or family tenure extending over many generations. For that kind of land ownership, stable village society is necessary. The work of clearing and cultivating is what is important in hoe tillage communities, and to those individuals or families who have cleared and worked a plot go the rights of usage. The size of the communities based on hoe tillage can range from those smaller than successful food-gatherers to large states with populations exceeding a million people, which were found in Central America and Peru by Europeans in the sixteenth century.

With plough agriculture, land acquires a different value. Agriculture involving short fallow periods and rotation of crops can maintain the fertility of the land for long periods of time. Agriculture can also feed a considerably greater number of people than are necessary to till the land. Thus, a large number of specialists in crafts and others who are non-productive can be maintained by agricultural societies. This is the basis for urban society. Land now becomes an economic asset of great value and permits the appearance of the landowner as a role distinct from that of cultivator. Owners of land can claim title to the surplus available in agricultural societies, and they can enjoy leisure and command the services of craftsmen. Priests and monarchs who claim control of the land as their divine right can do the same thing. The rich rewards in crops from plough cultivation can support a dense population fed and supported through a system of slavery or through a feudal system, involving tenures, leases, and obligations to landlords and rulers.

Plough agriculture is associated with knowledge of plants and soils, the use of draught animals, the use of animal manure as fertilizers, water-lifting devices, and crop rotation. It is often also associated with irrigation. The earliest development of agriculture appeared within the fertile valleys of great rivers in the Near East, Southeast Asia, China, India, and North Africa. With the cultivation of the land, the relatively sparse groups of hunters and gatherers were replaced by the more numerous aggregates of populations in villages and cities. There is some question as to the timing historically of the rise of villages, whether they preceded, followed, or accompanied the development of agriculture (Hole 1966:605-11). Whatever the timing, settled villages were one of the consequences of cultivation. Permanent villages led to increased population densities, the appearance of a division of labor based on crafts, and eventual consolidation of urban centers.

It is important to remember that the development of agriculture and the subsequent growth of urban civilizations based on cultivation was highly variable. There were many areas which developed agriculture without great empires and urban civilizations. In the five areas of river valleys which did first develop urban centers—the Near East, Mexico, Peru, China, and India—there were similarities of development which can be generalized along with specific social and cultural patterns. There was class stratification, marked by ownership and control of the land and its resources. There were political and religious hierarchies that regulated the irrigation system, the collection of taxes, the storage of grain, and the timing of planting and harvesting. Knowledge, science, and religion were under the control of the priests and rulers. In each of these civilizations there was a complex division of work, based on full-time craftsmen, servants, soldiers, and officials who were fed through the efforts of the primary cultivators, whose product in part was turned into the state and redistributed to the non-producers in the employ of the state. There were monumental public works financed through tribute and taxation. There were the beginnings of writing and systems of accounts relating to stored food and wealth. As regards broader social trends, these included urbanization, stratification, militarization, and bureaucratization within these societies. In each of these cultures there was established a distinctive form of art and architecture which reflected the religious values and myths of the society. At its base, such civilizations and cultures were made possible by the development of the cultivation of land for food.

CHAPTER TEN

Trobriand Gardeners
and Their Magic

BRONISLAW MALINOWSKI

THE PRACTICAL TASKS OF THE GOOD GARDENER, TOKWAYBAGULA

Let us now . . . follow the seasonal round of garden work. This
falls into four main divisions. First comes the preparing of the soil
by cutting down the scrub and burning it after it has dried. The
second stage consists in clearing the soil, planting, erecting the yam
supports, and making the fence. The third stage has for the most
part to be left to nature; the seeds sprout, the vines climb upwards
round the supports, the taro plants develop their big leaves and their
roots; while human intervention is confined to weeding, which is
done by women, and a preliminary pruning or thinning out of the
tubers and training of vines by the men. Meanwhile the magician
is at work, casting spells favourable to growth. Finally, after the
crops have matured, we come to the last stage, the harvest. Apart
from the magic of growth just mentioned, each new type of work
is inaugurated by a magical rite, and these form a series which
correspond to the sequence of practical activities.

Garden work is never done in heavy rain or in windy and what
to the natives would be cold weather. During the intolerably hot
hours of the day, at the season of calms, the gardeners usually return
home or rest in the shade. Whether for communal or individual or
family work, the farmers generally go early to the gardens, return
between ten and eleven to the village, and then start out again,
perhaps after a light meal and a siesta, to work from about three
or four o'clock till nightfall. Since some of the gardens directly adjoin
the village and the most distant are not more than half an hour's
walk away, there is no difficulty in interrupting and resuming work
at the convenience of the moment.

The technical efficiency of the work is great. This is the more remarkable because the outfit of the Trobriand farmer is of the most rudimentary nature. It consists of a digging-stick (*dayma*), an axe (*Kema*), an adze (*ligogu*) and, last but not least, of the human hand, which in many of their activities serves as an implement and often comes into actual contact with the soil. The digging-stick is used for turning up the soil at planting and thinning, at harvest and weeding. Axe and adze play an important part in the cutting of the scrub, the thinning out of the tubers and at harvesting. Skill with the hand is important during clearing, planting, weeding, thinning and at harvesting. These then are the tasks and the tools of a "good gardener" (*tokwaybagula*)—one of the proudest titles which a Trobriander can enjoy.

But besides hard work, and a technical skill based on a sound knowledge of the soil and its properties, of the weather and its vicissitudes, of the nature of crops and the need of intelligent adaptation to the soil, another element enters into Trobriand gardening which, to the natives, is as essential to success as husbandry. This is magic.

The Magic of the Garden

It may be said that among the forces and beliefs which bear upon and regulate gardening, magic is the most important, apart, of course, from the practical work.

Garden magic (*megwa towosi* or simply *towosi*) is in the Trobriands a public and official service. It is performed by the garden magician, also called *towosi*, for the benefit of the community. Everybody has to take part in some of the ceremonial and have the rest performed on his account. Everybody also has to contribute to certain payments for magic. The magic being done for each village community as a whole, every village and at times every subdivision of a village has its own *towosi* (garden magician) and its own system of *towosi* magic, and this is perhaps the main expression of village unity.

Magic and practical work are, in native ideas, inseparable from each other, though they are not confused. Garden magic and garden work run in one intertwined series of consecutive effort, form one continuous story, and must be the subject-matter of one narrative.

To the natives, magic is as indispensable to the success of gardens as competent and effective husbandry. It is essential to the fertility of the soil: "The garden magician utters magic by mouth; the magical virtue enters the soil" (Text 36, Part V, Div. VII, § 2). Magic is to them an almost natural element in the growth of the gardens. I have often been asked: "What is the magic which is done in your country over your gardens—is it like ours or is it different?" They did not seem at all to approve of our ways as I described them, saying that we either do not perform any magic at all, or else let our "misinaris" do the magic wholesale in the *bwala tapwaroro*—the house of the divine service. They doubted whether our yams could "sprout" properly, "rise up in foilage" and "swell". In the course of one such conversation, held in Omarakana with Kayla'i and Gatoyawa, I jotted down the following pointed comment on our method (Text 81: Part V, Div XI, § 9): "The missionaries state: 'We make divine service and because of this the gardens grow.' This is a lie." It should be noted that the native word for 'lie' covers anything from a purely accidental mistake, a *bona fide* flight of imagination not pretending to be anything else, to the most blatant lie. The natives do not accuse the missionaries of deception, but rather of a certain feeble-mindedness or, as Professor Lévy-Bruhl would put it, of a prelogical mentality when it comes to gardening magic.

I am afraid that converted natives who act as missionary teachers have *towosi* magic surreptitiously chanted over their gardens. And white traders married to native women have, under the pressure of public opinion and of the wife's influence, to engage the help of the local *towosi* to chant over their gardens; so monstrous did it appear to everybody that a cultivated patch of soil should go without the benefit of magic.

The round of gardening opens with a conference, summoned by the chief and held in front of the magician's house, to decide where the gardens are going to be made, who will cultivate such and such a plot, and when the work will be started. Directly in connection with this, the magician prepares for the first big ceremony, which is to inaugurate the whole gardening sequence, while the villagers procure a quantity of special food, usually fish, to be offered as a ceremonial payment to the magician. A small portion of this gift is exposed in the evening to the ancestral spirits, sacrifically and with an invocation; the bulk is eaten by the magician and his kinsmen. Then he utters a lengthy spell over certain leaves which will be used on the morrow. Next morning the magician and the men of the village go to the gardens and the inaugural ceremony takes place. The *towosi* strikes the ground and rubs it with the charmed leaves— acts which symbolise in speech and sentiment the garden magic as a whole. This rite officially opens the season's gardening as well as its first stage: the cutting of the scrub. Thereafter each stage of practical work is ushered in by the appropriate ceremony. After the cut scrub is sufficiently dried, he imposes a taboo on garden work, ritually burns the refuse, and introduces the planting of certain minor crops by a series of ceremonies extending over a few days. Later on, a sequence of rites inaugurate successively the main planting of yams, the erection of vine supports, weeding, preliminary thinning out, and finally of harvesting. At the same time in a parallel sequence of rites and spells, the garden magician assists the growth of the crops. He helps the plants to sprout, to burst into leaf, to climb; he makes their roots bud, develop and swell; and he produces the rich garlands of exuberant foliage which intertwine among the vine supports.

Each rite is first performed on one of the standard magical plots, the *leywota*. This is important from the practical point of view, because the men who cultivate these plots are bound to keep time with the rhythm of magical ritual and not lag behind. At the same time they must also be worked with special care. They are scrupulously cleared and cleaned, perfect seed tubers are selected, and since they are always made on good soil, they represent not only a very high standard of garden work but also of gardening success. Thus, in punctuality, quality and finish of work, and in perfection of results, these plots set a definite pattern to all the others, and this excellence is mainly attributed to the influence of magic.

THE GARDEN WIZARD

The *towosi* or garden magician is an hereditary official of every village community. As a matter of fact, the position of *towosi* coincides with that of the Chief or the head-man, if not in identity of person, at least in the principle of lineage. In native mythology and legal theory, it is always the head of the kinship group owning a village who is the garden magician. This man, however, frequently delegates his duties to his younger brother, his matrilineal nephew, or his son. Such handing over of the office of garden magician was especially frequent in the lineage of the paramount chiefs of Omarakana, on whom the duties of charming the gardens weighed too heavily.

The mythological system of the Trobrianders establishes a very close connection between the soil and human beings. The origins of humanity are in the soil; the first ancestors of each local group or sub-clan—for these two are identical—are always said to have emerged from a certain spot, carrying their garden magic with them. It is the spot from which they emerged which is usually, though not always, the sub-clan's soil, the territory to which it has an hereditary right.[1] This hereditary ownership of the soil—mythological, legal, moral and economic—is vested in the head-man; and it is in virtue of these combined claims that he exercises the function of garden magician. "I strike the ground," as I was told by Bagido'u, the proudest garden magician of the island, "because I am the owner of the soil." The first person meant, "I, as the representative of my sub-clan and my lineage."

We . . . see in our study of magical texts (Part VII) that the traditional filiation of garden magic is kept alive by every officiating magician. In some of the spells he has to repeat the whole series of the names of those who have wielded the magic before him. At one or two stages of his magic, he offers a ceremonial oblation, consisting of a minute portion of cooked food taken from the substantial present he has received, to the spirits of his predecessor. Such presents from the community are the expression of their gratitude and their submission to him rather than a commercial gift. They are the recognition of his services, and in this spirit they are offered to him and to his forerunners. This ritual offering of food, which is an integral part of the magical proceedings, is called *ula'ula*.

The members of the community, however, usually offer the magician other presents as well. At the beginning of the gardening cycle he is usually given small gifts of food, such as coconuts or bananas; or else he may accept a bunch of betel-nut or such objects of daily use as baskets, axes, mats, spears or cooking-pots. This type of gift, called *sousula*, is meant to repay him for the hardships undergone in the exercise of his calling. As one of my *towosi* friends explained to me, putting it in the concrete form characteristic of native utterance: "When I go about making magic in the gardens, and I hurt my food, I exclaim: *"Wi! Iwoye kayegu; gala sene si sousula."'* "Oh! (the object) has hit my foot; not very much their *sousula* payment (i.e. they don't give me enough to repay me for all my hardships)."

Again from time to time the magician receives a present of valuables called *sibugibogi*: a large ceremonial axe-blade, belts or ornaments of shell-disks or a pair of arm-shells. This gift is usually offered after a bad season to propitiate him, or else at an especially good harvest to express gratitude.

In carrying out of his duties, the magician is usually helped by some younger men: his younger brothers and his sisters' sons are his natural successors, whom he will have in due course to instruct in magic, teaching them the spells, telling them the substances to be used, advising them how to carry out the ritual and what personal observances they have to keep. Of this instruction, the most difficult is the learning of the formulae. Even this, however, does not require much special training, for garden magic is a public ceremonial, the spells are heard often by everybody, while the ritual is well known and anyone is able to tell you exactly what observances the magician has to keep. Those who have to inherit garden magic and practise it, and are therefore more interested in it, will be acquainted with every detail early in their life. They are the magician's natural helpmates and acolytes. Whenever the ceremony is cumbersome, they take part in it; or they repeat on other garden plots the rite which the chief magician performs on the standard plots. And they assist him often in the collecting of ingredients or preparing of magical mixtures and structures.

Besides these, he has non-official helpers among the younger people and children, who carry some of his paraphernalia, assist him in putting up certain magical signs and do other such minor services.

I have just mentioned the magician's taboos. These consist almost exclusively in the abstention from certain foods. In no circumstances may he touch the meat of certain animals and fish, or eat certain vegetables. Generally these are sympathetically connected with the substances which he uses in his ritual or with the aims of his magic. The magician is also not allowed to partake of the new crops until after the performance of a special ceremony, which consists as a rule in an offering to the ancestral spirits. A third type of abstention is the fast which he has to keep on the days on which he performs any ceremony.

From all this it can be seen that a garden magician's office in the Trobriands is no sinecure. Not only does he have to carry out a series of inaugural rites, following closely the practical work of the gardens, not only does he stimulate the growth of the plants in his spells of encouragement; but he also has to observe a system of by no means easy abstentions and fasts, and last, but not least, to carry out a considerable amount of practical work and control.

The garden magician is regarded by the community as the garden expert. He, together perhaps with his elder kinsman, the chief, decides what fields are to be cultivated in a given year. Later on, at each stage, he has to find out how the work in the gardens stands; how the crops are sprouting, budding, ripening, and then he has to give the initiative to the next stage. He must watch the weather and the state of the cut scrub before the burning. He has to see whether the gardens are sufficiently advanced before he performs the planting magic, and so at every stage. And when he finds that people are lagging behind, or that some of them, by neglecting a communal duty, such as the fencing of the garden plots, are endangering the interests of the whole community, it is his function to upbraid the culprits and induce them to mend their ways and to work energetically.

Time after time, as I sat in my tent reading or looking over my notes, or talking to some of my native friends, I would hear the voice of Bagido'u of Omarakana or Navavile of Oburaku or Motago'i of Sinaketa rising from somewhere in front of his house. In a public harangue, he would accuse such and such a one of not having completed his share of the fence, thus leaving a wide gap in the common enclosure through which the bush-pigs or wallabies could enter; and now that the seeds were in the garden and beginning to sprout, the wild animals would soon be attracted and might do a great deal of damage. Or again he would announce that the cut scrub was practically dry and that the burning would be inaugurated in three or four days. Or again he would impose one of the public taboos on work, saying that as in a few days the large *kamkokola* would be erected, everybody must stop all other work, and bring in the long stout poles necessary for the magical structure and for the final yam supports.

Thus the *towosi* exercises not merely an indirect influence on garden work, by giving the initiative and inaugurating the successive stages, by imposing taboos, and by setting the pace, but he also directly supervises a number of activities. In order to do this he has constantly to visit the gardens, survey the work, discover shortcomings, and last but not least, note any special excellencies. For public praise from the *towosi* is a highly appreciated reward and a great stimulus to the perfect gardener, the *tokwaybagula*.

The natives are deeply convinced that through his magic the *towosi* controls the forces of fertility, and in virtue of this they are prepared to admit that he should also control the work of man. And let us remember, his magical power, his expert knowledge and his traditional filiation to his magical ancestors are reinforced by the fact that he is the head-man, or, in a community of rank, a chief of high lineage, or a nephew or younger brother of such. When the office is in the hands of the chief's son, he again only holds it as the delegate of the rightful head of the community. Furthermore, the acts of magic are an organising influence in communal life: firstly because they punctuate the progress of activities at regular intervals and impose a series of taboo days or rest periods; and secondly because each rite must be fully performed on the standard plots, and these plots must be perfectly prepared for it, whereby a model is established for the whole village. Magic therefore is not merely a mental force, making for a more highly organised attitude of mind in each individual, it is also a social force, closely connected with the economic organisation of garden work. Yet magic and technical activities are very sharply distinguished by the natives in theory and in practice—but to this point we shall have to return presently.

NOTES

1. At times a sub-clan obtains rights of ownership in a district to which they have migrated.

CHAPTER ELEVEN

Work Patterns in a Mayo Village

CHARLES J. ERASMUS

In his *Economic Anthropology*, Melville Herskovits disagrees with what he labels the "coconut tree theory" concerning the work habits of nonliterate peoples, "the point of view that holds the 'savage' to be a man who . . . neither is required to exert himself nor is willing to do so when he can obtain even the necessary minimum to support life by abstaining from effort." Using quantitative data found in several ethnographic descriptions, Herskovits shows that considerable effort is expended by primitive peoples in their productive activities. He therefore takes exception to the inconsistency of those like Thurnwald, who, while claiming that nonliterate peoples often do more work than is necessary for survival, feel that they lack the "concentration and discipline," acquired only through working with machinery, that would compel them to overcome their tendency to "yield to the feeling of fatigue." According to Herskovits, "nonliterate peoples, like ourselves, do as much work as they feel they must to meet the basic demands of getting a living, plus as much more as their desire to achieve any given end not encompassed by those basic demands calls for. Unlike workers in a machine company, however, they take their ease at their own pleasure." (1952: 88–91)

In this paper we shall present additional case material on the subject of work patterns among nonliterate peoples as a further test of the validity of Herskovits' generalization. The field data presented here were gathered during 1948 in the Mayo Indian village of Tenía, which lies on the southern coast of the state of Sonora, Mexico, about twenty-five miles south of the Mayo River. While Tenía is both a "nonliterate" and a "nonmachine" village, it provides an example of a community which has become fully participant in a cash economy but whose members still adhere to the nonliterate pattern of taking "their ease at their own pleasure." We shall begin with a description of village economic activities and family variation in those activities, followed by the presentation of quantitative data on the daily rhythm of work and leisure.

Tenía is a village of some two hundred inhabitants divided among thirty-two households. Economic activities of the men include deer hunting, fishing, gathering, agriculture, cattle raising, cutting and selling firewood, and the manufacture of maguey fiber products (carrying bags, saddle pads, woven saddle girths and hammocks), etc. Women occasionally gather wild plant food in the thorn forest near their homes or in the fields, keep poultry, sheep and goats, and weave blankets. Only eleven men in the village still hunt deer and most of these hunt only after winter rains when the deer are fat and their tracks are clear. Six family heads do a limited amount of fishing during *lisa* season from July to September, wading into the surf with circular casting nets. Gathering of wild plant food is engaged in to a limited degree by twenty-six families to supplement the food staples of corn, beans and coffee. Maguey hearts are collected during the winter months and cactus fruit and wild greens (found in and near cultivated fields) during and after the summer rains. Of the thirty-two households, twenty-six engage in agriculture. These families average about three and a half acres of cleared land apiece. Corn is sown after the first summer rains in July or August and is harvested in October or November. Only five households plant a winter crop of corn. Black-eyed beans and squash are frequently planted in the summer and chickpeas in the winter. Six households hand-irrigate small vegetable gardens from wells during the dry season. The small amount of rainfall in the area makes dry farming extremely difficult and yields are usually poor.

Twenty-five households own cattle, the number ranging from one to fifty head. Five of these families have more than thirty each while the rest average about five head apiece. The milking and cheese-making season begins around the end of the summer rains in September and lasts through the period of winter rains until February or March. During the summer dry season from March until June the cattle must be watered daily at the village wells. Most of the year the cattle range freely in the thorn forest.

Sheep and goats are kept by eighteen families and are usually considered the property of the women. Throughout the year they are herded in the thorn forest during the day by small boys and corralled at night. All but three families of the village own draft animals such as horses, mules or burros. Two thirds of the households keep a pig or two and nearly all have a few chickens.

Men in twelve households regularly cut firewood in the thorn forest between November and June, and an additional ten households participate in this activity occasionally. Lime used to soften corn for tortillas is manufactured by nineteen households. It is made from shell gathered from old refuse sites along the coast and burned in round pit ovens. Lime is manufactured mainly in the winter but production has declined as the cutting and sale of firewood has become more popular. Maguey fiber products are manufactured throughout the year by male members of twenty-two households. Hammocks are the only maguey fiber product made seasonally since a market for them exists only during the summer. The maguey is gathered in the thorn forest and is not cultivated. Women in fifteen households weave blankets from the wool of their sheep throughout the year but especially during the winter when they bring the best price.

Each year during Easter week, Mexicans from the Mayo River vacation at the beach near the village and hire local men to repair or build temporary mud and wattle camping structures. Women of the village wash clothes for the visitors and sell them tortillas, bread, chickens, eggs, etc., and boys carry them water from the village wells. Individuals in sixteen households occasionally travel to the Mayo River to work during the tomato-harvesting season, and a few young unmarried men sometimes leave the village for short periods to work for wealthy farmers clearing new land near the river. Men in three mestizo families regularly engage in buying cattle from fellow villagers or from individuals in neighboring communities in order to sell them at a slight profit to butchers in towns along the Mayo River. Men in at least ten other households occasionally buy up local items such as lime, maguey fiber products, and cheese to be sold in the river towns. These minor commercial ventures are usually made by someone who has goods of his own to sell and is anxious to make his trip as profitable as possible. Two families operate small stores in the village apparently more for prestige than for profit since the local demand is hardly sufficient to justify the existence of even one store.

There are a few individuals in the village who work at specialties not generally engaged in by the rest. One woman occasionally makes pottery for local sale, and another makes hairbrushes of green cactus fruit. Two men sometimes make circular casting nets, one works as a carpenter on occasional local jobs, another makes adobe bricks on request, and three women with sewing machines frequently make clothes for other villagers.

One of the most striking features of the village economy is its great variety of occupations, the majority of which are engaged in to some extent by a large percentage of the families. However, since the villagers must purchase their food staples during most of the year, they are, in a sense, specialists within the larger cash economy embracing the rapidly growing towns and mechanized farming zones along the Mayo River to the north. Their agricultural production is insufficient to meet any major portion of their food needs because of the dry desert climate and the lack of inexpensive means to develop dependable irrigation. While goats are occasionally butchered locally, cattle are almost always sold to butchers in the river towns. They are said to constitute a form of savings and are usually sold only to meet some emergency. However, those families with the most cattle may sell two or three head each year as well as the cheese made during the milking season. Pigs are nearly always sold to buyers from the river communities and even chickens are seldom eaten locally. Hunting is too sporadic to be an important source of food, and when a deer is shot it is butchered and most of the meat sold or given to other villagers the same day. *Lisa* caught during the fishing season are dried and salted and sold in villages further inland. Cactus fruit and wild greens and roots are sometimes gathered during the summer months when the price of corn and beans is high at the stores. However, wild plant food other than cactus fruit is generally considered inferior and is eaten chiefly by the poorer families. Baked maguey hearts are well liked by all, but most of those gathered are sold along the river. Maguey fiber products and lime are also sold mainly in the river communities. Firewood is usually sold to buyers from the river towns who carry it away in trucks.

Let us now turn to the subject of the daily rhythm of work activities in Tenía. Because of the small size of the village it was possible to use the entire population as the "sample" for a quantitative study. As various topics of ethnographic interest carried the investigators (the author and his wife) to different parts of the village each day, notations were made of the activities of each villager seen and the time at which each observation was made. To eliminate the notation of activities which might have been altered in some way by the investigators' presence, the activity recorded was that in which the subject was engaged at the moment he was first observed. Individual charts were made for each man, woman and child in the village and on these charts were noted the page numbers from the field log where the activity descriptions were to be found. These page numbers were recorded on the charts according to the hours of the day when the observations were made. Thus, the individual charts served as indexes to the field log as well as a means of making sure that equal attention was being given to all families and all hours of the day. Periodic examination of the charts showed which households and which hours of the day were being neglected so that visits about the community could be planned to compensate for these discrepancies. Over a period of approximately three months (July to September, 1948) some 5,000 recorded observations were made of which 2,500 were on adults, 2,000 on children and 500 on the aged.

The results of the 2,500 observations on adults are shown in graph form in Figures 11.1 and 11.2. Activities for each sex have been divided into three major categories: economic, household and leisure. A breakdown of these categories is included in Table 11.1, most of which is self-explanatory. "Buying and selling" includes commercial trips, storekeeping, and negotiating local sales, etc. "Working for others" refers to work performed in the village for wages. Fellow villagers may employ one another occasionally for chores such as clearing land, repairing a house, or rounding up cattle. Those households owning the most cattle sometimes employ women of poorer families to wash clothes or cook, particularly if the woman of the house is ill or otherwise indisposed. Bread and pastries are considered a luxury and are seldom made except with the expectation of selling enough to pay for that which the family itself consumes. Men often assist in tending the adobe oven. Tortillas are not sold within the village, but two women make them daily for a bus-stop "cafe" on the highway some three miles away. "Treating sick patients" refers to the curing practice of one woman who was attempting to establish herself as a *curandera*. Due to the long dry period suffered in 1948, gathering was probably less important during the summer than would ordinarily have been the case.

Within the category of household activities, the title "Errands" refers to trips to the village stores or visits to neighbors' houses to purchase or borrow some minor item. Observations on "Butchering," while only a small proportion of the total, are much more numerous than the number of animals killed. This results from the fact that several neighbors invariably arrive on the scene to offer their assistance, for which they are always rewarded with a piece of meat. "Eating" is classified as a "Household Activity" in order to equate the activities of both sexes for Figures 11.1 and 11.2. As shown in the table, far more observations were recorded on this activity for men than for women. While men usually take their meals seated at a table and are served by the women, eating among the latter is often an indistinguishable part of food preparation.

It is interesting to note that the percentage of observations on leisure is the same for both sexes. In the case of men the item "Personal" refers mainly to shaving, bathing or haircutting. In the case of women, observations under this category consist almost entirely of combing and delousing one another's hair. Recreational activities of men include playing musical instruments and looking at pictures in Mexican periodicals. Women sometimes look at periodicals

Table 11.1 Sex Division of Daily Activities in a Mayo Village

	MEN	WOMEN
	Percentage of Observations	Percentage of Observations
Economic Activities		
Maguey fiber industries	13.9	.5
Agriculture	6.9	.2
Making or repairing tools	6.7	
Buying and selling	5.6	1.4
Tending cattle	4.0	*
Tending other animals	3.8	1.6
Fishing	1.8	*
Working for others	1.6	1.8
Lime	1.6	
Making fish nets for sale	.8	*
Hunting	.5	
Collecting firewood for sale	.5	
Gathering	.4	1.1
Carpentry	.3	
Preparing and spinning wool		4.6
Weaving blankets		1.5
Making bread, pastries, tortillas or cheese for sale	.3	1.8
Treating sick patients		.3
Total	48.7	15.0
Household Activities		
Preparing and serving food	.9	24.3
Mending and sewing clothes		5.4
Washing and ironing clothes		4.0
Getting water for the house	1.3	3.9
Caring for children	1.0	3.7
Cleaning and arranging house or house furnishings	*	4.0
Repairing house or house furnishings	3.6	
Milking	.6	3.1
Errands	.8	1.8
Collecting or chopping firewood for the house	1.6	.3
Making herbal remedies		*
Butchering	1.6	
Eating	9.1	3.7
Total	20.5+	54.2+
Leisure Activities		
Lying down	10.9	4.1
Sitting	8.1	10.6
Chatting and visiting	8.0	9.1
Personal	2.3	6.1
Recreation	1.4	.8
Total	30.7	30.7
Grand Total	100.0	100.0

* Less than 0.1% (only one observation).

or amuse themselves by making paper flowers to decorate the picture of a saint or an inside house-wall. Men are observed lying down during the day much more often than women, but their work is more strenuous.

Observing Figures 11.1 and 11.2, we find, as would be expected, that economic activities dominate the men's day and household chores dominate the women's. While most of the villagers awaken and commence their daily activities between dawn and sunrise, the women of the household in general rise before the men, who frequently remain in bed until their morning cup of coffee is ready. During the cool hours of the morning the men turn most wholeheartedly to their economic pursuits as the women busy themselves at household chores, particularly the preparation of tortillas. But as the morning wears on and the heat intensifies, work gradually tapers off, and leisure activity increases. Women's economic labors are the exception to this tendency since they are comprised to a large degree of the spinning of wool yarn and weaving, both of which can be done without too much physical effort while sitting in the shade of the house *ramada*. Leisure reaches a peak during the intense heat of early afternoon, but as the day grows cooler, leisure drops off and work again increases.

Despite the existence of a slight rhythm in daily activity influenced by the diurnal changes in the temperature, there are obviously no hours of the day when all the villagers may be found doing exactly the same thing. On the contrary, during a walk through the village at almost any hour, one may witness the entire gamut of village activities. Not only do households differ at any one moment, but the same household follows no identical routine from one day to the next.

If we convert the observation percentages of Table 11.1 into absolute hour estimates, we find that during the thirteen-hour day covered by our observations approximately four hours are spent at leisure and nine hours at work, a division which is the same for both sexes. In the case of men about six and one-fourth of the nine working hours are devoted to what we have called economic activities. We must also note that because of the previously mentioned difficulties of equating the data on the two sexes, we included observations of men eating under their "Household Activities." According to the observation percentages, the average male spends about one and one-fourth hours of the thirteen eating. Thus, total working time including household chores other than meal-taking amounts to approximately seven and three-fourths hours of the total thirteen.

Three factors affect the accuracy of the above data. First, we must consider the season of the year during which the observations were made. Since the days are longer in the summer than in the winter, the amount of time available for working was greater during this summer period. However, the summer is the most difficult season for the village. Transportation is hampered greatly by the rains which often make the roads impassable (even when none falls in the vicinity of Tenía). Consequently, fewer trucks visit the village to buy firewood, pigs, etc., and fewer trips are made to towns along the river to sell lime and maguey fiber products. The market price for all village products is lowest at this time while food staples such as corn are usually scarce and very expensive. Unfortunately, the seasonal factor is a difficult one to appraise without comparable data for the winter months, and since no such data were gathered it is impossible to accurately estimate the extent of bias in this case.

A second possible source of error would be the bias in favor of recording a disproportionate amount of leisure activity around the house resulting from the failure to observe all work activities which took members of the various households beyond the range of observation. Fortunately, in nearly all cases the fields, corrals, wells, and lime ovens, etc., belonging to a family were either visible from the family's house or lay alongside the path leading to it. Nevertheless, such occasional activities as gathering, hunting, and commercial trips sometimes took individuals outside this circuit. To offset this potential bias, inquiries were made at the time of a visit as to the whereabouts and activities of family members who were not present, such verbal "observations" accounting for less than ten per cent of the total. A further check was made by calculating separately the proportion of leisure and work engaged in during the same period by five men who worked exclusively at the weaving of maguey fiber products in their own homes. Results showed the equivalent of half an hour more work per day, or an increase of approximately fifteen minutes each in economic and household activities (other than meal-taking).

Third, some of the work activity performed during early morning and late afternoon did not enter into our calculations since observations were incomplete for those hours. However, work did continue in the village until as late as 8 P.M. in some instances. Considering factors two and three, we would therefore estimate the total working time of Tenian males during these summer months (including household chores other than meal-taking) at between eight and nine hours a day of which between six and one-half and seven hours were dedicated to what we have called "Economic" pursuits.

The data on the young and aged show, as would be expected, that they spend a greater amount of time at leisure in proportion to work activity than the adult group already discussed. Parents usually begin to assign minor chores to their children by the time the latter are three or four years old. Between the ages of four and six years, children spend less than a third of their day at work tasks. Past the age of six or seven, however, both sexes devote about the same amount of time to work as to leisure although the seriousness with which a task is performed is by no means as great during the earlier years. This equal division between work and leisure persists until marriage in the case of males. Girls past the age of eighteen, however, seem to devote the same amount of time to work as married women. While boys are capable of earning their own living by the age of eighteen and while they usually contribute to family food purchases, they are not under the same obligations as a married man with a family to support nor are they confined to the house as in the case of girls the same age. Consequently, the years of young manhood are the most carefree for the male.

One chore invariably assigned to little girls is that of carrying water to the house. In pairs or small groups they file down to the nearest well in the arroyo several times a day. As the little girl begs to undertake new tasks, her mother or an older sister begins to teach her to wash her own clothes or to make tiny tortillas. Gradually, her activities expand to caring for younger siblings, cleaning about the house, going on errands, milking, and preparing food. By the time she is thirteen a girl is quite capable of doing any household chore. At the age of fifteen or a little earlier, she may also begin to learn sewing, dressmaking, weaving, or the making of pottery, but an economic proficiency in these tasks may not develop for several years.

The first chores assigned small boys include running errands, getting water for the house, watering animals and collecting firewood. As early as six or seven years of age, boys may begin herding their mothers' sheep and goats in the thorn forest. Usually two boys will herd together and they frequently do more playing than herding. As they grow older, boys participate more and more in tasks involving assistance to their fathers or older brothers and proportionately less in household chores. Boys of seven or eight may be seen weeding fields and boys of ten or eleven may already have learned to plow. By the age of sixteen, boys may begin to weave maguey fiber saddle girths and the more simple type of hammock. After eighteen, however, they seem to spend much less time at household chores than either younger boys or married men normally devote to those activities.

Men and women over sixty years of age spend approximately half their day at leisure. Men in this age group are seen sitting and lying down twice as often as the younger men. While aged women spend less time at food preparation and housework than younger women, they seem to spend slightly more time at economic activities, primarily at spinning wool yarn.

CONCLUSIONS

The data presented here on the work habits of a nonliterate group seem to confirm Herskovits' generalizations based on previous examples. The total amount of time Teníans spend at work would probably compare favorably to that spent by semiskilled laborers in the vicinity of Washington, D. C., for example, during the same hot summer months. A major difference is that each adult Tenían is his own boss and can work or rest as he feels inclined.

The fact that Teníans spend as much time at work as they do came as a surprise to the observers. Had they made an estimate based entirely on their impressions, they would have arrived at a figure substantially lower than that indicated by the quantitative data. When a large proportion of a population can be observed at leisure at almost any hour of the day, a strong impression of indolence may result. This in itself might easily account for the strength of the "coconut-tree" picture of primitive work habits in the past. It also surprised the observers to find that the men spend the same amount of time at work as the women, for it had seemed to them that the women were far more active than the men. Perhaps the fact that the men were more inclined than the women to spend leisure moments during the day lying down was sufficient to erroneously distort the comparative impressionistic picture of the work habits of the two sexes.

The amount of time spent at work, however, is not necessarily an index of the efficiency with which the work is performed. The majority of the villagers produce only enough to meet their few basic needs, mainly those of food and clothing. For the majority of the inhabitants of the area the indigenous community of some 120 square miles that includes Tenía and several other towns and villages is a final refuge area where they are free to live as they please and to enjoy a nonintensive exploitation of the resources of the virgin thorn forest which still covers most of it. Since the land is held in common by the inhabitants, all have equal rights to its raw materials and to any virgin land they wish to clear and cultivate. To some of the more acculturated the present system of exploitation seems inefficient in comparison with the intensive machine agriculture being practised along the Mayo River. However, a full realization of the agricultural potentialities of this area would depend upon the development of reliable irrigation, and the present inhabitants do not have the capital necessary to make such a development. This leads some to welcome the proposal that the land be opened up to exploitation by wealthy farmers living along the Mayo River. Such individuals reason that while much of the communal land would be lost to the rich the resulting development of the agricultural potentialities would make a more intensive and profitable type of land use possible for all. But the majority of the inhabitants lack the self-confidence of those more acculturated individuals who believe themselves capable of benefiting from a breaking up of the communal land. Distrustful of both the government and the "whites," they feel that any change would be for the worse and would only leave them with less than they had before. It could probably be said that the existing work patterns of the villagers are quite efficient within the limitations of their own fears and aspirations.

As we have seen, the village of Tenía is regionally specialized in that its members depend largely on the exploitation of local raw materials in order to buy essentials such as food and cloth. What Herskovits terms "subdivision of labor" or "intra-industrial special-ization" is practically nonexistent (1952: 126). Division of labor is primarily by sex. While not every household participates to the same degree in all the economic activities of the village, most are capable of performing them all. Those adult males who would be incapable of performing a few of the more specialized skills, such as those required in maguey fiber weaving, are not dependent on the specialists in those fields for their products. Hammocks, for example, are never purchased locally since they are seldom used in the village. However, any adult male is capable of spinning the same maguey cord used in hammock weaving should he need it for some other purpose. There are a few exceptions, but they cannot be said to play an important part in the local economy. Women who cannot weave blankets may purchase them from others. One woman, as we have mentioned, occasionally makes pottery, for which there is only a limited local demand. Three old men often collect maguey leaves and extract the fiber for sale to younger men who spin and weave it. Similarly, three older women are frequently paid to spin the wool yarn used by younger women in weaving their blankets. The last two examples are really divisions of labor by age and are not true industrial subdivisions. No household and no individual in the village is economically dependent upon the rest for special services or for a market for his special skills. Each family is largely an independent production unit.

Quite the contrary is true of towns along the Mayo River, such as Huatabampo and Navojoa, where a multitude of specialized jobs and services have grown up not only in the towns themselves but on the many large mechanized farms where Indians and mestizos now work as hired laborers. While even here the rhythm of daily activities does not always show the same fixed regimen as in an industrialized area in the United States, there is a fairly definite schedule of working hours to which a large proportion of the population now conforms. The only individuals in Tenía who come anywhere near to approximating such a daily standardization of working hours are the two storekeepers, although they frequently close their stores or leave them in the hands of relatives when they feel inclined. The families of both storekeepers are supported by their cattle, not by their stores. Even in the marketing of their produce, the villagers do not find it necessary to conform to any strict regimen of working hours. The demand for local produce is fairly constant despite price fluctuations and very often it is disposed of to middlemen. A villager carries goods to the river for sale only when he has enough to make his trip worth while or when he needs the money.

It would seem to us that the "nonliterate" pattern of alternating work and leisure according to personal inclinations is related to a low degree of intraindustrial specialization. The development of economic and technological specialization to a point where the members of a given population become mutually dependent upon one another for a variety of personal services that cannot be efficiently performed without a standardization of working hours would seem to be the underlying factor of limitation which augments the probability of a change from a "nonliterate" to an "industrial" work pattern.

CHAPTER TWELVE

Organization of Labor among the Kapauku

LEOPOLD POSPISIL

WORKING HABITS

Kapauku start their working day at approximately 7:30 A.M., after they have finished their breakfast and discussed the plans for the day. They leave the village in small groups by way of a meandering path, so narrow that often they have to wade through tall reeds and grass still wet with cold morning dew. To overcome the cold of the morning they walk fast; the men even like to run for short stretches, skillfully avoiding the deep mud, puddles, and the excrement with which domesticated pigs clog the paths, at times making them hardly passable. As soon as a given small group of men or women reach the work area their temporary association is dissolved, and they assume the attitude of pronounced individualism and independence which characterize the agricultural working habits of the Kapauku.

A man usually works alone in his garden, only occasionally taking with him his young son or an apprentice. He works steadily, usually in a systematic and well-organized fashion. When working, Kapauku men do not stop to take breaks or to smoke. They work at a fast pace, as if in competition with their neighbors. In other words a Kapauku is a hard worker when he toils of his own will and according to his own program. He becomes so absorbed that, in time of war, an enemy sniper can easily ambush him. Because of this danger, young boys or even girls accompany their fathers and brothers to the gardens during war time to stand guard. A Kapauku female, although slower paced, nevertheless works as steadily as her husband. Indeed, since her work is more monotonous and slower, one gains the impression that she is even a steadier worker than the male.

Workers of both sexes prefer to toil alone. Their task must be clearly outlined for them to feel stimulated into high production. "I have to clear this land, from here up to there." "It is my job and nobody is going to do it for me or even help me with it." "The sooner I accomplish it the better for me." (These are loosely translated statements made by some of my informants.)

The Kapauku dislikes to share responsibility. He is always suspicious that a co-worker will exploit him and derive undeserved prestige from work to which he did not contribute enough effort. Also, a Kapauku likes to see his task clearly delimited so that he can say, for example: "I have to cut the trees as far as the neighbor's fence." To work with somebody else on the same plot means that one's task is not so well defined as it might be, which is undesirable to a Kapauku. For this reason, co-wives have their separate *medeke* sections in the same garden. If an individual wanted to help his co-wife or friend, for example, he (or she) would invariably subdivide the total work to be accomplished, and then work and finish a discrete portion of it (e.g., a man would clear a well-defined half of his neighbor's plot in order to help him).

As we may suspect from these statements, Kapauku hired laborers are rewarded not on the basis of the length of time spent on the job, but according to the amount of work actually accomplished. Aboriginal labor contracts always stipulate the amount of work to be done for a certain amount of pay and are never concerned about the time to be spent in accomplishing the task. Consequently Europeans who hire Kapauku "per day or hour" make a serious mistake. They deprive the native of initiative and pleasure derived from work and planning, and turn him into a slow, unreliable worker. "If I am paid by time, the longer the work lasts the better for me," said one of my informants, reflecting upon the white man's practice.

The hard-working Kapauku takes a break at approximately 11:00 A.M., when he kindles a fire and roasts a few sweet potatoes for himself. Sometimes he may just squat and enjoy the tubers which already have been cooked for him by his wife. While a man often eats in solitude, a woman usually prefers to join friends of her own sex in order to exchange important information and to enjoy lunch in a merrily joking and laughing company. After lunch, which may take as long as an hour, both sexes return to their work. Although a woman generally continues to work until four or five o'clock in the afternoon, a man, unless unusually preoccupied, leaves for home at about two in order to participate in local economic transactions or political life.

Since the Kapauku have a conception of balance in life, only every other day is supposed to be a working day. Such a day is followed by a day of rest in order to "regain the lost power and health." This monotonous fluctuation of leisure and work is made more

appealing to the Kapauku by inserting into their schedule periods
of more prolonged holidays (spent in dancing, visiting, fishing, or
hunting; in the Kamu Valley the last two activities are considered
recreation). Consequently, we usually find only some of the people
departing for their gardens in the morning, the others are taking
their "day off." However, many individuals do not rigidly conform
to this ideal. The more conscientious cultivators often work intensively
for several days in order to complete clearing a plot, making a fence,
or digging a ditch. After such a task is accomplished, they relax for
a period of several days, thus compensating for their "missed" days
of rest.

Division of Agricultural Labor

Except for the sexual division of labor, skill in all types of agricultural work is part of the general knowledge of the Kapauku. In
other words there are no agricultural experts or specialists, and there
is no Kapauku who would not have received, as a boy or a girl,
thorough training in the cultivation of plants from the parent of his
own sex. Certain tasks are considered to be exclusively in the domain
of one of the sexes; other tasks are only preferentially so. The rest
of the work is shared more or less equally by both sexes.

The following activities are considered purely the responsibility of
the men: planning agricultural production, digging ditches, making
garden beds (bedamai), felling trees, building fences, tying sugar cane
to supporting posts; also planting and harvesting bananas, apuu (a
variety of yam), tobacco, and chili peppers, planting native ginger,
and harvesting native squash and introduced maize. It is regarded
as improper for a woman to indulge in any of these activities; only
very exceptionally does one discover a violation of these rules. If a
woman is ever seen performing any of the difficult male tasks, her
husband is blamed and may be ridiculed or even reprimanded by
the head of the household, by his in-laws, or by the headman of
his sublineage. As a counterpart to the purely masculine tasks, the
planting of sweet potatoes and jatu as well as the weeding of sweet
potatoes, jatu, apuu, chili peppers, maize, manioc, dade, bottle gourd,
native ginger, native and string beans, tomatoes, and onions, are
purely female tasks. Although I know of exceptions to the rules
concerning the weeding regulations, I have never witnessed or heard
of a case of a man planting his own sweet potatoes. No matter what
his status, whether he is a widower or an unmarried orphan, he
always finds a woman to perform this task for him. For a man to
plant sweet potatoes would be regarded by the Kapauku as improper

as it would be in Europe for a male to wear a skirt or to wash the dishes. It is simply not done.

In addition to the clear-cut categories of specific agricultural tasks assigned to one sex or the other, there are two sets of activities that are performed preferentially by one of the sexes with members of the other sex permitted to participate only to a limited extent. The following type of work is regarded as belonging primarily to men: burning gardens; planting sugar cane, manioc, squash, and introduced maize; weeding squash, sugar cane, bananas, and tobacco; and harvesting sugar cane, manioc, and ginger. Conversely, it is mostly the women who plant and weed taro, and who harvest sweet potatoes. All other agricultural work is shared about equally by both sexes. Accordingly, most men and women clear the ground growth on new plots, guard crops during their maturation period, and plant *pego* (edible reed); *idaja* (spinach-like green); *dade* (a small shrub with edible leaves); *kagame* (tomato-like green); *damuwe* (parsley-like green); bottle gourd; cucumbers; native and string beans; Irish potatoes; tomatoes; lettuce; and onions. They weed *kagame, damuwe,* cucumbers, Irish potatoes, lettuce, *idaja,* and *pego;* and harvest taro tubers, *jatu,* and leaves of taro and gourd in addition to all the other crops that they planted (e.g., *pego, idaja, dade, kagame,* etc.).

We may draw some generalizations from the discussion of the sexual division of agricultural labor. First of all, it is obvious that tasks requiring strength and the expenditure of great amounts of energy in a brief period of time are, as a rule, assigned to men (for example, digging ditches, felling trees, and building fences). In contrast, women are held responsible for the kind of work that usually is more monotonous, more time consuming and, especially, that requires daily attention. Accordingly we find Kapauku women doing all the extensive planting and most of the harvesting of the sweet potato gardens (90.1 per cent of all cultivated land in 1955), and virtually all of the weeding. With the exception of sugar cane, the few plants in whose planting, harvest, and weeding the male does participate to any extent occupy negligible areas. Moreover, even the planting, weeding, and harvesting of sugar cane (planted only on 5 per cent of the total garden area) is not an exclusively male task. Women may, and do, participate in this work especially when the males of their household are engaged in war, trade, or visiting distant friends and are away for a long period of time. These arrangements mean that the male farmer is not "bound to the soil" but is allowed to participate in war or in trade expeditions to other regions, which may require as much as three or four months' absence from his gardens. Although some of the woman's work, such as supplying the household with fresh sweet potatoes, requires daily performance, she still may manage to leave for a few days to visit her relatives or to participate in a distant feast. This is made possible by the institution of polygyny or by the presence of several women in households where the co-resident women agree to substitute for each other on such occasions.

The rules pertaining to the division of labor are broken only exceptionally by a few individuals. A widow, before she remarries, or a wife whose husband has become incapacitated, may be compelled to perform purely male work such as felling trees, digging ditches, or even building fences. However, these are really rare exceptions, and everyone pities such an individual. Sooner or later some male is found to relieve the woman from her awkward and difficult occupation. On the other hand, a male, under no circumstances, would plant sweet potatoes or *jatu;* and only with utmost reluctance would he consent to do some of his wife's other duties. He would almost always manage to find a woman who, either for pay or for an exchange of services, would perform these tasks for him.

From this outline of specific types of work categorized according to the sex of the workers who traditionally perform it, it is apparent that total care for some of the plants (which involves planting, weeding, and harvesting) is assigned, in a given case, to a single sex. While sweet potatoes and—except for its harvest—*jatu* belong to the care of women, sugar cane, tobacco, *apuu,* native squash, introduced maize, chili peppers, and manioc may be regarded as "plants of the Kapauku males." Only the weeding of *apuu,* chili peppers, maize, and manioc are excepted from this generalization. These cultigens are weeded by women because all of them are usually planted singly or in small patches in sweet potato areas which have to be weeded by the female. It would be strange and highly un-economical if the women were expected to neglect in their weeding tiny areas in the large gardens which they must weed anyway.

The relative burden of agricultural work imposed upon the sexes will be discussed later in the section on the time factor in Kapauku agriculture. We may conclude the discussion on the division of agricultural labor with a few statements concerning the duties of children and elderly people in agricultural production. After he has reached approximately his seventh year of age, a boy is gradually transferred from his mother's supervision to that of his father. At this time the father begins educating his son in agricultural production, and the child slowly starts to contribute to the household economy. The child's training is never overintensified and is more sporadic than constant. Often the boy himself decides whether he will follow his parents to the garden or not. There he will be taught, in a very informal way, to clear underbrush and, later on, to cut smaller trees.

When the boy is about 12 years of age he begins to learn how to build fences and how to fell larger trees from the secondary forests. Instruction in digging ditches and in the cutting of primary forest is usually postponed until the boy has reached adolescence. Neither the child nor the adolescent is ever forced into work. The prospect of having his own garden and a pig—a prerequisite for becoming a rich man—is adequate incentive for the boy to take work in the gardens seriously. However, until he becomes adult a Kapauku male does not systematically contribute food to the household. His services in guarding piglets are often economically more important to his parents than are his accomplishments in agriculture.

The Kapauku girl's agricultural endeavors, on the other hand, are more steady. Because most women's work does not require great strength, relatively early in life (about 12 years of age) a girl learns all that she needs to know about plant cultivation. To make her feel as important and independent as possible, her father gives her part of one of his gardens which she marks as her responsibility by sticks pushed into the ground, thus making *medeke* a boundary between "her plot" and those of her mother and sisters. She does not own the land; it is hers only to care for. She plants the sweet potatoes, does all the weeding, and finally brings the produce home, cooks it, and proudly presents the food to her father and brothers. Her steady work in the garden is a definite asset to the household's agricultural production.

In old age the male retires earlier than the female from some of the difficult work. At about the age of 60 years, the man stops felling primary forest; by the time he is 68, his agricultural work consists only of clearing underbrush on the plots of his sons. A woman may not start her retirement until she becomes about 65 years old; even then, some healthy females continue to be fully productive in agriculture. In the Botukebo community all the old women, and all but three old men (1/13, 8/3, 13/5) were still participating fully in agricultural activities. Among the Kapauku is it more often disease than old age that removes an individual from his work.

CHAPTER THIRTEEN

Organization of Work
among the New Zealand Maori

RAYMOND FIRTH

Most of the large enterprises were communal affairs, i.e., they were performed by all the people of the community—village or *hapu*—working in concert. There are a number of native terms to indicate co-operative labour. An institution of some interest is the *tuao* or "working bee," a method by which a company of people voluntarily gathered together to accomplish some communal task, generally in connection with agriculture. Such a party of workmen assembled together is termed *ohu*. Thus in describing the planting of the *kumara* a native said, "*Mehemea he ohu, ka wehewehea kia toru, kia wha ranci, nga tangato whakaara; kia tokowha hoki nga tangala hai tuahu*"—"If it is a working party, three men or perhaps four may be detached as breakers-up of the soil; and an equal number also to form the mounds." And, again, another native said: "It mattered not how numerous were the plantations of a district, all would be completed in a short space of time by the *ohu* or working bee, a voluntary band of diggers and planters."[1] Colenso gives *ahu* as a synonym for *ohu*, "*Ina hoki te pepeha a Rangi. 'Ko te ahu a Rangi'; kei Maungatipa tena ahu*"—is given as an example. "Hence the boast of Rangi 'It is the company of Rangi'. That company was at Maungatipa." And again, "*Mo to ratou ahu nui ki te hanga i te waka*"—"For their great assembling together to construct the canoe." To combine or co-operate in work is termed *paheko* or *pahekoheko*, according to Williams. *Apu*, again, is another synonym for *ohu*, meaning a company of labourers gathered together for work in the cultivations, while *apa* means also a party of labourers, but implies that they are dependents, vassals, or even slaves.[2]

In some cases a single community was not possessed of sufficient labour power to undertake an enterprise of great magnitude, or for some other reason desired assistance, and called in the aid of relatives

186

or friends. In the erection of a large carved house, for instance, this was frequently done. Experts from other *hapu* or tribes would lend their services for the more specialised work, while large numbers of people from other villages might assemble to take part in the unskilled labour of hauling timber and hoisting the massive posts for the framework. Such work will be dealt with more fully in examining the system of rewarding labour; but the main principles of organisation are essentially the same as those mentioned previously. The system of invitation to work and the rendering of mutual assistance is well discussed by Brun under the name of *Bittarbeit*.[3] Such was a favourite practice of the Maori.

From the theoretical standpoint all communal work, or work where a number of people are engaged, may be divided into two types. The first is represented by such an undertaking as the hauling of a log from the forest. Here all the workers, with the exception of the leader and the skid-handlers, perform an identical piece of work, that of pulling on the ropes. For practical purposes there is no real differentiation in their functions. The second type of work is represented by the planting operations in agriculture, where the people of one party loosen the soil, those of another pulverise it and make the mounds, while others distribute the seed, and still others plant it and finish off the work. In the lifting of the crop, again, there appears to have been a certain amount of separation of economic functions. Some men attended to the digging alone, others collected the tubers into heaps, others put them into baskets, while others carried these to the store pits, where the task of stowing them away was performed by old men, often the leading men of the *hapu*. No interference with each other's work was allowed among these groups, and the people had to comply with a definite set of magical regulations.[4] Here the economic functions of the various sets of workers are sharply differentiated. Each has its own part of the undertaking to perform, its legitimate and definite place in a regular sequence of operations.

Work of the first type is termed by the economist "simple combination of labour", and that of the second type "complex combination of labour". It is important to make the distinction between them, since the organisation in each case is of a radically different pattern, requiring a different scheme of regulation and leadership of a different order. This has been pointed out by Professor Malinowski in his clear and concise *exposé* of the problems of primitive labour.[5]

In undertakings which have to be accomplished by a complex combination of labour the sphere of co-ordination is much wider than when all the workers have to perform the same series of actions. In the latter case integration of their activity is essential; in hauling a log all must pull together, otherwise the individual effort, however great, is wasted. Organisation of a certain type is required to effect this synchronisation of effort. But in agriculture, or the building of a house, the problem is more acute. Not only must co-operation be secured within each band of workers, but the result of their united efforts must be fitted into its proper niche in the series of tasks on which other parties of workers are engaged. Supervision, not only of one, but of several types of operation is required.

THE LEADER OF WORK

At this point we may proceed to an examination of one of the most important factors in accomplishing this organisation, i.e., leadership. In the preceding description of typical economic activities the need for co-ordination of the work has been fully stressed, and data have been given to illustrate the manner in which the leader helped in fulfilling that function. The theoretical bearing of these points may now be further analysed.

In small-scale undertakings the leader of the work is generally one of the principal performers in it and to any casual eye may not be distinguishable from the rest. As the type of undertaking grows in complexity and size, however, the person of the leader begins to stand out with greater clarity, until in certain enterprises he takes no part in the actual manual labour, but devotes all his energies to the supervision and direction of the affair. This differentiation of function on the part of the organiser may be correlated to some extent with advance in industrial complexity.

The operation of hauling a large tree trunk, which the Maori had to do for canoes and house timbers, provides a good illustration of this point. It is graphically described by the author of *Poenamo*.[6] In this case the workers numbered about eighty men, all quite naked. The log to be dragged out was some 3 feet in diameter and 80 feet long, and was decorated at the head with branches of flowering trees and waving tufts of feathers. On this end of the trunk stood the oldest chief of the *hapu*, brandishing his *taiaha* (staff) aloft in his right hand, and imparting to it that peculiar quivering motion so characteristic of the Maori. Rapidly he repeated a long chant, lifting up one foot and stamping it down again, the body being thrown back on the other leg. Every moment his voice became louder and louder, until it almost reached a scream. He grasped the weapon with both hands and sprang into the air, coming down with an action as if he were smiting an enemy to earth. At this instant the workers yelled forth a single word, as a finale to the chorus. As one man they simultaneously stamped on the ground, and then gave one great heave on the rope, which was doubled round the end of the tree. The huge mass forged ahead several feet.

Again the chief sprang into the air, flung his arms on high, and yelled out a word; the gang repeated it with a louder yell, sprang into the air and landed as one man. Then another pull, and away slid the timber a few feet more. Again and again this was done, at each heave the log advancing a few feet. At last, after one tremendous pull, the gang ended their shout by prolonging it until it died away on a comparatively soft note. This the chief took as an intimation that they desired a breathing space. So they rested, soon to begin again the same series of energetic movements.

In most of these hauling tasks skids were used and a special party was detailed to attend to them, picking them up from the rear and replacing them in front as the log passed over them.[7]

The peculiar customs observed in undertakings such as this—the antics of the chief, his prominent position on top of the object which is being hauled, the weapon which he wields in his hand, and the chant by which each fresh effort is prefaced—are patently devices of leadership by which he may impress his personality upon the workers and secure increased control. His lofty post and the brandishing of his weapon keep the attention of the people concentrated upon him and so enable him better to co-ordinate their activity. The rhythm of the chant also aids as a stimulus to effort.

In enterprises involving complex combination of labour another set of qualities, as well, is required in the leader. Pre-eminently he must have a knowledge of technical detail and a competent grasp of the whole economic situation. Hence we find that in such undertakings as the planting of the *kumara*, or the construction of a new house, the direction and leadership of the work was undertaken by the *tohunga*, the expert, skilled in the technique of that particular craft, and, moreover, versed in all the magical spells and ritual procedure necessary to secure the favour of the gods and the success of the work. He specified the time to begin, allotted the different sets of people their portion of the task, supervised the efficiency of the labour, and ordered the whole course of work, in accordance with practical and magical requirements.[8]

If the chief were a man skilled in the magical lore of the craft, then he himself might assume the direction of the activity. Thus a native of Te Kaha, Bay of Plenty, which is noted for its abundance of food products, says, "The most famous adepts of these parts at directing the labours of planting and in chanting the work songs were Tamehana Tarahanumi and his wife. It was owing to his fine work in directing the task of planting, as also the excellence of his work songs, that these clans [*hapu*] experienced no pangs of hunger."

He also mentions that this chief was seen directing a party of over forty workers; all were engaged in using the *ko* (digging stick). "As director Tarahanumi carried a *tewhatewha* (native weapon) in his hand, but did no digging himself. The diggers kept perfect time in the various movements in using the *ko*." Should a member of the *hunga ko* (digging party) in such work prove to be unskilled, he was sent back by the directing expert to join the planters in rear.[9]

The term *ngarahu* or *kai-ngarahu* is given by Williams as meaning "commander" or "leader in work". In each of the major economic activities the leader was denoted by a specific term.

A few words may now be said on the interrelation of social position and economic function, as illustrated in the leadership of the chief. In communal tasks of any kind the chief held a position of command in the work. He often took the part of the director of the undertaking, assigning different sections of the task to various sets of people, keeping them up to the mark of efficiency, and watching that the correct time-sequence of operations was observed. In this capacity he might work equally with his people, or might take no part in the actual labour, but merely exercise supervision over the whole.

On the other hand, his authority was often exercised as the initiator of economic enterprises. He supplied the spur, the incentive to action, as it were, either by his oratory and demonstration of the need for the work, or through the more substantial medium of gifts and a feast—a cogent argument which always appealed to the Maori! He would propose that a certain piece of work, say the erection of a new carved house, be undertaken, and the people after discussion would accede to the suggestion. Their motive in so doing was to take advantage of the feasting, the sociability, and amusement which such a communal affair always provided, while to have such a building in the tribe meant increased renown for all. The proposal of the chief was due to his interest in the welfare of his people, coupled with the desire to add to his own prestige. The chief Tarcha, in 1868, when describing the carved house now in the Dominion Museum, said, "Such a building as this is only erected by men holding a high position among the tribes; it is a sign of chieftainship, and the proprietor becomes a noted man. The whole tribe assist in building it when called together by the chief for that purpose."[10] In such a case the chief played the part of an entrepreneur, repaying the labour expended on his behalf by gifts to the specialists engaged, and presents of food at intervals, culminating in a gigantic feast to all and sundry on completion of the work. As one who gave the stimulus to production, because he was the possessor of stores of wealth, the chief might either direct operations himself, if he had the requisite technical and magical knowledge, or, more often, he commissioned a *tohunga,* an expert, to do so, rewarding him for his services with presents of garments, ornaments, and food.

An enterprise of this kind offers perhaps the clearest case of the duality of function which can be observed in the positions of chief and priestly expert. The latter was *par excellence* the actual director of work. Equipped, as a rule, with a deep knowledge of technical procedure and traditional rules, versed also in all the magic of the craft—spells, ritual, and *tapu* observances—he was eminently fitted to assume the post of skilled adviser or practical leader. And so we find to a certain extent this division of economic function, the chief providing the initiative and the *tohunga* the direction of the undertaking. This was illustrated in the description of Te Pokiha's fishing with the great net. The old chief supplied the stimulus to the whole affair, and assumed all the social obligations in connection with it, while the executive responsibility and technical supervision were placed in the hands of the *tohunga,* Te Whanarere, the expert in fishing lore. The division of the functions of leadership on these lines was, however, by no means invariable. But in large tribal enterprises this procedure was usual.

The exact nature of the economic leadership exercised by a chief was always dependent to a great extent on his status by birth. This is especially noticeable in the case of the *ariki,* the high chief, descended in the first-born line. Correlated with his social standing he had magical and religious powers of a peculiar kind, of such nature that he, and he alone, was qualified to perform certain economic functions. He was both chief and priest in one, and leader *sui generis.* So in ceremonies connected with firstfruits, the lifting of *tapu* from land to be cultivated, the breaking down of a *rahui* (the magical prohibition imposed on fisheries, forests, or shell banks), or the consecration of economic talismans (*mauri*), his was the post of leader. Even though he might be lacking in practical ability and his normal authority and influence pass to a younger relative, yet would he be called upon from time to time to use his peculiar powers in the economic interests of the people.[11]

The head man of the village or tribe thus always had great authority in economic affairs. It will be useful to summarise here the factors on which his status depended.

(1) His command of technical skill and knowledge of economic lore, coupled with his industry.

(2) His authority as leader of his people in social matters and head of the kinship group. From this he received a kind of derivative or transferred power of great force.

(3) His wealth, as the owner of valuable property and custodian of the most important tribal treasures.

(4) His sacerdotal position and *tapu* as a chief.

The degree of possession of these qualities varied according to the individual, but in general the prestige of this type which he held gave the chief his wanted position as leader and adviser in important economic enterprises.

It may be objected that leadership in magical ceremonies, such as characterised the *tohunga* of higher grade, did not enter into the economic sphere. But as will be shown in the following chapter, magic is intimately bound up with the success of all economic undertakings, and performs, indeed, a valuable function therein. The magical regulation of economic affairs is one of the most useful factors in organisation.

Apart from the ritual observances, and the regulations imposed upon work by magical beliefs and procedure, there is also a vast body of customary rules not directly dependent upon any religious sanction, but carrying with them the force of tradition. Conventional methods of procedure and technical rules built upon the basis of experience are a very efficient agent in helping to weld together the efforts of the workers into a coherent and purposive scheme of activity.

STIMULI IN COMMUNAL WORK

Some attention must be directed now to one aspect of co-operative work which is of the greatest importance in contributing towards the efficiency of labour in primitive societies. I refer to the stimuli which are in use to promote work, the "palliative concomitants" as they are termed by Professor Malinowski in his analysis of the problems of primitive labour.[12] These may be distinguished from the group of incentives examined in a previous chapter—the desire for reward, social reputation, etc.—by the fact that they do not represent the aim of the work, but simply the means of making it more pleasant.

Among the Maori there were several of these stimuli which relieved the tedium of protracted effort and introduced a sparkle of interest into the occupation. One of the most important was the pleasure of work in company. Most communal industry was an affair of the whole population, men, women, and children turning out *en masse*, and in the rest pauses indulging in conversation, banter, and the exchange of news and scandal, all of which gave a distinct fillip to the affair. The actual labour itself, too, was stimulated by the knowledge of the presence of others, likewise engaged, which thus had a distinct psychological value.

Another factor of importance is rhythm. This subject has been treated with great erudition by Karl Bücher,[13] who has collected a great quantity of material indicating the value of rhythm and songs in work. No attempt will be made to examine his results here, but simply to make a study of the Maori data. The Polynesian people have a great love for songs, and, even in these degenerate days, have a well developed sense of rhythm and a feeling for euphony. To this the Maori is no exception. Native singing, though sometimes rather monotonous owing to the succession of quarter-tones and fine modulations which are hardly appreciated by the European ear, is often very pleasing, while both in this and in the posture dances the rhythmic effect is well marked. With this partiality it is no cause for wonder that the Maori utilised songs, chants, and rhythmic measures very freely in his communal work. In log hauling, in digging, in canoe paddling, and in other tasks requiring the co-ordination of the effort of numbers of persons all performing the same type of movements, these songs were common. As a rule a definite song leader was appointed, whose duty it was to give the time or to intone the body of the chant in exact and measured style, to be joined by the workers in the chorus. The song leader in a canoe was called *kai-tuki* or *kai-hautu;* as a name for the fugleman when a canoe is being dragged Hare Hongi gives *kai whakahau*, and Best *kaea*.[14]

These rhythmic work songs may be divided into four main classes:

(1) *Toto waka, to waka,* or *tau waka,* canoe-hauling songs, used when a canoe is being dragged over a portage or a log through the forest. Best also gives *rangi waka* as a synonym for these.

(2) *Tuki, tuki waka, hautu waka,* or *rangi rangi,* canoe-paddling songs.

(3) *Ko kumara, tapatapa kumara,* or *whakatopatopa kumara,* chants used when digging the fields for cultivation.

(4) Songs used when engaged in other minor operations as grinding of adzes, etc.[15] The generic term for such songs is *tewha*. Williams also gives *ngaringari* as a name for a song to make people pull together when at work.

There is not space here to consider each type of work song in detail. Since the principle involved in the use of each is the same it will suffice to describe briefly the songs used for hauling and paddling canoes.

In dragging a partly finished canoe from the forest to the water, which might be a considerable distance, ropes were fastened to the framework or to projections inside, and men might also haul upon the sides of the craft itself. The work was heavy; and coordinated effort was imperative. The scene was essentially the same as that already described in the case of log hauling (see *ante*). Here we are concerned, however, not with the leadership of the work, but with the rhythmic chants sung and their bearing on the efficiency of the labour. The men by the canoe, when the word was given by the fugleman, extended one arm forward and the other back, grasped the topsides, and with chests pressed against the canoe, simultaneously impelled it forward and marched along beside it, while at the same time the others heaved on the ropes.The call of the fugleman and his chant served to ensure unity of effort on the part of the two sets of haulers, to induce them to take the strain at the same moment and to heave all together. Usually the body of the chant was intoned by the leader, while from time to time the working party responded with a word or phrase as chorus. A lengthy hauling song is given by Shortland,[16] which shows the correspondence between the words of the chant and the movement of the work. Short staccato phrases accompany a brisk heave, while a sustained pull on the rope is characterised by the onomatopoeic effect of long vowels and drawn-out syllables. In giving a long and strong pull to overcome a difficulty in the ground, the song is modulated accordingly, while a lengthened phrase, chanted all in one breath, is uttered as the gang walk away with the load.[17]

So was the canoe dragged along. A similar chanted accompaniment assisted the crew when paddling the vessel, with remarkable effect. C. O. B. Davis, long acquainted with the Maori, says that it is a most imposing sight to see a large war canoe, elaborately carved and tastefully decorated with feathers, urged forward by a hundred or more men, the paddles moving like clockwork and glistening in the sun.[18] This regularity was attained by conformity to the *tuki waka* or canoe song, which the chief or captain chanted from his post amidships, weapon in hand, stepping lightly from thwart to thwart, swaying now to this side and now to that with the rhythm and motion of the vessel. Samples of the *tuki waka* or canoe songs are given by a number of writers.[19] James Cowan has collected several of interest, one of which may be given here as an example of this type of composition. It is said by natives to be a part of the old canoe chant originally used on board the ancestral vessel Takitimu during her voyage to New Zealand many generations ago.[20] It indicates clearly the rhythmic nature of these *hautu waka*.

The leader begins:

Free translation

Papa le whastitiri, hikahiko ts uire,	The thunder crashes, the lightning flashes,
I kanapu ki te rangi; ru ana te whenue.	Flashes in the heavens, and the earthquake shakes the land.

Then waving his paddle or his weapon he chants:

He tia, he tia,	Dip lightly, dip lightly!
He ranga, he ranga	Now a long stroke, a long stroke!
Whakarere iho te kakau o te hoe	Plunge deeply your paddles
Ko a Manini-tua, i Manini-aro	The paddles Manini-tua and Maniniaro,
I tangi te kura, i Tangi-wiwini	Tangi-wiwini and Tangi-wa
I tangi te kura, i Tangi, wawana	wana.[21]
Tera te haeata takiri ana mai	See, dawn is breaking yonder
I runga o Matatera	On the peak of Matatera.
Ana Whaiuru, Wahaiuru,	Now, Whaiuru, Whaiuru
Ana Whaiato, Whaiato,	Now Whaiato, Whaiato.[22]
I arara tini, i arara tini,	Now a long, strong stroke!
I arara ri-i!	(Here the paddlers pause, while the canoe sweeps through the water under the impulse of the last stroke.)
E ko tena, tena;	Now, again, again!
E ko tena, tena;	Again, and again!
E hara ko te wai o taku hoe,	That was not the water from my paddle,
Ko te wai o taku hoe.	The water from my paddle.
Hei koti, hei koti, kei koti-i-i!	Now dig in, cleave it,
	A long, strong stroke!
E ka rere te rere i te waka	Now we're going along,
E kutangitangi, e kutangitangi;	How the canoe flies!
E kura tiwaka taua,	How fine the paddles sound
E kura tiwaka taua!	All together!
E kura wawawa wai,	My grand canoe,
E kura wawawa wai-i-i!	My treasured canoe,
	A treasure of the waters!
	(A long, strong stroke.)

The effect of such a canoe chant on the paddlers is excellently shown in the vivid description given by T. H. Potts in his too little known book *Out in the Open:*

"Each plunge of the paddle is directed by *te tangata hautu,* who shakes his paddle or quivers his fingers in exact time with the chant with which he encourages the rowers. Time is kept with most wonderful precision—the thirty paddles in the canoe dash aside the waters at the same instant. The stroke most frequently used is one strong plunge of the paddle, which is succeeded by a mere dip, which lasts while the way is on the canoe given by the preceding strong stroke. . . . Hark to the cry of *te tangata hautu,* 'Hoe, hoe, hoe, kaha, hoe kaha!' Swiftly is the craft urged forward. A *pa* or settlement comes in sight after rounding a turn; the *kupapas* (natives) increase the force of the plunging *hoe;* both canoes dash onwards in a terrific spurt. One feels the long craft bounding and quivering beneath the vigorous stroke. *Te tangata hautu* in a *ngeri* (song), frantically chanted, urges the panting *kupapas* to renewed exertions. *Hoe kaha, kia kaha, kia mau!* Then the burden of the song is taken up by the whole crew with a startling crash of sound. Spray dashes over the sides of the vessels and we rush through the water as though borne onwards by a wild crew of demons excited to the verge of madness. The settlement passed, all reason for showing off their strength ceases, and the sweating crew ease their paddling to a short quick stroke called *tupari.*"

From this account it is fairly easy to perceive the manner in which the working song acted as a stimulus to efficient performance of the task. Analysis of the actual effect produced shows that there are four main elements therein.

1. The expenditure of energy is rendered more efficient by providing regularly spaced time-points at which it can be synchronised. The rhythm facilitates co-ordination of individual effort.

2. The movements of the leader, the words of the chant, and the effect of participation in the responses or chorus divert attention from the physical strain of the work and so tend to relieve fatigue.

3. The song helps to raise the social temperature of the activity, or, to put it more concretely, it induces a feeling of greater cheerfulness in the workers.

4. The appeal of the leader and the ideas conjured up by the words of the song working through mental association act as a stimulus to the physical energies.

In this manner the working songs of the Maori are seen to have a distinct economic utility in increasing the efficiency of communal production.

NOTES

1. Best, *Maori Agriculture*, 158, 101.
2. For terminology of communal work see W. Colenso, *Mauri-English Leziken;* H. W. Williams, *Dictionary*, under words cited; also Best, *Mauri*, ii, 379–80.
3. *Wirtschaftsorganisation*, 39–40. The incidental statement, however, which he makes on the authority of Walsh and others, that in agriculture the Maori was compelled by custom to finish the planting in one-day cannot be accepted.
4. From John White's unpublished MS. (quoted by Best, *Mauri Agriculture*, 115).
5. *Nature*, 26 December 1925; *Argonaut*, 159–62. In the latter Malinowski has distinguished these two types of work under the terms "communal" and "organized" labour respectively. "These two conceptions are not synonymous, and it is well to keep them apart. As already defined, organized labour implies the co-operation of several socially and economically different elements. It is quite another thing, however, when a number of people are engaged side by side, performing the same work, without any technical division of labour, or social differentiation of function. Thus the whole enterprise of canoe building is, in Kiriwina, the result of *organized labour.*But the work of some twenty to thirty men, who side by side do the lashing or caulking of the canoe, is *communal labour"* (op. cit., 159). The distinction drawn is a very real one, but the choice of terms is rather unfortunate. Both types of labour may be communal, both are certainly organised. For without some degree of organisation, however rudimentary, some mutual arrangement, some direction of affairs, no undertaking which involves the co-operation of a number of persons, could have much chance of success. And the term "communal" simply implies reference to action by the *community;* it can bear no significance of antithesis to organisation. To contrast the two terms, then as if they were mutually exclusive, seems only to invite confusion.The usage of the older writers of "simple" and "complex" combination of labour, though perhaps a trifle clumsy, calls attention to the central fact of differentiation of economic function and may be allowed to stand. That his terms of "communal" and "organized" labour do not really present a valid contrast is shown by Malinowski himself in his subsequent description of labour in gardening. There are, he says, as many as five different kinds of *communal labour* in the gardens (p. 160). But it is clear from his account that, apart from the name, the main distinction lies in the different kind of *organisation* of each. For instance, the *tamgogula* and *lubalabisa* forms of communal labour "do not differ very much except by name; and also by the fact that, in the latter form, more than one chief or headman has to direct the process" (p. 161). But this direction clearly means *organised labour.* In other words "communal" and "organised" labour are not mutually exclusive types. The really relevant distinction which it is imperative to make in analysis is not that between "communal" and "organized" labour, which may describe different aspects of the same undertaking, as Malinowski has himself pointed out, but between differentiated and undifferentiated economic function in the case of the workers concerned.
6. J. L. Campbell, *Poenamo*, 79–82.
7. Various other descriptions of the hauling of logs and canoes bring out the same points—the outstanding figure of the chief, the exact co-ordination of effort, the rhythmic hauling song, etc; cf. Hochstetter (*New Zealand*, 270), who mentions seeing men, women, and children dragging a large canoe from the Awaroa creek to the Manukau. The leader, clad in a red shirt, and with a "battle-axe" (? *tewhatewha*) in his hand, skipped about "with the quaintest gesticulations", and with a chant, led the procession. See also J. W. Stack, *Kaiapohia*, 182; John White, A.H.M., iii, 102, for the pulling of Horouta canoe; J. S. Polack, *Manners and Customs*, i, 168, hauling of a log. In some cases the log took as much as three months of continued work to transport from the place where the tree was felled to the water side. A good description

of canoe hauling (with sketches) is given by Elsdon Best, *The Maori Canoe* (D.M.B. 7), 1925, 62–70.

8. For descriptions of the direction of work by the *tohunge*, v. W. L. Williams, "Kumara Lore," J. P. S., xxii, 36–41; J. Cowan, *Maoris of N. Z.*, 116, 172–8; cf. also John White, *Maori Superstitions*, 219; S. P. Smith, "The Tohunga Maori," *T.N.Z.I.*, xxxii, 253–70; A. T. Ngata, "Past and Future of the Maori," *Weekly Press*, 1892, Nos. 1448–50; W. B., *Where the White Man Treads*, 14; Best, *Maori Agriculture*, passim.

9. Best, *Maori Agriculture*, 101–2.

10. Proceedings, T.N.Z.I., i, 41.

11. Mr. Geo. Graham told me (1927) that *re* Paora Tehaere mentioned in Chapter III, though the lineal descendant of the old chief, Te Kawau, is not a man of ability and has no great authority among his people, he was nevertheless sent for only some few months before to remove a *tapu* from a piece of land at Purewa which was needed for railway purposes. Cf. also John White, *Maori Superstitions*, 223. An *ariki* who was a thief lost all influence over his people except in matters of imposing and removing *tapu*. It was desired that the *tapu* be lifted from a certain piece of land for cultivation. The *de facto* leader of the tribe could not do so; the *ariki* was appealed to. He refused, but at the united request of the people he performed the ceremony.

12. *Nature*, 26 December 1925.

13. *Arbeit and Rhythmus*, 6th ed., 1924. The more theoretical part of this work is not free from blemish, especially as regards Bücher's attempts to derive the origins of poetry and music from the rhythm of work. For criticism, see e.g., O. Leroy, op. cit., 85–7.

14. This last is a term also used to denote the leader of a flock of *kaka* parrots in flight.

15. Cf. Best, D.M.B., 4, 54, 60, and A. Shand, "Moriori Grinding Song," J.P.S., i, 81–2.

16. *Trad. and Superst.*, 1856, 163–5.

17. Hare Hongri, an accomplished member of the native race, and well versed in Maori lore, has some useful notes on this topic (J.P.S., xvii, 167). Cf. Sir Geo. Grey, *Motsatea*, 90–3, for a hauling song said to have been used when Tainui was dragged from the forest ("*Ko te tau tenei i toia mai ai a Tainui ki waho o te wao nui a Tani*"). Cf. Cowan, *Maoris of N.Z.*, 67–8, for another version, shorter and with considerable variation. There it is described as the *unu waka*, or canoe releasing song used to assist the hauling of Tainui over the Tamaki portage; see also *Moteatea*, 224, for another *tau waka*; Best, T.N.Z.I., xi, 250–1, for a timber-hauling song; ibid., *The Maori Canoe*, 66–9, for canoe-hauling chants; R. Cruise, *Journal*, 300; A. S. Thomson, *Story of New Zealand*, i, 136–9, 167.

18. *The Renowned Chief Kawiti*, etc., 10. Early travellers frequently remarked on the wonderful sychronisation effected in native paddling by the canoe song.

19. J. Cowan, *Maoris of New Zealand*, 82, 184–7; E. Shortland, *Trad. and Superst.*, 167–8. Cf. also for description W. Colenso, T.N.Z.I., xiii, 57, etc.; F. von Hochstetter, *New Zeland*, 297; J. A. Wilson, *Ancient Maori Life*, 31.

20. The original, obtained from Tuta Nihoniho by James Cowan, is given with a translation by Hare Hongi, J.P.S., xvii, 97–8, 104–5. There are some verbal differences from the rendering given here.

21. Names of sacred paddles belonging to the Takitimu.

22. Names of Hawaikian chiefs.

V

Introduction
Non-Market Cultures: Work and
Attitudes toward Time

Don Parkes stated (1980:292):

The study of time, whether as universal, biological, psychological, or sociocultural, has an integrative role among otherwise disparate disciplines. It provides a focus on a fundamental component of social organization and social conduct.

Wilbert Moore said (1963:9): "If activities have no temporal order, they have no order at all." Despite the significance of time as indicated by the above quotes, few anthropologists, aside from Hallowell (1937), Richards (1939) and Evans-Pritchard (1940), have shown a deep interest in the subject. It is only recently that a number of studies have appeared which deal with work as it relates to time (Harris 1975; A. Johnson 1975, 1978; Erasmus 1955, 1977; Gough 1975; Lee 1968, 1976, 1980; Minge-Kalman 1977, 1978; Minge-Klevana 1980; Pospisil 1963; Sahlins 1972; Whiting and Whiting 1974). These studies represent a wide diversity of methods and perspectives. Some studies attempt to assess how time is spent at work as compared with the way time is used during leisure. Other studies deal with household work as compared with subsistence work and work for wages. By and large anthropologists who have studied time have been interested in the cultural attitudes toward time more than in quantitative measures of time spent in various pursuits. But in many studies the quantitative and qualitative dimensions of time are intertwined and inseparable.

In all societies, but especially in non-market societies, time expressions both of duration and tense, are associated with social events or community achievements. Events remembered as social happenings become a time reference. For example, in our own society a person might say, "When President Kennedy was in office, such an event happened," or, "Last year, during the World Series, I did such and such." In non-market societies a long duration of time might be figured as a generation during which a certain group of elders were leaders in the society. Short durations can be related to cooking times—the time it takes to cook some rice, or to roast maize, or to boil a handful of vegetables. Periods which are devoid of any significant social activity are passed over without any terms to denote them.

It can be said that the social life of a community is reflected in the time expressions used. The names of days or seasons is reflected in the collective life. The Eskimos of Greenland divide up the day according to the ebb and flow of the tides. In the Society Islands, daytime is when the sea rises and night when the sea begins to flow toward the land. On the Marquesas Islands, night is "the hour of ghosts." Among the Yoruba, who keep cocks, they distinguish the day as "the cock opening the way," (daytime) and "cock-crowing before sunset" (nighttime). Nilsson 1920:38–9). The Banyankole use the term "milking-time" for 6 o'clock in early morning and 7 o'clock in the evening. In the social life of the ancient Greeks, the marketplace had great social significance and time was related to the market in the expression, "when the market-place is full," "before the market-place has filled up," "when a man rises from the marketplace to go home." All of these expressions are from the Iliad and the Odyssey (Nilsson 1920:36). Finally from Homer (Iliad, XI, 86) (1960) we see the connection between time and work in the expression, "when a wood-cutter prepares his meal after having fatigued his arms by felling large trees." The Greeks had good and bad calendar days for breaking in cattle. Taoism prescribes certain days for repairing houses or temples or for cutting out clothes. The calendar of the ancient Hebrews was based on the work that had to be performed during the year—planting season, harvest season—and many of their holidays were celebrations of work activities performed during the yearly agricultural cycle.

The reckoning of time is important as a means for the social interaction of a collective. All cultures need some notion of time and place. Social events require the presence of a number of individuals from different groups. This necessitates some common means of time designation which will be mutually understood by those involved. Religious ceremonies, rites, season festivals, hunts, military expeditions, markets, intertribal meetings—all require the cooperation of many persons at a fixed time and place and need a common time reckoning. The length of the week, which varies in different societies, is often based on economic activities and social events. The length of weeks among some non-industrial cultures is a result of when market days fall. The market must take place with sufficient regularity and frequency to permit neighboring communities who do not keep large stocks of food on hand to be able to obtain them from one another during market days.

Systems of time in a small, closely integrated community are not adequate when the field of contact expands. In industrial societies individuals from various social and cultural backgrounds must be coordinated. If they are to be synchronized in their work and other activities, they need a precisely defined time measurement and hence the need for a time instrument like a clock. As societies change from hunting and gathering, pastoral, and agricultural cultures to industrial ones, natural events no longer suffice as a framework for time reckoning. The social functioning of time systems was the very basis that led to the astronomical and mathematical basis for time systems. Natural events varied and did not occur simultaneously. Non-market societies use local, qualitative time systems based on concrete events. They are highly varied and unique. Urban societies use quantitative, homogeneous time systems, which are one-dimensional and the same for all communities.

Wilbert Moore (1963:6) said that time is rhythm, recurrence, and change. Each society has its own unique rhythm and sense of time. Agricultural people have a time rhythm that includes specific rest days from work, often based on religious values. Specified rest days are limited or unknown among hunting and gathering groups or fishing people who take their rest periods at random. A metropolis will have a time reference quite different from that of a small village. Time reckoning is dependent upon the functioning of the community. The mode of life and work performed determines which phenomena shall represent the beginning and close of workdays, workweeks, seasons, and the year. In those instances, as in non-market societies, where natural phenomena are used to fix the limits of time periods, the choice of activity is dependent upon the changes in climate and the biological transformations of plants and animals. In such societies time as such has no value in itself. People pursue their work until it is done, and then they may take up another task or do nothing, depending upon the season of the year.

Allen Johnson (1978:53–4) describes the contrast in his sense of time as he moved from an industrial culture to a non-market culture. He made several visits to the Machiguenga in the Amazon Forest in South America and then returned home to the United States. He reports that, whenever he made a field visit to the Machiguenga, after a period of two or three days he began to sense a definite decrease in time pressure which was both physiological as well as psychological. The feeling of a leisurely pace in life reflects the fact that in their work tasks and other activities the Machiguenga are never hurried or desperate. Each task is allotted its full measure of time and free time is never felt to be boring or lost but is accepted as natural.

When Johnson and his wife, both anthropologists, returned to the United States they immediately felt the pressure of time and a sense of hurrying. Johnson cites the economist Lindner (1970) who theorized that as a society produces and consumes more goods it experiences an increasing scarcity of time. Lindner sees this working in the following way. Increasing efficiency in work means more goods. In order to keep the economic system going, more consumption must occur to buy back the increase in goods. Thus, free time is converted into consumption time. Time spent neither at work nor in consuming is increasingly viewed as wasted time. Even on vacation in industrial societies, people are under pressure to consume. They are constantly badgered to "get their money's worth," to see more sights, to cram more activities into their vacation time, to spend and consume more. As compared with non-market societies, people in industrial cultures spend lots of time caring for the increased number of material goods they possess. The Machiguenga spend three to four times more working time making things than they do in the maintenance work of cleaning and laundering. The French pattern is just the reverse (A. Johnson 1978:54). This helps to explain the fact that labor-saving devices in households of industrial societies does not lead to more leisure time for housewives.

Summarizing, time and its relation to work and life is a measure of the character and quality of life in a society. It is also a reflection of how the social structure is organized and how the society functions. Societies that are affluent in goods and services seem to have a scarcity of time—they are time-poor. Cultures that have relatively sparse material wealth seem to have lots of time to spend on their tasks and have no notion of wasted time—they are time-affluent.

CHAPTER FOURTEEN

The Use of Time

BEATE R. SALZ

INDUSTRIAL WORK AND INDUSTRIAL DISCIPLINE: THE PROBLEM AND A BACKGROUND

The previous chapters have been devoted to a consideration of the skills, education, and health of prospective Indian workers as relatively isolable and obvious qualities which as such are of the most immediate interest to an incipient industry and which, by themselves, are held to be most amenable to testing and comparison in terms of given standards. The real and putative circumstances and conditions influencing these three qualities of the human "raw material" have also been taken into consideration and weighed in order to arrive at a first conclusion regarding the Indians' fitness or capacity for industrial work and its present-day requirements.

The following two chapters are to continue and conclude this survey of "single" qualities by examining an apparently integrated group of habits or routines which are pertinent to the question of industrial discipline. Modern industry holds certain expectations regarding a number of seemingly distinct qualities: it refers to them as "punctually," "regularity" of appearance at work, "reliability" of attendance, "steadiness," "sobriety," "perseverance" on the job and assigned tasks, observation of working schedules, etc. It is apparent that, when reduced to a common denominator, all these discretely enumerated qualities have to do with time. The scheme into which the following considerations are cast has to do with the problem of time in social life, with the nature of "discipline," and with allied categories, namely, "work" and "leisure" as distinct cultural conceptions.

"Discipline," in the more technical sense, is here understood as "the fitting of individual actions in such a way that the character of each and its relations to the rest can be accurately controlled in the interest of the end to which the whole is devoted. The importance

203

of discipline lies in *being able to count on the individual doing the right thing at the right time and place*.[1]

Discipline, in this sense, has to do with time. Time, indeed, is here the key concept. From an *economic* point of view, time is a budgeted commodity; *timekeeping*, on the other hand, in terms of its *social* function, provides a "useful point of reference" by which to co-ordinate "diverse groups and functions which lack any other common frame of activity."[2]

It will be seen that the present *scheme* of inquiry and analysis (in contrast to the *question* to which these two chapters are addressed) owes much to points raised by Henri Bergson (1944, esp. pp. 360–74), especially with regard to the "natural articulation" of time as over against scientific time. We substitute for science (which "admits of no essential moment, no culminating point, no apogee") the requirements of modern industrial organization of production. This substitution is perhaps not too unjustifiable since "scientific time and space are, in a sense, closer to . . . the average individual" of modern life, who "apparently . . . has become so habituated to the scientific time conception, which has infiltrated into the common sense point of view, that he finds it difficult to remove himself to a level which is psychologically more primitive." The modern (urban-industrial) individual thus tends to describe (and feel) time in Newtonian terms rather than in more "empirical" terms (Benjamin 1937:279; Johnson 1947, esp. pp. 15–31, and *passim*).

Outside modern physical science itself and its philosophy there are other hints as to the real and palpable differences in the apprehension and articulation of time, and of timed or timeable phenomena, situations, and events: these come from a comparison of "Standard Average European" and non-European languages and language structures and forms (Whorf 1941; Hoijer 1953), although there is a question whether and how far linguistic patterns and conceptions of time inferred therefrom influence actual behavior-in-time, or vice versa.

At any rate, for present purposes, it is being assumed that individual, "inner," private time is not only the strictly individual affair which it is (in terms of psychology) but may have groupwise, generally common features and thus a like general structure for peoples of like social and particularly, cultural situation. In other words, we have shifted *durée*, individually empirical, "experienced time" from the individual psychological to the sociological level; and we have concretized it.

Other observations have contributed to the present approach to time. Thus the phenomenon of the divergences in the use of time between modern urban and rural populations is, of course, known in a general manner. Rural sociologists sometimes comment on these differences, though only in very general terms and without drawing particular conclusions therefrom.[3] West characterizes well the distinctive characteristics of rural work as contrasted with most urban work: ". . . great variety in rural tasks," "the individual control of speed with which these tasks are performed," freedom from noise, tedium, and enforced, unsocial co-operation with other workers, and "the immediate, personally understood and simple relationship between work and livelihood" (1945:100).

Also the quite general tendency of deploring the budgetwise use and consumption of time in modern civilization according to the clock, the speed and artificial "rhythm" of modern urban and industrial life as over against the "natural" rhythms and leisurely flow of life ascribed to rural and peasant groups, is called to mind. Such perhaps romantic, nostalgic comparisons and expressions of petulance and resentment toward modern time regimes bespeak quite well an actual difference in "felt" or personally experienced time on the level of groups.

In this context it is not without interest to note that problems of "acculturation" are occasionally singled out for treatment in terms of time-behavior. "For example, an important item, among many such problems may be found to be Puerto Rican *work rhythms and tempos at variance with those which New York employment imposes.*"[4]

Of further illumination for our posing of the problem are Richards' observations regarding "the rhythm of work" among the Bemba of Northern Rhodesia, by which she means the difference (from our point of view) in the kinds and amounts of tasks performed daily, the apparently "erratic" change in working hours, the sheer bodily rhythms—in short, everything which distinguishes Bemba handling or "conceptions" of time, of periods, of work habits and work rhythms from those of industrially implicated man.[5]

"Time-budgets" are beginning to figure in recent ethnographic literature, particularly in studies on the economy of non-Western or non-Westernized peoples. These studies tend to emphasize the time spent on activities that are geared to main and supplementary ways of making a living within a given economy and within a given culture. There are few detailed observations along these lines. And as these tend to be related to given propositions of the science of economics, they tend to omit from their tabulations those activities that cannot somehow be identified as "productive." Else they are designed to give the lie to the "myth" of the lazy, undisciplined primitive man and his desultory working habits.[6]

It may be added that for the present question it is not significant whether differential time regimes are functions of specific cultures or directly or indirectly causally related to specific occupations (thus perhaps being "determined" by climate, the latitudes, the seasons, geography, etc.—as they well may be); our primary interest here is to show that *differential time regimes exist* and that their coexistence may have practical significance.

For if the modern industrial organization of work is viewed as a system of timing, a survey of the use of time such as is here proposed may serve as an analytical and diagnostic device by which to appraise traditional time uses in their potential bearing on industrial requirements.

Time, accordingly, is the broad frame of reference within which to examine the use to which Ecuadorean Indians put *their* time habitually and customarily; the manner in which it is divided up into "work" and "nonwork" activities or the Indians' distribution of events in time; and the systems and patterns in which work itself is carried out so as to gauge the nature of the work process itself in time.

The terms "work" and "nonwork" have just been employed and must be explained. For purposes of this discussion, "work" is not understood to be only that activity by which something is produced or effected according to intention, plan, or purpose. The definition here also, and very emphatically, includes the *attitude, set,* or *approach* toward the specific task of producing or effecting and the *spirit* and *behavior* in which this goal-directed activity is carried out. In other words, work is intentionally sober and unadorned activity related to the execution of a task or project.

Whether or not the product of such activity or the activity itself has a market value, and whether the task requires effort, sacrifices, or expenditures of any sort, or whether these are subjectively felt, is for the present purpose not of primary importance. Neither reward nor punishment enters into the present definition of work. It is meant to be applicable to the activity called "work" in modern industrial society as well as to the activities in a society such as the one under discussion.

The considerations leading to this unorthodox formulation of the concept of work as an operational concept are well illustrated in a generalization regarding the native populations of the Pacific Islands: ". . . in such cultures it is hard to draw a clear line, as Westerners do, between work and recreation. Much of the fishing, gardening, clearing, and other pursuits counted by Westerners as work is done in friendly cooperative groups under pleasurable conditions which approach recreation, while preparations for a feast, practicing a dance or clearing a sports ground for a meet may have all the vigor, discipline, and competitive spirit of hard work" (Handbook . . . 1948:185).

As will be noted at the proper place, the distinction between "work" (however defined) and "recreation" (as above) or, better, "leisure" would be out of place in regard to certain activities of a nonindustrial society, such as that of Ecuadorean Indians. In order to avoid the use of a concept which is bound to be misleading here, the admittedly clumsy terminology of "work" and "nonwork" has been chosen.[7]

"Leisure" is a phenomenon (and a "problem"[8]) that is specific to modern society, on the one hand, and of special strata of aristocratically oriented societies, on the other. This is one reason why the concept is inapplicable to Ecuadorean Indians, as will be shown, and why a neutral term had to be selected which would not conjure up our own notions.

By way of a not too far-fetched illustration, reference may be made here to the problems encountered by the Spanish in the sixteenth and seventeenth centuries in their attempts to exact from the Indians of Peru (then including most of present-day Ecuador) and Bolivia a required amount of work and to educate them to "systematic habits of work." Some aspects of the matter, pertinent to our discussions, are pointed out thus (Kubler 1947:392–94):

> The Spaniards do not seem to have comprehended that, for the Indian, no work was worth doing which was not infused by ceremonial symbolism . . .; work was punctuated by ritual and festive occasion; work itself was ceremonially performed [in precolonial times]. In Christian life, work and worship were separate concepts. The day of rest evoked no response from the Indian whose understanding of leisure was in terms of ceremonial exercise. Under Christian direction, the tributary was expected to do unadorned work for six days, divorced from all forms of ritual behavior. His daily devotions were a separate category, and labor, far from being a form of piety, was degraded into physical toil, without spiritual compensations.

Although the treatment of the problem may be somewhat novel, the problems to be discussed are, of course, old and well-known ones. Their presentation will be perhaps rather unorthodox, but they are cast into this form in an attempt to furnish a somewhat more distinct background to the problem arising from industrial requirements that consist in training "human beings to renounce their desultory habits of work and identify themselves with the unvarying regularity of the complex automation," the modern orthodox mechanized factory, and to make the independent craftsman, for example, "renounce his old prerogative of stopping when he pleases, because he would thereby throw the whole establishment into disorder."[9]

WORK HABITS AND WORK PATTERNS

The discussion of Indian work habits and patterns is divided according to the two methods or systems that can actually be distinguished, one that is individually performed, the other that is performed collectively or co-operatively.

A. Individual Work

In the case of individual work the larger part of the generally very scanty information again derives from observations made of Otavalo and similarly situated Indians. The daily round of chores and routine tasks of a basically farming population such as this one, generally living and working some distance from populated centers, is limited, humdrum, and sufficiently unspectacular to explain the scarcity of detailed information.

Such as these observations are, they refer to the alternations between given tasks, or the pattern of changing from one kind of work to another. Household and farming chores do, of course, impose to some extent their own regularly changing pattern of activities within the working day, as every housewife knows.[10] In the case of household industries such as weaving, work has been characterized as a constant alternation between and changing among heterogeneous tasks. Thus, though a man may be busily working from sunup to sunset, it is not sustained work at one task but a going from one to another and still another and back to the first, such as from weaving to hauling water to cleaning wool and back to weaving (Buitrón 1947a)—a working pattern which is no doubt relaxing but which certainly is not that of orthodox industrial production. There is, as we are informed (Buitrón 1947a; Parsons 1945: 51, 60, 61, 156, passim), remarkably little specialization of labor in connection with tasks within the household and in farming work, men and women performing a great many identical tasks and women helping men in almost everything. Weaving in Otavalo is practically the sole work performed exclusively by men and this only if done on the pedal loom. Where crafts prevail, men tend to do the skilled work, while women and children give proportionately more attention to farming and the care of livestock (Moomaw 1946:188). Children, depending on their ages, help in any task. From all this it can be inferred that the men's alternating work pattern just described is not imposed only by the inherent requirements of household and farm, since women and children could, in principle, look after these.

However, there is a rudimentary division of labor along the lines of modern industrially organized work. Some Indian weavers have enlarged their household "manufacturing establishments" to such an extent that they employ others (*peones*), who are paid by the piece; these weaver-peons are explicitly stated to observe a nonalternating pattern of work in that they apply themselves all day to a single task only (carding, spinning, weaving, dyeing, etc.).[11]

An observation kindly communicated by Mr. John Collier, Jr., throws some interesting light on the kind of discipline maintained within such an enlarged household enterprise (described to be working on orders, not "speculatively" for the market): there, the head of the family and master of the enterprise would not permit one of his sons to take out even a few minutes to satisfy the curiosity of his visitor regarding the preparation of some dye mixtures. The context of the incident made it clear that no resentment of an outside intruder or secretiveness was involved but that it was merely a matter of loss of time and the maintenance of shop and/or family discipline that were at stake.

It is in such larger household enterprises as *alpargate* ("sandal") making or the weaving of straw hats or rugs that the various operations are broken down and divided up among the members of the family or household, including the children (Buitrón and Buitrón 1947:61; J. Davis 1946:63–4).

One other feature of work patterns deserves mention, because it too reflects upon the treatment of work and the working process as a non-continuous one. That is the manner in which work is assigned, as in haciendas, or engaged for and undertaken by free peons or independent artisans. This feature constitutes a "task" system or a "task-within-time" system. Thus, in haciendas, the *huasipungeros* are assigned to various farm operations every morning, each assignment consisting of a definite task (*tarea*)[12] such as plowing or weeding a field of so many furrows of specified length. Similarly, they are held to take turns performing special services, for instance, serving a term of so many months as cowherd or house servant.

Free laborers (*peones*) hire themselves out "by the job" (*per obra*) as well as, though more rarely, by the day. Independent artisans such as masons and bricklayers, stonecutters, woodcutters, etc., who work from place to place, undertake work by the job and do a fixed amount of work for a fixed sum of money, sometimes within a stipulated period of time.[13] Similarly, the peons employed by the few larger weaving enterprises (or incipient factories, from the organizational point of view) in the Otavalo area are paid by the piece woven or the amount of wool spun, regardless of the time they spend on a given task (Buitrón 1947a).

Working time, then, is used for continuous, but disjointed activity, each activity tending to be a whole task without being necessarily related to the next in actuality or in concept. The alteration of tasks in time might, under given circumstances, be related to, or accentuated by, back-and-forth movements occurring in space.

With the exception of carriers and traders, who often and regularly journey long distances, Ecuadorean Indians on the whole are not travelsome.[14] What traveling there is normally occurs within the area surrounding a population center, be it ever so small, provided it has a church or chapel, a cemetery, a market, inns, some administrative officials, etc., and some opportunities for casual little jobs. Within such an area, Indians may move freely to and fro, but such mobility is deceptive because of its short range and because of its circuitlike character. Ecuadorean Indians' attachment to their homes is much emphasized by observers: they do not venture forth on long-distance traveling (as Guatemalan Indians, and to some extent also Peruvian and Bolivian Indians, do so conspicuously). What is of interest here is that a basic lack of venturesome mobility leads to a high degree of spurious mobility, which is mentioned here because it may affect directly the work pattern and accentuate the disjointed character of working. Thus Rivet, in proof of the attachment of Indians to their homes, miserable as these may be, says: "Cases of Indians are cited who work far away from home and who, after a hard day's work, make a long trip at night to visit it and return the following day to accomplish the daily task."[15] The majority of the free peons of a sector of Pichincha Province, which is said to be purely Indian, work in and around the city of Quito; some of them stay at the place of work from Monday to Friday and go home over weekends. But others commute back and forth daily (by foot), making a daily trip of 20 kilometers (12.5 miles).[16]

B. Collective Work

In contrast to the meagerness of information regarding individual work patterns, descriptions of collective or co-operative work institutions and patterns are both more frequent and more extensive. Passing reference has been made already to one feature of these traditional work arrangements, namely, their festive character. Being clearly extraordinary affairs, these *mingas* (also called *ayni, convite, cambia mano,* and by other terms) are conspicuous and have invited the attention of casual and expert observers alike far more than those everyday, continuous, and hence unspectacular activities which would throw light on individual work habits.[17]

A distinction should be made between *mingas* as arranged by Indians themselves and those which are ordered by local Indian or non-Indian civil or ecclesiastic authorities or by the large landowner.

In the first type, the *minga* is strictly an in-group affair, "a reunion of friends, neighbors, relatives for the execution of work for one of the members of the group." For a harvest, for other farming tasks too extensive to be executed by an individual farmer and his household, or for the building of a house or the transport of construction materials, an Indian raises a contingent of necessary hands by inviting his relatives and friends to help him in the particular undertaking on the basis of formal and informal reciprocity. While such work parties function essentially on a co-operative and reciprocal basis, the organizer of a *minga* furnishes food and drink, and the *mingueros* themselves may contribute housebuilding materials. They may also receive gleanings of the grain harvest or gifts of corn harvested. What with the serving of food and drink and the conclusion of the enterprise by dancing and general feasting, such a *minga* has all the earmarks of a fiesta rather than of work. All "have a magnificent time and it is more a fiesta than work."[18]

The second type of *minga* is held at the instance of bodies or persons generally not members of the in-group. Local public authorities call *mingas* for cleaning or repair of public squares and streets, for road work, for the building of a trail or sections of highways, for the digging of irrigation ditches, or for other works of a public nature. Functionally, at least, such *mingas* take the place of taxes. *Minga* service is obligatory, and summons for such work service have to be honored on pain of having some personal or household good confiscated to be redeemed by work or a money payment. Nevertheless, work performed on that basis may also partake of the festive character of Indian-arranged *mingas*, depending on the nature of the task to be accomplished and on the generosity of the local authorities, or of the single official arranging for a *minga*, in furnishing the drinks. Tools and also food are provided by the *mingueros* themselves.

Church *mingas* for the repair of church or chapel, etc., tend to be on a smaller scale and are informally arranged at the instance of the local *padre* through Indian chapel officials. *Mingas* for the benefit of a hacienda are nominally voluntary, and participants are formally invited rather than called up for service as in the public works *mingas*. Whether these *mingas* are undertaken by the Indians willingly or unwillingly, they too tend to be accompanied by liberal rations of *chicha* or *aguardiente.* "Chicha," as Rivet puts it, "is the promised recompense for the worker."[19]

While there is no indication that these collective and convivial work parties engender anything comparable to the machinelike rhythm of work which is said to be characteristic of collectively organized and executed tasks among other nonindustrial or preindustrial or primitive peoples, the alacrity and speed with which work in *minga* is executed[20] have been commented upon, quite apart from the good will and spirit prevailing under the best of circumstances. Since this type of collective work has been given attention here in so far as it may be relevant toward estimating work habits or patterns which might be brought into industrially organized work, the matter is summarily discussed.

There is no doubt that Indians can be organized into collective work, but hardly on the ground that *minga* furnishes the appropriate model. This conclusion needs some emphasis in view of the hope sometimes expressed in the literature dealing with the "Indian problem" which takes the existence of *mingas* as the traditional and natural expression of Indian co-operativeness and hence as capable of being utilized for modern institutions and activities. The evaluation of *minga* vis-à-vis industrial requirements is arrived at by considering three aspects not pointed out or made explicit in the literature that has been used here.

Negative evidence for the nonapplicability of *minga* in industry is derived from the fact that not a single instance has been cited of its use in craft work or, for that matter, in any kinds of work except those specified above (agriculture, construction, public works).[21]

Mingas, with the possible exception of those that are held for public works or only with a hacienda's own *conciertos,* are seasonal affairs. Where farming tasks are involved the point is self-evident, but it applies equally to housebuilding *mingas,* which are usually held during the agriculturally slack periods. This is one reason why *mingas* must be considered extraordinary events rather than matter-of-course and everyday work arrangements.

It has also been shown repeatedly that food and drink may constitute, among other things, the reward for efforts made on behalf of someone else. Workers bidden in groups for a special piece of work are, as has been seen, regaled by the bidder. Hence there is a chance that, in the event of an occasion requiring special or extra efforts, Indian workers will expect like treatment, be it by way of extra compensation, be it by way of "refreshment." Industry on occasion may, therefore, have to furnish the accustomed drinks— not necessarily as incentive but simply in answer to ordinary Indian expectations.[22]

Provisions of this sort are unusual, to say the least, in modern industry. The tendency is rather in the opposite direction, for reasons of "discipline" if for no others. Yet it needs pointing out that a totally "dry" industrial situation may not always answer native customs and expectations.[23]

In sum, institution and work pattern of *minga* provide no precedent for the standard industrial work pattern. *Minga* does not meet that requirement of industry according to which work ought to be performed soberly, regularly, and continuously. *Minga* does indicate, however, that common undertakings and work co-operation are not alien to Indians. It is on this ground—and the sporadic and apparently shrinking existence of common landholdings—that Indianists sometimes tend to hold certain hopes for the future shape of Indian economy. For Ecuadorean Indians, however, such hopes do not seem well-founded as far as industrial production is concerned. This type of collective undertaking lacks the substantiality of objective, functional work—in other words, of sustained activities geared exclusively to production.

C. The Problem of Adapting Native Time Regimens and Work Habits to Manufacturing Industry

The most general conclusion that can be drawn from the matters presented in these two chapters is that work as a whole for the individual tends toward diversification in time and in kind. Apart from the seasonal, there are special kinds of diversification that are related to household-farming-craft and service combinations. Whatever these combinations are, the exercise of any particular occupation other than that of daily tasks tends to be reserved for agricultural off-seasons or to be wedged between daily agricultural chores. Furthermore, work other than daily routine tends to be intermittent due to the punctuation of time by nonwork occasions. These occasions are numerous but relatively few in kind. Such as they are, they require massive, rather than evenly distributed, consumption of time. Moreover, from the Indian point of view and from the point of view of *his* social relations, they are unavoidable and imperative, a matter that has already been hinted at, but which will find more extended discussion at another point. In all, work is not only diversified in kind, but also exhibits discontinuities in time.

Both these features of work appear to be accentuated if daily work processes and individual work patterns, as in cottage industry, are considered. Daily work processes are discontinuous, and daily tasks are diverse and heterogeneous. The latter, moreover, are not related among themselves but related by virtue of the setting within which they are performed. Similarly, assignments to work and hiring out for work tend to be piecemeal, consisting of isolated tasks. The discontinuousness of the work "process" may be further emphasized due to special conditions such as distance between home and working place and the ensuing traveling back and forth, whatever the reason may be therefor (attachment to home, lack of facilities for lodging at the working place, etc.).

The manner in which Indians use their time, their habits and patterns of work, in no way predisposes them to the industrial production regimen and to the sustained routines by which uniform tasks are executed over relatively long stretches of time daily and every day; nor to a system of production that is based on budgetwise allocation of time to intentionally productive and intentionally non-productive ("recreation and leisure") categories; nor to one wherein, finally, time is of the essence not only for technical (i.e., budgetary and calculative) reasons, but also for reasons of social organization (i.e., considering the social function of time*keeping*).

In all these respects, the work and time-scheduling methods of Indians are not applicable to industry if the industrial system is viewed as a system of timing. There is a divergence between their habits of using time and those required by, or characteristic of, modern industry. The periodicities and rhythms of industrial life are not "naturally" those of Indian life. What is to be expected on the average and initially from prospective Indian industrial workers is a tendency toward a disjointed kind of work pattern that will express itself in daily performance as well as in delays and tardiness, irregular attendance and absences of varying durations, and a high degree of labor-turnover.[24]

An exception to this prognosis is perhaps presented by those who have already been habituated to or schooled in sustained work at uniform tasks and continuous daily work processes through large family-household industries and through the familiar and recognized authority. Such workers, however, will not be numerous, and they will presumably have fewer incentives than any other types of workers to enter modern industry. The same observation would seem to be applicable to Indians who are engaged in trading occupations, although they are the ones who have "acquired a notion of the value of time" that would in part answer that of industry.

The customary "task system" poses some special problems. First, supervision of those habituated to that system will tend to assume special importance and is likely to require a far more detailed organization in the assignment of tasks than is normally expected in industry (the necessity for oral instruction due to general illiteracy is here recalled).

Second, the "task system" has some implications with regard to hiring or job contracting and remuneration. Inasmuch as work consists, in the ordinary Indian situation, of a series of distinct jobs or tasks, time remuneration, as customary in industry and as preferred in most labor legislation, is not apt to strike a familiar chord among Indian workers. For instance, it is reported that Indian and Cholo workers, newly inducted into mining work, frequently fail to realize that large (for them) balances of wages are being kept for them by the paying office; instead, they ask the boss for little "advances," just as they used to ask the hacienda *patrón* for little advances against future crops and work obligations.[25] Thus there may be anticipated a pronounced disparity in understanding of work and remunerations as between these and modern industrial workers. For Indians the work unit, the finished product, is a completed task, and it is the completed task or product that is paid for. In other words, the conceptual and contextural precedent for remuneration is piecework remuneration, not remuneration for any slice of time spent working. It is hard to see how the confrontation in the industrial situation with a continuously incomplete task will make sense to the Indian, must less that a reward is bestowed for it. After all, Indians deal, no matter what the task, with visible wholes, not parts, of a product, even where operations themselves are divided among various individuals. The whole is, quite literally, not lost sight of, even in large household industries, where there is division of operations but not real specialization.

It should be clearly understood that piecework remuneration in industry is not advocated here as an incentive for Indians to work harder, or to avoid idling or cheating on the job; as such, piecework is of doubtful value since incentives have to come from somewhere else. Besides, Indians *are* industrious and work-habituated, thus "disciplined" to that extent. The justification for piecework remuneration rests here on existing work habits and work patterns and on this form's being understandable to Indians. In fact, this is a practice they may expect from an industrial employer, much as they might expect, analogously, the furnishing of food and drink as part of their regular remuneration or in support of any special efforts.

NOTES

1. Parsons 1937:507, paraphrasing Max Weber's concept of "discipline."
2. Mumford 1934:27. In reference to the succeeding, see also his suggestive remarks on the history of the clock as the key-machine of the modern industrial age, and his formulations of its consequences for the ethos, *habitus*, mentality, or pattern of average urban and industrial Western culture (pp. 12–18, 196–99, 269–73, 345).

3. See Sorokin, Zimmerman and Galpin (1930–32, III:360), where attention is drawn to this matter and a very sketchy set of data offered comparing timed activities of Russian industrial workers with those of Russian peasants.

4. From a report on Puerto Rican Communities in New York, research study on community organization conducted by the College of the City of New York, Prof. John Collier, Director, in *News Letter* of the Institute of Ethnic Affairs, Inc., Washington, D.C. (Vol. III, No. 2 [March 1948]:6; my emphasis).

5. Richards 1939:392–98; see also the context in which Herskovits (1948:271–72) discusses that matter.

6. Bücher 1909:408; also Thurnwald 1932:213–14. For examples of work-time budgets in anthropological literature, see Firth 1946:93–97; Foster 1942:35–38; Herskovits 1940:71–79; 1948:268–72; Tax 1953:85 ff.; Wagley 1941:25–26.

7. On this point and for much of the following discussion, cf. Curle 1949; Firth 1948.

8. From the growing body of literature and (apparently inconclusive) materials on leisure in modern society, see, e.g., Greenberg 1953; Denney and Riesman *in* Staley 1952:245–81, and particularly the roundtable discussion, "Leisure and Human Values in Industrial Civilization," pp. 50–91 with the illuminating remarks of its Hindu participant; also pp. 205–7.

9. Mumford 1934:173 and 174, quoting Andrew Ure, "The Philosophy of Manufacture . . .," London, 1835.

10. See Parsons (1945:185) and Santiana (1949:243–44) for the only—and at that, very sketchy—descriptions of a "typical day," which include that kind of tasks. Also Collier and Buitrón 1949:63–64.

11. Buitrón 1947a. For a fuller description, including time scheduling, of household textile industries in Ilumán, see IEAG 1953, No. 3:164 ff.

12. The unit of work performed in Chimborazo haciendas is a *raya*, one man-day's work, women's and children's work being counted as one-half *raya*, and as such is entered in the daily work books and other accounts of the hacienda and kept track of by the *huasipungeros*. See IEAG (1953, Nos. 10 and 11:19, 35, 47–49, and *passim*), for these and other details connected with work-assignments on haciendas.

13. Buitrón and Buitrón 1947:61–62, 66–67, 71; Buitrón 1949c, Table 2. A wedding fee, to be paid by the groom, may include (besides a cash payment) a *tarea* of fifty stones for the church (IEAG 1953, Nos. 10 and 11:60). See also Saenz 1933a:108–10, on hacienda work regimes; Serrano Moscoso 1946, summarizing labor legislation and labor contract provisions; and Moomaw 1946:166–67.

14. Buitrón and Buitrón 1945:10; Garcés 1941:23, 24; Parsons 1945:10 (also for the points following in the text).

15. Rivet 1903; similarly, Moomaw 1946:172. See also such behavior of a *huasipungero*, assigned by his master to woodcutting far away from his homestead, as described in Icaza's novel (1934).

16. Buitrón and Buitrón 1947:72. That "time values" change among certain groups is explicitly declared by Rubio Orbe (1953), in reference to Otavalo Indian vendors of textiles who travel long distances using autobus, railroad, and even airplanes.

17. On *mingas*, see Buitrón 1947a; Cisneros Cisneros 1948:187; IEAG 1953, No. 3:48–50; IEAG 1953, No. 11:135 (who also mention a new form, *minga de Oyari*, which is an abbreviated *minga* held from daybreak to breakfast-time among *huasipungeros* and Indian farmers who, after concluding the job, return to their regular daily tasks); Collier and Buitrón 1949:116–23; Garcés 1941:31; Murra 1947:820; International Labour Organisation 1949:94–96; Parsons 1945, *passim*; Rodríguez Sandoval 1949:95–96; Saenz 1933a:95–99, 111, 129–30, 190; Santiana 1949; Zambrano 1951:190.

18. Buitrón 1947a, commenting on such a housebuilding party.

19. Rivet 1903. The types of *mingas* held on behalf of persons or bodies who do not reciprocate in like manner by contributing personal help on another occasion have often been cited as survival forms of forced labor or tribute labor (*mita*), which was current in precolonial and colonial times and during republican times. These *mingas* have, on this ground and on others, been assailed as abusive of the Indians. It is difficult to draw the line between the voluntary and the forced aspect of *minga* in these cases, and there is no doubt that such systems lend themselves to impersonal and personal abuses, even though features may be incorporated that bespeak the meaning of voluntariness and reciprocity that is of the essence of *minga*. Thus there may be present the *hacendado's* bounty of *chicha* at a potato-harvesting *minga*, but the overseer's whip may figure just as prominently (see Franklin's eyewitness account of what is to all intents and purposes a *minga* [1943:80–81]). For a publicly arranged *minga* for the building of a trail, see Ferdon 1945. Daily newspapers sometimes carry announcements of local administrative officials for a *minga* to be held, say for the building of a section of highway or railroad, to which the populations of the respective localities are bidden.

20. Indians' working "rhythm" is slower than that of members of the other ethnic groups; and they are "less agile" than Whites and Mestizos, "lacking in nervous energy, and rarely execute forceful movements" (León 1952; cf. Florney 1945:33 with his description of Indian pace of work and his own irritation). One of the reasons given for Indian boys not taking part in playing football at school is that "they are very heavy-footed (*pesados*) and are no good" (*no sirven*) (IEAG 1953, No.3:228).

It is certain that Indians normally will not "snap to work" nor exhibit the kind of pep to which we are used, say, in an American soda jerker. The problem, if it is one, permits of several explanations and may be a matter of incentive and interest, of health, or simply one of habituation, analogous to the question of physical makeup and motor habits already discussed.

21. Cf. Zambrano (1951:190), considering all craft work: ". . . this work is carried out individually or by families and has nothing of the communal."

22. This should be distinguished from the fact that rations of food and drink are often part of the actual compensation for regularly and individually employed workers, such as hacienda peons. The above point should also be distinguished from the discussion regarding the necessity for industry to furnish its workers with food, from the point of view of health and physical efficiency.

23. A reminder of the grog-drinking British Navy and the dry American Navy seems not too impertinent here; also of the tea and coffee "addictions" and the work-breaks of, respectively, British and American workers.

24. Developments made during the second World War regarding arrangements of industrial work within the plant seem very pertinent to this particular point. These developments are reported to have occurred in the arrangement of work processes in mass production and consist of changes in the assembly layout *in concept* from the orthodox layout in *space* (or time). See Drucker 1946; also Digby 1949; cf. Staley 1952: 32 ff. on alternatives of organizing work processes in a factory.

It is to be wished that industrial and educational psychologists of the *Gestalt* school would interest themselves in this particular problem, as well as in the whole question discussed in these two chapters and in those problems which relate to skills and technical education discussed in the previous chapters. One such approach that has come to notice regarding training in specific skills is that presented by King 1947–48.

25. Franklin 1943:81–82. Cf. IEAG 1953, Nos. 10 and 11. This point and those raised further in the text may be compared with a suggestion that "it is conceivable that the pattern of working men's habits and social attitudes might be changed by altering the wage time span, that is, by paying wages at monthly or quarterly intervals instead of at weekly intervals" (Cohen 1949: esp. pp. 155, 156).

CHAPTER FIFTEEN

Time Allocation in a Machiguenga Community

ALLEN JOHNSON

The manner in which individuals spend their time is a basic dimension of ethnographic description. Under such headings as "the daily round," "the annual cycle," or "the division of labor by sex," most ethnographies eventually describe the broad outlines of time allocation in the community. This information is then used by theorists to construct comparative generalizations.

In general, however, ethnographic estimates of time inputs or product outputs are rarely quantified. Sahlins (1972), for example, has recently brought together some of the best quantitative production figures available to anthropologists. Employing studies such as those of Lee (1968) among the Bushmen and McArthur (1960) among Australian Aborigines. Sahlins (1972: 41–99)argues that hunters and gatherers typically work relatively few hours per day in obtaining ample food returns, a conclusion of particular interest for culture-evolution theory.

Despite the achievement of a relatively high level of quantification in a few studies, some serious measurement problems remain. The most serious concerns the representativeness of the data. Detailed study of time expenditure has usually been restricted to a narrow time period, such as four days (Lewis 1951: 63–71), or four weeks (Lee 1978: 36–39), during which the researcher attempts to observe, or to elicit through intensive interviews conducted once or twice daily, the ways in which a small number of individuals spend all their time throughout the period. But conclusions reached by this method are weakened by the limitations on the sample: first, in most subsistence economies seasonal variation in production is so great that a brief sample of one part of the year is rarely a reliable estimate for the entire year; and second, conclusions drawn from an intensive study of a few individuals cannot automatically be extended to the remainder of the community. A researcher's belief that the time period and the individuals in question are "average" (that is, intuitively representative) is not very much to the point; a representative sample is strictly speaking a random sample, and any departure from randomness is a cost which should be offset by clear research benefits before it is accepted.

A second measurement problem is that full-time studies of human activities are both time consuming and exhausting, because direct observation of activities is the only reliable technique for most purposes.[1]

A third problem is the absence of uniform means of reporting data. Sahlins (1972: 14–21, 57), for example, cites labor figures for hunter-gatherers and swidden agriculturalists which are not strictly comparable because of differences in reporting the data by the ethnographers. Thus, data on New Guinea horticulturalists refer only to labor in gardens, whereas data on the Bushmen refer to all food-acquiring activities, and the figures for Australian Aborigines extend even further to include cooking and the manufacture of implements. The data are perhaps adequate to demonstrate Sahlins' general point, but more precise analysis would increasingly find these data-incomparabilities unacceptable.

A solution to these problems could be sought in devoting more field time to the study of time allocation. Experience shows, however, that this strategy rapidly exceeds the point of diminishing returns. For although time-expenditure data are often crucial in anthropological explanations, they are seldom the only matters at issue; rather, they constitute one data set in far more extensive arguments. Devotion of major amounts of field time to collecting time-allocation data results in degrees of accuracy too detailed to interest most anthropologists, while simultaneously sacrificing such other basic information as exchange relations or kinship structure, which anthropologists also consider essential.

RANDOM VISITS

The data reported here, collected with the above considerations in mind, represent the tabulated results of a large number of random spot-checks on activities of members of a community of Machiguenga Indians in the Upper Amazon of Southeastern Peru. The technique was designed to make use of sampling procedures and computer processing (Johnson 1970) to increase the efficiency of a fieldwork project in which accurate estimates of time expenditure were needed.

The data were collected by Orna Johnson and myself as part of a more general investigation into Machiguenga cultural ecology, family organization, and sex roles, conducted between June 1972 and August 1973. Ten months of that period were spent in the community of Shimaa, along a tributary (Kompiroshiato) of the Upper Urubamba River in the Department of Cuzco, Peru. The Machiguenga of the Kompiroshiato typically live in small groups, either as single families, or as clusters of closely related families, varying from less than ten to as many as 30 individuals in a settlement. They derive most of their food from slash-and-burn gardens, cultivated largely by the men, supplemented by smaller quantities of food from the tropical forest and rivers, in the form of fish, grubs, wild fruits, and occasional large game such as monkeys or peccary. Small family groups are almost completely self-sufficient, except for occasional needs for trade goods such as aluminum pots and machetes. Machiguenga hunt with bow and arrow, manufacture their own cotton fabrics, and in the past have preferred to do without trade goods rather than become closely bound to traders or missionaries.

Through an increasing number of bilingual public schools, run by Machiguenga school teachers, accessibility to trade goods such as shotguns, manufactured cloth, and medicines is beginning to grow. The community of Shimaa has a bilingual school. Some households in the vicinity (within about two hours walking distance of the school) have been associated with the school for as long as eight years, others for much less than that, and a few have only arrived within recent months. In the meantime, others have left, preferring the self-sufficient forest existence to which they are accustomed. Those in the school communities are not yet strongly affected by the school, in the material sense at least. Only a few men or women own manufactured articles or clothing, and on the average less than 2 per cent of their time is spent in labor for wages or trade goods. The Machiguenga school teacher is the only member of the community who owns a shotgun.

Population

The population sampled included all households within reasonable walking distance (up to 45 minutes) from our house, so that they could be visited regularly. Under the scattered settlement of the Machiguenga this resulted in thirteen regularly visited households, with a total of 105 members.

Sampling Procedure

The sample included all members of the thirteen households. Visiting all households at the same time proved impossible as walking distances were so great. Therefore, the community was divided into two parts, upstream and downstream, which were visited alternately at random hours.

Households were visited only during daylight (6 a.m. to 7 p.m.) both because travel after dark is hazardous, and because visiting at night is not encouraged by the Machiguenga. Hours were selected in advance with a table of random numbers, and households were visited during the hour specified. Visits were not made every day because special events occasionally interfered; in any week, however, many visits were always made. Tabulations show that visits were evenly apportioned by hours of the day and by season. Visits were made on 134 different days, resulting in 3–195 cases (observations of individuals).

Recording Data

Visits were generally brief, which is well suited to Machiguenga visiting patterns. Visits could be as short as five minutes or as long as 45 minutes if other information were desired. The ideal was to describe the activities of housemembers at the instant before they became aware of the ethnographers' presence, but this was not often realistic, so sensitive are the Machiguenga to their surroundings. Activities of all members were described in longhand in notebooks, and the whereabouts of absent members inquired into. When feasible, such information was immediately verified by personal observation, but often individuals were fishing or hunting and such checks were impossible.

Coding Data

After the first month of visits, coding procedures were devised. Longhand notes were transferred after each visit onto coding sheets for later keypunching. The codes included time, place, person and activity. Activity codes were three letters arranged in order of generality, so that the first letter of the code specified a main activity, the second letter specified a subsidiary activity within the main heading, and a third letter, if necessary, specified a still more detailed subdivision. The main activity codes were:

1. Eating, including meals, snacking, or drinking beer, specifying which foods (maize, manioc) and how prepared (boiled, roasted).

2. Food preparation, including what food and how prepared.

3. Child rearing, whether nursing, holding, patting, etc.

4. Manufacture, specifying item and stage of manufacture.

5. Wild foods, including hunting, fishing, collecting.

6. Garden labor.

7. Idleness, including sleeping, awake doing nothing, awake chatting, recreation at beer party, etc.

8. Hygiene, including laundry, bathing, defecation, etc.

9. Visiting, including who visited and what exchanged.

10. School (applies only to ages nine to eighteen).

11. Wage labor (mainly for Machiguenga school teacher in exchange for tools).

Processing Data

The coding sheets are based on the 80-column IBM card, and are easily punched by professional keypunchers at low cost and low error. The data for this paper were processed using the Cross-Tabs II-program for the distributions in Tables 1–3, and the SPSS T-TEST program for the significance tests in Table 4. Midway in the research I returned briefly from the field to have preliminary data processed. These materials were most helpful in developing research questions for the latter phase of the research.

By randomizing the observations, problems of representativeness of the data were eliminated. By including whatever people were doing at the moment they were observed, the data constitute an essentially unbiased description of all activities, not just those, such as productive labor, which were of particular interest at the time of research. The brief time spent in recording activities took only a small fraction of the total field time. In fact, the visits brought us into frequent contact with community members who could then be interviewed for other purposes. Finally, observations were coded in the field and processed by computer during the fieldwork, so that results of the investigation could be used in guiding research as an integral part of fieldwork. The technique seems well suited to many anthropological purposes, by providing essential, well-quantified data on particular subjects without inhibiting the wide-ranging data collection commonly sought in holistic anthropological research.

TIME ALTERATION

Tables 15.1 and 15.2 exemplify the data obtained by the method outlined above. The time period covers the thirteen daylight hours from 6:00 to 7:00 p. m. The tables clearly reveal the transformation of time allocation from infants to toddlers, occupied with idleness and eating, to the diversity characteristic of adults, who reach a low of 18–19 per cent of idleness. This low figure for idleness is quite surprising; can it be that primitive horticulturalist/hunter-gatherers, living under low population density, are engaged in productive labor more than 80 per cent of their daylight time?

To be sure, the answer depends on how the notion "productive" is construed. We might follow Sahlins (1972:57) in considering only the amount of time spent in gardens as productive labor. Apparently

Table 15.1 Male Activity: 6:00 a.m. to 7:00 p.m.

ACTIVITY	INFANT (age 0–1)	TODDLER (age 2–5)	YOUTH (age 6–13)	UNMARRIED ADULT[1]	MARRIED ADULT
(in percent)	$N_0 = 100$	$N_0 = 358$	$N_0 = 290$	$N_0 = 22$	$N_0 = 550$
Eating	16.1	12.9	6.8	(0)	9.1
Food Prep.	0	0	1.5	(0)	1.5
Child Rear.	0	0	1.1	(1.7)	0.1
Manufacture	0	0	1.2	(0)	10.4
Wild Foods	0	0.4	9.2	(7.2)	15.6
Garden Labor	0	0.2	8.5	(8.5)	18.5
Idleness	61.2	61.4	41.4	(56.0)	18.1
Hygiene	6.3	1.5	1.8	(0)	2.5
Visiting	12.0	21.4	12.4	(5.2)	8.0
School	0	0	9.7	(17.8)	0
Wage Labor	0	0	0	(0)	1.6
Other	4.4	2.2	6.4	(3.6)	14.6

1. N_0 = number of observations
2. Due to the small number of observations, the data in this column are weak and presented only for the sake of completeness.

Table 15.2 Female Activity: 6:00 a.m. to 7:00 p.m.

ACTIVITY	INFANT (age 0–1)	TODDLER (age 2–5)	YOUTH (age 6–13)	UNMARRIED ADULT	MARRIED ADULT
(in percent)	$N_0 = 115$	$N_0 = 288$	$N_0 = 403$	$N_0 = 344$	$N_0 = 815$
Eating	12.3	16.5	11.3	9.5	7.0
Food Prep.	0	1.0	10.2	11.0	18.1
Child Rear.	0.8	0	3.3	6.4	8.8
Manufacture	0	0	1.0	14.6	15.9
Wild Foods	0	0	2.5	9.2	6.6
Garden Labor	0	0	1.1	3.0	6.6
Idleness	61.6	60.7	49.7	20.0	19.1
Hygiene	6.0	5.7	5.2	4.1	4.5
Visiting	18.5	14.1	4.2	4.9	5.8
School	0	0	8.3	11.8	0
Wage Labor	0	0	0	0	0
Other	0.8	2.0	3.2	5.5	7.6

N_0 = number of observations

once a group has been classified as slash-and-burn horticulturalists, Sahlins takes their garden time as an estimate of total productive labor. This definition, applied to adult married Machiguenga, finds the men productively engaged only 18.5 per cent and the women only 6.6 per cent of the time.

But I think this approach is overly typological. Simply because we might classify the Machiguenga as slash-and-burn horticulturalists does not mean that garden labor provides all their subsistence. Consideration of all food-getting activities reveals the men active in production about 35 per cent of the time, and the women 13 per cent. Furthermore, from here it is a small step to include as productive activities manufacture and food preparation. Some might also want to include childrearing and time spent in eating, hygiene, and even certain kinds of visiting. In that case, men appear to be productively employed 65.7 per cent of the time, and women 73.3 per cent (Table 15.3)

Depending, therefore, on which measure of productive labor we wish to use, we could conclude that Machiguenga men spend less than two and one-half hours or more than eight hours per day in essential subsistence activities, and that women spend less than one hour or more than nine hours per day. The advantage of providing a complete record of the activities performed by different categories of individuals should be clear: comparative theorists are then free to define variables in accordance with their theoretical aims rather than having to accept the incommensurable figures each idiosyncratic fieldworker may choose to publish.

A further breakdown of time allocation appears in Table 15.4 giving a more complete view of the division between the sexes. For example, differences between men and women in the gross category, "manufacture," are not statistically significant; but subheadings within that category reveal that men do nearly all the work involving woodworking, whereas women are predominantly concerned with making cotton cloth, and these differences are statistically significant. In obtaining wild foods, men are the only hunters, but men and

Table 15.3 "Productive" Activities: 6:00 a.m. to 7:00 p.m.

	Married Men	Married Women
All Food	34.1% (4.4 hr.)	13.2% (1.8 hr.)
Manufacture	10.4% (1.4 hr.)	15.9% (2.1 hr.)
Food Prep.	1.5% (0.2 hr.)	18.1% (2.4 hr.)
Child Rear.	0.1% (—)	8.8% (1.1 hr.)
Eating, Hygiene, and Visiting	19.6% (2.5 hr.)	17.3% (2.2 hr.)
TOTAL	65.7% (8.5 hr.)	73.3% (9.5 hr.)

women both fish and collect fruits, grubs, etc. In horticulture, women's only significant contribution is in the harvest. In sum, the Machiguenga division of labor by sex is extreme in terms of observed behavior. Yet each sex puts in a relatively long working day, if that term is broadly defined.

DISCUSSION

A large number of special-interest tables could be generated from the data collected in the random visits. Tables which have already been of use include the distribution of tasks by time of day, the distribution of tasks by season, and the frequencies of visiting between different households. Presentation of these and other tables will be reserved for appropriate publications, but a number of general points have emerged which bear on the value of such data and techniques for collecting them.

The principal advantages of describing time allocation in this manner are:

1. The resulting data are quantified at a high level of measurement, and can be compared with exactness across cultures.

Table 15.4 Division of Labor by Sex (Married Adults)

ACTIVITY (in percent)	MARRIED MEN (n = 15)	MARRIED WOMEN (n = 20)
Eating	9.1	7.0
Food Prep.*	1.5	18.1
Child Rear.*	0.1	8.8
Manufacture	10.4	15.9
Woodwork*	6.7	0.6
Cotton Cloth*	0.1	13.5
Other	3.6	1.8
Wild Foods*	15.6	6.6
Collecting	2.9	2.5
Fishing	5.7	2.3
Hunting*	5.7	0
Other	1.3	1.8
Garden Labor*	18.5	6.6
Clearing, Burning,		
Planting	3.7	0
Weeding*	5.8	0.3
Harvest	6.1	5.1
Other	2.9	1.2
Idle	18.1	19.1
Hygiene	2.5	4.5
Visiting	8.0	5.8
Other	16.2	6.6

* Differences are significant at p < .01 level (t-test).

2. Erroneous conclusions reached intuitively can be corrected. For example, after months of being with the Machiguenga in a variety of settings, I came to believe that the women were idle much more of the time than the men. Table 15.4 reveals that there is no significant difference in idleness between adult males and females. Women's work is more often conducted in a sitting position and at a slower pace than men's work,[2] and that probably led to my incorrect impression. Whenever anthropologists estimate time allocation without some objective research method, errors like this are bound to arise.

The randomness of the visits introduces an element of unpredictability into the anthropologist's routine, counteracting the natural tendency to be predictably in certain places at certain times. It thereby provides the anthropologist with a wider range of experiences than he or she might otherwise encounter.

A few rules of procedure should be observed in conducting random activity surveys:

1. Visits should be random (or occasionally stratified) samples of:

(a) the population.

(b) the time of day.

(c) the days of the year. Random visits scheduled in advance should not be missed except for good reason, such as special events or situations of personal danger; and a minor inconvenience, such as a rainy day, should not interfere, since this would lead to just the kind of bias to be avoided (in this case, a bias against rainy-day activities).

2. All activities should be recorded, not just those of special interest, since the overall configuration of activities is the theoretically most useful form of the data.

3. All activities should be coded unambiguously according to person, time, location, and activity. Activity codes may be as detailed as necessary. As long as codes have unambiguous meanings, those assigned in the field may be punched directly onto IBM cards without time-consuming recoding later.

CONCLUSION

The data reported in this paper represent a random sample of daily activities of members of an Indian community of the Upper Amazon. Estimates of time expenditure are basic data in ethnographic reporting, but to be useful for cross-cultural theory construction they should reach a high level of measurement and constitute a truly representative sample of the activities of the community being described. Owing to a natural tendency to find patterns through implicit mental processes, the memory of both the ethnographer and the informant in such matters is liable to be faulty. Since these mental processes are culturally determined in part, reliance on memory is bound to distort descriptions of time allocation in some unpredictable direction determined in cultural notions of what constitutes "spending time." The ready availability of computer-processing of masses of quantitive data has opened the door to descriptive techniques which avoid such biases, yet at relatively little increase in field-time costs.

NOTES

1. Informant interviewing may be a useful supplement, to estimate time spent in locations where the researcher was unable to follow, but this cannot stand alone as a reliable technique.

2. Measures of calorie energy expenditures by task show that Machiguenga women consistently expend fewer calories at work then men.

Section 2

Mixed Cultures

VI

Introduction
Mixed Cultures:
A Clash of Work Values

Cultural values are shared conceptions within a group or culture concerning beliefs and behavior considered desirable. They are the ideal to which members of a culture aspire and therefore they influence the behavior of community members. Values may apply to very general principles, to situations, or to very specific events or things. As with any set of rules in a culture, values can be, and are, often violated. However, when values are violated, the violations occur within the overall cultural context; the very violation is testimony to the strength of the cultural norm. The values of a society tend to form a coherent system. Every society has a ranking of values and a systematic connection between its values and behavior. Values functioning as a system is reflected in the fact that general patterns of orientations can be identifed in a culture based on its society's values and norms.

Florence Kluckhohn (1953) has identified five dimensions of value orientations along which cultures can be described. She maintains that cultures differ from one another according to their value orientations and that the differences in values impact other more concrete aspects of the culture. This is important for those studying work, since work is one of the concrete aspects of culture significantly affected by value orientations. Kluckhohn's five dimensions are:

1. Humans' basic nature, which can be conceived as either good, evil, or a mixture of the two. A part of this is the belief as to whether human beings can change or are immutable during their lifetime.

2. Humans' orientation toward the past, present, or the future.

3. Humans' relationship to nature: subordinate to it, an integral part of it, or master of it.

4. Humans' primary purpose in life: being, being-in-becoming (self-actualization), or doing (achievement).

5. Humans' primary relationship to other human beings: individualistic, lineal (family), or collateral (one's peers).

The orientation to time, the relationship to nature and the relationship to other human beings have been previously discussed in this book, relating these values to work. Kluckhohn points out that these value orientations differ from society to society, and also differ within complex societies with varying classes, ethnic categories and religious groups.

All societies have a more or less integrated pattern of beliefs, values, structures, and practices. They also have to varying degrees elements and patterns that are disruptive and dysfunctional. These disruptive elements cannot simply be torn out of a culture, which is a whole, containing positive and negative elements intricately interwoven. What seems like a dysfunctional element may in fact be a logical and inevitable part of a broader pattern that is important to the entire culture. It is when an entire value system is under attack, when its basic work organization or its religion is threatened, that disorientation and malaise set in and the culture's lifeways are threatened. When this happens, there are symptoms of social disorganization, in the form of demoralization, unrealistic escape mechanisms, and social conflict.

Values can be implanted through the dictates of authority and authority figures, through tradition and custom, and through education, both formal and informal. Values may also be based upon individual preferences, family upbringing, religious beliefs, political views, and occupational perspectives. In small-scale, non-market cultures, there is no wide diversity of values based on occupation, education, and class. There is a homogeneity of behavioral patterns and less individual choice of values because of the integrated nature of the culture. Everyone has almost the same level and type of education, and they pursue the same work tasks. Alternatives and choices arise in non-market cultures when these societies have contact with industrial societies which offer work for wages, new technologies, and new products to consume. Alternatives also arise when individuals leave their non-market cultures and migrate to industrial social settings.

Values which are prevalent in a culture are often accepted by the members of that culture in a way that is not expressed, but assumed, that is not articulated, but felt, that is not conscious, but subconscious. They are taken for granted and for that reason are very powerful.

An attack on such fundamental values is an attack on the individual and the group. Cultures are whole social fabrics, and if an attempt is made to change a part without taking into consideration all other aspects of a culture the effect can be chaos and disintegration (C. Kluckhohn 1962:337).

Clyde Kluckhohn relates how the Navaho Indians of the southwestern United States have been going through a process of change, forced and unforced, in which there is a fundamental clash of values. The Navahos' value system is based on collectively organized reciprocal services in work. As a culture the Navaho do not stress the individual competitiveness that one needs to make one's way in the larger white society. When Navahos enter white society there is nothing there to replace the collective interdependence that they enjoyed in their own culture; the result is dislocation, resort to escape mechanisms, and chaos for the individual.

The Navahos had no choice in the matter of becoming a mixed society. The world around them was taken over by an advancing industrial society, and the Navahos were torn between their own former values and those of the larger, more powerful white society. The values of the white society were urged, if not thrust, upon the Navahos by teachers, missionaries, Indian agents, and others from outside their tribes. The values of the white society were also part of the lure of work for wages to which the Navahos responded, especially when times were difficult economically.

Some of the outsiders did conscientiously try to take account of Navaho customs. But, as was often the case, no account was taken of the underlying Navaho values, and the outcome has been seen as deplorable by both Navahos and whites alike (C. Kluckhohn 1962:341). It has not been possible for the Navahos to wall themselves off in their communities and insulate themselves from American ways like the Pueblos did. Nor have Americans nor the United States government been exemplary in their sensitivity and understanding of Navaho values. The result has been a clash in values in which the most painful impact has fallen upon the Navahos.

Mixed cultures are inherently filled with value conflicts because of the interplay of two cultural worlds. The study of such cultures is particularly significant for examining the process of social change. Value systems are the most resistant to change because they are so deeply embedded in individuals and reaffirmed by social institutions. Communication is a key factor in the process of integrating the values of a society. In a non-market society, communication is direct, face-to-face, and mutually intelligible. In industrial and other market societies communication is diverse, diffuse, very often ambiguous, and controlled by those who control the mass media sources. Diversity is beneficial in market societies because it offers a wide range of choices of ideas and values. But it can be non-beneficial because it is difficult to establish consensus. One of the main problems of market cultures is their lack of clearly formulated sets of values to which members of the society can subscribe. Members of non-market cultures find it easier to communicate with each other, and they have a time-honored set of beliefs and values to which almost all members of their society are committed.

The selections which follow deal with persons in non-market cultures who are drawn into a market environment through migration to urban centers or by the inroads of market economic relationships into the non-market society. In these situations one can observe all the conflicts of work values previously discussed—time-oriented work versus task-oriented work; a rigid system of control at work versus a flexible, unhurried approach to work; the view of work as a means to an end versus seeing work as an end in itself.

The clash of work values that takes place when people from non-market environments enter market conditions involves not only work relationships but the entire personality system of the migrant. The non-market person has been brought up in a world based on close-knit family relations and kinship support. In a market economy they are atomized and isolated. The values and behavior appropriate to their villages and communities do not prepare them for the competitiveness of market societies. In many non-market cultures, although not all, aggression is repressed in order for the community to maintain its system of cooperativeness. When Eskimos are confronted with hostile behavior they respond by leaving the person exhibiting the hostility or greeting it with silence and ridicule. This behavior is not uncommon in non-market societies and when the clash of values becomes unbearable it may happen. In the 1960s, in Greenland, the Thule Eskimos relocated themselves as a community following a dispute with the United States military command on their territory.

The situation of mixed cultures—societies with differing value systems, communities which stand between two worlds, migrants who move from one culture to another—is a crucial one at this time in world history. The earth has become a much smaller planet with differing societies and cultures increasingly having more contact with each other. There are few, if any, cultures which are totally isolated. The mass media and other types of communication are bringing to people throughout the world information and knowledge about diverse societies with differing value systems. The contact between societies with different values raises the question as to how, and how long it takes, to shift values from one culture to another. It is particularly important in modern society with its intergroup prejudices, vested interests, and cultural rigidity operating within a cosmopolitan social maelstrom. Anthony Wallace (1951), in a study of Iroquois cultures, states that no cultural characteristic can be successfully changed within one generation if it involves fundamental value systems and beliefs. Hallowell (1952) says that it cannot be done in less than three generations. Felix Keesing (1966:416) believes that if the mother who has the major intimacy with the young child is sufficiently convinced of the rightness of a new tradition that values might be successfully transmitted in two generations. Keesing also states that in the first generation, at least, where individuals are wholly conditioned in childhood to one value system and are then called upon to make adjustment to another, it is unlikely that whatever modifications they make will reach down to the core of their value system.

The greatest value conflict and anxiety arises in cases where the basic values tend to be thrown into doubt or collapse. Anthropologists have observed that even with religious conversion by people in nonmarket societies, older beliefs continue to persist. An American Indian, while consciously a Christian, may report dreams of religious drummings, witches, thunderbirds, and other phenomena of his or her background. Work is such a persistent, daily activity that it must be confronted constantly, and where there is a conflict of values it cannot be easily avoided, if the individual wishes to remain at work in a market culture. The selections which follow only touch on the question of the clash of values, but they deal with the first generation of contact, which, as indicated, is the most severe in its impact.

CHAPTER SIXTEEN

Money Work, Fast Money and Prize Money: Aspects of the Tahitian Labor Commitment

BEN FINNEY

The expansion of market-oriented and industrially organized activities over the world entails a revolutionary change in mode of livelihood for literally millions of people. Those formerly dependent on subsistence and cash crop production are rapidly turning to wage labor. This growing *labor commitment*—to borrow a term from Moore and Feldman[1]—by which is meant the wholehearted acceptance of wage labor as a permanent mode of livelihood, is a process that demands the attention of all social scientists. I believe that anthropologists have a unique contribution to make in understanding labor commitment among the various peoples of the world. Their tradition of lengthy study, of learning the local language, and of analyzing their subjects' categories can be used with profit in such situations. They should go beyond statistics on labor involvement, or questionnaire-elicited "attitudes," and focus on how people perceive work, and the alternative modes of employment open to them. One of their goals should be to map out the cognitive view of work that lies behind the choice of wage labor as a mode of livelihood.

A brief example of such an anthropological treatment of the question is drawn from Polynesia, where—despite the European stereotypes of carefree and idleness-loving islanders—there is a growing labor commitment.[2] The recent transformation of the Tahitians from farmers and fishermen to a people largely dependent on wage labor provides the substance for this paper.[3]

JOB AVAILABILITY IN POLYNESIA

Tahitians need not leave their home islands to seek work, for there are plenty of jobs in and around Pape'ete, the capital of Tahiti, and all the surrounding islands that constitute French Polynesia. Pape'ete is a bustling port town jammed with Polynesian immigrants, Chinese storekeepers, European officials, military personnel and tourists. Its harbor, crowded with trading schooners, freighters, cruise ships and naval vessels, links French Polynesia with the outside world as does its airport where jet flights arrive and depart almost daily to and from North America and Australasia. Almost 40,000 people live in the Pape'ete urban area; this urban mass accounts for about three-quarters of Tahiti's population, and close to half the approximately 90,000 people inhabiting all of French Polynesia.[4] Almost all Tahitians in the Pape'ete area are workers, many living in slums that have recently sprung up along the outskirts of town[5] A majority of those living in rural districts of Tahiti commute daily to jobs in the urban area. Some Tahitians living in the most remote districts, and on neighboring Mo'orea Island, work in town and return home only on weekends. A Polynesian proletariat has been created in Tahiti.

This proletariat is a fairly recent phenomenon, for until the last decade most Tahitians were peasant farmers and fishermen who depended on copra, vanilla and other crops for their cash income. In previous decades there were some jobs available in plantation agriculture, in the phosphate mines on nighboring Makatea Island, and with trading firms and businesses in Pape'ete which did provide many Tahitians with an introduction to wage employment, but the total number employed at any one time was small.[6]

In the late 1950's the balance turned from peasant occupations to wage employment. Increased French government spending, and, for Tahiti, a huge investment of metropolitan funds in tourist facilities and other new enterprises, brought an economic boom that provided thousands of jobs in construction, transportation, government services, new businesses, and even a few small factories. Immigrants from outer islands began pouring into Pape'ete seeking work and many living in rural Tahiti began commuting to jobs in town. The 1962 census showed that over half the economically active Tahitians were wage laborers.[7] Recent French expenditures for the construction of nuclear testing facilities in French Polynesia have accelerated this economic boom. In mid-1965 officials estimated that over three-quarters of all able-bodied Tahitians were wage laborers.[8] To prevent further desertions of farms and plantations by Tahitian peasants eager for wage employment, plans were then being formulated to import laborers from Portugal.

Granted that Tahitians have recently shown a preference for wage labor over peasant occupations, the question is still open concerning the degree to which Tahitians are committed to a life of wage employment. To answer that question we must first examine the economic calculations made by Tahitian peasants-turned-workers, and second, the Tahitian cognitive view of work.

THE ECONOMIC CALCULATIONS

Upon first analysis the increased "economic" benefits offered by a life based on wage earning would seem to provide sufficient explanation of the Tahitian eagerness for wage employment. Tahitians now have available to them a wealth of consumer goods—radios, imported foodstuffs, beer and wine, motorcycles, automobiles, and even television sets—which increased buying power derived from wages enables them to purchase. Most Tahitians calculate that wages, particularly today's inflated wages, are higher than what they could make in cash and kind by continuing to farm, fish and produce cash crops. In addition, the extension to Tahiti of the French system of family allocations for dependent children has increased further the advantage of the wage earner, since only he, and not the self-employed peasant, receives these substantial benefits. The Tahitians have long participated in a money economy; they now seek to maximize their returns in it by working for wages.[9]

But economic calculation alone does not explain the wholehearted manner in which Tahitians have taken to wage employment. It would be an exaggeration to say that sheer economic pressure has been the only force impelling Tahitian peasants to seek wage labor. Most could still earn a living from the land, and for a few at least, considerable profits—higher than the returns from most jobs—could be made from food crop production. But it is the Chinese farmer, not the Tahitian, who farms food crops (usually on land leased from Tahitians) and earns these high profits. The eagerness of Tahitians to abandon peasant pursuits can only be fully understood by examining their cognitive view of work.

THE COGNITIVE VIEW OF WORK

In general, Tahitians consider "work" (ohipa) to be onerous. But some types of work are considered more onerous than others. "Farming work" (ohipa fa'apu), a category which includes both subsistence and cash crop production, is negatively viewed by most contemporary Tahitians. Unlike Redfield's ideal peasant type, few Tahitians express reverence for the soil. Most denigrate farming as being dirty, difficult and unexciting. "Money work" (ohipa moni) as wage labor is known, is positively valued as the modern and exciting way to earn a living. Most Tahitians, in fact, find it hard to conceive of a life without "money work," as the following example illustrates: In talking with me, the Tahitian cook of a large tourist hotel happened to mention that he once served aboard an American yacht that called on Tikopia, the isolated Polynesian outlier in the Solomon Islands.[20] When I asked what impressed him most about this island populated by his distant Polynesian counsins, he replied: "There is no money work there.'

"Money work" is desired not only for itself, but also because of the immediacy of wage payments. "Money work" yields what Tahitians call "fast money" (*moni 'oi'oi*) which comes every week on payday, instead of "slow money" (*moni taere*) which comes at long and irregular intervals from cash crop harvest. It is "fast money" which provides funds for car and motorcycle installment payments, for the daily diet composed of imported foodstuffs, for beer and entertainment, and not the "slow money" which takes so long to come, and is infrequently paid.

The Tahitian desire for immediate instead of delayed reward brings into focus another important feature of their cognitive view of work which bears on the problem of labor commitment. Anyone familiar with how Tahitians work for themselves, or for other Tahitians, know they are capable of sustained and conscientious work. For example, self-employed Tahitian pearl shell divers cheerfully perform extremely arduous and hazardous work, and at a pace that astounds the observer. In fact, their zeal for more and more pearl shell sometimes leads to fatal accidents as they step up the frequency and duration of dives and fail to rest sufficiently between them.[11] Yet many Europeans characterize Tahitians as lazy and unreliable workers. They complain that Tahitians in their employ are not punctual, and that they take every opportunity to malinger, particularly when not directly supervised.

This conflict between Tahitan work performance in European and Tahitian contexts is, as one would expect, largely due to differing conceptions of how work should be defined, scheduled and compensated. This is a classic case of the conflict between the European idea of looking at work in terms of time, and the probably more widespread idea of regarding work in terms of tasks to complete. To paraphrase Goodenough's analysis of this conflict,[12] Europeans tend to organize work in relation to the clock. Work is a continuous process in which people are employed to put in so many hours a day. After the allotted eight hours are up, the worker stops even though the job may not be completed. He returns to the job the next day, or a worker on the next shift takes up where he left off. But the Tahitian, like many workers from nonindustrial societies, sees work not as time-oriented but as task-oriented. Tahitians prefer to conceive of work in terms of a definite task to complete—a field to clear, so many coconuts to husk, or a trench to dig. Payment, when working for others, preferably comes at the completion of the task; not after so many hours or days of work.

Wage work that is defined in terms of task is called "prize work" (*ohipa ta re*),[13] a term which contrasts to work defined in terms of time, which is called "hour work" (*ohipa ta hora*) or "day work" (*ohipa ta mahana*). Though he may take his time in completing a task organized by "prize work," most often the Tahitian rushes to complete it as soon as possible. A popular etymology of the term "prize work" connotes this approach: Tahitians say the term stems from contests between workers in ancient days whereby the first to finish a set task won a prize.

Employees who understand this Tahitian preference try to organize their jobs by "prize work." (Notably, these employers share a high regard for Tahitian work capabilities.) In some jobs, such as field clearing, this is easily arranged. The worker is told to clear a field, and is promised so much for its completion. Other jobs, however, are not so conveniently arranged as "prize work." One trucking firm, engaged to haul gravel from a steam bed to a construction site, tried to pay its driver per load carried, but found the results disastrous: accidents and traffic citations issued to speeding drivers increased greatly.

In a factory on Tahiti that I studied, European employers successfully evolved a mixed system of "prize work" and "hour work." The factory produces dried, grated coconut meat for export to France. The essential manufacturing operations involve (1) husking the coconuts, (2) chipping the inner shell from the coconut meat center, (3) scraping the brown rind from the coconut meat, and (4) tending the grating and drying machines.

After several years of experimentation with straight hourly work, and on final recognition by the management of Tahitian task-orientation, the first three work stages were organized as "prize work." The men who husked the coconuts, and the women who subsequently chipped and scraped them, were given a quota of so many nuts a day, above which a premium was paid. As it was not feasible to organize those tending the drying and grating machines by "prize work," these workers were paid by the hour. Notably, their jobs were the least popular in the factory.

Anyone doubtful that Tahitians are capable of fast and sustained work should observe these factory workers whose tasks are organized by "prize work." The men huskers start in the cool of the dawn, work for three or four hours until the sun becomes hot, then take the mid-day hours off, for lunch, a nap, or perhaps some spearfishing. In the cool of the evening they return for an hour or two to finish their quota. When husking, they work at top speed, usually without taking any breaks, to finish their quota in the minimum amount of time.

The women chippers and scrapers work as fast as the men, or even faster. From the time the morning whistle blows to 7:00 a.m. until the lunch whistle at 11:00 a.m. these women sit on tiny stools amid husked coconuts, chipping and scraping at a furious pace. Many work the four hours without a break, not even for urination. After a quick lunch they return for an hour or two to finish their quota. Their day's work done, most return home to wash clothes, care for their children and prepare the evening meal. The performance of these factory workers testifies to the high work capabilities of Tahitians when their efforts are organized by "prize work."

The discussion so far concerning Tahitian labor commitment may be summarized in the following paradigm:

In the conceptual domain of "work" (*ohipa*)
"money work (*ohipa moni*)
which yields
"fast money" (*moni 'oi'oi*)
is preferred to
"farming work" (*ohipa fa'apu*)
which yields
"slow money" (*moni taere*).
Within the category of "money work"
"prize work" (*ohipa ta re*)
is preferred to
"hour work" (*ohipa ta hora*) or
"day work" (*ohipa ta mahana*).

LABOR COMMITMENT

At this point the reader may be willing to accept the fact that wage labor is currently popular among Tahitians, but may be wondering whether the Tahitians labor commitment, or employment opportunities, or both, will continue at their high level. The question is therefore whether or not the Tahitian proletariat is a permanent creation.

The analysis presented so far indicates that most Tahitians would prefer to continue living from wage labor. Yet I have heard many Tahitians who have just joined the labor force say that they will only work awhile before returning to their rural occupations, or that they will alternate between wage employment and peasant production. I suspect, however, that if employment opportunities continue, the majority of these men will remain regular wage laborers. The factory cited earlier provides a case in point. This factory, which was started in 1950 by French entrepreneurs, is located in a rural district of Tahiti 20 kilometers from Pape'ete. In the first few years of its operation it drew exclusively on the local Tahitian peasant population, giving them their first major opportunity for regular employment. Although there has been a considerable labor turnover since 1950, few of these workers have returned to a peasant status. Most have gone on to higher paying jobs in Pape'ete, just a half-hour commuting trip away. Furthermore, it is notable that most of those now working at the factory seem adjusted to the idea of working the year around. Although by law they are entitled to three weeks paid vacation, practically all elect to continue working without a vacation, and to collect their vacation pay as a bonus.[14] If my analysis of the Tahitian cognitive view of work is correct, and if the history of the work force at this factory is any indication, most Tahitian workers will elect to remain workers if wage employment opportunities continue. In other words, Tahitian workers are developing a deep labor commitment.

Maintenance of the 1962 level of employment should not be too difficult, barring major political or economic upheavals. Tourism is rapidly expanding, and requires much labor. In addition, such new local industries as commercial fishing and coconut oil processing should also help sustain a large labor force. Maintenance of the current (1965) high employment level should be more difficult, however, for many of the new jobs stem directly from France's nuclear testing program in the islands. Once test facilities are completed, and testing is underway, the demand for workers may decline. Continued French military development of the islands could, however, take care of any employment slack. Like other parts of the world, military expenditures loom large in the Tahitian employment picture.

CONCLUSION

The technical advisor or administrator concerned with promoting economic modernization should be aware of the cognitive views of work shared by the people he is concerned with. To be sure, looking at a change situation through the categories of the people involved offers only one perspective on the problem, but it is an important perspective. Such a perspective would, I believe, help avoid the kind of errors in directed change mentioned by the late John Provinse in a letter to the Editor of this journal.[15] Provinse was concerned about the numerous unsuccessful attempts to induce groups in North America, the Near East and Southeast Asia to become sedentary agriculturalists when it would appear that craft or industrial employment would have offered these groups a more congenial path to economic modernization. In such cases an analysis of the cognitive view of work, common in each group, along lines similar to the analysis of the Tahitian situation offered here, would perhaps have provided information necessary to guide the advisor or administrator who would recommend or direct changes in mode of livelihood.

NOTES

1. Wilbert E. Moore and Arnold S. Feldman, *Labor Commitment and Social Change in Developing Areas*, Social Science Research Council, New York, 1960.

2. The ready availability of jobs in Hawaii, New Zealand and Tahiti has meant that Polynesians there could find employment with a minimum of residential movement. However, for those islands where job opportunities are few, those seeking employment have been forced to emigrate to metropolitan centers. For example, Cook Islanders and Western Samoans find work in New Zealand, while American Samoans are attracted to Hawaii and the West Coast of the United States. See Norma McArthur, "Contemporary Polynesian Emigration from Samoa and the Cook Islands," *Journal of the Polynesian Society*, Vol. 63, pp.336–339.

3. These are rough estimates based on the 1962 census and interviews with officials in 1965.

4. The term "Tahitian" (*Ta'ata Tahiti*) can refer specifically to the local Polynesians of Tahiti and the other Society Islands, or it may include all Polynesian residents of the Society Islands—even if they originated in other islands of French Polynesia. For simplicity, I prefer the latter usage.

5. Gabriel Marc, *Comptes Économiques de la Polynesie Française 1960–1961–1962*, Institut National de la Statistique et des Études Économiques, Paris, 1964, pp. 18–19.

6. Since this paper is based primarily on recent observations and the recollections of informants, there is no attempt to trace the history of Tahitian wage laboring from the 1800's when the first plantations were founded. Those familiar with Tahitian history will recall that some plantation owners of the last century considered the Tahitians to be neither willing nor very able workers, and preferred to import Chinese laborers or other Pacific Islanders supplied by "blackbirders." I suspect that analysis would show that the apparent change in Tahitian labor commitment between the last century and now is best explained in terms of the contrast between the near slave conditions on the 19th century plantation and the relatively free and equitable employment situation today, rather than by any drastic change in Tahitian views of work.

7. Although increasing numbers of Tahitians are entering business, professional and Administration positions, they are greatly under-represented in these fields in comparison to European and Chinese residents. See Ben Finney, "Race and Class in the Society Islands of French Polynesia," *Proceedings of the VIIth International Congress of Anthropological and Ethnological Sciences*, Moscow (in press).

8. For data on the income and expenditure patterns of Tahitian workers studied during 1961–1962 see Ben Finney, *Polynesian Peasants and Proletarians*, Polynesian Society Reprint Series No. 9, The Polynesian Society, Wellington, 1965.

9. Robert Redfield, *Peasant Society and Culture*, University of Chicago Press, Chicago, 1960, pp. 63–65.

10. In a recent book on the Tikopia, Firth notes the yacht visit reported here. Raymond Firth, *Social Change in Tikopia*, George Allen and Unwin, London, 1959, p. 43.

11. Pierre-Jean Truc, "Le Taravana," *Journal de la Société des Océanistes*, Vol. 15, 1959, pp.227–236.

12. Ward Goodenough, *Cooperation in Change*, Russell Sage Foundation, New York, 1963, pp. 485–486.

13. "Command Work" (*ohipa ja'au*) is a synonym.

14. This and other examples that could be cited indicate that the Tahitian worker's response to opportunities for increased earnings is more often "rational' than 'traditionalistic', to use Weber's terms.

15. John H. Provinse, "Letter to the Editor," *Human Organization*, Vol. 24, 1965, pp.185–187.

CHAPTER SEVENTEEN

Industrial Employment of Rural Indigenes: The Case of Canada

CHARLES W. HOBART

In recent years there has been much discussion and troubled questioning of the treatment and fate of indigeneous people in Canada. While it has been hundreds of years since they experienced the wanton killing Bodley documents for other Aborigines in *Victims of Progress* (1975), in other ways their experience of neglect is typical of many other indigeneous people. The interest of the Canadian government was long restricted to the mineral resources of the "storehouse of the North." Thus, government initiatives toward negotiating peace treaties with the Indians of the Northwest Territories came only after discovery of oil at Norman Wells (Northwest Territories) in 1920 (Fumoleau n.d.). No treaties were signed with any Inuit because there were no parallel inducements. After Treaty 11 was signed with the Indian bands in the Mackenzie drainage in 1921, development activity was accelerated: a refinery was built at Norman Wells, mining developments at Port Radium on Great Bear Lake began in 1932, followed by gold mining around Yellowknife in 1934, and development of the large Pine Point mine began in the late 1950s. All of these were essentially "lily white" operations, employing few if any indigenes.

The attitude of the government toward native people remained essentially neglectful until after World War II, characterized by "inaction," "myopia," (Jenness 1964), and "absence of mind" (Granatstein 1976:21). It was only the surfacing of Canadian sovereignty issues in the Arctic islands (Dossman 1976) and perhaps Mowat's (1959) popularizing the plight of "the desperate people," the Keewatin Inuit, that prompted the government to adopt an attitude of more active wardship toward the northern indigenes.

The tendency to ignore the impacts of resource development projects on native people came to an end during the hydrocarbon exploration boom in the Mackenzie Delta and the high Arctic islands in the late 1960s and the early 1970s. The changes these developments were inducing in the north, the assumptions on which development was predicated, and the present and future effects development would have on natives began to be increasingly questioned. Usher's description of conflict between native trappers and hydrocarbon exploration interests on Banks Island (1971), Brody's work on Inuit and Whites in the Eastern Arctic (1975), and Paine's essays on social change in the Eastern Arctic (1971, 1977) all grew out of, and helped to focus, this rising concern. Discussion and controversy peaked during the Mackenzie Valley Pipeline hearings under Mr. Justice Berger on the proposed pipeline down the Mackenzie Valley. The arguments advanced by many of the witnesses at these hearings were reflected in the two volumes of the Berger Commission Report (Berger 1977), and many of the antidevelopment position papers were published in a book edited by Watkins (1977).

There are many who yet feel that the major issues in the Canadian North today relate to resource development. However, this paper is not concerned with debating the wisdom, justice, or timing of such activity. We must assume that resource development activity will continue, because between 1960 and 1981 the Canadian government, through tax incentives, encouraged investment of $3.5 billion in hydrocarbon exploration in the north; because the Supreme Court of Canada in a November 1979 decision upheld the right of mining companies to prospect in northern areas despite Inuit efforts to block this activity; and because no less than six major development projects in the Arctic have been approved since 1979, or are on the verge of gaining approval. Accordingly, this paper takes as its starting point the facts that much industrial employment is currently available in the Canadian Arctic, that numbers of northern indigenes are already involved in this employment, and that opportunities for more native employment will probably come swiftly with the six projects now afoot. Moreover, there is a rapid rate of native population growth, particularly among the Inuit who are now increasing at a rate of 3% per year. There is also a parallel increase in their wage earning interests and capabilities as a result of universally available education largely patterned on southern Canadian models, and near universally available southern television broadcasts. Thus, we can conclude that substantial increases in wage employment among northern native peoples must be expected.

This paper analyzes the consequences of industrial employment experiences of Indian and Inuit (Eskimo) people in Canada during the past 20 years, with special emphasis given to relocation and rotation or commuting employment experiences. There are brief discussions of the native workers' mastery of industrial skills; on the stressful effects of industrial employment; on the worker and on the worker's family with particular reference to support, child rearing, and conflict; on the community, with emphasis on the maintenance of cultural traditions and community viability; on the harvesting of traditional resources; and on the maintenance of traditional cultural patterns.

SOURCES OF DATA

The information presented in this paper comes from some previously published work as well as from a number of unpublished research reports with which I have been associated. The published sources report on a series of studies of the work adjustment of workers, and the social adjustments of workers and their families to industrial employment that typically involved relocation of workers and their families to more or less distant work sites. In all cases the workers and families were Inuit; none were Indian. The unpublished reports included four projects on the effects of rotation employment on workers, families, and communities; one on the effects of relocation employment; and four on the attitudes of people toward rotation or relocation work options. The studies of the effects of rotation employment included two dealing with Inuit and one with Indians, while the attitudes studies included Inuit, Indians, and Metis (Canadians who have some Indian ancestry but who do not have treaty Indian status). The work sites were located in the Northwest Territories, Arctic Quebec, and in northern parts of Alberta and Saskatchewan.

INDUSTRIAL EMPLOYMENT AND THE WORKER

Most of the Indian and Inuit men who have had industrial employment in Canada were little better prepared for it than many of the indigenous people from remote areas of South America or Africa. When this northern employment first began to increase in the late 1950s and early 1960s, most could speak little or no English. Only a small minority at that time had attended school at all, so that most knew little or nothing of reading, writing, or arithmetic in English, although some of them could read and write in their native language. Lacking steady employment experience, they had neither the clock-time orientation nor the work discipline expected of workers elsewhere. Consequently their approach to when work should begin in the morning tended to be casual, and if the weather turned fine for hunting or traveling, or if a herd of caribou was sighted, workers failed to appear for work the next day without bothering to notify their work superiors. This was consistent with traditional norms that what a man did was his business alone.

Similarly, their backgrounds at that time provided them with no understanding of the need to take care of equipment or to be concerned about preventive maintenance. The result was that equipment was left out to rust, machines were sometimes run until they "froze up," and native workers commonly acquired a reputation for negligent or abusive use of equipment.

Often there were communication problems, many of which originated in traditional behavior patterns. The Inuit in particular were quite likely to nod smilingly when they were given instructions, though they might have had little idea of what they were being told. They were loath to ask questions because that is traditionally seen as being impolite, something done only by young children. Moreover, even when workers did understand the words that were said they often did not grasp initially what they were supposed to do because understanding instructions involves understanding the work "scheme" or "game plan." When this understanding was lacking, there could be no comprehension of the instructions given.

THE WORK PERFORMANCE

The consequence of these difficulties was that native workers often required a longer "shakedown" period, to become adequately oriented to their jobs and to the work situations in which they found themselves, than did comparably placed White workers. This period was further lengthened by work absences and irregularities as men took time out to go hunting to provide their families with game meat, thus discharging traditional obligations that are still significant in terms of food preferences.

In time, however, native workers became excellent workers, thoroughly competent and dependable at the work they were assigned. One of the most dramatic early evidences of this is the history of their employment at the Rankin Inlet Nickel Mine in the Canadian Northwest Territories during the early 1960s (Williams 1974). The initial attempts to operate this mine using an all-White work force failed because the turnover rate was so high that a satisfactory level of production could not be achieved. Eventually, a manager was appointed who advocated operating the mine using local native labor. He did so successfully until the shutdown of the mine three or four years later, when the ore body was exhausted. During most of this time, up to 75% of the work force was native, including some who occupied highly skilled and responsible positions, such as the mine plumber and the mine electrician. While some of the Inuit who worked at the mine had prior industrial work experience at an American air base in the Canadian Arctic during World War II, many were quite without relevant experience. Indeed some had been living in snow huts during the winter and dressing in caribou skin clothes, in many respects living a precontact existence, until they were relocated from their traditional hunting lands a few years earlier following several severe starvations.

The successful work adaptations of these Inuit is even more surprising, given their living circumstances. When the mine began employing them, none were native to the Rankin Inlet Mine site; all had to relocate there. Some of the starvation victims were provided with small cabins, 49m^2 or less in size, to house their typically large families. Others lived in houses of similar size provided by the Canadian Department of Indian and Northern Affairs, but many were forced to build makeshift shacks from materials scavenged from the mine dump. The diet and the rest needs of many Inuit workers suffered. Wives bought foods from the store without any conception of nutritional requirements; some wives are reported to have purchased food supplies consisting only of candy. Similarly, during the summer period of 24-hour daylight, children and unemployed adults typically lost any track of "day" and "night," sleeping only when exhaustion overcame them. Many workers were unable to get the rest they needed in their tiny, crowded houses during periods of long daylight and dragged themselves to their jobs, at times more asleep than awake. Some retreated to a company-provided bunkhouse where they could get adequate rest (Williamson 1974).

The most impressive evidence of the high level of work proficiency achieved by these Inuit is found in the judgment of the mine safety inspector that the all-Inuit mine rescue crew at the Rankin Mine was the best crew in the Northwest Territories (ibid.:1974).

The Nannisivik underground lead-zinc mine on northern Baffin Island is having a similar experience with the native people, mostly Inuit, who currently make approximately 20% of its work force. One of the "jumbo drillers" is native, as is the best "ore buggy" driver. The mine foreman, a veteran with 20 years' mining experience in the North who has trained the all-Inuit mine rescue team, reports that it is the best he has ever seen. He says that if he were trapped underground, he would want an Inuit crew to be trying to reach him, stating flatly, "If the crew was Inuit, I know that I would get out; if it were a white crew, I would not be so sure" (Baffin Region Inuit Association 1980).

The maintenance shop foreman, who is responsible for the training of native apprentices, another veteran with 24 years of experience, reports that his native trainees learn faster than any others he has ever worked with in six or seven countries around the world. In particular, he praised the speed with which they "catch on," their craftsmanlike skill with hand tools, and their enthusiasm. Limitations in their arithmetic training set ceilings for some who require arithmetic upgrading training, but generally he finds them to be peerless.

The successful adaptation of Inuit to underground-mine employment is particularly noteworthy because many expected that the Inuit, used to the treeless, wide-open spaces of the Arctic tundra, might find that mine shafts deep underground induced claustrophobia. On the contrary, it appears that objections among the Inuit to working underground may be less common than among a random sample of Whites. The relative mildness of the underground climate has clear advantages over the above-ground climate in the North much of the year (ibid:1980).

Inuit have adapted successfully to many other forms of employment as well, including jobs as locomotive engineers, heavy equipment operators, truck drivers (work which many find highly satisfying) and oil field drilling crew members (Stevenson 1968; Williamson and Foster n.d.). Small but increasing numbers are attaining professional employment: there are currently one or more native doctors, engineers, and surveyors, and increasing numbers in teaching and managerial or supervisory positions. Clearly these are a very small proportion of the total, and include people who come from unusual educational backgrounds; the important point, however, is that breakthroughs have already occurred in these areas, and it must be expected that larger numbers of native persons will qualify themselves in the future.

THE SOCIAL ADJUSTMENT OF THE WORKERS

There is evidence of both the satisfactory and the unsatisfactory social/psychological adjustment of native workers who have industrial employment. Some of the most impressive evidence of their satisfactory social adjustment comes from comparative ratings that work supervisors have made of native and White workers. For example, one study showed that 24% of the native workers were rated "excellent" in terms of "camp citizenship"—"being reasonably friendly, cooperative, and considerate of others, not causing friction or trouble"—as compared with 16% of the White workers employed at comparable job levels (Hobart 1974). A similar study found that 49%

of the Inuit workers were rated "excellent" on camp citizenship as compared with 28% of the White workers (Roberts 1977).

Although native workers are often shy in their dealings with Whites, there is evidence that in mixed work crews both Indian and Inuit employees often establish strong, companionable relationships with White co-workers and supervisors. Thus, northern native trainees at on-the-job training sites in southern Canada were rated as "friendly" and "considerate" by respectively 95% and 63% of their co-workers. They were rated as "friendly" and "cooperative" by respectively 78% and 72% of their training supervisors, and as "fitting well into the work group" by 58% of these supervisors. These ratings are particularly significant since in the employment situation in which these data were gathered, the native workers enjoyed holiday and travel expense benefits not accorded to the White workers, and indeed were being trained to replace White workers. Despite these bases for jealously, friendly relationships were the rule—a tribute to the open-mindedness of the White workers and to the effectiveness of both native and White workers in overcoming the barriers of language and ethnicity (Hobart 1975).

Nevertheless, there is evidence that native workers in industrial work situations where Whites predominate do experience tension, probably at higher levels than the "acculturative stress" Berry has described (1976), because of the greater integration with Whites. The tension does not come out in the form of fighting, unless the native workers are able to obtain liquor and get drunk. This happens only rarely at typically "dry" northern work sites, but where liquor is obtainable fights have taken place. Otherwise, however, the native workers' internalized controls are typically too strong to permit open conflict, so that fights between two natives, or a native and a White worker are virtually unknown.

While there has been interest in acculturative stress for more than a decade (Berry 1976; Chance 1965) we are not aware of any methodologically sophisticated efforts to assess the distinctive tensions associated with employment in industrial settings. Some apparent sources of stress experienced by native rotation workers are worrying about their wives and children and about the fidelity of wives during their absences from home. Several studies have shown that worrying about the health and well-being of the wife is reported by between 54% and 87% of absent husbands, and similar worries about their children are reported by between 60% and 84% of absent native fathers (Hobart 1975; Baffin Region Inuit Association 1980; Roberts 1977).

Dramatic evidence of concern about the fidelity of absent wives comes from a study of workers' adjustments during the first year of their involvement in a rotation employment program. The employment was seasonal, lasting from mid-November to the end of April. During this period, monetary income in the small village of 730, from which approximately 54 rotation workers were recruited, increased considerably, by 75%, and there was a 29% increase in liquor consumption. A study of violent woundings during this period showed that although the total increase was only 12%, the number where the victims were married women doubled from four to eight. It appears that some of the men, while absent from home at the work site, brooded about the behavior of their wives. Liquor imports, available only by air shipment from the government liquor store, were distributed on the same day that the men returned from the work site. Drinking parties began very soon thereafter, and in time, with normal Inuit inhibitions suspended because of inebriation, men who had been brooding beat their wives. The incidence of violent wounding of wives declined to normal levels during the next three years, but the increase is clearly reflective of stresses that the workers experienced initially.

Workers experience a different pattern of stresses in those cases where they relocate with their families to a work site that is distant from their home communities. The main advantage of such an arrangement is that the worker has his family with him. He does not suffer from homesickness, or worry about the well-being of wife and children, or about what his wife may be doing. Instead, he experiences two other difficulties. The first is that his family may have considerable difficulty adjusting to the new community, particularly if it is primarily a "White man's town," contrasting sharply with the native community from which they came. Under these circumstances, the wife, and perhaps the children, may experience such difficulty in adapting (discussed in the next section) that he quits the job and moves his family back to the home settlement.

The other source of strain derives from the fact that in most parts of the Canadian North, to be a native man is to be a hunter, and a man's status in his community is still largely determined by his hunting prowess. To be unable to keep their family adequately supplied with game meat would be disturbing to many men, even though they were earning large paychecks. However, effective hunting requires considerable knowledge of the terrain and of game movements in the area where game is sought. Hunters who relocate typically experience little carryover of relevant knowledge to new areas, and their employment may leave them little time in which to build up their knowledge of the new area. Moreover, if this area is cut up by mountains and fjords, the danger of getting lost is real and not to be taken lightly in Arctic climes. As a consequence, in one northern relocation community none of the native men hunt to any significant degree, and they suffer a corresponding loss to their self-esteem. The result of these several sources of stress is that native workers often leave the relocation community after a few months to move with their families back to their home settlement (Baffin Region Inuit Association 1980).

ADJUSTMENT OF THE FAMILY

The demands made on the family by rotation employment of the male head are quite different from those experienced when the whole family relocates to the work site. Moreover, wives and children both experience rather different kinds of stress. Considering rotation employment impacts first, studies suggest that between 32% and 38% of wives generally report worrying about the welfare of their husbands while they are away at work. Loneliness is another commonly reported reaction. Wives may experience other less subjective difficulties as well, such as a shortage of meat when men work long work rotation periods, as reported by 29% and 40% of the wives interviewed in two studies (Hobart and Kupfer 1973; Roberts 1977). This condition is exacerbated when men do not send wage money home so their wives can buy food. This oversight is not uncommon because many native people think of food as wild game or fish, while money is to be spent on nonfood items such as boats, motorized toboggans, guns and ammunition, candy, and liquor. However, where the work period is lengthy this failure may cause serious problems. Money is sometimes gambled, as well, and families have been known to suffer when their men lost all their earnings. Thus, some families have experienced a degree of privation as a result of rotation employment when men were away at work. However, the closeness of extended family ties and, in most places, the continuing strength of the sharing ethic, as well as government social assistance programs, ensure that none ever go hungry.

A minority of workers' wives report specific troubles experienced during their husbands' absences. Several studies indicate that about 10% report difficulties in handling their children while their husbands are away, and about the same say they experience unwanted attention from other men (Hobart and Kupfer 1973; Roberts 1977; Baffin Region Inuit Association 1980).

Despite these problems, the shortage of wage employment in most northern native communities is such that wives are generally enthusiastic about rotation employment, with typically 80% or 90% reporting that they want their husbands to have such work the next employment season. The same proportions say they would like their husbands to work for "as long as possible." The reasons that they give typically refer to the material advantages of the employment, although some mention the work skills that their husbands are learning and the satisfactions the men get from this work (Hobart and Kupfer 1973; Roberts 1977)

Like their mothers, children suffer both subjective and objective losses. The former includes children missing their fathers while they are away. The objective losses appear to be restricted to sons, and involve inadequate training in hunting skills and lore of the land that they experience when the rotation schedule requires the absence of their fathers for long periods of time (Hobart and Kupfer 1973; Roberts 1977; Baffin Region Inuit Association 1980).

The evidence from several studies indicates that both workers and their families experience greater dissatisfaction and maladjustment if they relocate from their homes to a distant work site. There are a number of reasons for this: separation from family and friends; separation from the familiar settlement and surrounding hunting areas; often, removal from an essentially native settlement to a White-dominated settlement; loss of familiar pastimes and friendly associates; communication problems with Whites; unsatisfactory quarters; nonavailability of some familiar and preferred foods; increased access to liquor; difficulties between the families' own native children and non-native children; difficulties experienced by children in school, etc.

While men in this situation may experience problems in adjusting to their new work situation and may quit abruptly as a result, and while children may experience problems as well, as noted above, the problems experienced by the women are most disruptive and typically precipitate the families' sudden return home. The problems relate centrally to the women's lack of acculturation to southern Canadian patterns. Men who relocate typically have enough industrial experience to adjust to the more White-controlled situations they experience, and the flexibility of most children often enables them to adapt well to the new situation. Wives, particularly during the 1960s, often had no industrial work experience, and little contact with more White-oriented communities. On the other hand, they are commonly emotionally dependent on continued close association with other native women, relatives, friends, and neighbors. Accordingly, they often find removal from the home community an absolutely devastating experience, and often begin to drink heavily to escape loneliness and the emptiness of their lives. Stevenson writes of his visit with several Inuit families, living in miserable little shacks on the outskirts of a northern Alberta town where their husbands were involved in building a railroad. He found wives drunk and miserable, and describes one in particular who, speaking in the Inuit language, described her despair with awful clarity: "There is no place for me in this land" (Stevenson 1968).

The material benefits of both rotation and relocation employment are easily enumerated. Teachers report that children are better clothed when employment is available and their diet contains more fresh fruit and vegetables, as well as more candy. Certainly they are given more toys and have more spending money. Less tangible, but more important, are the social and psychological effects that result when fathers who have been on welfare are not only able to become self-supporting, but can buy canoes, motors, motorized toboggans, and other hunting equipment that they were not able to purchase earlier. These things make children proud of their fathers, and give them an attractive vision of the future involving employment and cash income available to buy the equipment needed by a successful hunter. Several studies have shown that many boys identify with this future, indicating that they would like to have rotation employment when they grow up. Girls also say that despite the loneliness of separation, they would like for their future husbands to have such employment as well (Hobart and Kupfer 1973; Roberts 1977; Hobart in press).

A negative possibility is that children might suffer during the drunken parties that appear to increase, at least initially, when relocation or rotation employment is available. At such times, and especially during winter, young children in particular might experience inadequate nutrition or protection from the cold, or even physical mistreatment and abuse at the hands of drunken parents. At least six different studies have probed these possibilities, and in every case the findings have been negative (Hobart and Kupfer 1973; Hobart 1974, 1976, 1978, in press; Roberts 1977; Baffin Region Inuit Association 1980). To date there is no evidence that infants have suffered physical abuse or neglect as a result of industrial employment.

A final possibility, for which we have empirical evidence, is that the dental health of native children might suffer as a result of industrial employment because parents are able to buy more sweets and soft drinks for their children. Evidence is available from two Canadian Inuit communities, in one of which about 25% of the men had rotation industrial employment, while in the other there was virtually no industrial employment. The evidence from dental surveys of school age children showed that there were no significant differences between the dental health of children in these communities. In both cases their dental health was very bad, indicating that the tastes of children, the indulgence of parents, and the merchandising policies of the store in both communities made for high incidence rates of tooth decay (Hobart in press).

EFFECTS OF INDUSTRIAL EMPLOYMENT ON COMMUNITY ACTIVITIES

Participation in industrial employment might have adverse effects on at least three aspects of community life: participation in community activities; recruitment to and performance of leadership responsibilities in the community; and perhaps most basic of all, levels of interpersonal interaction among community residents, which leads to the crystalization of issues in community life, identification, and discussion of strategies and of alternative solutions. Each of these would be jeopardized by widespread relocation employment because of the loss of population, and perhaps particularly, the better trained and more energetic members.

One might expect that rotation employment would more greatly endanger these aspects of community life than would industrial employment based in the home community. However, the available evidence appears to point to the contrary. Men working in their home communities typically have jobs requiring them to work 40 hours a week, and in addition they have heavy obligations to hunt and fish and feed their families. Those who fail to do so are not seen as good providers and do not qualify as "men," in the traditional *hunter* sense of that term. They also have obligations to take their sons out hunting and fishing in order to train them in hunting, fishing, traveling, and land-living skills. In many areas, hunting and fishing trips require two or more days; as a result men who have full-time permanent employment experience very heavy demands on their time. Their participation in community activities generally may suffer. However, their overextended schedules are most apparent in respect to participation in the daily interactional life of the community, their involvement in community issues, and their ability to exercise leadership in the community.

Since the rotation work period is usually no more than two weeks in the Canadian North, rotation workers are able to involve themselves more heavily in community life than are locally based, full-time industrial workers. According to the typical schedule, rotation workers are at home one week out of three or two out of four. While there, they have no work obligations. True, they must go hunting and fishing during part of this time, but they are left with much time for visiting, discussing, and participating in local decision-making processes. Several studies have suggested that community activities, and particularly those charging a fee, are better supported in communities where many are engaged in industrial rotation employment, than otherwise (Hobart 1974; Roberts 1977). In high employment communities, Settlement Council meetings are scheduled to coincide with periods when rotation-employed council members are at home, and emergency meetings are held without them. The most salient point, however, is that rotation workers have the money to purchase the hunting equipment, and the leisure time to establish themselves as respected providers in the community. They have the leisure as well, while they are in the community, to participate in community discussion and crystallization of issues. As a result of both of these characteristics, they are likely to be seen as respect worthy, significant people in the community, whom others may look to for leadership.

EFFECTS OF INDUSTRIAL EMPLOYMENT ON TRADITIONAL SUBSIST-
ENCE AND RESOURCE HARVESTING ACTIVITY

The harvesting dealt with here includes hunting various kinds of land and sea game—caribou, moose, seal, walrus, whale—and birds; trapping and hunting a wide range of furbearers for their pelts; and fishing. Although the means used have changed, hunting and fishing are undeniably traditional activities, pursued by native peoples in the Canadian North ever since their arrival in these regions thousands of years ago. Hunting and fishing are still of immense significance to these people for a number of reasons. The most obvious is that game foods are the single largest source of income—income in kind— in most native communities in the Canadian North today. With relatively few exceptions, native people prefer the traditional native game and fish foods to the store-bought foods that Whites have made available. We have noted earlier that hunting prowess is a major basis on which men are accorded respect, and that it is an important aspect of men's self-image. It is generally true that to be a native man is automatically to be seen as a hunter and to see oneself as a hunter. Finally, the process of traveling on the land, away from the expectations and pressures, the spoken or unspoken queries, judgments and disapproval of Whites, is for many natives a necessary, recreative, soul-restoring experience.

Trapping must be seen slightly differently. Although native people have dressed in furs and hides ever since they migrated to cold areas, they had relatively little use for the fine furs that command high prices on commercial fur markets. Thus, fur trapping is not strictly a traditional activity, but rather has been induced by the demand for furs by Whites. However, it has come to be seen as at least semitraditional and, along with "hunter," as symbolic of native identity because it is pursued in conjunction with hunting and fishing and it draws native people out onto the land that they love.

It might be expected that the dietary preferences of native people would work to sustain hunting and fishing activity among native people, and that the high prices now paid for fur would work to sustain relatively high levels of trapping, even in the face of increased availability of industrial employment. This is generally true, but some distinctions and clarifications must be made.

Consumption of store-bought food is increasing throughout the Canadian North. The reasons for this include the rapidly growing population and the depopulation of many parts of the North with the gathering of seminomadic natives into permanent settlements since 1960, which together have caused a shortage of accessible game and fish stocks available to feed the rapidly increasing and more clustered native population. The increased distances to herds and to fish stocks have made hunters dependent on motorized toboggans and power boats, which some do not have. Finally, a probably increasing minority of children who have been away to the hospital or to residential schools have learned to enjoy store-bought foods.

The residents of poor villages, situated in relatively poor trapping areas (as many villages are) and lacking industrial employment, are driven to consume more store foods because of the scarcity of transportation equipment to carry them the distances to where game may usually be found. Moreover, as we noted earlier, natives who have relocated to distant work sites may hunt relatively little.

Men with full-time industrial employment in their home communities are often able to buy the transportation and other equipment for successful hunting, but as we have said, they often lack adequate free time. Many of them lend their hunting equipment to older sons, to younger brothers, fathers, etc., and as a result game and wild food supplies in such villages are maintained at high levels. But such industrial workers lack the leisure time to make extended hunting and fishing trips, whereas those with rotation employment have both the money for equipment and the leisure during their time at home to hunt relatively frequently. The latter are better able to develop a satisfying integration of traditional interests and activities with their industrial employment than any other category of industrial workers.

Several studies have shown that instead of having an adverse effect on traditional hunting and trapping activities, substantial levels of rotation employment in native villages tend to result in increasingly effective traditional resource harvesting. The most detailed study investigated the effects of rotation employment in Coppermine in the Northwest Territories on hunting, fishing, trapping, and production of semitraditional handicrafts—carving, sewing, and traditional artifacts (Hobart in press). Adequate quantitative data on hunting harvests are not available to permit specific estimates because of imprecision among hunters reporting their kills. However, long-time residents of Coppermine, with whom the matter was discussed, reported that the involvement of about 25% of the male labor force in rotation employment during the winter season, and of up to 15% throughout the year, had not reduced the availability of good game in the community. In fact, such food probably became more available, the informants reported, because the increased prosperity in the settlement meant that there was more transportation and hunting equipment available to hunters than ever before.

The story is similar with respect to fishing: accurate statistical data are not available but there was certainly no decline in the availability of fish in Coppermine during the rotation employment period. Indeed there was apparently an increase as a result of the greater number of boats and out-board motors in the community (ibid., in press).

Coppermine people did not find it necessary to make changes in their plans to travel to spring seal hunting and fishing camps as is traditional, beyond those already necessitated by the educational schedule. Yet another study of the effects of year-round rotation mine employment showed that while this made it necessary for workers' families to reduce their lengths of stay at the hunting or fishing camps, few families abandoned these traditional camping experiences (Baffin Region Inuit Association 1980).

Data presented in Table 17.1 show that although the figures for trapping returns in Coppermine reflect considerable fluctuation, there is no evidence of decreased trapping activity during the 1972–77 rotation employment years, and indeed the level of trapping appeared to have increased. Table 17.2 suggests that the same appears to have been true in respect to semitraditional carving and handicraft production.

In summary, the kind of industrial wage employment available to native people has considerable effect on their continued participation in traditional subsistence and resource harvesting activity. Note that in most areas of the Canadian North it is not possible for trappers to adequately support themselves from trapping alone: they require the cash infusions available only from at least seasonal wage employment in order to purchase and operate the expensive equipment (e.g., skidoos, motor boats) that is necessary. If they accept employment that requires them to relocate to a distant work site, their ability to hunt effectively is inhibited because they lack adequate blocks of time, because much of their knowledge of terrain and animal movement patterns may not be relevant in the new setting in which they find themselves, and because of fear of getting lost in some areas. Those who accept full-time, permanent employment in their home settlements have the money to buy the hunting

Table 17.1 Indications of Trapping-Hunting Activity in Coppermine, 1968–69 to 1978–79.

Year	No. of Trappers	White Fox		Other Fox		Wolves		Polar Bear		Seals		Total Value[a]
		No.	Value	No.	Value	No.	Value	No.	Value	No.	Value	
1968–69	89	211	$ 2,983	40	$ 461	6	$ 192	—	$ —	1,944	$13,037	$ 16,653
1969–70	143	549	6,963	101	1,168	8	280	3	666	2,279	24,429	33,506
1970–71	116	2,098	29,624	68	645	6	240[b]	2	560[b]	2,098	29,624	60,693
1971–72	162	1,642	18,452	29	216	3	133	1	339	1,642	18,452	37,592
1972–73	89	134	2,315	34	545	2	62	—	—	1,956	27,169	30,100
1973–74	114	4,250	115,061	218	7,793	23	1,110	1	1,000	2,146	38,178	163,509
1974–75	160	1,230	21,340	43	1,007	162	8,670	1	650	1,570	26,841	59,075
1975–76	148	1,808	45,076	148	5,859	111	10,230	—	—	1,880	35,925	98,748
1976–77	141	3,188	106,899	230	11,073	40	6,490	—	—	2,279	37,307	164,534
1977–78	133	848	25,313	185	12,912	43	5,919	2	2,800	1,872	22,202	69,146
1978–79	156	1,679	69,482	723	66,180	1063[c]	165,456	5	7,500[b]	1,618	19,890	331,734

a. Total Value includes value of fine furs.

b. Value estimated.

c. Includes 284 wolves used locally or shipped to Holman, not included in value totals.

Source: Data supplied by Fish and Wildlife Service, Government of the Northwest Territories.

equipment that they need, but often they do not have the blocks of free time necessary for hunting in many areas. If they obtain rotation employment, they have both.

EFFECTS OF INDUSTRIAL EMPLOYMENT ON CULTURAL RETENTION

The issue of retention of traditional culture has become increasingly important. Anthropologists speak of "a world on the wane." Native people, often the more acculturated, mourn the passing of their traditional culture. Social psychologists point to the costs of the relative loss of identity that native people inevitably experience with loss of that culture. As resurgent ethnic minority movements show in Spain, England, Canada, and some areas of the Middle East, among others, cultural survival and cultural retention are of immense significance to millions of people. What are the effects of industrial employment in this critically important area?

There is no need to elaborate the point that industrial employment does have profound effects on retention of the traditional culture. The shift from a hunting-gathering economy, even a somewhat technologically sophisticated one, to an economy based on industrial wage employment is massively consequential. Extensive changes become necessary in language, in conceptions of seasonal and daily time, in motives and values, and in the patterning of many relationships in the community, to name but a few.

In Canada, these changes have the strongest impacts where the worker and his family relocate to the work site, which inevitably has a Euro-Canadian cultural orientation. Cut off from relatives and

Table 17.2 Furs and Handicrafts Purchased by the Coppermine Eskimo Cooperative, 1970–78

Year	Payments for Carvings, Handicrafts[a] and Furs
1970	$ 38,000
1971	52,800
1972	67,000
1973	82,500
1974	N/A
1975	97,000
1976	111,500[b]
1977	127,200[c]
1978	274,255[d]

a. Estimated from figures supplied by the Canadian Arctic Cooperative Federation Ltd.

b. Includes $62,562 for carvings and handicraft purchases.

c. Includes $90,879 for carvings and handicraft purchases.

d. Includes $148,829 for carvings and handicraft purchases.

Source: Hobart 1978.

traditional associates, in a strange geographic and human-made environment where established patterns of interaction, sharing, and time usage are frustrated, the individual and the family are much less buffered, much more vulnerable to rapid cultural change than they were in their home settlement. In short, families in this situation find themselves in a "White man's town," where the employing industry structures the life of the community in many ways, without the activity or interaction-based reinforcements of their traditional culture.

Workers with full-time industrial employment in their home communities find themselves in an intermediate position. They do have all of the environmental and community based supports for the more traditional culture including the ability to engage in familiar culture-relevant activities and interactions. On the other hand, most of their working days are spent in industrial situations interacting with other industrial employees with respect to issues and in contexts that have little, if any, traditional relevance.

More consequential yet, in the long run, is the fact that the worker's children, and indeed many other people in the community, may be favorably influenced toward the worker's life style by the convenience of the hours he works, the comfortable work environment that he enjoys, and the obviously substantial paycheck that he dependably receives. In this situation, the seeds of change, and perhaps of cultural replacement, are planted in the heart of the home community. The appeal that such employment can make is obviously attractive, particularly in impoverished native villages where cash earnings from hunting and trapping are smaller, more uncertain, and involve harder work and greater personal risk than industrial employment.

Industrial rotation employment offers the opportunity for maximum wage income with minimum cultural impact. The most significant point is that the worker's family and home community is buffered from the industrial work setting and the influences emanating from it by the intervening distance. The daily routine of the community is quite unaffected; the men, women and children present going about their daily lives without experiencing any immediate industry-induced influences. The absence of some men when at the industrial work site is generally analogous to their absence when on hunting or trapping trips, though with less personal risk and thus less need for worry on their behalf, as the residents of Coppermine recognize (Hobart in press). The only link between the settlement and the work site is the rotation workers: should they decide that the personal, cultural, or other costs of the employment are too high, they could quit their jobs, thus severing the link, and the home community would in many ways be little changed from the preemployment community.

A further advantage is that the settlement is not exposed to the influences and pressures, whether intended or unintended, that single-industry towns may experience (Lucas 1971). In such towns, the dominating industry has a vested interest in many different areas of town life, and finds ways to make that interest felt. Moreover, there is no influx of White personnel, as there certainly would be if the industrial operation were located adjacent to an existing settlement. The settlement remains a native community, without a growing White challenge to continuing native control.

This is not to deny that rotation industrial employment does induce culture change as a result of the workers' work activity, work associates, and source and amount of income. The effects of increased income (beyond a certain level) may be used to purchase a more southern-oriented home environment, and there may be changes in the identifications and expectations of the workers' children. However, the essential points are that these changes are more under the control of the worker: he can terminate them at will, and there are far fewer latently induced or persistent impacts as a result of rotation employment. Thus, it is difficult to conceive an arrangement better designed to offer relatively high paying industrial employment, coupled with minimization of inevitable acculturative influences.

CURRENT INTEREST IN INDUSTRIAL EMPLOYMENT AMONG NATIVE PEOPLE

One might expect that interest in industrial employment would be at a low ebb among indigenes in Canada today. In the Northwest Territories, native land claims are being negotiated with the Canadian federal government, and many native people fear that initiation of new development activity will jeopardize their claims. The native organizations that have become politically active have pitted themselves against any further development until land claims are finally settled. The polarizations of loyalties, which the aboriginal rights issue has sharpened, have further strengthened nativist sentiments and the glorification of distinctively native patterns, so that the prestige of hunter-trappers has been increased. This was apparent during the course of the Berger Hearings, when the significance of hunter-trappers was repeatedly emphasized, while the contribution of wage workers to community life was typically ignored.

But underneath the rhetoric, wives and husbands both know the importance of paychecks for the home and for resource harvesting equipment. This is seen in the large proportions of native people who hope for industrial employment opportunities, as a number of studies made since 1976 have shown. Because in almost all cases there are no prospects for significant developments adjacent to native settlements, these studies have inquired about interest in rotation or relocation employment. Despite the dislocation of the familiar patterns of interaction and relationship of the workers such employment would involve, the interest expressed is often very strong, as the data in Table 17.3 show.

DISCUSSION

The relevance of this Canadian experience to other developing countries depends on the similarities and differences that determine the applicability of the Canadian experience. Perhaps the most significant contextual aspects of the Canadian experience are the high level of affluence in Canadian society, the economic and cultural gulf separating the native Canadian from other Canadians, the small size of the native population (constituting only 1.5% of the total), the remoteness of the industrial work sites under consideration in the Arctic from the center of Canadian population between 1,000 and 2,000 km to the south, and the harshness of the Arctic environment. All of these differentiate the Canadian experience from situations in most other developing countries. The remoteness and the harsh climate make it difficult to recruit experienced workers from southern

Table 17.3 Employment Interests among Selected Samples of Canadian Northern Native Peoples.

Location	Sample Size			Interested in Rotation Employment		
	Male	Female	Total	Male	Female	Total
Gjoa Haven NWT	20	17	37	95%	82%	89%
Fort Chipewyan Alberta	220	216	436	90	79	85
Coppermine NWT	77	78	155	68	72	70
Central Alberta (Metis)[a]	456	482	938	66	38	52
Central Alberta (Indians) NOT ASKED						

Location	Sample Size			Interested in Relocation Employment		
	Male	Female	Total	Male	Female	Total
Gjoa Haven NWT	20	17	37	65%	29%	49%
Fort Chipewyan Alberta	220	216	436	92	81	87
Coppermine NWT	77	78	155	63	64	64
Central Alberta (Metis)[a]	456	482	938	41	26	34
Central Alberta (Indians)	407	348	755	81	71	76

a. Includes nontreaty Indian status, and mixed ancestry Indians.

Canada for long-term, permanent employment in the North. This has been a major inducement to industry to recruit northern native workers and to make the unusual initial adjustments that their employment required. Moreover, because the Canadian federal government had treaty obligations for their welfare, and because of the increasing size of both the northern native population and of the social assistance payments required for their support, the government has actively encouraged industry to make employment opportunities available to native people.

Nevertheless, there are significant similarities between the Canadian situation and what is occurring in other developing countries of the world. Perhaps the most important is the vastness of the economic and cultural gulf separating the dominant middle and upper classes of the centers of metropolitan dominance from the far less acculturated indigenous peoples of the more remote hinterland areas. In many countries, of course, lower class and working class people reflect substantial indigenous origins and thus bridge the gap between the two extreme groups to some extent. Another point of probable similarity relates to the issue of cultural retention. This may not commonly be seen as an important issue among many aboriginal groups today, as was also generally true in Canada before the 1960s. However, the perceived importance of this issue will increase rapidly as aboriginal groups become more acculturated and as the dominant metropolitan culture makes increasing inroads on traditional cultures, so that their survival is seen to be problematic.

A search of the literature has failed to disclose comparable studies of the effects of industrial employment on native communities in other countries. Accordingly, it is not possible to contrast my findings with those from other parallel studies. Nevertheless, the following points are broadly applicable. As agricultural and industrial development encroach on the traditional lands of aboriginal peoples, their ability to maintain traditional subsistence patterns is progressively destroyed. Alternative sources of livelihood must be found to at least supplement remaining traditional resources, and some of these will involve industrial employment. If such employment is blindly introduced without regard to impacts on indigenous individuals, families, and communities, the result will be the disorganization and destruction of "victims of progress" seen around the world: anomie, apathy and depression, alcohol and drug abuse, violent crime, mental illness, a people without a vision, a dying people.

The reaction to these tendencies is often the attempt to reassert the traditional culture, which offers promise of meaning, order and purpose. But the restoration of precontact conditions is almost never possible.

It is in the context of these alternatives that the Canadian experience is relevant and instructive. The ability of Canadian indigenous people to master work disciplines and work skills, even those requiring technically sophisticated abilities, is encouraging, and this capability certainly exists among native peoples in other countries. We attach particular significance to the distinctive advantages of rotation employment for individuals and communities without prior industrial work experience. Some advantages, not previously noted, should be mentioned. The controlled context in which the worker lives at the work site, in the midst of work-experienced others, increases the probability of optimum work performance since he gets a well-balanced diet and adequate rest. This context facilitates the learning of work skills and disciplines and the effectiveness of on-the-job training. Absenteeism is nonexistent and tardiness is very rare at the rotation work site. Thus, indigenous workers can establish a foothold in industrial employment while retaining involvement in the traditional economy and buffering the home community from disorganizing acculturative contacts. These native communities may retain as traditional a life-style as environmental circumstances and their inclinations permit. Continuation of traditional resource harvesting is safeguarded and so is retention of the cultural tradition which articulates with the traditional economy and social organization of the band or tribe. In turn, this increases the probability that appropriate cultural syntheses will emerge that will facilitate the nontraumatic transition of the indigenous people from obsolescent and nonviable traditional ways to the stage of increasing involvement in the larger society that is often inescapable.

The Canadian setting has been both advantageous and disadvantageous in facilitating nondisruptive industrial employment among native people. It has been advantageous in opening employment opportunities because affluence in the society, growing governmental insistence, and the inaccessability and disinterest of alternative labor sources made the incorporation of indigenous people into well-paid industrial labor almost inevitable. However, the Canadian situation has posed distinctive problems in minimizing the disruptive consequences of this employment. The massive differences between the native and southern Canadian cultures, the magnitude of the income disparities between that earned from industrial employment as compared with more traditional economic pursuits, and the differences in facilities and creature comforts between the work sites equipped according to southern expectations and the more primitive conditions existing in home settlements are all disruptive in their implications. This prompts the conclusion that the Canadian context offers no special advantages in facilitating nondisruptive employment of native indigenes, by comparison with other countries.

Chapter Eighteen

The Personal Adjustment of Navajo Indian Migrants to Denver, Colorado

Theodore D. Graves

Introduction

One Wednesday morning in mid-September a young Indian stepped off the bus at the Trailways depot in downtown Denver, Colorado. Like most Navajo migrants, Harrison Joe was in his early twenties and single. He had graduated two years before from the Special Navajo Program at Intermountain School in Brigham City, Utah. This program, now discontinued, was a five-year course for Navajos with little or no prior educational experience. It emphasized basic language skills and vocational training and was all the education Harrison Joe had ever had. Nor had experience served as a substitute. The majority of Navajos who come to Denver have never been in a city before, and neither had Harrison Joe. Other than boarding school his only off-reservation experience was two months picking potatoes in Idaho, at $120 per month.

At Intermountain, Harrison Joe received vocational training in upholstery. But this didn't help him find a job near his reservation home. During the two years following graduation his only wage labor work was ten days for the tribe at $10 per day. So he decided to try relocation. Denver was his first choice because he had a relative there and it was close to home. The Bureau of Indian Affairs (BIA) which "sponsors" most Navajo migrants, agreed to pay his way to the city and to help him find a job there, under a special government program in operation since 1954.

And so on arrival in Denver, the first thing Harrison Joe did was to ask his way to the BIA Office of Employment Assistance. There he was given intake interviews and a haircut and was taken to a rooming house where several other Indian relocates lived. His first weekly subsistence check was issued: $30, which after paying $21 for room and board still left him with a bit of pocket money. On Friday and Saturday the Office also gave him job counselling and sent him out on three nonproductive job interviews.

Though unsuccessful at finding a job those first few days, Harrison Joe had no difficulty finding friends. The first morning in town he met another Navajo at the Bureau office, and his new roommate at the boarding house was also Navajo. Thursday evening he went looking for his "uncle," a young man about his age with a couple of years of urban experience in both Chicago and Denver. But he had moved. Friday, Harrison Joe tried again, and this time found him sitting in the park with some other migrants. So the whole group spent the evening together. On Saturday afternoon another Navajo took him out to see the town, and later to watch TV at his apartment. Sunday, Harrison Joe struck up an acquaintance with a former Navajo roomer at his boarding house who was to become his closest friend. Together they went to the "Pink Elephant," a popular Navajo bar where they spent the evening with his "uncle" and other friends. Though this was fun, the evening was marred on his way home by a fight with another group of Navajos, who taunted the shy stranger.

During his next week in Denver, a temporary five-hour job as a bricklayer laborer and another day heaving cinder blocks were Harrison Joe's only work. All of his job interviews were unsuccessful, and he was beginning to feel discouraged. That Saturday, BIA subsistence funds again in his pocket, he set out to explore the town. Meeting no one he knew, he again dropped into the Pink Elephant, where he spotted his "uncle" chatting with another clan brother from Gallup. This fellow, also a new migrant, had found no work and had been beaten up. He, too, was getting discouraged and talked of returning home.

Harrison Joe's third week in the city was equally unsuccessful. By Tuesday the BIA had given up trying to get him work in upholstery, and instead got him hired as a cinch maker in a saddle shop. The next day he was fired because he was too slow and came to work two hours late. Thursday he tried to get a job on his own at the Colorado State Employment Office. Because the lines were so long, however, he didn't even get to fill out an application form. By this time he was so discouraged that after he picked up his BIA subsistence check he packed his bag and decided to return home. But instead he spent the evening talking with one of our researchers. Friday morning, when he stopped at the BIA office, they got him a job as a trainee leather trimmer, to begin the following week, so he decided to stick around and give the city another try.

Saturday was an eventful day. He earned $3 cutting lawns and, with this added to the $9 left from his subsidy check after paying room and board, he felt quite flush. He decided to wander down to Larimer Street, Denver's skid row, where other Navajos had pointed out a friendly bar. "Navajos, two of them, were around," he reported later, "and they bought some beers for me, and we started drinking." In typical fashion, each bought drinks for the others, and they moved from one bar to the next. Exactly what transpired during the evening is unclear. At some point Harrison Joe got into a fight and was badly bruised and cut on one arm. He may also have been slipped a Mickey and rolled (his perception of the events), or perhaps he and his friends simply drank up his $12. "I don't know how much I drink," he admitted.

In any event, there were some "police standing there and me drunk. One Navajo took off. And I just sit there, don't know if I had been passed out. And I was in jail." Because it was his first offense he was released Sunday morning, but was required to return to court Wednesday. Broke, tired, and hung-over, he hiked to the house of a friend, who took him out for a couple of beers to sober him up. Then he went home to bed.

Monday, Harrison Joe began work as a leather cutter trainee. Tuesday he was fired. Wednesday he went to court and was given a $10 suspended sentence. Thursday he picked up his $30 maintenance check from the BIA and without a word to anyone, left town.

Harrison Joe is fairly typical of the majority of Navajos who come to Denver in search of better employment opportunities. Migration to the city creates for them a difficult emotional conflict. On the one hand they want the material goods their Western education has taught them to value but that limited job opportunities on the reservation prevent them from attaining. On the other hand they retain a deep emotional attachment to their kin and the reservation for which the city offers few substitutes (Graves and VanArsdale 1966). The average migrant arrives in Denver with other handicaps. He has limitations of language, race, and culture, and Indian education still lags behind that of the American public at large. It is therefore not surprising that over half the migrants remain in the city less than six months. But often the migrant is equally ill-equipped to compete back home. The better educated Navajos who remain on the reservation command the best available jobs. Thus the migrant is apt to slip into a cycle of urban migration and return, each phase of which ends in personal failure. Small wonder that large numbers of these "marginal men" seek release from frustration and failure in drunken stupor.

Research on the personal adjustment problems of Navajo migrants in Denver has been in progress at the University of Colorado since 1963. The present paper reports some of the economic, social, and psychological factors associated with the quality of their adjustment. It is a distillate from a book-length manuscript (Graves, in preparation) and can present only highlights from our findings, with emphasis on but one of the three theoretical "models" that guided our work (Graves 1966). But even in this brief summary our multi-dimensional, "concatenated" approach to explanation will emerge.

THE PROBLEM OF INDIAN DRUNKENNESS

One index of the psychic difficulties these migrants experience is the frequency with which they are arrested in Denver, almost always for a drinking-related offense. The high rate of Indian arrests in comparison to other U.S. minority groups and to the dominant white community has been documented by several researchers (Graves, in

Table 18.1 Comparative Rates of Arrest of Various Ethnic Groups in the United States— 1960

	Total arrests	Alcohol related Arrests	Official % alcohol related
Total population	2,200	940	43
White	1,700	780	47
Negro	5,900	2,000	33
Indian	15,000	11,000	76
Chinese-Japanese	1,100	270	24

Taken from Stewart, 1964, Table 2, p. 61. Rates shown are per 100,000 population.

Table 18.2 Comparative Rates of Arrests of Various Ethnic Groups in the City of Denver, Colorado—1960

	Total arrests	Alcohol related arrests	Official % alcohol related
Total population	5,300	2,700	51
White	4,800	2,500	53
Anglo	3,500	2,000	57
Spanish	15,000	7,000	46
Negro	12,000	3,600	30
Indian	60,000	51,000	86
Chinese-Japanese-Filipino	1,100	470	41

Taken from Stewart, 1964, Table 14, p. 65, as corrected by Graves. Rates shown are per 100,000 population.

preparation; Honigmann and Honigmann 1968; Stewart 1964; Ferguson 1968; Whittaker 1962). Tables 18.1 and 18.2 present figures based on official FBI statistics and census data for the nation at large and the city of Denver, Colorado, as summarized by Stewart (1964:61, 65). Note that Indian arrests are ten or more times those for whites, and at least three or four times those for other minority groups.

Figures of this kind, however, are subject to the criticism that the population base on which these rates are calculated may be badly distorted. This problem is particularly acute in an urban area such as Denver. Rapid Indian turnover in the city makes accurate census-taking nearly impossible, nonresident Indians temporarily in the city for recreational purposes may account for many arrests, and the urban Indian population is made up predominantly of young, single males in the lower strata of the population, who are disproportionately liable to drunkenness and arrest. Their racial distinctiveness, furthermore, and their pattern of public drinking makes their drunkenness particularly conspicuous, regardless of any latent prejudice some police officers may harbor.

To control for such factors in our study, individual police records of 488 migrant Navajo males were collected, representing 94% of the known Navajo migration in Denver over the last ten years. In addition, we collected similar records on 139 Spanish-American male migrants (Rendon 1968) and 41 lower-class Anglo males who occupied jobs in the city similar to the Navajo (Weppner 1968). Since Denver police consider Spanish their major problem-group, these subjects served to control for possible police bias in arrests, as well as for any problems of unfamiliarity with the city which a new migrant might suffer. The lower-class Anglo group served to control for the possible effects of reputed lower-class drinking "culture."

Despite these controls against bias, the Indian group exhibited an arrest rate of 104,000 per 100,000 man-years in the city, which is more than twenty times the Anglo rate (5,000) and over eight times the migrant Spanish rate (12,500). At least 93% of the Navajo arrests were for drinking-related offenses, far higher than for the other two groups. Even this figure may be too low, however, if a careful follow-up were made of each arrest to check the possibility of alcohol involvement. In exactly such a study of 610 Indian arrests in San Francisco, for example, Swett found that "consumption of alcohol was a contributing factor, either to the offense or to the arrest, in every case" (1932:2). Furthermore, when we examined the *types* of crimes for which our migrant subjects were being arrested, it appeared that the rate of arrest for serious crimes, whether against persons or against property, were clearly *lower* than for the population at large. Obviously it is not that Indians are more "criminal" than other minority groups, as Stewart (1964:65) implies, they are simply more drunk. It is to an explanation of this phenomenon that we must now turn.

THE STRATEGY OF EXPLANATION

An explanation of these gross group differences can be sought in either of two ways. The typical anthropological approach is to examine factors in the history of the Navajo, or of American Indians in general, to discover aspects of their cultural tradition, particularly with respect to alcohol use, that might explain their apparent low threshold for drunken excess (Heath 1964; Stewart 1964; Ferguson 1968). For example, most North American Indian groups lacked aboriginal intoxicants; they acquired a taste for hard liquor within the context of a "frontier" society; their long history of prohibition gave them little opportunity to learn and practice patterns of "moderate" social drinking; and so forth (Dozier 1966).

The poverty of culture as an explanatory concept is apparent, however, on two counts. First, despite the depressing overall picture of migrant drinking just presented, about half the Navajo who come to Denver never have a run-in with the police and appear to be keeping their drinking within tolerable limits. Yet all are products of this same cultural tradition. Recourse to specific features of a culture's development or to limitations in its adaptive behavioral repertoire simply fail to help us understand these significant *intra*-group differences.

Second, even if we were able to achieve some satisfactory level of explanation of migrant Indian drinking through an appeal to unique features of Indian "culture," our general understanding of drunkenness as a behavioral phenomenon would be relatively little advanced. Each "cultural" explanation of group differences is ideographic, an explanation that can apply only to that group (or very similar groups) in that place and time. But how then are we to explain drunken excess among American Indian groups such as the Apache and those south of the border who *did* possess intoxicants aboriginally, or among half-breeds whose socialization to Indian tradition is often attenuated, or among the Eskimo whose cultural tradition and contact history are quite different? And won't the American Indian experience have anything to contribute to an understanding of the growing problem of drunkenness among their Spanish-American neighbors, or stepping farther afield, among educated South African Bantu?

The strategy of explanation adopted in the present study is quite different, and I believe far more fruitful in the long run. All analyses have been conducted within a single ethnic group, the Navajo, thus

controlling for effects of cultural heritage. Drawing on more general
social science theory about the social-psychological etiology of excessive alcohol use, analytic variables have been selected on which
individual Navajo migrants may differ. Thus whatever empirical
relationships we find between indices of drunkenness and other
structural or psychological variables among Navajo migrants have
potential explanatory significance for other groups with drinking
problems as well.

This strategy does not imply that Navajo culture is irrelevant for
understanding excessive drinking among them. For example, the
modal position of Navajo subjects on the analytic variables we have
investigated results in large part from the way their culture patterns
the typical learning experiences of the Navajo child and subsequently
conditions his likely position within the wider American society.
Furthermore, the typical *form* that Navajo drinking takes (Health
1964; Ferguson 1968), its social and public nature, makes it particularly susceptible to notice by the police, so that arrest rates can be
used as a convenient and objective index of drunkenness rates,
something that could not be done if Navajo drinking were generally
more covert.

Finally, drunkenness has come to occupy a prominent place in the
adaptive repertoire of many Indian people: its narcotizing effects are
leaned on heavily as a way of coping with, by temporarily escaping
from, feelings of personal inadequacy and failure. This is only one
of many functions of alcohol use, of course, and one that most
drinkers, Indians and non-Indians alike, are aware of and depend
on from time to time (Jessor, Graves, Hanson, & Jessor 1968; Jessor,
Carmen, & Grossman 1968). It is possible, however, that in the
typical response hierarchy of Indian people drunkenness has a lower
threshold for selection when adjustment problems arise than alternative, more constructive adaptations.

Such a response tendency, if it exists, could be ascribed to the
peculiarities of Indian cultural tradition. Alternatively, however, it
may also be explained in terms of the typical structural conditions
within which their problems of adaptation occur. This is my own
reading of the facts. I find no convincing empirical evidence that
there is something unique about the way Indians use alcoholic
beverages, or that other people in similar circumstances would not
behave in a similar fashion (Jessor, Graves, Hanson, & Jessor 1968).
In fact, it is my contention that the vast majority of Indian drunkenness can be explained purely in terms of structural and psychological variables relatively independent of their particular cultural
tradition and that any residue of difference between them and other
minority groups that remains may as well be accounted for by the

limitations of our theory and measurement as by some Indian "cultural predisposition."

THEORY AND METHODOLOGY

The theoretical orientation adopted in this study is a synthesis of two major intellectual traditions. One embodies theories of psychopathology, which treat drunkenness as one of many "neurotic" responses to conditions of psychic stress. Critical elements in these theories are such things as *conflicts* between competing but mutually incompatible goals, or the *disjunctions* that result from unfulfilled aspirations. The other is made up of socialization theories, which treat drunkenness as learned behavior. Critical elements are the social *models* provided, and the pattern of social *reinforcements* and *punishments* by which behavior is social modified and directed.

These two bodies of theory are complementary: each explains exactly what the other leaves out. Disjunction-conflict theories of psychopathology provide powerful psychological *motives* for drinking, social learning theories account for the *channeling* of these motives into specific behavioral form. Their synthesis results in a true social-psychological or "field" theory of urban Indian drunkenness (Yinger 1965).

My approach has been to treat drinking as a rational and purposive act, an adaptive maneuver in a migrant's continuing efforts to achieve personal satisfaction. The determinants of this act are hypothesized to lie in the interaction between a particular set of objective conditions and a particular set of personal attributes for perceiving, evaluating, and coping with these conditions. Such a simplified "decision-theory" framework is straightforward enough when applied to specific choices such as whether to return home to the reservation (Graves and VanArsdale 1966). But drunkenness is a *recurring* act; our interest is not in whether a migrant drinks, but how often he drinks to excess. This requires us to search for explanatory variables that can be related to group differences in *rates* of drunkenness by increasing or decreasing the probability that a drinking response will be displayed by a variety of actors in a variety of situations through time.

Finally, a word must be said about the nature of alcohol itself. People drink for many reasons. An adequate theory of drinking behavior should therefore provide room for a diversity of individual motives, such as the many social-convivial ends consumption frequently serves. But drunkenness is a peculiarly attractive response to conditions of frustration and conflict. Its narcotizing effects provide a simple, inexpensive, and readily available means for temporary escape from psychic misery. When trying to account for high rates

THEODORE D. GRAVES

of drunkenness within any group, therefore, these physical properties of alcohol must certainly be recognized.

Based on these theoretical considerations, four general hypotheses have been formulated concerning sources of intragroup variations in Navajo migrant drinking behavior.

Hypothesis I: *Those Navajo migrants who are least successful in obtaining the economic rewards of urban life will display the highest rates of drunkenness.*

A migrant may come to Denver for many reasons. But the main thing he is seeking is a good job, one better than the limited reservation resources can provide. Failure to obtain steady, well-paying work in Denver should therefore prove to be a major source of disappointment and frustration, which alcohol could help him to forget.

Hypothesis II: *Those Navajo migrants with the greatest opportunity for acquiring skills for successfully holding down good jobs will display the lowest rates of drunkenness.*

Failure on a job may occur either because it is too difficult or because the migrant has limited personal resources for coping with its demands. One source of their urban difficulties, therefore, should be found in the poor training and limited experience that many migrants bring to the city.

Hypothesis III: *Those Navajo migrants who experience the greatest disjunction between their personal goals and their expectations of achieving them, or the greatest conflict between competing, mutually incompatible goals, will display the highest rates of drunkenness.*

Although a marginal economic position should be the major structural source of migrant motives to drink, they may differ in the way they perceive and evaluate their marginality. And material things are not the only goals toward which migrants aspire. For a more complete understanding of reasons they may seek drunken escape, therefore, a direct assessment of these psychological variables is also required.

Hypothesis IV: *Those Navajo migrants experiencing the weakest social pressures to drink and the strongest social controls against drinking will diplay the lowest rate of drunkenness.*

In Denver the major social pressures and constraints relevant to a migrant's drinking stem from his wife and his fellow Navajo peers. This fourth hypothesis directs us to examine the effect of these social relationships on migrant drinking behavior. In interaction with strong psychological motives to drink, these factors should provide substantial understanding of the high rates of Navajo drunkenness and arrest observed.

To bring empirical evidence to bear on this decision model, data were collected on 259 male Navajo migrants and former migrants, including essentially all who were living in Denver during 1963–1966 ($N = 135$), as well as a one-third random sample of all former Denver migrants who had returned to the Navajo Reservation ($N = 124$). Our main instrument was a lengthy formal interview of about two hours duration, which included background information, complete job histories, and a battery of psychometric and sociometric tests. In addition, interviews and ratings were collected from most employers of Navajo Indians in Denver (Weppner 1968), all migrant records from the Bureau of Indian Affairs were abstracted, participant observation of Navajo recreational activities in Denver was conducted (Snyder 1968), and case studies in depth were made of representative migrant individuals and families (McCracken 1968; McSwain 1965; Ziegler 1967). From this wealth of data, findings of substantial internal consistency and reliability are now emerging.

In the present paper arrest rates in the city will serve as our major criterion measure. These have the virtue of being "nonreactive" (Webb et al. 1966) and extend over the entire period each migrant remained in the city. Self-report data on drinking rates and drinking-related problems were also collected, but for a number of reasons these have not proved to be as useful. Not the least of these is that half the self-reports were collected after the migrant returned to the reservation and therefore may reflect a post-migration adaptation.

The use of arrest rates places some limitations upon the analysis, however. In the case of the Navajo (and probably all urban Indians) the assumption that the greater the drunkenness the greater the arrest rate is not unreasonable, given the high percentage of arrests that are drinking-related offenses and the predominantly public form that Indian drinking takes. But because the relationship between drunkenness and arrest is probabilistic rather than mechanical, *group* rates will be more dependable than *individual* rates, making correlations between a migrant's personal attributes and his frequency of arrest unstable. This problem is exacerbated by the fact that many migrants, like Harrison Joe, remain in the city only a few weeks or months, so that the temporal base on which individual rates might be calculated is often very small.

As a result of such considerations, our analytic procedure has been as follows. To relate arrest rates to various "independent" variables, these are dichotomized at the median, or in some cases at a natural break in the distribution or at some psychologically significant point. Then we estimate the arrest rate for those migrants with high and with low scores. First we count the number of arrests among those "highs" interviewed on the reservation, multiply this figure by three (since we have a one-third sample) and add it to the number of arrests acquired by "highs" interviewed in Denver (where we had essentially a total sample.) The same procedure is then followed for estimating the number of man-years the "highs" spent in the city, and arrests are divided by man-years, rounded to two significant decimal places, to yield an estimated rate per man-year for the "highs." These steps are then repeated for migrants falling in the "low" category as well. In standard form these two figures are then converted to rates per 100,000 man-years in the city (simply multiplying each by 100,000) to permit direct comparison with data such as were presented in Tables 18.1 and 18.2.

This procedure may sound complicated, perhaps even a bit underhanded. It is not. Nevertheless, since it will be used throughout this paper and is critical to the argument, it is essential that credibility not be lost at this point. The following demonstration may help to illustrate and clarify the procedure and perhaps allay suspicions of mathematical legerdemain as well.

The arrest rate for our migrant population in Denver has already been presented; it was based on actual records from almost the entire group. Suppose we were to estimate this same rate from our interviewed sample. How would this estimate be calculated, based on the procedure outlined above, and how would it compare with the actual rate?

The 135 migrants interviewed in Denver had 245 arrests, while the 124 interviewed on the reservation had 137. Since the reservation group is a one-third sample of all returnees, we multiply their arrests by three to get an estimate of the total returnee arrests: 411. When these are added to the Denver group we obtain an estimate of 656 arrests for the total population. The actual number by count was 665, giving us an error in estimate of about 1½%. Similarly for man-years in the city. The group interviewed in Denver account for 352½ man-years, while the group interviewed on the reservation account for 86⅓. Multiplying the latter figure by three and adding the two we obtain an estimate of 611½ man-years in the city for the total migrant group. This compares with 639 man-years by actual count, or an error in estimate of about 4%. Finally, to calculate the arrest rate, we divide the estimated number of arrests, 656, by the estimated number of man-years in the city, 611½, and multiply by 100,000. This yields a figure of 107,000 arrests per 100,000 population, as compared with the actual rate of 104,000, for an error in estimate of less than 3%.

Also worth mentioning at this point is the question of the "statistical significance" of the data to be presented subsequently. Since arrests are not independent events, i.e., the same person may be arrested more than once, there is no statistical procedure by which the "significance" of a difference between the arrest rates of two groups can be tested. This problem is exacerbated by the unequal sampling ratios employed in the Denver and returnee strata, since data from the latter subjects must be multiplied by three to provide population estimates, introducing further nonindependence. As a consequence, no tests of statistical significance will be presented in this paper. Instead, we will be forced to apply far more stringent criteria to an evaluation of our results: (1) is the magnitude of the group differences in arrest rate found large enough to have *social* significance, and (2) is the *pattern* of associations found consistent and in line with a reasonable set of theoretical expectations? If these two criteria are met, then the issue of statistical significance would be irrelevant anyway. For those still concerned with the problem, however, some evaluation of the results can be based on the error in estimate of group rates just presented. If group differences in arrest rates are no larger than 3,000 to 5,000 per 100,000 man-years in the city, for example, they are probably not large enough to be stable, and therefore not worth interpreting. But almost all of the differences to be presented here are of the order of 20,000 or more. It is therefore very unlikely that our interpretations are empirically unfounded despite our inability to demonstrate the formal statistical significance of our results.

ECONOMIC FACTORS

As I have emphasized in a different research context, the major structural pressure to drink experienced by Indians in U.S. society derives from their marginal economic position. The theoretical basis for this statement is to be found in the work of Merton (1957) and others. When goals are strongly held for which society provides inadequate means of attainment, in the view of these theorists, the resulting means-goals "disjunction" produces pressures for engaging in alternative, often nonapproved adaptations, of which excessive drinking is one common form. In decision theory terms what this means is that the anticipated rewards (goals) for engaging in socially approved behavior (means) are relatively low. The resulting disappointment and frustration leads to the selection of *other* courses of action (such as drunkenness) that may not be so highly approved but provide substitute rewards. Using a rural sample of both Indians and Spanish-Americans, I found that among those strongly oriented toward the dominant society and its material values, those with poor and irregular jobs consistently had higher rates of drinking and associated problem-behavior, as well as stronger psychological *feelings* of deprivation and alienation, than those holding down relatively steady jobs. By contrast, among those with relatively little commitment to the dominant group values, the kind of jobs they held had practically no relationship to drinking rates or associated psychological feelings (Graves 1967a. See also Jessor, Graves, Hanson, and Jessor 1968 for the more general situation among nonacculturating groups as well).

Among migrant Indians, the situation is different than among these rural-reservation groups. Essentially all migrants are strongly attracted to economic goals, which is a major source of their dissatisfaction with reservation life and motivation to migrate. Furthermore, those who remain in the city longest display the strongest economic value orientation (Graves and VanArsdale 1966). We therefore hypothesized that any index of economic failure in the city would be associated with higher rates of drunkenness and arrest among all migrants.

This hypothesis was repeatedly supported, regardless of what measures of economic success we employed (Tables 18.3 and 18.4). Wages have great psychological salience for these migrants, and the reader should particularly note the association between arrest rates and an indirect measure of feelings of *relative deprivation* that we derived from this fact. When the migrant's starting wage was *lower* than the highest wage he had received before migrating, as was true for slightly over half of all migrants, it is probably fair to assume that he might well begin to wonder if the many sacrifices associated with migration were worthwhile. This structurally based psychological situation is associated with a subsequent arrest rate of 116,000 per 100,000 man-years in the city, more than double the rate of 54,000 among those migrants whose starting wages were at least as high as they had experienced before migration.

But absolute levels of economic achievement are also associated with arrest rates; jointly these form an even more powerful predictor. Those who experienced unemployment rates of 15% or more during their first few months in Denver and who had a starting wage of no more than $1.25 per hour, which was also as low or lower than they had experienced before migration (16% of all migrants), had an arrest rate of 214,000 per 100,000 man-years in the city. By contrast, those with less unemployment and higher starting wage in both relative and absolute terms (11% of all migrants) had an arrest

Table 18.3 Initial Economic Experiences in the City Versus Denver Arrest Rates

	Percentage of all migrants	Arrest rate per 100,000 pop.
Initial % employed		
more than 85%	50	73,000
85% or less	50	128,000
Starting wage		
more than $1.25 per hour	38	77,000
$1.25 or less per hour	62	93,000
Starting wage relative to highest premigration wage		
same or higher than premigration	48	54,000
lower than premigration	52	116,000
Combined pattern of variables		
favorable on all three of the above	11	34,000
favorable on two out of three	32	85,000
favorable on only one indicator	41	88,000
unfavorable on all three of the above	16	214,000

Table 18.4 Subsequent Economic Experiences in the City Versus Denver Arrest Rates

	Percentage of all migrants	Arrest rate per 100,000 pop.
Subsequent % employed		
full employment	66	66,000
some unemployment	34	179,000
Present wage		
more than $1.35 per hour	45	57,000
$1.35 or less per hour	55	167,000
Present wage relative to highest premigration wage		
higher than premigration	51	43,000
same or lower than premigration	49	165,000
Combined pattern of variables		
favorable on all three of the above	22	44,000
favorable on two out of three	32	55,000
favorable on only one indicator	33	157,000
unfavorable on all three of the above	13	448,000

rate of only 34,000 per 100,000, about one-sixth that of their less fortunate brethren.

Although these initial economic experiences in Denver are powerful predictors of a migrant's subsequent drinking problems, the association between economic position and arrest rate deepens with time in the city (Table 4). For example, those who continued to have periods of unemployment during their last few months in Denver and who were making less than $1.50 per hour, which was a wage no higher than they had received before coming to Denver (13% of all migrants), had an appalling arrest rate of 448,000 per 100,000 man-years in the city!

In part this depressing relationship between economic position and arrest rate probably results from the fact that continuing deprivation is more psychologically disturbing than initial deprivation, when hopes may linger for better times to come. But it also derives from the effect of the migrant's drinking on his economic position. Complaints about their drunkenness is the major factor that differentiates employer ratings of Indian employees from those of Whites in comparable jobs, and these complaints are clearly related to lower Indian wages or dismissal (Weppner 1968). As one employer put it, describing his experience with one of our subjects, "He'd take off three or four days at a time because of drinking. We took him back three or four times but hell, there's no use putting up with it." This feedback from the migrant's drinking behavior to the structural and psychological "determinants" that in turn give rise to it is a theme we have tried to pursue in this study wherever our time-linked data permit. Thus we can trace the development of a vicious cycle between structural position, personality, and behavior that is difficult to break once it has been set in motion.

Background Factors

This developmental cycle does not begin in the city, however. Background preparation for urban life also contributes to economic success in Denver, and thereby to a better personal adjustment. We were particularly fascinated by the possible influence of a migrant's father (or father surrogate) in providing both direct and indirect training for successful wage-labor, via now familiar processes of social learning and "modeling" (Bandura and Walters 1963). Our hypothesis was that successful parental wage-labor role models would be associated with better economic performance in the city by their sons, and therefore better personal adjustment. All the links in this chain of inference cannot be presented here, though this hypothesis received support at each point examined. Table 18.5 presents the end product, the association between parental models and subsequent urban arrest rates. As can be seen, those migrants whose fathers provided economically successful wage-labor role models had arrest rates of 62,000 per 100,000 man-years in Denver, less than half the rate for migrants whose fathers were engaged in more traditional reservation occupations and were economically unsuccessful as well (135,000 arrests per 100,000 man-years).

Table 18.5 Economically Successful Parental Role Models Versus Denver Arrest Rates

	Percentage of all migrants	Arrest rate per 100,000 pop.
Father's occupation		
father has nontraditional occupation (wage-labor)	39	75,000
father has traditional occupation (farming-herding)	61	97,000
Economic position of family or orientation		
perceived as better off than neighbors	60	75,000
perceived as worse off than neighbors	40	117,000
Combined pattern of variables		
nontraditional occupation *and* family was better off	26	62,000
mixed pattern	48	83,000
traditional occupation *and* family was worse off	26	135,000

Table 18.6 Education and Vocational Training Versus Denver Arrest Rate

	Percentage of all migrants	Arrest rate per 100,000 pop.
Years of education		
11 years or more	14	33,000
8–10 years	31	75,000
5–7 years	45	128,000
4 years or less	10	87,000
Vocational training		
skilled	41	66,000
semiskilled	45	117,000
none	14	83,000
Combined pattern of variables		
8 or more years of education *and* skilled vocational training	21	51,000
mixed pattern	43	77,000
less than 8 years of school *and* no skilled vocational training	36	145,000

Education and vocational training provide even more direct preparation for successful economic performance and were therefore also expected to be associated with a better urban adjustment. The evidence in support of this hypothesis is presented in Table 18.6. Migrants with eight or more years of formal education that included skilled vocational training also had arrest rates of less than half those with less education and no skilled vocational training (51,000 versus 145,000 arrests per 100,000 man-years in the city). Note, however, that a small amount of education or training is associated with higher arrest rates than almost none at all. Perhaps this results from raising the migrant's aspirations higher than this level of preparation can help him achieve. Commonly these migrants, like Harrison Joe, who came to the city with semiskilled training for which there is a limited market, expect to receive good jobs in their chosen field right away and are disappointed when they don't.

Other forms of premigration experience were also implicated, but not always in the manner one might anticipate. For example, premigration wage labor experience, though it usually resulted in better urban jobs, was also associated with higher arrest rates. From other data it appears likely that favorable premigration experience raises migrant aspirations farther than the reality of urban life can satisfy, thus producing a sense of "relative deprivation" among many otherwise "successful" migrants.

In sum, if we were to look at no other variables than a migrant's economic position in the city, we would still have achieved a major understanding of his drunkenness and arrest problems.

CHAPTER NINETEEN

Papago Indians at Work

JACK O. WADDELL

ANGLO CULTURAL MAXIMIZERS
Commercial Farms

A Papago farm hand who relies on relatively steady work on a southern Arizona farm is involved in a hierarchy of social structures that provides a progressively diminishing intensity of contact and interaction with fellow Papagos as he extends himself beyond the farm. That is, the commercial farming enterprise is so structured that the most intense and direct social experiences are in terms of other Papagos in the farm setting, with a minimization of contact with other Papagos as social relationships are traced outward from the farm setting to non-Papago involvements in towns and cities.

Most farms with which I have become familiar have made provisions for their farm laboring families to live in the many adobe, wood, or block dwellings that have been constructed on farm property over the years. Within such encampments, it has been possible for Papagos, particularly the ones more regularly attached to the camp or farm, to appropriate the dwellings in accordance with changes in the numerical structure of the household. A nuclear household may either be relatively isolated from all other nuclear or extended households at the farm, or it may be adjacent to other nuclear households. In the cases where there are close relatives, adjacent nuclear households may actually function as a form of extended family and utilize common cooking and eating facilities and manifest other forms of cooperative interdependence. A number of individuals from a number of related nuclear families may rely on the stable incomes of one or two individuals plus whatever other members might contribute from occasionally joining chopping or picking crews.

It is a general characteristic of commercial farm organization to segregate the homes of farm laborers from the residences of supervisors. Papagos can further semi-isolate themselves, within farm camps, through the manner in which they occupy certain sections of them. The camps usually have ample buildings to permit a kind of Papago farm community or neighborhood of relatives to develop, although the larger camps are more complex since a number of ethnic groups may be represented. Even in this case, Papagos usually can maintain the integrity of their corporate households. The most intense and direct interaction is with other Papagos, usually related, in adjacent sections of the camp. Lesser contacts with members of other camp households, including those of other ethnic groups, also occur. The tendency of certain farms to have high concentrations of Papagos tends to be reinforcing and Papagos know where to go in order to find certain concentrations. After all, many of these are built up and sustained by a flow of relatives over several generations or seasons.

Although there are irrigating teams, cleaning crews, and other occasions for group work and informal contact in fields among Papago workers, I would generalize by saying that the formal requirements of farm jobs are performed largely in relative solitude—driving a tractor, irrigating a field, or chopping or picking in a crew that is spread over a cotton field. Any informal contacts between employees usually take place without the knowledge or concern of supervisors.

Other significant relationships provided by the farm structure and organization are the formal and informal interactions with foremen and farm operators. A foreman or an operator usually makes initial contacts to explain the nature of the day's work or to get the worker started, making periodic checks throughout the day. Occasional informal contacts with a foreman seem to be significant; since it is common for the foreman's house to be near the camp, and the foreman may become the channel through which personal requests for services such as transportation are made. The foreman's children may play with children in the camp, and he may have a familiarity with informal activities in the camp because of its proximity and his more direct relationships with the laborers.

The structured relationships are largely due to the organization of the farm itself but subject to the greatest amount of Papago modification. A next level of structured relationships would consist of those that occur within the rural farming town center. The store becomes the focal point for informal contacts with Anglo, Mexican, or Chinese store managers; but Papago farm hands' relationships with the general stores are essentially economic in nature.[1] In some places, such as Stanfield, Marana, and Sahuarita, for example, the store becomes the source of contact with other Indians from other farms and reservation villages in the vicinity. These meeting places provide an additional source for sharing the present state of the farm labor market in terms of jobs available in an area.

Public drinking by Papagos in the town centers usually takes place in rather well-known establishments. The names of particular taverns where Papagos go are well known in Gila Bend, Casa Grande, Coolidge, Florence, Marana, and Sahuarita. Thus, the town centers, through their taverns, also become media for drawing together Papagos scattered throughout the farming region. In this way, rather than breaking down Papago contacts with other Papagos, rural towns—through stores, taverns, jails, and other congregating places—actually function to integrate Papago informal activities and thus contribute to ethnic maintenance and cultural identification.

I found that a number of my informants had occasion to go to Sells to consult with a representative of the agency about income tax reports, the handling of money, or some welfare problem relating to some member of the family. The state, county, and BIA agencies are not always together as to which has jurisdiction in particular cases involving off-reservation Papagos, since Papago families off-reservation may be in touch with a number of such agencies. My general impressions are that Papagos whose experiences have been predominantly off the reservation do utilize the services of BIA agencies but with less frequency. The modified kinship settlements on farms orient individuals and families to the more immediate rural town centers or urban areas for the services of state and county agencies or to Anglo individuals for the personal advice that might have formerly been performed by the Indian service representatives.

There are other Anglo structures that extend into the countryside to link Papagos to the larger social order. Protestant and Catholic churches attempt to minister to individuals and families within the camps; state agencies, through public health nurses and welfare case workers, pay visits to families within the camps; selling agencies send traveling salesmen to call on homes with their products; and law enforcement agencies have official business in camps. These contacts are, however, most meaningful largely in terms of the individual agents representing the various institutions.

There are significant cultural values relating to industrialized commercial farming that are extremely relevant to Papago participation in a non-Papago social environment. The fact that commercial farms are concerned primarily in producing market crops that will result in profit implies that farm management must employ whatever instrumentalities best ensure this kind of production. Whether to exploit machines, human effort, or both largely hinges on this.

The immediate effect of this production-profit value on Papago and other unskilled laborers consists in the rationalization of industrialized farming that there are great risks in producing for a market. The farm must battle against unforeseen losses due to inclement weather, bacterial infestations, fluctuations in national market economy, the uncertainties of a labor force, etc. As one way of offsetting this risk, it must rely on a largely unskilled labor force to which it cannot pay, nor need it pay, very substantial wages.

As further rationalization to offset this apparent "inhumane" practice, the farm operator can claim a number of "humane" practices that are not found in urban industrialized labor appropriation. The farm can claim that it provides rent-free facilities to its employees. Likewise, it provides wage opportunities for those who would have difficulty marketing their unskilled abilities in other kinds of work. Even more significant is the rationalization that farms are more tolerant of Papago life ways in that the demands of the job actually alter Papago social organization, activity interests, and other values very little. There is a form of institutionalization, which I call condescending institutionalization, in which certain operations of an industry are actually geared to the behavior patterns of the particular people being utilized by that industry. This form of institutionalization contrasts with what I call bureaucratic institutionalization, where operations are not geared to or dependent on the habits of a particular group of people but, rather, are standardized to utilize only those who qualify and continue to meet the job requirements.

Farms condescend in institutionalizing their dealings with Papagos in that they are cognizant of family ties, aware of festive occasions that take Papagos away from their jobs, acknowledge that the jobs they provide fall within traditional and well established activity interests, and can adjust occupational rewards and punishments to Papago drinking patterns without losing access to this labor resource. I call it condescending institutionalization because it admits the availability of an inferior, subordinate group of workers whose very deficits are exploitable and can be appropriated to the best interests of commercial farming goals. Several operators and foremen have complained about the erratic and undependable behavior of their Indians but at the same time choose to depend largely on Indians for their sources of labor. There is good evidence to suppose that farmers have long come to be as dependent on this kind of institutionalization as have their Indian employees. This is particularly true of some of the smaller, less highly industrialized or mechanized farms.

The extent to which farm operators and supervisors become friends and neighbors to the working force, including Papagos, must be restricted. Homes are provided for laborers; but they are segregated from the homes of management, since the success of the operation depends on a relative amount of social distance. Laborers are kept within reach for use on necessary activities, but social distance is maintained. Common laborers, with their "different" values and usually "depraved" economic situations, cannot be treated as equals or as friends because equality and friendship would imply mutual and reciprocal manifestations of such status. With unequal economic statuses, if operators treated laborers as friends and neighbors, they fear they would soon be overdrawn in requested favors and the functioning of the farm organization, which depends on employer-employee relationships (not friend to friend relationships), would be seriously challenged. The functional solution, long ago achieved, is a brand of paternalism similar to the *patrón* system, where proprietors and workers alike know just how far to extend themselves in their interpersonal relationships. It is a controlled relationship that may be distantly friendly but not a friendship. The employer may respond to a request for aid or favor, but it is not as a neighbor, friend, or equal. He responds instead, as employer who is seeking to maintain a relationship with a relatively reliable and trustworthy economic commodity—a laborer.

This brand of paternalism is not inhumanitarian; it is, instead, expedient humanitarianism in which both employer and employee understand what to expect and what not to expect in terms of the other. I found a considerable degree of attachment and interest on the part of some farmers toward some of their more steady Papago hands, even when the farmers spoke negatively of Papagos as a whole. The humaneness lies in the rationalization that the farm is tolerant toward what is assumed to be the Papago style of life. Since the arrangement is economically advantageous as well, both farmer and Papago worker can be relatively content. The Papago farm worker whose lifetime has been spent in this kind of relationship to a farm or farms may have misgivings about it; but generally I have found far greater contentment, or better, lack of manifest resentment than I have in those situations where occupational experience has attempted to venture outside of the farm labor market.

Farm life, centered in a camp and involving a limited range of familiar occupational activities currently is not particularly a system unto itself. The countryside, as an extension of more populous, industrialized urban centers, is constantly invaded by the values of the larger system. Perhaps the most influential inroads of Anglo industrial culture into the farm camps where Papagos live are traversed by agents of the welfare complex, that complex of institutions which operates on the value premise that the people who are out of step with the economic, health, and spiritual benefits of the Anglo technological tradition are in need of directed efforts to aid them in articulating with these benefits. Much of the activity related to this concern is directed by governmental or public agencies and supported by a number of institutions at the horizontal (national) and vertical (local) levels (Steward 1950: 115). Public health instruction, economic services, various other social services, and spiritual guidance and indoctrination are some of the instrumental values to which Papagos on farms are being introduced.

The influence of the various public institutions, however, is largely through individual agents. The extent to which the institutional values are effectively transmitted depends largely on the quality of the particular interpersonal relationships between Papagos and the individual agents of the cultural values embodied in the local and national institutions they represent.

The agents of Anglo institutions that most frequently have contact with Papago households and camps are school teachers, migrant ministers and priests, public health nurses, deputies, salesmen, and independent Anglo benefactors. While there are the usual formal expectations of their services (special tutoring, indoctrination, performance of rites, health instruction, arrests, sales, etc.), the influence the personal agents have in transmitting Anglo values depends on their personal qualities and the extent of their interest in certain individuals and/or families. Public health nurses, for instance, not only advise in matters of domestic health but, if close to a family, might talk to a young person about saving money or the kind of work for which he might prepare. These influences, since highly personalized, are never evenly distributed over a single camp but are usually centered on the more receptive households. Papago men seem to be far less influenced by these contacts than are the women and children.

Ajo Mine

A Papago miner at Ajo similarly is involved in a hierarchy of social structures in which his interactions with non-Papagos undergo qualitative changes in duration, nature, intensity, quality, and directionality as he extends himself beyond his Papago household and the Indian village.

The Ajo Indian village is a segregated segment of the community of Ajo and consists of a number of individual nuclear households. Households that are related by kinship ties are generally dispersed throughout the village, due to company regulation of housing rental and due to the fact that turnover at the mine does not usually permit acquisition of adjacent houses by related families. There is, however, some informal and uncondoned "swapping" of houses which creates a few neighborhood aggregate households of kin. The overall community arrangements are more favorable to individual nuclear households. During the periodic shutdowns, most Papagos in the Indian village return to their various kinship villages on the reservation; or reservation relatives frequently come to visit in Ajo. The vital kinship links are still largely in terms of kinship villages, not the Ajo village.

Partly due to the complexity of the Indian village and partly as a result of company encouragement, the Indian community is stratified. The smallest and lowest rent houses are usually clustered together and are more frequently occupied by Papagos with the highest turnover and lowest skill levels. Next are clusters of larger houses at slightly higher rent that are generally occupied by employees with greater seniority and occupying higher skill levels. Also, there is one section of the village where homes are owned, usually by Papago families of several generations in Ajo. They are usually the most permanent Ajo Papagos. Lastly, there is a marginal section between the Indian village and upper Mexican town where a few Papago families occupy modern bungalow type houses. The heads of these households are Papagos who are involved in political activity for the village and who generally have stable positions if not higher job levels with the company. The company has been instrumental in encouraging Papagos who it feels could best occupy these better houses. As would be expected, there is a great deal of rivalry and interpersonal conflict that results from these internal status differences.

Other significant structural features of the Ajo Indian community are the several pan-village sodalities. Besides integrating a number of unrelated and independent Papago households in the different "strata," the sodalities seem to contribute to an Indian (primarily Papago) cultural identity that the diverse origins, the wide range of acculturation types, and the stratified nature of the community would otherwise tend to weaken. In addition, the sodalities serve as links to the larger Anglo community, including Mexican town—the Feast of St. Catherine draws Anglos and Mexicans as well as reservation Papagos; a women's club helps plan for "Indian Day" in the schools; the village councilmen consult with personnel of local agencies regarding problems relating to Papagos in the larger community, etc.

Most Papago contacts within the larger community are self-initiated and consist of individual contacts in various facilities in town, such as the stores, recreational facilities, and welfare agencies. There is wide variation in the extent of participation. The mining company, through its cooperative store, its housing authority, its company hospital, its employment opportunities and policies, and its overall influence in the community through its officialdom, functions to integrate the segregated ethnic communities.

There are some central value orientations that are instrumental in encouraging the behavior and attitudes of Papago miners to conform to certain social and economic demands. The formal occupational structure and the policies relating to the mine operation embody values that are extremely significant; since they largely stimulate the social differences in the village and the town proper, thus having an important bearing on the structure of interaction for Papagos.

First, there is the wage system that is structured according to the level of skill demanded for particular work roles. Even the minimum wage for an unskilled worker is considerably more than even the highest paid farm hand receives. Since unskilled jobs are gradually being eliminated through mechanization, skill and training are becoming even more important. Whether one is hired depends on a high school diploma, and success on a whole battery of standardized tests. While seniority still functions for older employees, skilled competence is the only assurance for advancement to higher skill-pay levels and more responsible and prestigious jobs. The skill levels are still sufficiently spread out to provide a wide range of skills and responsibilities, but it is an implicit feature of the structure that certain jobs and certain performances have a greater value and worth attached to them. The best indication of this worth is in the wage and the job title, and the motivation is directed upward in these terms.

Ideally, the structure is bureaucratic in that the many levels are open to all who can qualify for them, and all employees have equal opportunity to rise in the system. Those who cannot qualify at higher levels cannot ascend the opportunity structure, and those who cannot meet minimum requirements do not qualify for a job in the first place. This feature is therefore a very selective one, since Papagos who do qualify are those who either have long-term seniority or who have incorporated the motivational values and the necessary skills to qualify in the first place.

The occupational structure at the Ajo mine, in other words, embodies the values of a technologically and industrially advanced society—namely, the importance of supervisory and administrative know-how; the significance of equal opportunity as an ideal value; the right to organize and express grievances or to arbitrate them; the importance of material manifestations (type of home, clothes, goods, etc.) of one's success in the system; and the importance of formal education as an index of one's ability to do a job.

Notwithstanding these cultural ideals, Papagos and other Indians at Ajo are a discretely identifiable segment of a highly segregated mining community. This is, in part, due to historical precedent wherein the demand for a large unskilled work force in the past and the availability of Papagos drew a large number to the mine. With the rapid changes of the past few decades, the mine's own rationalizations have functioned to further segregate the Indians as something different, while at the same time promoting the ideal of equal opportunity. Some of these rationalizations are that the mine has been understanding by helping to provide the Indians with a community all their own in which they can carry on many of their own activities. At the same time the company has helped to provide better housing and facilities than the Indians demanded for themselves.

The employment office has also made allowances for Papagos as the mining industry has undergone radical technological changes that have demanded new kinds of skills. Formerly, most Papagos who came to work on the track could usually get a job for a few days, and, as turnover was high, these unskilled labor jobs could usually be performed at will. This seems to have been the occupational stereotype supported by both Papagos and the company for many years. This has been radically transformed in recent years, particularly by the company and by some Papagos. It is actually a source of disappointment among some Papagos to see this stereotype eliminated, since it has likewise barred unskilled and untrained Papagos from getting jobs for which they could qualify.

There are still allowances, made largely with Papagos in mind, for irresponsible drinking habits and lack of concern for the time demands of a steady job. The warning slip system for dealing with delinquency on the job is an accommodation of the company to these essentially Indian characteristics.[2]

Another rationalization is that while all are to be treated equally, Papagos must be treated unequally if they are to have equal access to the occupational system. Hence, while all applicants must qualify by passing standardized tests, Indians are given second chances to pass. If Indians do pass the tests, they are usually put to work if possible; while this is not true for other ethnic groups, who may have to wait.

The company also points to figures that indicate how Indians have elevated themselves over the years. One can see in the Ajo mine operation a combination of both bureaucratic and condescending institutionalization. I would suggest that the latter is the earlier manifestation, wherein former mining operations could function adequately by being geared to the habits of the common labor force. As operations changed, demands for greater and more diversified skills led toward the bureaucratization of the industry, whereby competence and skill became more essential than a muscle force. The high complement of Indians with seniority and the continued need for certain lower skilled performances have, nevertheless, maintained some of the condescending attitudes toward Indian employees.

The process seems to be in the direction of greater bureaucratization and less condescension. This has necessarily affected many Papagos, both those that are caught in the bureaucratic system and those whose jobs have been eliminated because of it.

Urban Occupations

The urban Papago worker has a considerable range of social experience, depending largely on his particular occupation and the specific kind of residence pattern he assumes. It is possible for a worker to be relatively insulated from intense and direct relationships with middle class Anglos if he attaches to a Papago residence compound in the Papago urban enclave and assumes one or several of the stereotypic work roles in the urban setting. In the residence compound his interactions are predominantly with Papago relatives whose social experiences are similar to his. In the stereotyped work role (i.e., yard work, nursery, railroad gang, etc.), he is party to the condescending institutionalization that reinforces the Indian stereotype for both himself and his employer. Other than economic relationships at stores; socializing experiences in taverns, on the streets, and in recreational facilities; or confrontations with public agency personnel, his interactions are largely in terms of other Papagos or other lower status ethnic group members.

Other urban Papagos, particularly those of second or third generations in Tucson, who have stabilized work roles, although still of low status, may have incentives to be more detached from the cultural group; because they have sufficiently grasped Anglo values to have hopes for their children, even if it is too late for themselves. They may move away from the center of the enclave into homes of their own, interspersed among other ethnic groups, or they may have retained homes in neighborhoods that have been abandoned by the Papago enclave as it has been pressed southward.

Of course, there are many transitory Papagos who do not succeed in attaching themselves to any particular Papago residence unit. These individuals simply float around certain downtown or South Tucson areas, having interaction with other Papagos on the streets but remaining unattached to any stable residence unit.

A last group would be those Papagos who, by their enculturation and training experiences, have assimilated the necessary values and motivations to have experienced some successes and satisfactions in their occupations and in their social relationships with non-Papagos. The values and interests of Anglo society have sufficiently motivated them to the point of selectively de-identifying with much that has characterized social life in the urban Papago enclave or social life in the reservation villages. They are more articulate with Anglos and are capable of articulating the condescending concern toward other Papagos that is characteristic of Anglos.

It is difficult to treat each of these four kinds of urban social orientations as a unit, but it seems justifiable to assume that they constitute a vertical mobility structure within the urban Papago "community" in which one group is largely stimulated by Anglo middle-class values. This Anglo-oriented Papago group in turn may function as a reference group for a younger generation derived from a more stable lower status group of Papagos. The latter, in turn, may serve as a reference group for certain individuals originating in the enclave compounds to which certain transitory Papagos may attach themselves and thus use the enclave community as a point of reference behavior.

Central Anglo values, then, funnel downward and become the basis of aspiration for Papago individuals throughout the Papago urban population. The most significant values are economic betterment and material acquisition, educational improvement, occupational preparation and training for higher statuses, better paying jobs, social participation in non-Papago types of organizations and sodalities, home ownership and improvement, and neighborhood affiliation that corresponds to socioeconomic status.

The discussion thus far has centered on general propositions about the social structure of occupational social fields. It has been suggested that these Anglo based sociostructural fields provide the basic social situations wherein Papago individuals experience different kinds and degrees of maximization in non-Papago culture, depending on the particular occupational field and the particular kinds of interactive experiences within it.

Papago Cultural Modifiers

In addition to the structural bases of interaction in each of the various Anglo dominated occupational settings, there are Papago social structures and values that must be accommodated to the occupational structures and values, through the media of individuals. What are some of the most obvious and significant of these modifying features of Papago culture that operate in the occupational field?

This study has treated kinship and other features of Papago social organization as significant dependent variables. In addition, leadership and ceremonial activities, informal group relations relative particularly to drinking and festive activities, and values about work and leisure activities have been assumed to be important in adapting behavior to the demands of an occupational involvement. Since the research design has concentrated on gathering data relative to these four areas, other significant areas, known and unknown, have necessarily been omitted or neglected in the data gathering stage. The following discussion is an evaluative conclusion as to the general significance of the four chosen areas for answering the question that has been the concern of this study; namely, what are the most significant demands that off-reservation occupational situations place on Papago individuals, and how do Papagos go about adapting their accustomed behavior to these demands?

Kinship and Social Organization

It does not seem satisfactory to unconditionally accept the proposition that the Papago extended family is altered at great psychic cost to Papago individuals when it confronts industrial society, where the nuclear family becomes a functional necessity. In the first place, the nuclear family is a meaningful Papago social unit that exists as one among a number of other relatively contiguous nuclear households made up of relatives. Kinship can be traced to many individuals in one's village or beyond, and domestic life and cooperation within this network of relatives takes many forms. This in no way obviates the nuclear household's importance or precedence, any more than the nuclear household prevents individual members from feeling obligated toward most distant relatives. Papagos speak of their obligations to relatives, relate meaningful experiences with them, and even lump classes of them together terminologically; but the nuclear household residence is a vital element in the socialization of individuals. The structure of kinship villages and their ecological relationships nonetheless provide a Papago individual with a social environment that is completely oriented to interactions with relatives of varying degrees of genealogical closeness.

Some of my data challenge my original notion that occupational mobility is always antithetical to extended family relations. It seems to support Litwak's (1960: 20) conclusion that in contemporary industrial society extended family relations emerge out of different institutional sources and are not totally dependent on geographic and occupational proximity in order for the extended family to be a functioning entity. In some cases the modified extended family relationships are more congruous with certain kinds of occupational mobility than are those of the isolated nuclear family.

The Papago cases seem to point to a number of ways that extended family ties can be modified to meet occupational exigencies. The modifications do seem to be functionally relevant to adaptations in particular occupational fields; and some types of occupational organization are more congenial to satisfactory modifications of extended family ties than are others. The facility with which Papago families are able to accommodate their family organization to certain kinds of occupational situations lies not only in the occupational structure; the Papago family has a cultural history of modification in its structure and in the relationships of its members. Economic expediencies (seasonal movement to mountain and field villages, taking in relatives to support, living in tent camps following construction crews, temporary encampments near sources of labor, etc.) seem to be primary causes for changes in family organization.

Thus, a family can be exclusively nuclear in terms of spatial arrangement (either due to the particular features of the occupational structure or due to internal features of the Papago family itself) and at the same time can be a functioning extended family network in terms of sentiment, economic cooperation, serving as informal channels of occupational recuitment, periodic festive activity, and providing sources of social reunion and leisure. The combination of nuclear and extended relationships is the functioning quality of the Papago family in adapting to the demands of making a living, and it has its foundations in the indigenous system, not exclusively in the more recent wage work complexes. The Papago family seems to be quite flexible in terms of adapting its organization to the facilities available in certain kinds of occupations.

I have been impressed by how widely distributed in space members of the Papago families with which I have become familiar seem to be. The majority of family histories and individual life histories reveal lifetime patterns of this extensive spatial distribution of individual members. It is difficult, therefore, to support the proposition that familiar kinship units and relationships are drastically disrupted by the exigencies of off-reservation occupational environments and thereby make Papago adaptation to jobs more difficult. The cases presented seem to support the proposition that Papago kinship boundaries are sentimental domains in which kinsmen over extensive spatial areas are linked together but that Papago family units and individual members in actuality are capable of considerable modification if the occupational situation is deemed to be an economically expedient arrangement.

The case studies presented seem to indicate that there is sufficient flexibility in the family and kinship structure; that any number of functional modifications in family arrangements are possible, even for the same family; and that any number of these arrangements are adaptive in nature; that is, they are capable of facilitating styles of life acceptable to the individuals involved. While there is expressed dissatisfaction at being apart from one's kinship village or one's relatives, I cannot attribute this dissatisfaction as a major difficulty in adapting personal behavior to the demands of a particular job. While family and kinship facets of role behavior are vital to Papago satisfaction and emotional security, it is difficult to consider kinship, by itself, as the crucial element in adaptive behavior in occupational social fields. The cases with which I have become familiar seem to indicate that Papagos adapt themselves personally to wage systems, despite what these occupations might immediately do to the family arrangements.

A long history of geographical mobility within an extensive but spatially limited area has produced a somewhat malleable form of family organization that is capable of adapting to a number of economic situations and still provides meaningful relationships with kinsmen. I do not see anything in the particular occupational complexes that are overwhelmingly incongruous with indigenous Papago patterns as far as kinship matters are concerned.

The farm organization seems more pliable for incorporating relatives, both with respect to the physical layout of farm camps and with respect to tendencies of farms to institutionalize relationships with related Papagos from certain reservation areas. It is not uncommon, however, to find isolated nuclear Papago households that have little direct relationships with kin; and I have found steady, reliable, and long-time employed Papagos from both extended family rural camps and from nuclear family isolate households largely cut off from a rural farm kinship community. Neither the assurance of extended family facilities nor the assumption of more isolated nuclear family organization is a guarantee of a stable relationship between a family and a commercial farm.

Ajo provides little in the way of a continuous experience for a worker among his many relatives. I found a few families that have been able to skirt company rules and form a neighborhood of related nuclear households into a kind of corporate family, but the majority of households are entirely nuclear arrangements. I found a prevailing lack of interest in Ajo other than as a necessary place to live while work is performed.

The nuclear family organization is the prevailing type within the Ajo Indian village, but the proximity to the reservation and the frequent shutdowns permit those who have extended family commitments on the reservation to fulfill them at anticipated intervals. As the company takes a more direct role in encouraging long-time Papago families to improve their status and living conditions to conform to Anglo values, the greater will be the threats to the workers' relationships with their fellow Papago kinsmen and friends who do not conform. I see Ajo as a much greater influence in stratifying Papago society and altering kinship ties than is the farm. More and more of the less acculturated Papagos are rejected by the Ajo complex and filter back to the reservation or to the commercial farm complex, and Ajo is becoming a selective social base for only the more assimilated Papagos.

The urban setting provides a wide range of family organization, and the type of family organization is significantly related to the extent of Papago vertical mobility in the urban socioeconomic structure. The South Tucson enclave provides a rather persisting base, through its residence compounds of related families, where individuals can find temporary or more prolonged support within an extended family context. Yet there are urban isolate nuclear families with progressively decreasing dependence on relatives and kinsmen as they stabilize occupations and become more socially mobile. It is in the urban setting that the family organization seems to undergo the greatest change, and this is related to the fact that Papagos have come to participate differentially in a socioeconomically stratified urban environment.

A review of the social organization data encourages me to conclude that while kinship may be an important element in a worker's overall adaptation to a job, I must look elsewhere for more pertinent explanations of adaptive behavior.

Leadership and Ceremonial Activities

Another area of social activity that I was initially interested in exploring in terms of its relevance to adaptive behavior in an occupational field was that of leadership and/or ceremonial activities and roles. I wanted to determine the validity of an assumption that extensive participation in the ceremonial calendar and leadership or decision-making responsibilities in kinship villages are antithetical to stabilization of an occupational pattern.

First, in those cases where the informants are relatively steady farm hands or whose residence patterns have been oriented toward prolonged off-reservation residences, I find some variation; although generally there is little evidence to suggest that they have any major functions in the activities of their villages. Of the 11 cases involved exclusively in farm activities and oriented residentially off-reservation, 10 were attached to some form of farm laborer encampment or residence; and the remaining case resided within an off-reservation Indian village. Only one of the 11 had a house in a reservation village while all of them had access to living quarters of either siblings, more distant collateral relatives, or affinal relatives during infrequent visits. The time demands of their particular occupational tasks, the distance to kinship villages, their prolonged periods away from their kinship villages, and their orientations to rural town centers and larger towns and cities indicate little in the way of involvement in the political and leadership aspects of their villages. Most contacts with villages are in the nature of visits with relatives for short periods when the work is slack or attendance at special festivities or ceremonial events involving kinsmen.

As already noted, farms have generally acknowledged the festive and ceremonial activities of their Papago employees. Those Papagos who have had prolonged relationships with farm employers and clearly established responsibilities in the farm operation can usually anticipate that their employers will permit them to take time off for such occasions if it is at all possible. Those who depend largely on seasonal labor and crew type work can leave at will without seriously affecting their chances to make a little money some other time. The former type make the most reliable steady hands, since they pay more heed to the time demands of their jobs and rely on the institutionalized condescension of their employers.

Indian villages off the reservation usually have political structures that are absent in farm camps and have informal leaders who are usually the eldest and most prestigious individuals. In addition there are elected leaders, frequently younger men, responsible for organizing village events and dealing with representatives of the Indian Bureau or other Anglo institutions. Further, there are individuals that Anglos in the nearby towns try to utilize to mediate their concerns; but such presumed leaders may also be sources of intravillage antagonisms. These political aspects are usually quite separate from an individual's occupation, and he can participate in work on nearby farms without his work conflicting in any way with political events in the village. The villages, since they usually lie adjacent to or close to an Anglo town, can gear their political and ceremonial activities to the time demands of the occupations (predominantly farm work) represented by village members.

Data gathered from Papago farm laborers indicate that while kinship village activities and obligations may be important to them, they apparently are not that crucial in determining whether individuals do or do not adapt to relatively steady farm jobs.

The Ajo data have suggested a paradigm in which the interplay of leadership and ceremonial roles, and activities in the occupational and kinship communities can be depicted. The following paradigm classifies the possible types of situations, with the first two types being the most crucial in terms of adapting dual roles:

1. Responsibilities and obligations at a kinship village with none at the Ajo Village.

2. Responsibilities and obligations at a kinship village as well as at the Ajo village.

3. No responsibilities and obligations at either a kinship village or at the Ajo village.

4. No responsibilities and obligations at a kinship village but at the Ajo village.

The paradigm might be explained in another way. Those Ajo miners who have significant duties in their kinship villages and none whatever at the Ajo village are under the greatest pressure because of the time a steady job keeps them away. I do not think there are many who remain in Ajo if their commitments to their kinship villages are too strong. If an Ajo miner has responsibilities to both kinship village and Ajo village, there may be a strong pull toward the home village; but a commitment to the village in which he resides as a result of his steady job leads to a compartmentalization of roles, without which the pull toward the kinship village would threaten his commitment to the job.

No leadership or ceremonial commitments in either village would indicate either a highly transient Papago or one who lives within the village but who is somewhat detached from the activities of the Indian village. Such an individual would have no problem in adapting behavior relative to this aspect of the social field. He may or may not maintain a steady job at the mine, but for entirely different reasons. If there are no obligations at a kinship village but increasing leadership obligations at the Ajo village, an individual likely has the full support of company officialdom and would represent a local Papago elite. This latter kind of individual has the greatest chance of success with the company and thus in his job. A Papago in category two of the paradigm would have difficulty in achieving category four and vice versa. The mine operation's schedule of shutdowns makes categories one and two possible, however; otherwise kinship village activities could not be accommodated to the mining occupation.

The urban data are not sufficient to ascertain other than general impressions. There are individuals from some isolated Papago nuclear households, as well as some in the Papago enclaves, that maintain strong reservation ties and may have responsibilities in their kinship villages. Other individuals, due to long-term residence in the city, are almost totally unattached from any kinship village. There are festive activities and ceremonial events in reservation villages that involve almost all Papagos, especially when they relate to situations involving relatives.

The stereotypic urban occupations are more amenable to participation in many of these social obligations, while the higher status jobs curtail, although do not completely exclude, the carrying out of such obligations. A new kind of leadership role becomes apparent with higher socioeconomic status and among vertically mobile Papagos. It is a welfare leadership, where a Papago appropriates the middle class value of condescension toward the less fortunate and seeks to influence other Papagos through his example.

While kinship relationships and social responsibilities and obligations to kinship communities are significant variables, they still do not provide the kinds of explanations I am looking for in dealing with adaptive behavior in occupational settings. There are adaptations taking place, as the individual cases seem to reveal rather clearly; but taken alone they are not explanatory enough. There are institutionalized supports (farm acknowledgment of festive patterns, shutdowns at mine, and weekends off, etc.) that reduce the conflicts that might otherwise occur. Where there are conflicts, there are alternatives, such as compartmentalizing roles to do what one can as the job permits, or to take off regardless of consequences, or to try one's luck elsewhere.

Except in individual cases, the resolutions of various leadership or ceremonial roles do not generally seem insurmountable for those who have found it necessary to venture into the off-reservation wage system. Indigenous functions do not seem so rigid that they cannot be accommodated to an economic demand.

Interpersonal Relations and Drinking Behavior

It is in the area of informal Papago interpersonal relations that I have found some of the most meaningful data relative to discovering barriers that inhibit or restrict Papago occupational adjustment and acculturation. This area of investigation has been a most difficult one, however, and is much in need of further investigations. There are some generalizations that can be drawn from field observations and interviews. These generalizations should reveal the direction that further research might take.

There seem to be some rather distinct differences in the patterns of interpersonal relations of different Papago age groups. Also, there are some quite noticeable differences in the structure of interpersonal relations relative to informal group behavior in each of the different occupational complexes. At the same time, there are some general rules or norms relative to interpersonal relations among Papago men that have an important bearing on occupational adjustment. These will be discussed with particular emphasis on drinking behavior.

Older Papago men that I have come to know in various off-reservation settings have generally conveyed the idea that they drink for different reasons and in different quantities than do younger Papago men. In addition, they seem to drink in different places and on different occasions, although I found both young and old to be affected by older Papago values and rules regulating the custom of social drinking. Such a general assumption is, of course, untested and would be a very useful line of inquiry.

Older men, particularly on the farms, are interested in sitting around, after a day's work in the fields, in the cool of the evening conversing and playing games with other men or perhaps, if one is available, watching TV and resting. Younger men are more prone to head for nearby towns or to visit friends at neighboring camps. The steadiest farm hands among my informants were older men (50 or older), while the majority of the youngest of my informants (19–35) were usually part-time irrigators or, even more commonly, almost wholly dependent on a contractor in a chopping or picking crew.

Some of the middle-aged men (35–50) had steadier work but still exhibited a great deal of job jumping within the general vicinities of their usual residence, reflecting some of the pattern of the younger men. Much of this mobility and job-jumping seems to have some direct relationship to the interpersonal relations with those of one's own age group. Joining a chopping crew gives the individual a control over just when he desires to place himself in the wage market, and he can enter or withdraw at will. One day's work may give him enough money to invest in an evening of companionable drinking.

Several of my younger informants mentioned that they liked to keep on the go and not stay in one spot. Older informants (50 and older) have confirmed this general tendency on the part of younger men, and their own earlier patterns give some evidence of the same kind of leisurely attitude toward wage work. This is apparent even in the earlier patterns of Papago workers now engaged in nonfarm labor, such as at Ajo or in Tucson. Older informants have pointed out this difference in behavior to me; but seldom, if ever, did I detect censure or undue criticism of this erratic behavior of younger men. In fact, it seems to be understood as something to expect from younger men.

On the basis of prolonged personal contact with a number of informants representing all ages, types of wage work, and locations, it is possible to conceptualize what have seemed to be rather general norms behind drinking group or companionable drinking behavior.

It is of importance because I think the "norms" are highly relevant to occupational adaptation.

Drinking is not a disapprobation even if it occasionally leads to difficulties with legal authorities, although inappropriate excess may be frowned upon by other Papagos. Drinking in Papago culture has stemmed from a ritual-social context and carries with it the power to affirm affections and to seal friendships. Drinking what is offered is equally an affirmation of goodwill just as is offering it.

Drinking groups, therefore, are made up of individuals who reciprocally exhaust the source (money) and supply (liquor available); and each participant, although he may lack resources on one occasion, can still participate, knowing that there will be other times. Since the money resources of drinking friends are never the same, individuals are continuously obligated to return their gestures of affection on other occasions. Even when an individual has good reason for stopping and may desire to do so, he may run into another similar group of friends and may get involved, either contributing anything he has left or counting on someone else. Several informants have conveyed to me how they are "trapped" in an unavoidable situation; to handle it any differently would be insulting.

There is, of course, a good deal of drinking in which it is the intention of individuals to get drunk; and individuals who start drinking know that is how everyone will end up. Younger men, and older men who have had rather intense experience in non-Papago social situations (military, for instance) and are aware of status differences, undoubtedly use voluminous and prolonged drinking as a way of expressing or airing their status grievances to each other (James 1961: 740-1). Their awareness of their status inferiority among Anglos, while not verbally aired to employers, is expressed in the context of an ingroup involved in extended drinking. The explicit explanation for these drinking bouts invokes the older cultural value that one is supposed to drink with friends, while the drinking itself functions also to air the grievances an individual holds within himself when face to face with an employer or other Anglos.

If drinking and its end results (drunkenness, arrest, and confinement) are bad, they are bad only in the sense that they cross Anglos and their legal and welfare institutions. So a Papago can and does "feel bad" about where his drinking leads him, and he can share the guilt imposed on him by a court or by an awareness that his family has had to do without. But I have yet to find the attitude that drinking in itself is bad. When Papago individuals seek therapeutic assistance, regardless of the agent sought, it is due to a desire to meet the time demands of an occupational task rather than to relieve oneself of a "bad" habit.

It has not been uncommon to find Papagos who could work relatively long periods during the busy season, only to fall into extended periods of intoxication during the slack weeks or months. Even some of the most chronic drinkers I have had dealings with have exhibited this ability to control just how much time they really wanted to give to work or to drinking. I am not suggesting that alcoholism, in the disease sense, is not present; it is important, however, to be sure that "drinking-in-excess" is not just a convenient label based on recognition instead of a well-established definition (Hoyt 1960: 135).

Papagos, like many other Indian tribes, have a long history of being compelled to skirt Anglo legal restrictions relative to drinking, so they are well aware of what is "good" and "bad" or "right" and "wrong" (i.e., bootlegging). They know the Anglo "negative stereotype" (James 1961: 731) of Indians as "heavy drinkers but damn good workers when sober", and some learn to behave in accordance with the stereotype. There are, of course, old Papagos who drink heavily and do not work, just as there are young Papagos who are most dependable in the eyes of employers.

While this aspect of Papago behavior is general for all the occupational types represented, the structure of interaction provided by specific complexes would account for identifiable differences. The Ajo and urban bureaucratic occupational demands show less tolerance for uncontrolled drinking. In order for men to hold jobs, there must be some motivation to utilize whatever means are available to alter drinking patterns.

The farm provides an outlet, through seasonal work and contract labor, for those who cannot or do not wish to modify their drinking behavior. The steadiest of farm hands, however, usually have brought this aspect of social behavior into some kind of alignment with the demands of the job. It is far easier for employees on farms to sneak off to drink on the job, even though there are ultimate consequences as far as the job is concerned. A rationale of some young Papago farm laborers (confirmed by more elderly Papago informants) I have come to know is that one can always find a little farm labor somewhere, so one need not worry too much about where immediate drinking may lead.

Data gathered from my field work seem to support Bahr's (1964: 12,66) observation that there is a *miligan kiidag* (a necessity to work for wages) and an *'o'odham kiidag* (making local resources work for one's good). Companionable drinking is far more compatible with the time and performance demands of the latter than with the former, but *miligan kiidag* is important because it takes money to enjoy companionable drinking as well as to buy food and other necessities.

To commit oneself to steady work demands a modification of one's interpersonal relationships with one's peers. This seems to be one explanation why an occupational pattern takes so long in materializing, if it does at all. Rather than aiding in the adjustment, such things as partial education, partial assimilation of Anglo values, partial vocational training experience, etc., may only intensify the pattern of ambivalence and status inferiority. Individuals partially but unsuccessfully assimilated into Anglo institutional values seem to be even more aberrant in terms of their occupational patterns. These people, particularly, are apt to fall back to the peer group and share in the corporate retreat from social isolation with the aid of alcohol and companions.

Values Regarding Work and Leisure

The central concern in the analysis has been directed toward the disclosure of certain kinds of role adaptations which Papago workers have worked out for themselves in response to the social demands of particular occupational complexes. Adaptation in this sense refers to the process of learning to modify Papago social structures and cultural behaviors in order to conform to the demands of institutionalized occupational roles and the numerous other social roles that are afforded by the particular adaptational social fields connected with particular types of occupations.

Certain values and certain role demands, related specifically to the occupations Papagos perform, are important in analyzing adaptational behavior. With different kinds of wage work, there are different time demands—the hours and days that a status occupant must put in, both for the recompense he receives for his time and in order to maintain the status. In addition there are performance demands, or the tasks and activities required in the carrying out of the central role elements of a status, as well as the additional expectations an employer may demand, such as certain desired personality traits and social behavior.

Against the time and performance demands there are the ego demands, such as desires for emotional security and satisfactions, recognition by others, autonomy, and a host of other individual personality needs. Further, there are social demands related to the job, such as relationships with bosses and supervisors and associations with other workers. Finally, there are extra-work social demands that may either be compatible with the work status demands, in conflict with the demands of the job, or relatively neutral and irrelevant to the job requirements.

The following are some of the most significant generalizations my data suggest relative to Papago adaptation to certain kinds of work. On the farm, the amount of time a worker has to spend on the job varies considerably with the kind of job. A steady job as an equipment operator or a full-time irrigator demands long hours with few days off and well-established pay periods. These jobs may slacken during the height of the harvest season and may provide the steady hand with an opportunity to pick cotton or to take a little time off to visit the reservation. Very few of my informants who were steady irrigators or tractor drivers like to pick cotton and usually left this to other members of their families. The picking season becomes a vacation time for steady hands who do not have other tasks to perform. There appear to be status or prestige factors involved if this generalization proves to be quantitatively valid. Only under dire necessity do tractor drivers or irrigators turn to picking cotton.

On the other hand, there are Papagos, particularly young men, who work almost exclusively under labor contractors, even if they live permanently at a particular farm camp. They can select when they wish to join a crew and make a little money for immediate use, as there is usually no need to wait for the end of a pay period. The risk of a few days in jail or laying off work to sober up is no great threat to the job, since the individual can get back to it again when he desires.

The range of farm tasks Papagos generally perform falls within familiar bounds; that is, the tasks, in terms of what is to be done, what kinds of motor movements to employ, and what can be expected in return, are well established by years of routine experience. While interviewing or visiting in camps, I would occasionally observe little children at the edge of a cotton field dragging a paper sack and picking cotton, all in play, or perhaps hoeing with a stick. Parents have conveyed to me that while they worked, their children would be given little sacks or a stick to play with along the field's edge. One Papago tractor driver says his eight-year-old son likes to watch him drive the tractor and hopes he will be able to do it someday, just like his father.

Much of my projective data reveal familiar patterns of work that constitute ideals for future generations. While other kinds of wage work, involving new kinds of experience, are known and of interest, farm Papagos manifest a prevailing selectivity, reinforced by enculturative experiences, for certain kinds of routine farm jobs. Familiar physical environments or surroundings, along with the established features of the work itself, tend to fix some Papagos' patterns in terms of the farm. This inclination for farm work may be due to a lack of preparation for anything else, but the fixed or institutionalized dependence on certain kinds of farm work in turn operates to restrict interest in any other forms of wage work.

Communicating instructions to farm laborers is less complicated, although the channels do get muddled by language barriers or other social habit barriers. Routine work is usually its own instructor. A Papago need not be personally compatible with a foreman or supervisor as long as the time demands are kept within the institutionalized bounds and the tasks can be channeled from supervisor to employee.

The ego demands depend to a great extent on particular individual personality organization, but there are some general tendencies. I found a rather strong tendency to desire a considerable amount of autonomy or to be left alone on the job with little interference from supervisors. Along with this there is the desire to maintain routine work roles and the avoidance of undue responsibility or anything that would require an excessive reorientation of performance demands. Ego demands are also significant for understanding the influence of extra-work social demands.

Some of the requirements of social life that are not directly a part of the work performance may either support or conflict with the demands of one's job. Attachments to kinsmen and reservation villages, discomfort around Anglos, language difficulties, festive events, attitudes about how to spend one's time, absence of other Papagos, complications with Anglo authorities, and a host of other states of mind or social situations that occupational life demands are in conflict with the Anglo cultural requirement to maintain steady work.

On the other hand, having a settlement of relatives, friends, or other Papagos close by with living expense at a minimum, having places where liquor is obtainable and where companionable drinking can take place, being reasonably close to reservation villages, residing at camps where relatives through the years have established certain relationships with employers, living in rural surroundings similar to the environmental ecology of home villages, etc., all tend to complement the farm occupational roles as well as to restrict movement into nonfarm occupations. Failure in securely attaching to nonfarm jobs results in a flow of urban-oriented Papagos back to the rural areas or to the reservation.

At Ajo, there are definite time demands that hold for all employees, Papagos or anyone else. In former days, Indians had to be rounded up on the reservation in order to have a sufficient number of common laborers, mostly track men. It was then possible to work whenever one wanted to put in time, and there was considerable turnover. Now, all employees are on regular payroll, and workers must either report to work with a minimum of unexcused absences or be dropped.

Circulating shifts of personnel and a set rhythm of shutdowns for shift changes must be adhered to. There are set vacations, holidays, and sick leave privileges. All employees in the labor operation are paid by the hour, according to level of the skilled operation, at set pay intervals.

Performance demands vary considerably according to the grade or level of skill in the hierarchy of occupational statuses. Indians have tended to cluster at the lowest levels, largely in unskilled routine but important tasks. More recently a few have invaded the semiskilled, intermediate levels; but there has been no change with regard to the highest levels.

Papagos generally have avoided supervisory responsibility, preferring to remain as peers to others in predominantly Indian work groups. Most jobs at the levels where Papagos are most frequently distributed are largely routine jobs, once learned. There is a reticence about assuming new kinds of responsibility, and I frequently found that the biggest reasons given are lack of education and inability to measure up to what Anglos expect. I detected a considerable amount of expressed inferiority and unpreparedness for some of the higher jobs. There is no reason to question the sincerity of expressions of inadequacy, but I perceive that Papagos also see occupational mobility in the Ajo mine structure as a threat to the cultural identity of the Indian community. The higher status Papagos in the newer suburban-type houses are beginning to be the objects of gossip by the other families, and some Papagos decline company offers to move into the bigger and better houses. Their own acceptance of their "inadequacy" helps to confirm that Indians are different and functions to preserve a kind of cultural identity.

The influence of the company, then, is instrumental in compounding a form of factionalism by its policy of stimulating certain select Indian families to "set an example" for the other Indians. There are those who follow the example, some who could but do not, and many more that are not even considered. So there are some additional social demands of a job at Ajo outside of the job itself.

The extra-work demands in conflict with occupational performance are similar to those discussed with regard to Papagos on farms— strong orientations toward reservation kinsmen, activities in home villages, strong sentiment toward their homes, distinctive customs, etc. Compensating features of the Ajo situation, however, are advantageous company housing, predictable shutdowns for periodic visiting in reservation villages, the availability of company economic and medical services, and an Indian cultural identity through a modified Indian community with many of its own activities, to reiterate only a few. An Ajo job is a rather secure arrangement but due to its selective features, many Papagos fail to make the grade in it.

The urban environment is much too complex for so general a treatment. For those Papagos within the Papago enclave and dependent on stereotypic work roles, there are less rigid time demands. The stereotypic jobs are not too dissimilar from those found on the farm, since the individual can usually work at will and does not have to count on anything steady. Close relationships or paternalistic relationships are prone to develop in the stereotyped roles, much like that which occurs on farms.

The urban setting provides greater anonymity for Papagos, but most of the informal relationships are centered in Papago neighborhoods or in familiar congregating and drinking places. As Papagos attain other-than-stereotypic work roles, there are new kinds of social demands involving more intense relations with non-Papagos. Thus, the stratified nature of the urban occupational structure induces a certain amount of cultural de-identification as well as a motivation to rise in socioeconomic status.

NOTES

1. Store operators are usually selective in offering credit and usually do so only for the more established families. Some store operators I have found to be very helpful in assisting Indian customers in interpreting the meaning of letters, making out money orders, or answering other questions. There seems to be a wide range of difference in attitudes toward Indians manifest by different ethnic store operators. This would be an interesting subject for future investigation.

2. This is the rationalization of the company; that is, it instituted the warning slip system as a corrective device to control the extent of employee drinking and delinquency, a particular problem with Indian employees, although not exclusively.

VII

Introduction
Mixed Cultures: Cultural Adaptation and Change

When a society or culture is in contact with a more powerful one, the weaker society is often obliged to acquire cultural elements from the dominant one. Such a process began with the expansion of western European cultures four hundred years ago, and that process is still at work. The external pressure can take various forms. In the extreme case, the dominant culture conquers the weaker one and through direct force effects cultural change in the conquered society. For example, during the conquest of Mexico, the Spanish forced many of the Indian groups to accept Catholicism. Even where direct force is not used, dominated cultural groups find it hard to resist change. The history of Indian-white relations in the United States includes direct force but also involved occupying lands used by the Indians, which forced them to give up many aspects of their traditional ways of life. In order to survive, American Indians had little choice but to try to work and live in white society. When Indian children had to attend white schools where they were taught white values, the process was accelerated. Similar cases have occurred in Southeast Asia, on the islands of Oceania, in Africa, South America, and the Middle East.

Non-market cultures continue to give way to the sheer efficiency manifested by industrial societies in the twentieth century. The mass of scientific technology, the more productive methods of work, and the overwhelming resources of capital and consumer goods are pitted against the small-scale, hand methods of peasants, horticulturalists, hunters and gatherers, and herders. Sometimes, people from non-

311

market societies see the handwriting on the wall and elect to adopt cultural elements from the dominant society in order to survive. At other times they may resist change and even go so far as to revolt in order to perserve their way of life. The changes effected and the adaptation to change are never simple, and are often accompanied by disruption and disorganization. Sometimes a culture is able to borrow from other cultures peacefully, as in the case of Japan, so they can assimilate what is useful and enjoy what it considers to be the benefits of other societies.

There is the example of Gopalpur, a village in India. After many centuries of coping with and adapting to their environment, consisting of human beings and natural forces, Gopalpur villagers attained a state of equilibrium (Beals 1967:202). Government officials in India were pushing the people of Gopalpur to adopt new ways of working their agricultural plots and to buy improved agricultural implements. But, as Beals explains (1962:79), if the Gopalpur farmer did this, he would threaten his traditional relationship with the village blacksmith and the village carpenter. The blacksmith and carpenter were not only neighbors and friends but they had religious functions during such events as births, marriages and deaths. The carpenter and blacksmith offered the farmer an integrated set of tools with a lifetime guarantee of repairs and replacement, something not true for the new agricultural implements he was urged to buy. If the farmer had an improved plow his productivity might go up, but it would be at the expense of the pattern of cooperation and reciprocity that made life within the village integrated and part of a functioning whole. As Beals remarks, "In refusing to adopt new methods, the farmer of Gopalpur shows common sense, not conservatism" (Beals 1962:79). But while the farmers resist and the government officials debate, the merchants in the towns and the world economic order continue to press in upon the village for change.

A century ago Japan was a mixed, feudal society, with land distributed among vassals, a growing class of merchants and artisans and a developing market system for textiles, food, and handicrafts. By 1941 Japan had undergone profound changes in all sectors of life. "No other nation of the modern world had undergone such drastic and self-sought cultural changes under conditions of internal peace in an equally short period of time" (Norbeck 1965:10). One reason for Japan's success in cultural change has been its many centuries of receptivity to other cultures. They borrowed much from the Chinese. They took a great deal from the United States after World War II. Another reason for Japan's adopting ideas from the West has been that many of her traditional values were compatible with industrial cultures. High value was placed on education. Success, competition, and cleanliness were all part of Japanese values. The practice of thrift and industry were also part of their value system, as was the ethic of achievement. As Norbeck states (1965:20), "the Japanese value industriousness and the desire to succeed," both important ingredients in their taking naturally to industrial cultural mores.

While a great deal of Japan's changes have been internally induced, as well as the result of external borrowing, much of the culture change and adaptation in many non-market societies at the present time is externally induced. One way in which external pressures induce changes in non-market societies happens when members of the non-market culture move to a place that offers the possibility of working for wages. This happened in Tikopia, an island in the South Pacific near the Solomon Islands. When Raymond Firth first studied the island, it was a non-market, self-contained culture. There was a minimum of trade for industrial goods and some iron and steel tools. This situation changed with World War II. When Firth (1959) revisited Tikopia in 1952, he found over a hundred Tikopians had left the island to work in the nearby Solomons where commercial businesses were established. Money had been introduced in Tikopia, which affected their way of life. Cultivation of the land was more intensive. Extended kinship ties were weakened, with nuclear units becoming more important and the old style of cooperation between family units less important. In many cases, the land had been split up among nuclear families, with land rights becoming individualized. People were no longer willing to share with their extended family, particularly with respect to money earned and goods acquired in the Solomons. In short, the former ways were changing under the impact of changes in the way people worked and earned their living.

Change and adaptation to new conditions can occur when a non-market horticultural society comes to depend for its livelihood upon trading with commercial establishments tied to industrial societies. A case in point is the Mundurucu of the Amazon Basin (Murphy and Steward 1956). As trading developed, the Mundurucu increasingly gave up their own crafts and methods of work to devote themselves to producing cash crops to obtain the industrially made articles. The Mundurucu shifted from a society based on cooperative work and community autonomy to one devoted to individualized work and dependence upon an external market. As rubber became more important to industrial societies, agents were sent to the Amazon to encourage rubber production. The Mundurucu were caught up in that process. Rubber collection began to alter Mundurucu social patterns, moving men away from their jungle-based communities. Wild rubber trees are only to be found along rivers, which were a considerable distance from the habitat of the Mundurucu and can only be worked during the dry season from May to December. This meant that Mundurucu men had to separate themselves from their families for half a year to work the rubber trees. It is also work that is done alone or in small groups, which was quite different from the collective styles of work in the Mundurucu villages. The Mundurucu became increasingly dependent upon goods supplied by outside traders. They learned to use firearms, but needed lead and powder. They bought clothing from traders, but required needle and thread for repairs. These articles could only be bought for cash earned by rubber collection. Inevitably the old crafts disappeared—metal pots took the place of clay pots; manufactured hammocks replaced homemade ones. Gradually the village agricultural cycle ceased to be adhered to by the Mundurucu. The authority of the traditional chiefs was weakened. The point of no return was reached when significant numbers of Mundurucu abandoned their villages for permanent settlement near their individual holdings of rubber trees. These new settlements lacked the unity and sense of cooperation in the old village, and each nuclear family worked for themselves to raise their own standard of living.

It may appear from the material presented in this section that all borrowing and adoption of cultural items is a one-way process, from the more technologically advanced society to the less advanced. That this is not true can be shown if the case of the United States and the American Indian population is reviewed. A glance at the types of things and ideas borrowed from the American Indians is impressive. For example, plants domesticated by American Indians furnish almost half of the world's food supply today (Driver 1961:584). Among the plants developed by the American Indians are the potato, corn, beans, squash, and sweet potatoes. Among the stimulants is tobacco and among the drugs is curare, used in anesthetics, cinchona bark as the source of quinine, and ephedra in ephedrine used for clearing sinuses and nasal passages. There is also datura in pain-relievers and cascara used in laxatives (Driver 1961:587). The woolen poncho, the parka, and moccasins were also acquired from Indian cultures. The commercial cottons are derived mainly from the species cultivated by American Indians. American Indians music influenced such American composers as Edward McDowell (Hallowell 1957:207) and American Indian culture influenced authors such as Longfellow and James Fenimore Cooper. While American Indians have taken over large parts of American and European culture, there are many aspects of the American way of life that find their origins in Indian society.

Cultural change also occurs in non-market societies when cultivators produce a surplus which can be sold for cash. When this happens those who till the soil become identified as peasants. Peasants are a class of cultivators who pay taxes or rent for the use of their land, grow crops, and keep livestock for their subsistence, and sell their surplus to towns and cities. Peasants first appeared during the early stages of the growth of urban centers in Egypt and Mesopotamia. They exist in pre-industrial societies and are peripheral to industrial cultures, which rely on large-scale, mechanized agriculture to support the large number of non-food producers.

What changes when non-market cultivators become peasants? They still need to produce for their family's needs, but once they become peasants their way of life is altered because now they must produce for outsiders—for landlords and the state—who are able to enforce their systems of taxation and control through their use of the police and the military. When people who were formerly semi-autonomous become peasants, they find themselves dependent upon the larger society. Peasants the world over are faced with the problem of balancing the demands of their own families and local communities with that of the larger, dominant power outside their villages—the state and the landlords (Wolf 1966:13).

All societies, non-market as well as market, undergo change. Nowhere in the world do human affairs remain the same year after year. Societal change can be internal, based on innovators, or changing natural conditions, or changes in the adaptation to a culture's habitat. In the contemporary world, the most important stimulus to change is contact among people with different cultures. All the processes of interaction, borrowing, cultural diffusion, exchange of ideas and technology, and resistance to change, are often at work during such contact. The type of change which takes place is often a consequence of which society controls the major resources. Most non-market cultures have been forced to change by the powerful pressures of industrial cultures. Often this has meant serious cultural loss and social disorganization. The selections which follow are studies on the effects of cultural contact and how non-market cultures attempt to cope with new values and new ways of organizing work. Once the changes are set in motion there follows a chain reaction of consequences that require adaptation, adjustment, or an entire reordering of a society's way of life.

Chapter Twenty

Energy Development on Alaska's North Slope: Effects on the Inupiat Population

John A. Kruse, Judith Kleinfeld,
and Robert Travis

Introduction

Much of the research examining the effects of energy development on Indian and Eskimo groups concludes that such resource extraction projects bring few real benefits to local communities. Reviewing the impact of the Navajo Tribal Council's leasing of oil, natural gas, helium, and coal to energy corporations, Robbins (1978) argues that these sales have improved the economic position of only a small group of tribal members. This appears to be due primarily to the fact that total industry employment is quite small compared to the total Navajo work force. In 1977, these industries employed 1800 Navajo workers, 60% of the total industry employment. Such a light proportion of Native American employment in energy projects is quite unusual. Anders (1980) points out that during a period of intensive energy development, reservation unemployment actually increased for the majority of tribes that are members of the Council of Energy Resource Tribes. Yet, even where Indians gained employment, these Navajo jobholders represented less than 3% of the work force. Thus, the effect of energy employment among the Navajo was to create a small elite of high wage earners.

While few Navajos have been directly employed by the energy industry, the Navajo tribal government has received revenues from energy-related royalties, rents, leases, and bonuses. Indeed, 70% of tribal revenues derived from mineral leasing, a situation that places the tribal government in a weak bargaining position when its interests may call for cancelling leases or refusing to negotiate new leases (Ruffing 1978). Again, however, the payments have not been large

($16.3 million in 1977) and reflect prices that are far below fair market value for the resources extracted (Jorgensen 1978; Owens 1979; Ruffing 1978).

The impact of energy industry wages and tribal government payments on the Navajo economy has been further diminished by the fact that most expenditures are made off the reservation to non-Indian businesses (Owens 1978). While Navajo mean per capita and household incomes have increased since 1970 due to the earnings of a small group of high wage earners, the median Navajo household income has actually declined. In other words, a major effect of energy development among the Navajo has been to increase income inequality (Arthur 1978).

Research on the impact of energy development projects in Canada suggests a similar pattern of outcomes for Indian and Eskimo groups. The major potential benefits is employment opportunities in energy industries, and these jobs are not necessarily structured so that Native groups can take advantage of them. While some Indians have been employed in oil sands extraction plants, the Native communities in the Athabasca Oil Sands Region continue to experience high rates of unemployment and underemployment (Nichols 1979). Indeed, the proportion of the Native adult population who are employed has not risen despite the construction and operation of major oil sand plants in the region. During this period as well, Native incomes have declined as a proportion of the provincial average. In short, economic activity in the region resulting from energy development led to the growth of a large, prosperous White settlement, Fort McMurray, and bypassed the rural Native communities.

Examining noneconomic effects of these energy projects on Alberta Native communities, Justus and Simonetta (1980) contend that not only has the Indians' standard of living failed to increase but also that these communities have experienced increased alcohol and drug abuse, greater violence, and more family breakdown. In addition, Indian respondents reported declines in the availability of fish and game in the oil project area (Justus and Simonetta 1979). It is not clear from this research, however, to what extent such changes represent general historical trends as opposed to specific effects of energy development.

Under certain conditions, however, energy development may have positive effects on Native communities. One such example, although quite limited in scope, is Gulf Oil Canada's rotation employment program, in which Inuit men from the community of Coppermine worked at drilling sites for two-week periods followed by a one-week home break. Kupfer and Hobart (1978) report almost unanimous approval of the project on the part of the Inuit interviewed. The project brought the community substantial income, which was primarily spent on family necessities and hunting equipment. Moreover, wage work did not reduce the supply of Native foods. The men continued to hunt between their periods of work, increasing their

hunting effectiveness with investments in better equipment. While
alcohol consumption and violence did increase at the beginning of
the employment program, these were transitional effects (Hobart nd).
On balance, the effects of the work program appeared quite favorable.
The Coppermine case presents a hopeful sign for improved relationships between energy developers and Indian and Eskimo groups.
In most cases, however, the well-being of the Native American
population has not been improved by the energy development. The
present study offers an illustration of an instance where the economic
well-being of the general population did improve. This situation has
some aspects that are not common in other Native American experiences with oil development. First, actual oil field activities occurred
96 km away from the nearest Inupiat settlement. Second, the North
Slope Inupiat were able to gain local property taxing authority by
creating a regional government. Native Americans on reservations
are currently attempting to gain such taxing authority. However,
knowledge of this instance may increase the ability of tribal units
and pan-tribal organizations such as the Council of Energy Resource
Tribes to deal effectively with the opportunities and difficulties presented by resource development.

THE STUDY

This study examines the effects of oil development at Prudhoe
Bay on the Inupiat population of Alaska's North Slope. The Inupiat
population consists of about 400 persons of whom slightly over half
are adults. Approximately 2800 individuals, mostly Inupiat, live in
the regional center, Barrow. The remainder of the population is located
in seven predominately Inupiat villages of less than 500 residents
each. Using the opportunity to obtain tax revenues from oil properties,
the Inupiat established a Native-controlled local government, the
North Slope Borough. In 1973, the borough's total budget was
$528,000. Six years later, the annual budget grew to almost $60
million (McBeath 1981). Sixty percent of the borough's revenues in
1979 came from property taxes, which the borough, as a local
government, placed on oil properties, while the next largest category
(24%) came from intergovernmental transfer payments. The borough
government also launched a $511 million capital improvement pro-
gram (CIP) to improve schools, roads, housing, sanitation, and other
public facilities. Through local hiring programs in both the CIP and
government operations, the borough employed over half the Inupiat
population. Median household income rose while income inequality
did not. The Inupiat community also experienced increases in traumatic death and declines in traditional community values. However,
these changes appear to be a continuation of long-term historical

trends. It is not clear that these problems are specific impacts of resource development.

This study was supported through the National Science Foundation's "Man in the Arctic Program" (MAP), a six-year project designed to examine the effects of oil development on Alaska's urban and rural populations. This paper presents information on social and economic effects of energy development on Inupiat individuals and households. The data derive primarily from a household survey conducted in 1977 by the Institute of Social and Economic Research in cooperation with the North Slope Borough. In addition, public health and other agency records were used to examine changes over time in alcoholism, traumatic death, and other social problems. Other studies within the MAP program examine Inupiat political organization and the economic development of the region.

Methods

The results reported in this paper are based on the responses of 290 Inupiat adults to an hour-long personal interview. Before the structured sample survey was administered, 30 individuals participated in in-depth interviews designed to refine our research hypothesis. In addition, we were able to benefit from an analysis of the results of a survey we conducted in another rural region in Alaska (Gasparro 1978). Draft interview questions were reviewed by Inupiat leaders and were pretested among Inupiat residents. An Inupiat translation of the revised interview schedule was prepared and Inupiat residents were hired and trained as interviewers.

We selected all households in the communities of Point Hope, Wainwright, Nuiqsut, Kaktovik, and Anaktuvuk Pass and a 50% simple random sample of all noninstitutional households in Barrow. Two small North Slope communities, Point Lay and Atkasook, were not surveyed since they were being resettled. Within selected households, we randomly designated an adult member of the household (18 years or older) to be interviewed.

Interviews were conducted from October, 1977 to February, 1978. Respondents received $10 for their assistance. The final sample consisted of 75% of the 385 selected respondents. Twenty-four percent of our respondents chose to take the interview in Inupiaq. Non-Native interviewers conducted a small proportion of the Barrow interviews and the Inupiaq version could not be used in these households.

In presenting survey results, the Barrow interviews are weighted to reflect the proportion of Barrow adults in the total North Slope Native population. Sampling errors for responses involving the entire sample are about 4%. The interview schedule itself covered four major areas: wage employment, subsistence, community living conditions, and personal background characteristics. Factual self-reports of current and past behavior form the core of the first two sections while perceptions concerning 14 community characteristics and 7 institutions are the primary question form in the third section. The final section of the interview schedule contains questions concerning living experiences outside of the region and childhood exposure to wage and subsistence activities, as well as a complement of questions concerning income, expenditures, and education. A comprehensive statistical presentation of the results is available (Kruse, Kleinfeld, Travis, and Leask 1981), as are separate monographs on employment (Kleinfeld, Kruse, and Travis 1981), subsistence (Kruse 1982), social problems (Travis 1981), and institutional development (McBeath 1981).

HISTORICAL BACKGROUND

Environmental Setting

Alaska's Brooks Range forms the southern boundary of a 228,800 km² area referred to as the North Slope. The arctic foothills of the Brooks Range give way to a flat coastal plain containing thousands of small lakes and both wet and dry tundra. Despite low average levels of biological productivity in the region and its surrounding waters, bowhead whale, walrus, seal, caribou, Canadian geese, eiders, and sandpipers along with numerous other shorebirds and waterfowl seasonally migrate through the region. The availability of and access to resources is limited by the severe arctic winter, however, where the chances of wind chill temperatures of $-30°C$ are 50% or greater during six months of the year.

Population and Traditional Economic Base

The harsh climate and often meager availability of resources limited the aboriginal population to perhaps five thousand. These people consisted of two societies. The Nunamiut ranged across the Brooks Range and arctic foothills, basing their economy primarily on caribou. The coastal environment was exploited by the Tareumiut, who formed villages in locations affording good hunting opportunities for migrating sea mammals. Men were the primary hunters in both societies with women providing support to the men's subsistence activities.

Social Organization

As in most traditional societies, material insecurity was a strong incentive to engage in group activities that minimized individual risk

(Dalton 1971:11–12). Food sharing among related households was widespread. Social status depended not only on wealth but also on generosity. Group bonds were strengthened by the need to hunt caribou and the large marine mammals collectively as well as by the instruction of the young men in hunting techniques given in village ceremonial houses. Traditional religious beliefs primarily concerned human-environment relationships perceived as critical to hunting success.

Regional Intrusions

Apart from the intrusion of foreign trade goods and numerous arctic explorers in the 18th and 19th centuries, the first major outside contact occurred during the period of commercial whaling in the arctic (ca. 1854–1906). Missionaries and the establishment of shore trading stations followed soon after the first commercial whalers arrived. The next major intrusion came with the search for national oil reserves during and after World War II (1946–53). Oil exploration activities were closely followed by the construction of Defense and Early Warning (DEW) line facilities. During the 1960s the impact of national and state poverty programs aimed at upgrading the quality of health, education, transportation, and other community services was felt on the North Slope. Most recently, the presence of substantial oil fields has heightened outside interest in the North Slope region.

Effects of Early Intrusions on Economic Activities

The whaler's need for meat added a commercial value to subsistence resources. Men sought caribou meat to obtain Western foods and trade goods as well as for food. The commercial whalers also competed with Native whaling captains for labor, thus introducing wage employment to the North Slope (Sonnenfeld 1957:235). The drop in price of baleen in the early 1900s was not followed by a complete resurgence of traditional hunting patterns. Men also turned to natural resources having a commercial value: fur bearers and reindeer introduced by missionaries and the federal government.

When male wage employment opportunities again increased in the 1940s, the village of Barrow attracted residents from throughout the region. Although the new wage employment opportunities did not seriously conflict with hunting opportunities, preferences for Western food were exercised and per capita consumption of Inupiat foods significantly dropped (Sonnenfeld 1957–544). Whaling, however, increased. The number of whaling crews was traditionally limited by the wealth present in the community. Wage employment provided a new means of obtaining wealth, particularly because the whaling equipment could now largely be purchased rather than slowly amassed through past successful hunting efforts (Van Stone 1962:42). Interest in whaling probably remained high for several reasons. First, more secure food supplies increased the relative attractiveness of whaling over traditional mainstays of the subsistence economy, seal and caribou, both of which provided little meat per kill. Second, active whaling consumed only a few weeks a year and could be fit among other activities. Third, and perhaps most important, whaling continued to involve a large segment of the community and remained the most visible tie to traditional Inupiat activities (ibid.:165).

During the 1950s and 1960s, the DEW line and government construction programs sustained wage employment opportunities in construction. These jobs continued to be taken primarily by men. Women, however, started to enter the labor force as education, health, and other government service jobs appeared.

Effects of Early Intrusions on Social Organization

The attachment of commercial values to subsistence resources presented a conflict between traditional sharing obligations and the desire for Western foods, housing, and clothing (Sonnenfeld 1957:253). An individual who wished to take advantage of the new commercial hunting opportunities could now do so with a rifle instead of relying on group effort (ibid.:239). Whereas Inupiat hunters traditionally linked their success to an adherence to religious practices, they increasingly came to depend on the use of new technology. This, along with missionary pressures, led them to abandon practices with affirmed traditional religious beliefs. The Barrow community dismantled the ceremonial houses and no longer publicly recognized traditional religious leaders. The Presbyterian church became the predominant social organization, thus introducing residents to a prototype form of modern political organization.

Along with new technology and a new religion, Westerners introduced diseases and alcohol. Flu, measles, pneumonia, and tuberculosis epidemics decimated the population, dramatically reducing the viability of the individual household as a social and economic unit. In addition, alcohol misuse led to accidents and violent deaths and removed the will of many residents to engage in productive activities (Brower, Farrelly, and Anson 1942). When health conditions finally improved in the 1950s, high birth rates and low death rates dramatically increased the number of household dependents. The children of the baby boom of the late 1950s and early 1960s reached working age during the mid-1970s, the period of central interest to this study.

The Prudhoe Bay Discovery and Formation of the North Slope Borough

The discovery of oil on state leased lands at Prudhoe Bay in 1968 set into motion massive investments in oil production and transportation facilities. Employment at Prudhoe Bay exceeded 6,000 during the peak construction period in 1975 and has averaged over 3,000 since then. Thus the employment generated at Prudhoe Bay has been comparable to the size of the entire North Slope Inupiat population. Despite the tremendous employment potential at Prudhoe Bay, actual employment and income effects of the development have not been large. In contrast to the Navajo experience, however, the Inupiat have been able to capture and exploit substantial sums of oil-related wealth. The formation of an Inupiat-controlled regional government empowered to tax property and to provide a wide spectrum of facilities and services accounts for much of this difference.

As the oil industry geared up for production, several young Barrow Inupiat formed the Arctic Slope Native Association (ASNA) to press a Native claim to the entire North Slope (McBeath 1981). The land claims movement gained momentum and the ASNA broadened its objective to include calls for jobs, housing, and schools. Thus, the ASNA not only contributed to the statewide land claims movement but also established the need to form a regional government (ibid.).

The state opposed the formation of the North Slope Borough, viewing Prudhoe Bay oil as a statewide tax resource. Oil companies wanted to limit and stabilize their tax liability and fought the borough in the courts (Morehouse and Leask 1980). Following extended litigation, Native leaders succeeded in establishing the borough and its taxing authority in 1972 and soon began planning the multimillion-dollar CIP designed to provide local employment and to construct village facilities. Property taxes paid by North Slope Oil producers will pay for virtually all of the CIP program.

In addition to Prudhoe Bay oil development and the formation of the North Slope Borough, the Alaska Native Claims Settlement Act established a third major development force in the region, the Arctic Slope Regional Corporation (ASRC), which will receive almost 1.6 million ha of land and about $52 million. Eventually the regional impact of ASRC investment activities may exceed the impact of borough tax revenues. However, since 1972, the borough has received revenues equal to three times ASRC's share of the 1971 Settlement Act and is spending rather than passively investing these moneys. Of the two Native-controlled development forces, the North Slope Borough has clearly had the greater impact at this point.

The establishment of the North Slope Borough and the Arctic Slope Regional Corporation marked the end of a colonial era that lasted 120 years. While regional resources are still sought by state and national interests, the two Native organizations now have the power to influence outside forces for change and to institute changes themselves. Our central research question is thus how oil development has changed the lives of the Inupiat residents both directly as a result of the new employment opportunities and land use and indirectly through the mediating influences of the North Slope Borough and to a lesser extent, the Arctic Slope Regional Corporation.

POPULATION EFFECTS

Aside from producing tax revenues, the Prudhoe Bay oil development itself had little direct impact on the North Slope Inupiat. All employee housing and support services were provided at the site and most workers took direct flights between the enclave and hiring points in Anchorage and Fairbanks. The nearest Inupiat settlement is 96 km from Prudhoe Bay and virtually no intraregional surface travel routes pass through the area. As we discuss below, there is little evidence that the Prudhoe Bay development itself adversely affected wildlife populations.

Employment

Between 1970 and 1977, only 14% of Inupiat adults had worked for the energy industry and just 8% had worked for longer than 12 weeks. The existence of borough jobs paying comparable wages in the villages doubtless made the employment opportunities at Prudhoe Bay less attractive. However, even without competing local job opportunities, direct Inupiat participation in the energy development would probably not have been substantially higher. Personnel records for the construction phase of the trans-Alaska pipeline, for example, indicate that 17% of the adult Native population worked on the project and more than half of these persons worked only for 8 weeks or less (Naylor and Gooding 1978). Thus, despite the large scale of oil development activities in Alaska, direct benefits to Alaska Natives have not differed greatly from the experience of other Native groups with energy development. The formation of the borough, however, led to major gains in employment and income for a large proportion of the population. The Inupiat government transformed oil revenues into local high-paying jobs.

By 1977, five years after it was established, the North Slope Borough was the largest employer of the local Inupiat population. Almost half of the jobs held by Inupiat adults came from the borough government and school districts. The borough had at some time employed about 57% of the Inupiat adult population. Most men were employed as construction workers in the CIP program. While the borough contracted with outside firms to manage construction projects, actual construction work was performed by borough employees. In this way the Borough was able to implement a strong local hiring program.

The number of jobs related to general government operations increased as well, opening up new opportunities for Inupiat women. The borough also adapted the structure of its jobs to minimize conflicts with contemporary Inupiat life-styles. For example, the borough had a policy of granting leaves of absence for subsistence activities, and employees irregularly absent from work were generally rehired. Borough pay scales were high. The average weekly wage of North Slope Inupiat adults in 1977 was almost $500 per week and about 25% received weekly paychecks of $800 or more. Inupiat residents viewed the increase in the "number of good jobs you can get" as the single most positive change in community conditions that had occurred on the North Slope since 1970, before energy development. In 1977, almost 68% of Inupiat rated the job situation as favorable, while only 33% considered the job situation favorable in 1970. Residents who did not see wage work opportunities as improving, primarily lived in villages without major borough construction projects during our survey year.

Borough jobs did not succeed in eliminating unemployment among the Inupiat population. During 1976–77, unemployment among adults in the primary working ages (18–54) averaged 12% of the total male population and 8% of the total female population. In addition, an average of 32% of the male population and 26% of the female population were intermittent workers temporarily withdrawn from the labor force. Even during the month of peak employment (September) in the survey year, only 68% of the total male population between ages 18 and 54 and 52% of the female population in this age group were employed. While Inupiat women's labor force participation was close to the national female average, the labor force participation of Inupiat men remained far below national norms.

These moderate employment/population ratios resulted from three major factors. First, Inupiat men were primarily blue-collar workers (81%) who were vulnerable to being laid off as particular construction projects ended. Of male job terminations, 39% resulted from layoffs. Second, many Inupiat did not want year-round wage work. In response to a survey question about preferred work schedules, about 50% of Inupiat males and 52% of Inupiat females said they would prefer to work part of the year. Third, large numbers of young Inupiat adults who were born in the 1950s and 1960s were entering the economy in the 1970s and swelled the numbers of Inupiat adults in the labor force. However, the borough was important in providing jobs for the young adults. Among 18–24 year olds, 75% had received employment from the borough.

While the borough provided wage work to a large proportion of the population, the periods of employment were not typically long, due to lay-offs and personal preferences for part-year work. Inupiat men employed by the borough received, on the average, 17 weeks of employment, and Inupiat women, 23 weeks. Thus, the effect of borough jobs was to distribute some employment to a large proportion of the population, rather than to provide high-paying jobs to a small group.

Income

Higher wage rates and increased female labor force participation caused real incomes to rise at an annual rate of 6.5% between 1970 and 1977. In 1977, the median Inupiat family income was $17,347 (Table 20.1). The North Slope Borough was clearly successful in using oil production profits to increase the economic well-being of the general population. Equally important, the North Slope region has so far avoided increasing disparity in incomes, a common trend among regions experiencing rapid economic change. The poorest 20% of North Slope residents earned 3.5% of the total regional household income in 1977 and 3.6% in 1970. The North Slope income distribution is only slightly more unequal than Alaska or the United States as a whole.

The North Slope Borough enabled the Inupiat to share in the general growth of income in Alaska brought about by oil development. North Slope families experienced the same proportionate increase in income (2.5 times) between 1970 and 1977 as Alaskan families in general and exceeded the gains made by all U.S. families.

While incomes have increased rapidly and proportionately across the North Slope population, they are still far below urban Alaska. The average unadjusted per capita income in Fairbanks, for example, was $11,291 in 1976, compared to $3,745 among North Slope Inupiat. Twenty-nine percent of the North Slope Native population received incomes below the poverty level established by the U.S. Department of Agriculture Economic Food Plan Program in 1977.

Subsistence

The income gains experienced by North Slope residents were clearly not sufficient to eliminate the need for subsistence activities. Despite

Table 20.1 Native Family Income: 1960–77

Income	1960	1970	1977[a]
Under $2,000	34%	14%	3%
$2,000–$5,999	39	31	14
$6,000–$9,999	27	23	10
$10,000–$14,999	—	21	16
$15,000+	—	11	57
	100%	100%	100%
Median Family Income:	$3,438	$6,923	$17,347
Adjusted Median Income:			
(1960 Dollars)[b]	$3,438	$5,700	$ 8,982
Number of Families:	(237)	(451)	(260)

a. The $15,000+ category for 1977 when broken down further shows 14% of households with incomes between $15,000–19,999, 21% between $20,000–29,999, 10% between $30,000–39,999, and 12% with $40,000 or more.

b. Median income was adjusted using the Consumer Price Index for Anchorage. As such, the adjusted income should be interpreted as a crude approximate to North Slope Native household income in actual dollars.

Sources: U.S. Bureau of the Census, 1960 Census of Population, Alaska; U.S. Department of the Interior, 2(c) Report: Federal Programs and Alaska Natives, 1973; ISER North Slope Survey, 1977.

the availability of wage employment, most adults continued to engage in subsistence pursuits. In fact, 70% of all Native adults engaged in one or more subsistence activities in the 12 months preceding the survey. Respondents in 45% of the households perceived that half or more of their food came from these activities.

Subsistence activities were important even in households with incomes of $25,000 or greater. Indeed, men in such households reported engaging in subsistence activities during more months of the year than men in households with incomes below $25,000 (6.1 compared to 3.6 months, $p < .01$).

This positive relationship between income and subsistence activity is understandable in view of the increasing dependence on purchased equipment. Increased incomes were also used to widen the variety of subsistence products pursued. Men in households with incomes of $25,000 and over engaged in more subsistence activities than other men as well (4.8 compared to 2.9, $p < .01$). In short, the higher cash incomes resulting from oil development and borough formation, far from depressing subsistence interest, were related to heightened and more varied subsistence activities.

Changes in subsistence technology also dramatically reduced the time necessary for many subsistence activities, making it possible for Inupiat to combine wage work with a high level of subsistence effort. Respondents reported that 60% of all subsistence activities took place after work or on weekends. Another 7% occurred on leave or vacation time. One-half of the trapping and two-thirds of the seal hunting took place on weekends, after work or on leave time.

Despite the evidence of continued need and desire for subsistence products, most Inupiat adults (63%) reported that they spent less time on subsistence activities in 1977 than in 1970, and 75% said that they obtained fewer subsistence products in 1977. Whereas 82% of the adult population recalled that the amount of fish and game in their area was good or very good in 1970, only 27% made the same assessment in 1977. The major reason given for the reduced subsistence resource taken, then, was related more to the availability of resources than to the time available to hunt and fish.

The role of onshore petroleum development in the decline of regional fish and game population, if it exists, appears to be quite indirect and an effect of increased Inupiat income rather than severe degradation caused by development. One-fifth of our respondents did mention that they thought development activities have adversely affected wildlife populations or their habitat. Most respondents, however, felt that they needed more information to make an assessment. The size of the Central Arctic caribou herd, which occupies the Prudhoe Bay area, has not declined since development activities started, but researchers and local residents have observed that some migrating caribou, particularly cows accompanied by calves, tend to avoid the pipeline corridor (Davis 1980; Cameron and Whitten 1979; Finkler 1979). In addition, the quality of some streams was reduced as a result of inadequacies in the design and construction of the pipeline (Morehouse, Childers, and Leask 1978).

Most of the affected wildlife resources, however, were not among those heavily used by the Inupiat population. Village residents primarily take caribou from the Western Arctic and Porcupine herds rather than the Central Arctic herd. Both the Prudhoe Bay oil field itself and the pipeline corridor are about 80 km from the nearest village, so local wildlife resources have not been reduced. The effects of future outer continental shelf oil exploration and production activities in the Beaufort Sea on key subsistence resources may, of course, be entirely different.

The immediate reason for our respondents' negative assessment of hunting and fishing conditions in 1977 was a state restriction placed in 1976 on harvests of the Western Arctic caribou herd. In 1975, the Alaska Department of Fish and Game estimated that 20,000 caribou were harvested from the herd and that the population level had dropped from about 242,000 in 1970 to 75,000. Inupiat hunters and state biologists disagreed about the amount of the decline and its precipitating causes (Davis, Valkenburg, and Reynolds 1979). The biologists maintain that overharvesting was a major cause for the decline. We noted that higher income is related to higher time spent on subsistence and time spent on subsistence may be positively related to subsistence harvesting as well. We cannot confirm the latter relationship without harvest data. If true, however, a connection might be drawn between oil development, the higher incomes it indirectly provided, purchases of equipment and supplies that permitted individuals to acquire preferred foods and to engage in preferred activities, and, finally, increased harvest pressure on subsistence resources.

Caribou hunting was not the only subsistence activity to receive public attention since oil development activities began. Higher incomes meant that more men could afford to form whaling crews. The larger number of crews and expanded whale harvest attracted the attention of some members of the international scientific community. In 1978, the International Whaling Commission directed North Slope whalers to take no more than 12 bowheads instead of an annual average of 29 taken between 1970 and 1977. While caribou hunting restrictions have been recently eased as herd sizes have increased, the bowhead controversy continues.

As we have seen, subsistence activities continue to play an economic role on the North Slope. The data also suggest that food and activity preferences are likely to continue to involve subsistence activities even as incomes increase. The basis for these preferences appears to be broader than the individual. Traditional norms regarding the sharing of subsistence products continue. Sixty-four percent of Inupiat households distributed food to 77% of Inupiat households. Forty-eight percent of Inupiat households gave or lent money or equipment to others for subsistence activities. The spring whaling festival, Nulukutok, continues to be the single most important expression of Inupiat cultural identity. Given disturbingly high levels of alcohol abuse and other signs of social adjustment difficulties discussed below, the stabilizing role of subsistence may in the long run be as important as its economic role.

Social Problems

The North Slope has been the subject of numerous articles in national publications which contend that oil development has created high levels of social problems and undermined Inupiat cultural stability. In addition to these journalistic treatments, a major study conducted by the Center for Research on the Acts of Man (Klausner, Foulks, and Moore 1980) argues that the high and rising rates of alcoholism, suicides, and other types of social problems on the North Slope are an indirect result of oil development. According to this argument, oil development has concentrated new wealth and power in a small group of Inupiat who have the competencies to deal with Western bureaucratic institutions.

Inupiat adults indeed perceived serious social problems in their communities and also a general deterioration in the social fabric of community life since the 1970s. In 1977, for example, only 4% of Inupiat adults viewed the levels of drinking, drugs, fighting, and stealing in this village as good, whereas 36% perceived the levels as good in 1970. Death rates from causes as suicide, homicide, alcoholism, and accidents indeed rose on the North Slope during the period of oil development.

The central issue, however, is whether this increase represents effects of oil development or a continuation of a historical trend that began well before oil development. To explore this question, we examined trends in traumatic death rates on the North Slope since the 1960s. We also compared the rate of change and level of traumatic death on the North Slope from the 1960s through the late 1970s with that of a neighboring Inupiat region, which has experienced much less impact from energy development and a much slower rate of economic change.

If oil development was directly or indirectly responsible for the increase in traumatic death rates during the late 1970s, we would expect to see such patterns as (1) a higher absolute level of traumatic death on the North Slope compared to the neighboring Inupiat region; (2) a steeper increase in traumatic death during the late 1970s on the North Slope compared to the neighboring Inupiat region; and/ or (3) an increasing rate of traumatic death on the North Slope during the late 1970s compared to the 1960s. As Figure 2 shows, none of these patterns appear. The traumatic death rate on the North Slope increased to an even greater degree during the peiod before oil development, 1960 to 1971, than it did between 1971 and 1977. The rate of increase in the neighboring Inupiat region was substantially higher during the late 1970s than it was on the North Slope. Moreover, the absolute level of traumatic death on the North Slope in the late 1970s was only slightly higher than in the neighboring Inupiat region and it has been somewhat higher since the 1960s. While social problems may indeed be related to long-term economic and structural changes in Inupiat culture, these patterns do not suggest that energy development itself caused or accelerated social disorganization on the North Slope.

Alcoholism (and its consequences, such as in suicide, homicide, and other violent crime) is a serious community problem. We defined a "problem drinker" as (1) any person who was arrested on a criminal charge while intoxicated; and/or (2) any person who was held at least once during the year in the Barrow detention program, essentially a sleep-off center. Using this criterion, about 21% of the Inupiat adult population in Barrow can be considered drinkers who require intervention from the community. These problems are concentrated in males, particularly males in the 18–24 and 35–44 year old age groups. Severe drinking is also related to the high rate of homicide on the North Slope (30.7 per 100,000 between 1972–77), compared to the total U.S. population (9.6 per 100,000 during this time period). It is worth noting that while the patterns of change for suicide and accidental death on the North Slope suggests a continuation of historical trends, the region has experienced a large increase in homicide compared to earlier periods (5.2 per 100,000 between 1960–71). The comparison Inupiat region did not show such a dramatic increase in homicide during the 1970s. However, it should be kept in mind that these North Slope homicides are concentrated primarily in two Inupiat families and are not a communitywide phenomenon.

Community Conditions

By 1977, the borough had been in existence for five years and had spent over $99 million in capital improvement projects, education, and general government operations. How did Inupiat residents evaluate the changes in community conditions that had occurred since 1970, before energy development and the formation of the borough? Inupiat adults saw a mixed picture of positive and negative change. The greatest perceived benefit was the creation of jobs. In addition, residents noted improvements in air transportation (mostly an indirect effect of the CIP), the amount of home living space, and the quality of health care and village schools, which were controlled by the local borough school district. Residents also perceived negative changes including less fish and game; higher food and clothing prices; and more drinking, drugs, and fighting. On balance, 35% of Inupiat adults perceived that village living conditions worsened since 1970 and only 7% observed that village living conditions had improved.

Most residents (69%) believed that the North Slope Borough has generally met their needs but they were unsure whether the borough had effectively controlled oil development on the North Slope. The oil fields themselves were distant from the villages and the consequences of the development were ambiguous and indirect. When asked to evaluate the overall effects of oil development on the North Slope, one-third of the residents felt that they did not know enough to make an assessment. "Oil didn't come to our villages," one respondent pointed out. "I have not heard enough about it," explained another.

About equal proportions (20%) of residents perceived the overall effects of oil development as good, bad, and mixed. Those seeing the effects as positive stressed that "jobs are provided to the people." Those seeing the effects as negative stressed the decline of fish and game opportunities; for example, "Caribou have to be searched for; hunters go a long distance to find caribou." Whether correctly or not, this group tended to attribute the poorer yields of fish and game to oil development. "One river [where my husband] caught fish has no fish, because of the oil company." The Inupiat also expressed anxiety about the new availability of money and its effects on the traditional culture. "People's way of living has changed because of too much money," said one respondent. "Materially we're better off," pointed out another," "[but] the culture is being lost faster."

If the North Slope Borough had not been formed, perceptions of the effects of oil development probably would have been more clearly negative, for positive assessments were primarily based on increased employment opportunities. As we have seen, most of these new job opportunities were created through the borough, not the oil industry itself. In sum, despite the development of a strong political institution, the creation of jobs, and increased incomes, Inupiat adults were ambivalent about oil development in their region. As in the case of the Cheyenne (Nordstrom et al. 1977) and of Canadian Athabascan groups (Justus and Simonetta 1979), the Inupiat's ambivalence toward energy development was rooted in the perceived effects on social problems, fish and game resources, and the maintenance of traditional lifestyles.

CONCLUSION

As long as Prudhoe Bay tax revenues continue at current levels, the borough's economic strength remains secure, and with it the ability to continue government operations, construction projects, and local, well-paid employment. A stable tax base is expected at least through 1993. Most projections anticipate high Prudhoe Bay tax revenues through the turn of the century. Other oil and gas developments in the North Slope, such as at the National Petroleum Reserve and on the Outer Continental Shelf, may well maintain or increase the borough's tax base.

However, the extensive system of public facilities and social services that has been created on the North Slope requires substantial revenues solely for maintenance and operation. Inupiat residents must pay current users fees, such as utility costs and waste disposal charges, that require them to maintain stable sources of cash income. The Inupiat population has also become accustomed to a high level of cash income and frequent purchases of snowmobiles and other vehicles, vacations, and household goods. Energy development has created a marked dependence on the part of Inupiat individuals and the borough government on an unstable, nonrenewable resource. Oil revenues have not led to the growth of a diversified, self-sustaining regional economy. Indeed, the borough's policy of setting wages at nonmarket rates may impede economic development in other potential sectors (Huskey 1980).

While energy development has had positive economic effects in creating jobs and raising household income, the economic structure created by the borough presents some nagging problems. One issue is the potential disparity of Inupiat men and women in educational achievement and life styles. Inupiat men have entered primarily high paying, blue-collar work (80%), and are maintaining a life style that combines moderate levels of wage work and subsistence activities. Inupiat women, particularly the younger generation, appear to be decreasing participation in subsistence activities and increasing participation in skilled, white-collar work.

In the current North Slope economy, Inupiat women, much more than men, have financial incentives for educational achievement and for occupational mobility. Inupiat women who obtain a high school education or above, for example, earn over one and a half times the weekly wages and over twice the annual wages of women who are not high school graduates. For men, completing high school makes no difference to weekly wages and results in less than a 30% increase in annual wages (an increase which may well disappear if unemployment compensation is taken into account). These different economic incentives may affect male and female levels of educational motivation and other socializing experiences. In the youngest age group, a trend appears for Inupiat women to have slightly higher levels of educational achievement, more employment, and more education, work, and travel experiences outside the North Slope. This disparity indicates a reversal of earlier patterns, where Inupiat men had greater educational, employment, and travel experiences.

Similarly, the white-collar jobs Inupiat women hold provide more nonformal education then the blue-collar jobs held by men. Inupiat women's jobs tend to place them in close working relationships with professional supervisors who view their role explicitly as training Inupiat employees. Many of these jobs also have built-in training programs and career ladders, such as the education provided health and teacher aides. Inupiat men tend to work for construction contractors who are more concerned with getting the work done than in educating the Inupiat.

A goal of the North Slope Borough is to increase self-sufficiency by raising educational levels and by reducing dependence on imported professionals and other skilled workers. The current economic incentive structure and nonformal job training patterns may not be strongly supporting this objective, at least for the large proportion of men in blue-collar work. There may be an intrinsic conflict in the goals of the North Slope Borough both to distribute high paying jobs to the general population and to encourage educational achievement and skill development.

Another disturbing problem associated with energy development on the North Slope stems from the continued and perhaps increased pressure on subsistence resources. Higher incomes have not eliminated the need to harvest these resources and, in fact, appear to have permitted the Inupiat to increase their hunting effectiveness. Subsistence activities not only continue to produce preferred foods, they are also a social binding force and a source of individual rewards that have not been replaced by new job opportunities. At the same time, however, the potential for excessive resource harvests, whether actual or perceived, has focused state, national, and international interest on the viability of caribou, bowhead, and other animal populations. To date, this interest has been expressed as externally imposed regulations on resource harvests. Should the trend toward external control over subsistence resources continue, the Inupiat may find themselves in the potentially disastrous position of trading subsistence rights for jobs.

While the issues of individual development under the economic incentive structure remains a concern, the North Slope Inupiat have been generally successful in using the opportunities brought about by nearby resource development. The relevance of their experience to other Native American groups affected by energy projects may vary with the particular circumstances. For other Native regions of Alaska that have not organized themselves into borough governments, the North Slope Borough has become an important model. As energy development occurs on Alaska's Outer Continental Shelf or alternative revenue sources become available, other Native regions may well establish borough governments.

The implications of the North Slope Borough experience for Native American communities outside Alaska are less clear. On the North Slope, the taxation mechanism was critical to the Inupiat's ability to obtain substantial economic benefits from oil development. On reservations, development occurs under a different legal structure and there are substantial constraints to tribal taxation, which are only now being overcome. In addition, the Inupiat enjoyed some special circumstances, such as the location of energy projects in enclave developments away from their population centers and major subsistence resources, that may not apply to other situations. The importance of the North Slope experience lies not so much in the particular strategies and policies used by the Inupiat to direct energy development as in the example it provides of the possibility of using resource development to increase Native American wealth and power and the ability to pursue indigenous goals.

CHAPTER TWENTY-ONE

Problems of Management and Authority in a Transitional Society: A Case Study of a Javanese Factory

ANN RUTH WILLNER

The problems of managerial leadership in a transitional society can be examined in many contexts of organizational activity. The one employed in this article is that of an industrial organization in a primarily preindustrial setting in East Java, Indonesia. For the industrial context brings into sharp focus the dilemmas that confront those who attempt to impose unfamiliar organizational forms and norms on a society reluctant or only partially prepared to accept the behavioral innovations demanded by the new organization.

The leaders of most new nations are ideologically committed to industrialization and to the development of concomitant industrial structures modelled on prototypes in advanced industrial societies. Yet the introduction of new and complex forms of organization, such as a modern factory, in a traditional agrarian environment frequently sets up tensions between the operational requirements of the organization and the cultural norms and expectations of those members of the local community recruited to fill the organizational roles. Where such organizations were introduced under conditions of colonial domination, their operational goals received first priority. These could be attained, in the last resort, through the application of various forms of coercive control by largely foreign management whose authority could not easily be brought into question.

Political and social changes in nations that have undergone successful revolutions have altered the staffing patterns of organizations and the sociocultural determinants of organizational behavior. Most intermediate and many top managerial posts are filled by indigenous personnel. However desirous they may be of securing rank-and-file compliance with organizational needs, their problems are more complex than those of their foreign predecessors. For, unlike the latter, they cannot resort to arbitrary measures in maintaining discipline without arousing strong opposition among their subordinates to tactics now labelled "colonial." They must therefore obtain some degree of consensus.

Successful political nationalism, however, tends to produce dissensus in the sphere of authority. On the one hand, it strengthens the claims of those who have learned to advocate and accept rational and utilitarian bases for decision and action. On the other hand, it is generally accompanied by a cultural nationalism that reinvigorates prescriptions traditionally governing social interaction. Thus there may be little agreement on such questions as who has the right to be assigned roles of authority or what are the means by which authority can properly be exercised. Every such issue complicates the possibility of reconciling the impersonal requirements of organizational efficiency with the expectations of those who are part of the organization.

These dichotomies are elaborated in the following description[1] of patterns of authority in a Javanese textile factory during two periods of its history. The first period is that immediately preceding the Second World War when the factory, which I here call Pabrika, was owned and largely managed by Europeans. In 1954–55, when I observed its operations, it was Indonesian-owned but managed by a Dutchman. With the exception of three other members of the managerial staff of Chinese ethnic origin, the rest of the managerial and supervisory posts were held by Indonesians.

The factory at this time employed a labor force of 1000, about half of whom were drawn from predominantly agrarian villages outside the small town in which it is located. A seven-hour work day and rotating shifts enabled many to retain some ties with agriculture. One-fifth of the workers were women and one-fifth were migrants from other areas, some of urban provenience.

TRADITIONAL PATTERNS AND THE EARLY FACTORY SYSTEM

Of the many aspects of the factory routine, those relating to supervision and the enforcement of regulations and discipline appeared to have undergone the most significant changes between the early period of Pabrika's operations and when I observed them. The picture I derived from the reminiscences of older workers and supervisors suggested that this was the area which had formerly provoked the strongest resentment among the workers. For the new recruit, entry into the factory meant not only the necessity to adapt to a new type and schedule of activities. It also meant exposure to an unfamiliar pattern of interaction with rather alien kinds of people. In the first place, he found himself at the lowest level of a hierarchic order in which all authority emanated from above and unquestioned and prompt obedience was expected from below.

Neither hierarchy as a mode of organization nor obedience as a duty to status superiors seems strange in itself to the Javanese reared in the traditional social environment. For as a young child he becomes aware of a ranking system within the family and within the larger kinship group. He soon learns the different terms[2] by which he must denote and address his immediate and more distant kin and the behavior appropriate to each with respect to degree of relationship, line of descent, and age. He realizes that within the nuclear family paternal position is paramount and unquestioned and that he also owes a measure of respect and obedience to elder siblings and is owed the same by younger ones. Later he discovers the ranking system in the village that distinguishes its families on the basis of hereditary rights to land. And he learns to recognize the primacy of the village head and to accede to his instructions. While his encounters with members of the *prijaji* or gentry may be rare, he is nonetheless aware of the deference due them from him by virtue of their superior place in the wider society.[3]

Although stratification is a familiar element in almost every group in which a Javanese participates, the particular hierarchy of the factory differs in several respects from the hierarchal structures he knows. In the first place, the factory hierarchy is organized for a specific goal, that of production, and status within it is primarily determined by appointment theoretically based on abilities relative to this purpose. Traditional social groups may serve a multitude of functions. Status within them, as suggested by the above, is allocated by birth, age, and other ascriptive criteria that do not necessarily relate to the achievement of a particular goal. Leadership roles in the factory are specific to factory activity and may not overlap with the exercise of leadership elsewhere. Those with higher ascribed status in traditional groups appear to exert generalized leadership for a number of activities. Power conferred by leadership positions in the factory tends to be channeled downward and responsibility upward. In traditional structures those who hold power through status have concomitant responsibility toward those over whom they exercise it.

Supervision—The New Role

Moreover, the factory as a work organization introduces a set of intermediary roles generally unknown in groups organized for work in the traditional village. These roles are those of foreman, supervisor and other positions intervening between the employer and the man who performs the visible physical tasks of labor. The wage worker in the village deals directly with the man who wants work done and pays for it. The farmer hires field workers himself and he or a member of his family exercises whatever supervision may be necessary. Even when farming takes place on a tenant or sharecropping basis in which several parties profit from the proceeds, neither serves as a "go-between" between the other and the wage workers. Whoever is the cultivator has full discretion over the employment of laborers and the terms of work and payment until the harvest. When the plot is divided at harvest time, each party to the agreement then hires his own harvesters. Similarly, in small industrial establishments in villages and town, the proprietor is both the direct employer and serves as his own supervisor. And in most organized work activities, the employer works together with his laborers so that supervision as a discrete function is indistinct.[4]

The direct and face-to-face contact between employer and worker in these situations results in a work relationship in which the personal element is rarely absent. It allows for the continual possibility of negotiation and adjustment between the parties concerned. It makes possible loans and advances to workers in times of need. Thus there is no analogue[5] in village work structures for the figure who is just a link in a chain of command, directive but not responsive. He who is neither an owner nor visibly engaged in production but merely passes on orders with no power to negotiate the terms of their execution is an anomaly.

Nevertheless, however obscure the functions of those directly above him may have appeared to the new worker in Pabrika's early period, he might not have found it difficult to reconcile himself to taking orders from them. For these superiors were mainly Dutch and Chinese. And in the larger colonial society outside the village, a society in which stratification was partly based on ethnic origin, these people held high status. In the eyes of the villager they stood in the same relationship to him as his own gentry, government officials, and smaller figures of prestige and authority.

However, while the fact of ethnic dissimilarity might have legitimized these unfamiliar roles, this ethnic difference was accompanied by cultural differences affecting their interpretation. The behavior of those who occupied these positions, behavior offensive to the workers, rendered both them and their roles objectionable. The workers were faced with a group of superiors whose demands could not easily be anticipated, whose responses were startling, and whose very language could often not be understood. Even the most submissively anxious worker might not understand instructions barked at him in a mixture of Dutch and Malay or the most crude Javanese. His bewilderment or hesitation, taken for stupidity or obstinacy, was likely to produce impatience, annoyance, and vituperation in these "bosses." Action resulting in errors called down upon him loud-voiced anger and humiliating curses. A worker who stopped to rest or fell asleep from the fatigue induced by a long work day might be cuffed on the head[6] or beaten.

Work and Traditional Values

Such conduct offered a great contrast to that displayed by superiors in the customary environment. Perhaps because the Javanese is conditioned from childhood to respect and obey properly constituted authority figures and can anticipate and understand the content of their directives, these figures rarely find it necessary to exert visible effort or force[7] to obtain compliance. Indeed the very act of doing so might itself be taken as an implicit admission of their uncertainty of their right to make demands. If those to whom orders are given appear to hesitate in following them or in some other way subtly indicate some degree of resistance, similarly subtle and indirect means of persuasion are applied.

Resistance itself is rarely overt but takes the form of polite evasion. Prolonged non-compliance, which may often be accompanied by outward assent,[8] generally results in the issue being shelved or temporarily deferred until a more favorable occasion arises for obtaining acquiescence. For to bring an issue to the point of open conflict might disturb the harmony of the social order whose maintenance is deemed indispensable in the traditional Javanese view of society.

Such circumspection in avoiding overt discord is not only characteristic of encounters between social unequals but permeates nearly all face-to-face interchange. Thus the treatment workers in the factory received from their foreign[9] overseers, in addition to affording sharp contrast with that accorded them by traditional group leaders, also violated their notions of appropriate behavior between human beings irrespective of status. No matter how incensed a Javanese may feel towards another, he refrains from expressing irritation, anger, or vituperation directly toward that other or in his presence. Incipient or active hostility toward another finds an outlet in making him the butt of humor or in deriding him to others behind his back. But he who expresses an aggressive impulse overtly is regarded as immature, improperly socialized, and deplorably crude. And he who lifts his hand against another,[10] except under the most extreme provocation,[11] is considered no longer a true Javanese, certainly not civilized.

Just as bewildering to the factory recruit, if not as directly humiliating as the supervisory procedures, was his subjection to a strange system of penalties that seemed arbitrarily enforced. For failing to meet a standard of workmanship he might only dimly comprehend, he could lose part of his wages. For infractions of regulations of whose existence he might not have been aware or whose purport he could not understand, he could be fined, suspended, or otherwise penalized. Damage to equipment or theft might result in immediate dismissal. What is recalled as having seemed most unjust was the occasional instance, generally involving theft, of the punishment or dismissal of a whole group because none of its members would admit to being the culprit or accuse any of the others. And what seemed least comprehensible was that these penalties were impersonally administered with reference to the offense itself and often without—what to the worker seemed most relevant—concern with intention, cause, or extenuating circumstances.

My observations of work relationships in the traditional settings[12] produced little evidence of an analogous system of sanctions. Neither in the field nor in the handicrafts enterprise does there seem to be a precise standard against which the quality of work is measured. In the first place, since time and speed are not emphasized, there is more opportunity for a task to be performed meticulously and mistakes avoided. In the second place, approximation is acceptable and exactness of product is not demanded. *Pentjars,* or bundles, of paddy may vary somewhat in size but are paid for at the same rate. Some bricks or tiles or copper kettles are not as well made as others, but only the most obviously unfit are discarded and not paid for at the piecework rate. Sometimes a differential rate is paid to workers according to relative skill (most generally there is only a distinction between apprentices and experienced workers) on the assumption that each sustains over the average the quality of which he is capable and there are no deductions for pieces that later may be discarded.

In accordance with the prescribed decorum for inter-personal behavior described above, discontent with the performance of an individual is rarely expressed in direct or scolding fashion. A dissatisfied employer is likely to dispense with the services of an unsatisfactory worker with a face-saving pretext, such as telling him that he has not enough work in the near future or that some relative has suddenly turned up whom he is obliged to hire. Or he might, without being in any way sharply critical, convey sufficient lack of appreciation for the worker's efforts to induce the latter to decide to seek a living elsewhere. Similarly, a discontented worker does not complain of conditions of work or payment or announce that he can do better elsewhere but finds that some urgent situation in the family forces him to sever the connection temporarily.[13]

Direct dismissal as a punitive measure appears to be difficult, in any case, for several reasons. Work associations are rarely a mere exchange of labor for payment. They are often within the context of kin, neighborhood, and village ties involving a number of reciprocal obligations in which skill or performance may play a minor role. Beyond this and related to it is the tradition in agrarian communities that those with land rights or in other respects in superior economic circumstances should provide as many as possible opportunities for work for the landless and those in a needy position. This results in the apportionment of available work among as many hands as possible rather than the recruitment of labor on the basis of efficiency. The converse of this is the implicit recognition of the individual's "right to work" as a concomittant of community membership apart from considerations of skill or level of performance.[14]

If despite all precautions a disagreement should arise in a situation in which custom has not created a precedent,[15] its resolution would appear[16] to be based on a consideration of more factors than those directly pertinent to the issue itself. Perhaps the most important of these is that tension should be diminished and any sustained bitterness averted. Friends and neighbors often serve as mediators, attempting to press mutual concessions on the contestants rather than trying to assess guilt or support the claims of one to the exclusion of those of the other. Should the issue be taken to the village head or some other prestige figure, the ultimate decision generally favors neither one nor the other completely but is a compromise in which each party obtains some satisfaction.

The problems of supervision and authority can thus be understood in terms of the contrast between the structuring of work relationships in traditional Javanese society and in the factory system. In the early period of Pabrika's operations, this antithesis found little expression within the factory itself. The workers faced the full burden of making the transition and their problems of adaptation were further complicated by language and cultural barriers. Some managed to overcome the strains of adjustment; many, following the traditional way of withdrawal from stress, quietly retreated to the familiar environment.

THE CURRENT SEARCH FOR ACCOMMODATION

Today the contradictions between these systems are being acted out within the walls of Pabrika. And they are no longer exclusively personified by the workers on the one hand and the supervisory and managerial personnel on the other. Instead there exists an uneasy interplay of elements of both systems in the behavior of each of these groups toward the others. In circumstances that can best be characterized as a search for a pattern of accommodation permitting an integrated order, the workers tend to exercise a strong measure of control over the means by which they are controlled. This has come about as a result of the following factors:

1) The replacement of foreign supervisory and managerial staff by those of an ethnic background identical with or similar to that of the workers;

2) the entry of workers who have been exposed to both urban and revolutionary influences and are not reticent in making known their views;

3) the formation of unions through which these views can be channelized;

4) the appointment of a general manager familiar with Javanese values and behavior and capable of employing them himself.

The formal organization of the factory with its hierarchic structure has not changed. But the present recruit from the village finds that those in roles above his interpret them in ways that are not disconcerting. His foreman and supervisor[17] are likely to share with him a common language and a common understanding of how people treat each other. They issue instructions in calm quiet voices or in gestures that are meaningful to him. They are patient with his initial fumbling, recognizing that he needs time to accustom himself to this new world. Subsequent errors are more likely to arouse not anger but good-natured ridicule that will shame him into avoidance of mistakes that are likely to provoke it.

In fact in the present scene it is the middle group of foremen and supervisors who are taxed with the burden of reconciling the formal requirements of the factory with the expectations generated by the culture. Discussion with them makes it clear that they do understand the requirements of their roles. They know that their major task is to pass on to those under their jurisdiction the directions they have received from their superiors and to see that these are carried out. They recognize that with respect to the workers this involves more or less the following tasks: (1) to make explicit and clear the instructions for the job at hand, (2) to exert continued surveillance over the pace and quality of worker performance, (3) to issue reprimands when called for, and (4) to impose the prescribed sanctions within their competence when necessary.

According to management criteria, only the first of the above functions is consistently and satisfactorily performed by all the supervisory personnel. Although most keep a fairly steady eye on the workers, some appear to observe only sporadically the operations under their control, mainly when their own bosses are present. Fewer reprimand their subordinates with any conviction. And practically none dares to impose penalties without resort to higher authority. In principle, there is delegation of responsibility and allocation of concomitant power down the line. In practice, responsibility is often evaded and the exercise of authority shoved upward. In the words of one department head:

> Only the foremen are supposed to watch and direct the workers; my supervisor is supposed to control the foremen; my assistant should check only on the supervisor and serve as liaison between him and me; and I should spend most of my time in planning and conferences. What really happens is that the supervisor has to keep an eye directly on the workers as well as upon the foremen; my assistant must control the supervisor, foremen and workers; and I have to be in the shop most of the day to be sure everything goes smoothly.

This department head did not mean that he necessarily substitutes for his subordinates in any specific function, although that takes place also, but that his physical presence is necessary to insure their adequate performance. In his absence, a foreman might turn his back on a group of workers who are not following instructions, pretending not to notice them; the supervisor might somehow neglect to scold the foreman for his inattention; and the assistant might hesitate to inform the head that production is not proceeding smoothly. To affix responsibility for the resulting snarl-up would not be easy. For the foreman would explain that he had been so busy watching another group of workers at a crucial task that he had not had time to notice the first group. The supervisor would have been occupied in explaining the requirements of a new work order to the other foreman. The assistant might admit to an inkling that something was wrong, but since it was not his place to address the workers directly and there was nothing he could do about it at the time, he had not wanted to disturb his so busy superior.[18]

External Status and Factory Authority

Many of the foremen with whom I talked confessed to a sense of being almost constantly caught between conflicting currents. And although this can be said of the position of foreman in almost any factory, placed as it is at the point where demands from above and pressures from below tend to converge, it is doubly true at Pabrika. For if on the one hand managerial staff expect the foremen to obtain compliance from the workers, they also expect this to be done without coercion of the type that would arouse worker hostility and union protest. If the foreman is to gain acquiescence without resort to pressure, it is necessary for the workers to recognize the role of the foreman and to accept the individual assigned to that role. Many of the foremen cannot always depend on such acceptance. When uncertain they hesitate, in Javanese style, to put their authority to a crucial test.

I have earlier indicated that in the traditional system, he who directs the work of others, with the exception of work performed as a reciprocal obligation, generally has higher status than those who work for him. Obviously the landholder ranks higher in the village stratification system than the workers he employs. The small entrepreneur is often a *hadji* with the prestige acquired from his trip to Mecca. Work on community projects is organized and often directed by the village head not because of superior organizational skill on his part but in his capacity as village head. Thus conversely the right to direct labor may be seen as flowing from status derived from other criteria than the work situation itself.

Some of the foremen in the factory hold such status in the environment beyond the factory. Two of them are leading landholders in nearby villages and one of these is also well educated by town as well as village standards. It is significant that these two seem to find little difficulty in maintaining discipline among their workers. Another supervisory official who has no feeling that his authority is challenged is a Eurasian who in the earlier period was slightly assimilated to the European element in the town and was regarded as such by the Javanese.

It is conceivable that some of the others might have little difficulty in gaining acceptance as authority figures in the eyes of workers recently recruited from the rural area. For even though they themselves may have originally come from low-status groups of the population, by this time they have acquired some of the attributes of higher status. To the villager, their style of living and mode of behavior may seem more comparable to that of the town officials than to his own. And he is likely to regard them, at least initially, with similar respect and a shade of deference.

NON-TRADITIONAL WORKER'S CHALLENGE TO AUTHORITY

Many of the workers, however, are not from the traditional village background. Those with prior residence and work experience in larger centers than Namakota have themselves acquired some of the attributes of urban sophistication whose possession gives their holders higher status in the eyes of agrarian villagers. Many of them have had equivalent if not more education than their foremen, have become accustomed to similar material possessions and ascribe to themselves the traditionally associated symbolic significance these carry. Those who hold superordinate status in the factory are more likely to be regarded by them outside of the factory as their equals rather than their superiors. This attitude often carries into the factory where they can be seen retorting freely to admonitions of their foremen and not hesitating to tease and joke with them.

It is not easy to determine what constitutes legitimation of authority for this group. Some of its members appear to consider seniority as the sole criterion for the elevation of others to a position of direction over them. They do not question the right of men who have been in the factory for ten or twelve years to supervise their work.[19] Others seem somewhat amenable to authority exercised by someone whose skill is manifestly superior to theirs as long as this skill is amply demonstrated. One foreman told me that he constantly hopes for situations to arise in which workers need his direct assistance. Then his stock rises and his crew appear to respect him; in between these occasions they seem to regard his presence as superfluous.

Those workers with a background of revolutionary activity and ideology, most influenced by the new emphasis on democracy and egalitianism, tend implicitly and often explicitly to challenge the notion of any authority imposed from above. In their minds such authority carries about it the aura of colonialism and should similarly be abolished. Valid authority over a group, according to their interpretation of democracy, is that derived through selection by and voluntary agreement of the members of the group. This attitude is frequently encountered in other contexts than the political one in which it originated. Within the factory it finds expression in the intimations that workers should have some voice in the selection of those who supervise them, if not directly at least through right of rejection.

During the period of my residence, the general manager received a petition signed by over forty workers requesting the removal of a recently appointed supervisor. The major charge levelled against him was that he was "unproductive." When asked to explain what they meant by this term, the leader of the delegation replied that this supervisor seemed to spend most of his time observing and studying[20] and had not been seen working with his hands. Further investigation revealed that there was resentment at what the workers felt to be an aloofness and a sense of superiority on the part of this man toward them. There was also some grumbling at the fact that he was not Javanese, but from another Indonesian ethnic group.

This was but one of a number of instances in which workers have communicated objections by means of organized protest rather than individual withdrawal. Previously there had been overt resistance by workers in one section to taking orders from a foreman brought in from outside. They declared that they would prefer to have someone from their own ranks. This approach had been initially tried and then discarded when those so promoted had proved in management eyes to be even more than normally reluctant to assume effective authority over former colleagues and the latter even less than normally disposed to accept it from them. This was succeeded by an experiment of transferring workers who seemed to be promising supervisory material to other departments for a few months before returning them with higher status to their original ones.[21] The first retransfer on this basis also encountered worker resistance, from some on the grounds that the individual in question was "too young," from others because he was now "an outsider" from "another department." Ultimately, worker opposition in these cases was overcome by rather skillful rhetoric from top management.[22] But a formula has not yet been found for locating new supervisory personnel who are both effective and acceptable.

THE AMBIGUITIES OF THE MANAGERIAL ROLE

Given such attitudes on the part of even a small number of workers, it is not surprising that few of those in middle-level positions have the confidence to assert authority to the point where it may be challenged. Although none would admit to desiring a return to the "hard old days," it is clear that a situation in which a worker may dare to ignore one of them, turn his back on him, or complain over his head counteracts whatever sense of security is derived from their selection to their posts by management. For many of them share the background of the workers and to some degree are similarly influenced by the attitudes that affect worker recognition of them. Although they have therefore formally mastered the roles assigned to them, they have not yet sufficiently internalized them to implement them adequately.

Traditional Javanese values and modern egalitarian notions also appear to affect the way in which supervisory personnel fulfill the task of transmitting information upward. Yearly wage raises for workers are based upon the three criteria of work efficiency, quality of work, and regularity of attendance. The foremen are expected periodically to give objective evaluation of individual worker performance. It is not at all unusual for a foreman to grade all workers under him as satisfactory on all counts. For, apart from the group solidarity developed through working together, the foreman often lives in the same neighborhood as some of his workers and may have formed a number of other ties resulting from this propinquity.[23] The obligations resulting from such ties make it difficult for him to risk offending them by adverse judgments. They may go so far as to enable workers to induce foremen to record stoppage periods to their advantage. Possibly also bearing on the uniformly favorable grading is the attitude that an advantage should be indiscriminately apportioned, an attitude that may have its origins in the village tradition of sharing benefits and hardships or perhaps it is derived from the post-revolutionary emphasis on equality.

Management's scepticism of the reliability of such blanket approval has resulted in a technique that combines checking of record and attendance books[24] with a sort of bargaining process. The supervisor checks the records with the foremen and generally succeeds in working out with them some downward revisions; the department head engages in the same process with the supervisors and so on up the line. This is done on the assumption that with each step further removed from the worker there is less likelihood that personal considerations influence judgment. At the same time, those closest to the workers can avert recriminations from them by attributing unfavorable judgments to pressure from those above.

Many of the criticisms levelled against foremen and supervisors by most of the managerial staff are also applied to the managerial staff by the European general manager. In several respects he has attempted to follow a different course than that of his predecessor. Whereas the latter made most of the policy decisions unilaterally, he holds daily meetings with his staff for joint discussion and decisions. His predecessor reportedly spent much of his day observing the execution of his instructions and often directly supervising operations. He attempts to delegate as many functions as possible to his subordinates, appearing only briefly out of his office. He tells them that the department heads are more technically qualified than he, that they have wide latitude in the execution of decisions and should only resort to him when major problems arise. He defines his task to them as primarily that of planning, coordination, and liaison with the owners.

Thus far this "loose reins" strategy has been more successful in retaining the goodwill of his subordinates than in achieving its objective of forcing them to function as executives. Perhaps two have risen to the challenge and perform satisfactorily at the level required of managerial staff by the factory model without stimulus and pressure from him. The others seem to require at least his presence, if not his occasional prodding, to sustain them and they tend to relax their efforts in his absence.[25] Like the foremen and supervisors, they are only too eager to pass up to him the responsibility for the enforcement of discipline. The usual reason given in such instances[26] is the desire to avert possible difficulties with the communist-dominated union.

Implicit in statements of this type is a more basic motive—the disinclination to make embarrassingly obvious the latent ambiguities of their position. For all of the foreman and supervisors and many of the managerial staff are also members of the same union as the majority of the workers. Several are even members of the governing body of this union. The development of unions has facilitated the crystallization of worker sentiment and the participation of managerial personnel in union affairs is an additional factor conditioning their responsiveness to this sentiment. Although such participation could serve as a means of channeling union policy in a direction most advantageous to management aims and sometimes does, this is limited by the existence of a rival union and competition between the two for membership.

Those in the dual roles of middle-level or higher-managerial officials and active union members or officials profess to feel no real conflict between them. They see themselves in a median or conciliatory position, carrying out the traditional Javanese ideal of maintaining harmony by reconciling divergent interests. It is clear, however, that this inhibits their full identification as members of a distinct "management team." And it may be adduced as another of the factors[27] explaining their inclination to leave any drastic disciplinary action to the very top managerial officials.

In the last analysis this throws the major burden of decision in the sphere of authority on the general manager.[28] Unable to depend upon unequivocal support from his subordinates and aware of the psychological complexities of their position, he does not try to compel their strict adherence to the formal mechanisms of control as apparently did his predecessor. Instead, he assumes the paternalistic but non-authoritarian role they seem to demand of him and works with them in trying to evolve techniques which outwardly satisfy cultural expectations while achieving the goal of maintaining the factory in relatively efficient operation. And he is not above employing the circuitous Javanese modes of behavior himself in attaining his objectives.

Flexibility and the System of Sanctions

This is seen most clearly in the ways in which the system of sanctions is enforced. The formal outline of this system has not been greatly altered since the period when it constituted a major source of worker grievance. Workers are still subject to wage deductions for errors, suspension and dismissal for infringement of regulations. However, the regulations themselves are now the outcome of union-management negotiation. Most of the workers I encountered are fairly familiar with them, having been generally informed of them at the time of entry or shortly afterwards. Should one feel himself unfairly disciplined, he has the right of appeal. The very reluctance of his immediate superiors to administer punitive measures means that a worker has a good chance of carrying his case to the highest authorities with the opportunity to defend himself personally.

I received the impression that workers now venture evasion or transgression of regulations in the spirit of a game of chance in which the player is willing to risk the consequences of losing. In fact, the risk is not so great, for in practice the major penalties are rarely administered without investigation of the particular circumstances by higher management officials and often in consultation with the union heads. For example, a worker who has been recorded as dismissed for prolonged absence should not, according to the rules, be reinstated upon reappearance. In actuality, a good weaver stands an excellent chance of being taken back if he can justify his absence with a plausible explanation or even with an original and entertaining—if somewhat implausible—excuse. Occasionally, a worker trades shifts by private agreement with a worker on an alternate shift in the same department. As long as the machine is not left unattended, such arrangements are not objected to by management.

A worker who proves to be repeatedly inept, careless, or lazy is no longer dismissed on these grounds. Instead he is exposed to a technique that embodies the utmost Javanese finesse. He is progressively transferred to less demanding tasks which carry with them lower prestige. An ex-weaver assigned to a job that requires him to carry loads through the mill under the eyes of his former colleagues is likely to feel himself so degraded that he leaves voluntarily after several days. As a result workers who fall below the standard of skill of which they are known to be capable are sometimes brought to rapid recovery by the mere suggestion that they might be happier with a transfer to another part of the factory.

The most drastic penalty of dismissal is generally applied only in cases of theft and action leading to damage or danger to safety. Even here a concession may be made in extraordinary circumstances. For example, one of the men in the storeroom had worked out an elaborate system of checking and recording supplies which had enabled him to withdraw and somehow take out of the factory a sizeable stock of cloth for three months before he was caught. The offender pleaded at his hearing that his original intention had been to make only a single haul to fill one pressing family need for money,[29] but that the system he had evolved forced him to continue his depredations to avoid detection. The staff listened to this explanation and examined the system. They were so impressed with its ingenuity and the intelligence it implied on the part of the worker that instead of being dismissed, he was assigned a job that would utilize his initiative.

There is no doubt that such pliancy on the part of present management has contributed to the improved morale of the workers and to the growth of a more stable work force. On the other hand, continued divergence of practice from principle may well obstruct the development of integrated and self-sustaining procedures of supervision and authority needed by a factory system. The present ways of reconciling various worker pressures with the requirements of efficient production rely rather heavily on the father-figure of the general manager and on a sort of stop-gap improvisation. But perhaps improvisation is the only mode of dealing with an unstable situation that offers many variables and few constants. The situation in Pabrika is not unique. It merely mirrors in microcosm the confusion prevalent throughout organizational life in Indonesia as old norms of authority have been wholly or partially repudiated and generally accepted new ones have not yet emerged.

NOTES

1. This is part of an unpublished study, *From Rice-Field to Factory: the Industrialization of a Rural Labor Force in Java,* based on my field investigations. For support of the study I am indebted to Professor Bert F. Hoselitz and the Research Center in Economic Development and Cultural Change of the University of Chicago. What little knowledge I have of the disciplines of Social Anthropology and Sociology I owe to my sister, Professor Dorothy Willner, who cannot be held responsible for its shortcomings.

2. These terms indicate not merely degrees of kinship but differentiate between junior and senior kin of the same degree. There are separate terms for elder brother and younger brother, elder sister and younger sister, and similarly for elder and younger brother of parents.

3. It could well be said that every encounter between two Javanese involves a mutual recognition in gesture, language, and attitude of relative place in a stratified order.

4. Even when he does not share the work, his right in the land or his ownership of the enterprise might be seen as the factor authorizing him to direct it.

5. Perhaps the nearest analogue to the "intermediate" role is that of the village head in his capacity as recipient of orders from higher governmental levels to which he is expected to obtain village compliance. In the eyes of the villagers, however, he is the only visible authority besides being the symbol of the community and its intactness. Directives are not given to him in the village but at meetings with sub-district officials at their offices.

6. A whack on the head is more than an affront, for the head of an individual is sacred and not to be touched by another.

7. On the rare occasions when force is resorted to, it is not directly applied by the authority figure himself. Thus, a former district head, recalling that repeated efforts to persuade farmers to plant paddy at the time suggested by the agricultural advisors were of no avail, stated: "I was finally obliged to order two farmers to be beaten as an example to the rest."

8. It is customary to assent to requests or orders whether or not one has the intention of fulfilling them. Either the tone of voice or the rhetoric of the assent may convey whether it is merely a polite affirmative or substantive and, in any case, time will tell.

9. Occasionally such treatment was also meted out by Javanese foremen as well but, if my informants are to be believed, generally upon direct orders and in the presence of those above them. What was more typical of the exploitation of workers under them by Javanese foremen, although perhaps not necessarily regarded as such, was the "commission" taken from the wages of those workers whom they brought into the factory.

10. Even disobedient children are not as a rule spanked or slapped but nipped or pinched.

11. An example I was given of extreme provocation provoking violence was adultery. Even here, according to informants, retaliation is often indirect, such as by poison or soliciting the aid of a "black *dukun*." Outright violence is much more likely to be perpetrated by a group rather than an individual and usually after the group has been harangued or has whipped itself up to an emotional frenzy. The most noted type of individual violence—of which I have had no personal experience—is *amok*.

12. Here I am speaking of labor in agriculture and small enterprises in this area and not domestic services. Where I observed the latter in the homes of Javanese aristocrats, especially in the principalities of Central Java, it was not unusual for domestic servants to be sharply reprimanded for unsatisfactory performance and even occasionally physically chastised.

13. These pretexts do not, of course, deceive anyone as to the underlying reasons but are appreciated and, indeed, expected as a face-saving ritual.

14. I asked a farmer who was complaining of the high cost of labor why he did not select a few of the faster and more skilled field workers and employ them over a longer period of time, thus cutting his costs. The reply was that he couldn't risk the resultant disapproval of the community and the possible accusations of being penny-pinching and unconcerned with the welfare of his poorer neighbors. A small entrepreneur who was maintaining two extra hands during the off-season when he had little work for them in the shop but tried to keep them occupied with odd jobs around his compound said: "After all, they cannot easily find other work and they must eat. What else should I do, let them starve?"

15. For the disposition of shares of harvest and for the provision of a certain minimum of food to workers, custom is sufficiently strong to preclude the possibility of disagreement.

16. I have not directly observed the course of a disagreement between wage worker and employer in a village work situation but am drawing an analogy from disputes observed over debts and work contracted with artisans.

17. Almost three-fourths of the present supervisory personnel are Javanese and many have been recruited from the ranks of former workers.

18. An example of this, which was observed in some detail, occurred during the installation of some new looms. On a Thursday morning, under the direction of its foreman, a work crew began on the first loom. A technical advisor stood by checking the directions on the blueprint. The factory manager came in frequently to survey the progress and the general manager stopped by several times. By early afternoon, the first loom had been installed. The work on the second loom went faster and was finished by the end of the afternoon. This time the technical advisor looked in several times, the factory manager twice, and the general manager once to assure themselves that the complexities of installation had been mastered. On Friday morning, work began on the third loom. The general manager left in the middle of the morning for the city, the factory manager spent most of the morning in conferences and the afternoon at home and the technical assistant also did not appear after lunch. The foreman seemed to be giving the same instructions but somehow the work was proceeding more slowly. Two of the members of the crew did not report back after the usual Friday break for mosque attendance. By 4 p.m., when the general manager returned from the city, the third loom had not yet been completely installed. Called to account, the foreman explained that he had not been any less explicit or assiduous in giving orders than the previous day but the workers had responded more slowly and lackadaisically. Slightly stronger pressure on his part had not produced visibly better response. He had not dared to become really rough with the workers. Besides, there had been nobody there to back him up.

19. When questioning workers concerning their opposition to a new foreman in circumstances related below, I received numbers of replies to the effect that only a man who has done a certain sort of work for years would know enough to be able to tell others how to do it.

20. Since this was in the dyeing department which engaged in experiments with different dyes, the new supervisor was also being trained in the technical aspects of dyestuffs.

21. The underlying rationale was that time and distance might lessen the familiarity which was considered to be the major deterrent on both sides to the assumption of the new relationship, while the added experience might be accepted by the workers as justification for the new status of their former equal.

22. For example, in the first instance mentioned above, the general manager addressed the delegation, taking as a starting point the comments that the foreman was from another *bangsa* or ethnic subgroup. He stated that he was shocked to hear that his workers could speak so in this period of national unity. "After all, hasn't Bung Karno (affectionate diminutive for President Sukarno) said that now all Indonesians are one *bangsa*? Then the delegation was urged by him and other management officials to show by their acceptance of the foreman that they were good supporters of national unity.

23. I have observed workers and supervisory personnel in joint recreation, such as playing cards and gambling together. One supervisor is engaged in financing credit purchasing of bicycles by workers, i.e., he makes the initial payment to the dealers and collects from the workers on an installment basis. On the one hand, this is regarded by the workers as a form of assistance, despite his profit on interest; on the other hand, since collection of debts of this sort reportedly can no longer be legally

enforced, he is somewhat subtly intimidated to stay in the good graces of these workers to ensure that they retain their sense of obligation to repay him.

24. There is a daily book for each section of the factory in which is recorded the production of each loom or other machine, stoppages, problems, etc. If a worker complains that errors recorded against him or lower production is the fault of the loom rather than of his efforts, this book is used to compare his production rate with that of other workers on the same loom in different shifts.

25. Although the general manager spends much of this time outside the factory premises, conducting many of its affairs from his home across the street, it is as if his "being on call' serves as a catalyst for the normal conduct of affairs. During a period when he was on home leave, production declined steadily and he was cabled by the owners to cut short his vacation and return.

26. One instance I observed when an electrician, careless a second time after a warning caused a small fire. The regulations provided for immediate dismissal in such a case and either the foreman of the crew or the supervisor of maintenance, both present, was empowered to discharge him. Instead, they called the factory manager and suggested that he do so; he, in turn, went to the general manager. The latter firmly told the factory manager that it was his affair and he, in turn, prevailed upon the supervisor with the statement that the "big boss" expected him to do it.

27. It is not easy to attribute relative weights to the various factors that have here been advanced to explain the behavior of this group. For example, in the neighboring British-managed textile factory, there is a separate union for Indonesians above the rank of worker. Nevertheless, the British department heads and supervisors complain that the Javanese supervisors and foremen under them never translate literally their reprimands to the workers but always "soften" them and are generally "too easy" with the workers. The union membership of managerial personnel at Pabrika may be a less important factor than the others.

28. The three other management officials who are not affiliated with a union are of Chinese ethnic origin. And, although they are not subject to the same inhibitions as their Indonesian colleagues, they also tend to be circumspect and a bit wary because of the peculiar position of even those Chinese who are Indonesian citizens in the present nationalistic period.

29. Many of the workers, especially those from the rural environment, cannot understand why they cannot borrow money from the factory in case of personal need and repay in gradual stages through wage deductions. This arrangement, as had been earlier mentioned, is not uncommon in village work arrangements, especially in small-scale enterprises.

CHAPTER TWENTY-TWO

Household Economy during the Peasant-to-Worker Transition in the Swiss Alps

WANDA MINGE-KALMAN

A substantial part of the agricultural population in Europe today is made up of families who work on their own farms and also in wage labor. While transition from exclusively agricultural production to wage labor has traversed several generations of European families, we still know little about how the peasant-worker family, as it has come to be called, allocates labor to both the agriculture market and the wage-labor market. In particular, we know little of how the family composed of peasants in the parent generation and wage laborers in the children's generation—a commonplace in the final phase of the peasantry—organizes as a labor group. From a wealth of illustrative detail on peasants in Europe today. S. H. Franklin (1969: 55) concludes that

> the worker-peasant family as a socio-economic type remains
> largely uninvestigated. Never to my knowledge has an attempt
> been made to analyze the phenomenon of the worker-peasant
> family within the context of the theory of the peasant
> economy.

The most often cited theory of the peasant economy, at least so far as Europe is concerned, is Alexander V. Chayanov's work, first published in 1925. Chayonov's theory of the peasant economy, that is, "family farms normally run without wage labor," is a comprehensive theory of how family labor is related to family consumption at different stages of the family's developmental cycle. In the first stage the married couple becomes ever more burdened with children who are too young to work. Using empirical data from zemstvo statistics, Chayanov (1966: 59) shows that the consumer-worker ratio reaches its highest proportion around the fourteenth year of the family's existence. After this point, "as the children grow up the consumer-worker ratio will fall rapidly, approaching unity . . . ."

The important question concerning the transitional peasant-to-worker family today is: what happens when the children do not work with the family when they become old enough to work? Contrary to what happens in the peasant family, the consumer-worker ratio does not begin to balance at this stage in the peasant-worker family. In fact, the consumers (the children) may, during this stage, cost the workers (the parents) more than they did in the earlier years.

To be sure, since education became mandatory as the demand for skilled labor increased in Europe in the middle of the nineteenth century, children's foregone labor on the farm has burdened the family that continues agriculture—regardless of whether it has other wage laboring members. That is, whether one parent works for wages or both parents work on the farm, preparing the next generation for wage labor is a burden to the parents that is measurable, in part, by the foregone labor of the children and, in part, by expenses related to education. In the context of the theory of the peasant economy, the primary cost to the parents is the foregone labor of the children who now go to school from age six to sixteen—whereas, in peasant families of the past, the children worked throughout this decade.

The parents' cost in children's foregone labor is an omitted factor in the rapidly growing literature on the cost of children in industrial and industrializing[1] societies (for a summary of some of this literature, see Espenshade 1977). But it can, in fact, surpass the out-of pocket cost of children, as George Psacharopoulos (1973) has shown in his study of the foregone labor of children in wage-labor families in 24 countries. For each country he has obtained an average value of the labor of adolescents who are legally old enough to work. The cost to the family in foregone labor relative to the family's direct education cost is shown for four European countries on Table 22.1.

Table 22.1 Costs Per Student Year by Educational Level and Country (in U.S. Dollars)

| Country | Secondary | | Higher | |
	Direct	Children's Foregone Labor	Direct	Children's Foregone Labor
Belgium	—	—	4,860	2,220
Denmark	—	—	2,695	4,246
Great Britain	483	1,269	2,690	2,137
Norway	420	1,589	959	2,366

Source, Psacharopoulos 1973: Appendix D.

Hence, within the context of the theory of the peasant economy, what might occur in the peasant-worker family economy today is that the labor burden of the parents does not decrease when the children become old enough to work, but it might become greater for the parents.

I have roughly approximated the proposed relationships between changes in family consumer units (measured by an index of one adult = 1.0) and changes in the number of laborers in the family with a hypothetical curve. Although children begin to work at about the same time, they do not become full-time labor units for the family, and thus, the workers' curve levels. Furthermore, if adolescent children consume more material goods than parents, as one study has shown (Wynn 1972), the rate of increase in the parent's labor burden will be greater than a linear function of children's age. Compared to Chayanov's (1966: 59) theory of the consumer-worker ratio this curve suggests a change in the very nature of family labor allocation as it evolves from a peasant food-producing group to a group involved in wage labor.

The family's transition to wage-labor society can be better understood by an empirical examination of the hypothesis that as children allocate more of their time to education and less to the farm, the parents make up for the foregone labor and offset the additional education costs by allocating more of their own time to family-based labor.

Herein, I test this proposition with data from an Alpine village in southwest Switzerland where I did fieldwork in 1975–76. The high-altitude villages in the valleys of the Rhône River are excellent places to test such a theory of labor in peasant-worker families because the area is in rapid transition from a traditional peasant economy to a modern, industrial wage-labor economy.[2] The accelerated industrialization of canton Valais has recently attracted much anthropological attention. During the past decade, five anthropologists have done fieldwork in Valaisan villages, all prior to my own (see Berthoud 1967; Friedl 1974; Netting 1972; Weinberg 1975; Wiegandt 1975).

I use the term "peasant-worker" to refer to most of the families in the village since most are transitional families today. That is, although one or both parents are farming today, in only two of the 80 families will the children continue the family farm. They are taking wage labor instead. The rate of exodus from mountain farming— 90 per cent in fifteen years in this region—is characteristic of upland villages throughout the Alpine chain in five countries in Central Europe.

A further factor contributing to the suitability of this location is that the resident domestic group in the French-speaking Swiss Alps is a nuclear family—the most common resident pattern of the west European family (Laslett 1972). Methodologically, this is a simplifying factor since it is the two-generation family of parents and children in which I am primarily interested.

THE DIVISION OF AGRICULTURAL LABOR IN THIRTY-TWO FAMILIES

To study family labor I lived for one year in Le Levron, a Valaisan village in which half of the 80 families are peasants and half derive their primary income from wage labor but continue to work the land. I lived in the home of one of these peasant-worker families.

A greater proportion of Le Levron's population is active in agriculture today than that of most Swiss Alpine villages. More than other villages in the region, it has maintained some of the socio-economic traditions of Alpine agro-pastoral, high-altitude villages. For one thing, the village endogamy rate remains high—86 per cent of all resident couples in 1975; and unlike many villages in which emigration has decreased the proportion of young people in the population, 58 per cent of the 375 residents are under 35 years of age. For another, Le Levron children have a three-week vacation from the village school to tend the cows on the meadows when they are brought down from the high summer pastures each autumn—an institution that has disappeared from all other villages in the region.

The village is located on a wide, south-facing slope above the intersection of the Entremont and Bagnes Valleys. The terraced slopes are divided into tiny parcels of land, a result of the practice of partible inheritance. The average farm in Le Levron is less than three hectares, and the average number of parcels per farm is 36. Each family's parcels are scattered at varying altitudes, from their vineyards in the Rhône valley to the communally-owned summer pastures above the village. Such fragmentation hinders the mechanization of agriculture, and it also costs the villagers much time in transportation. They travel up and down the mountain on small hay wagons, and they may spend a few days at a time at one of their seasonal huts away from the village.

Today as in the past, cheese-making is the most important agricultural production. Each family has a few milch cows that provide milk for the communally-owned cheese-producing dairy as well as for family consumption. Other cash crops are wine grapes and strawberries. In addition, each family grows its own vegetables and grains for the cows. Le Levron is the only village in this region that still grows the four grains described by Arensberg (1963) as having once been the staples of the European agricultural economy.

In the typical peasant-worker family in this region, the husband/ father is the full-time wage worker, usually in a factory, although he may be a self-employed craftsman or work in tourist inns in other villages in the region. There is no tourism in Le Levron, and the majority of wage workers are employed in construction or in administrative offices in the nearest town, 40 minutes away by car. These families have not given up agriculture: they still keep cows that require twice-daily milking, 60 hours of haying per cow during the summer months, and approximately 120 person-days of cow tending in spring and autumn; and they still maintain labor-intensive grape and strawberry cultivation.

A time-allocation study was made of all agricultural labor (Table 22.2) in a set of families in which the parent generation works only in farming and in a set in which the mother continues the family farm while the father is employed in wage labor. My daily obser- vations of individuals working in the fields and stables were recorded on code sheets designed for this "spot-checking" method by Allen Johnson (1975). Because time duration is not measured, it is necessary to have many observations. At the end of a complete agricultural cycle I included only families on which I had made more than 40 observations. In these 32 families, I made a total of 3.433 person- observations. Table 22.3 summarizes the observations of the eighteen families who work only in agriculture in the parent generation and of the fourteen families in which the husband-father does wage labor.

It is not surprising that, as husbands take wage labor, wives do a greater proportion of the agricultural labor. Milking, which has always been done by the husband in peasant families, is done by the wife in peasant-worker families (see, for example, families S, G, and J). Strawberries, the most labor-intensive crop, are cultivated by women, partly because they were introduced as a cash crop after men had begun taking wage labor in this region.

A less-expected result of these observations is that most children work on the family farm only during peak days in the harvest season.[3] The haying in late June, for example, comes at the same time the strawberry harvest begins; hence, some children help at this time. And in the autumn they tend the cows to free the parents for the potato harvest which cannot be completed before the cows return from the summer pasture. This is not considered work but a holiday for the children. October days are cold and sunny with snow appearing at higher altitudes; the young herders build fires of larch- wood to keep warm and to roast sausages for meals; and each day the mountainside is alive with the sound of the 25-pound bells around the necks of 200 cows.

Table 22.2 Seasonal Division of Agricultural Labor in Le Levron

Spring	Summer	Autumn	Winter
Cows milked twice daily	Cows milked twice daily until June 10	Potatoes harvested	Cows milked twice daily
Pastures and fields cleared of debris	Cows all day on meadows June 3–10	Cows on meadows 6–8 weeks (all day every day)	Wood chopped for stoves each day
Manure carried from barn to fields	Vineyards defoilaged	Beets harvested	Kindling gathered in forest
Vineyards defoilaged. (Some families lived in Rhone Valley "quartiers" a few days each week.)	Hay harvest: cutting, turning, raking, transporting to barns	Winter cereals planted	Tools repaired
Barley sowed.	Strawberry harvest, late June through late July	"Vendange" (Harvest of wine grapes) in Rhône Valley	Barns, stables, and storage huts cleaned and repaired
Beets, potatoes planted	All gardens weeded		
Strawberry plants weeded	A few vegetables cut daily for family meals		
Vegetable garden planted: carrots, cauliflower, peas, green beans, celery, lettuce	Wheat and rye cut and dried		
All gardens weeded			

Table 22.3 Thirty-Two Transitional Families: Percentages of Total Labor Observations According to Family Member

	Wife/Mother	Husband/Father	Children	Total %
Eighteen Families with Only Second Generation Wage Workers (1,081 family-observations; 2,150 person-observations)	24% (516)	62% (1,333)	14% (301)	100
Fourteen Families with Both Generation in Wage Work 719 family-observations; 1,293 person-observations)	63% (813)	33% (427)	4% (52)	100

As Table 22.3 shows, only a small percentage of the observations are of children in either set of families. (Only resident children were included, which in the peasant-worker families are all children—an average of 3.9 per family—and which in peasant families are about half of the families' children—an average of 4.9 per family. Table 22.5 indicates how many children are still members of the domestic group.) As I have mentioned, of all children in the village, only one is planning to continue the family farm without an outside job; two (in the same family) are planning to continue farming as a secondary job, that is, in addition to wage labor. (None of the parents said they were sorry their children are not continuing agriculture.) It is not surprising, then, that the children's labor contribution is less than the theoretical expectation of children who are continuing the family farm.

Conclusion

In this study I have examined certain theoretical propositions about the economics of the transitional peasant-to-worker family. In the families studied there is a relationship between the level of education and the mother's time allocated to family labor. Since much of the foregone labor of children is labor that would have been allocated to the family farm (which is continued by mothers when fathers take wage labor), on the average, the mother's labor hours increase more than the father's as children's education level increases.

If changes in the division of labor in these Swiss families are not unlike other European families during the peasant-to-worker transition, one could surmise that in this transitional stage of the evolution of the family, there commences a qualitative change in the family as a labor unit: the children eventually cease to be part of the family labor group and the parents' resources, including their own labor time, are reallocated from strictly food production to preparing children for wage jobs which require more education.

In relation to Chayanov's theory of the peasant family economy, I have emphasized here that the foregone labor of children is a cost to the parents of educating children. This is a hidden cost which has not been included in the growing literature on the cost of children in western industrial societies as compared to less industrial societies (see, however, Minge-Kalman 1978).[4] I suggest that this is another omitted factor[5] in the widely held view that the post-peasant family is not an economically productive labor group.

NOTES

1. For example, John and Beatrice Whiting's research in a transitional Kiluru village near Nairobi shows that until 1972, when the government began taking over the cost, primary education cost the parents eight times more than the family taxes. Although primary school was not mandatory, 75 per cent of the children attended because of the decreased availability of land per person. The only alternative became wage labor.

2. The Alps have for centuries been a labor reserve, sending surplus labor off to cities or to mercenary military service in other areas. The differences in modern Switzerland today are, first, the labor market demands formal education and, second, almost all of the children are leaving the farms for wage labor even where there is land to inherit. The mass entry into wage labor includes women.

3. Children's labor at this time is necessary to the families who increasingly specialize in labor-intensive crops. Hence, as the children become less interested in farming and take wage jobs during the summer months, their parents cannot continue intensification which is crucial for mountain peasants today (Minge-Kalman 1977). Many Levron families give this as the reason for the decline in strawberry cultivation.

4. In west European countries most of the direct cost of education is paid by the state (O.E.C.D. 1977). However, soon after primary education became mandatory, the extracurricular cost of education exceeded the direct cost to the family (Banks 1957: 186).

5. Another factor which has usually been excluded from estimates of the cost of children in wage-labor societies is the mother's labor time which has recently been estimated to range from $75,000 to $155,000 in the United States (Espenshade 1977). This figure is the estimated value of earnings the woman might have had, but had to forego because of the need to care for her children.

Bibliography

Adams, Robert M. and Carl H. Kroeling, editors 1960 City Invincible. In Symposium on Urbanization. Chicago: University of Chicago Press.

Alasdair, Clayre 1974 Work and Play: Ideas and Experience of Work and Leisure. London: Widenfeld and Nicolson.

Alexander, K. J. W. 1964 Casual Labour and Labour Casualties. Transactions, Institute of Engineers and Shipbuilders in Scotland. Glasgow.

Anders, Gary C. 1980 Indians, Energy and Economic Development. Journal of Contemporary Business 9:57–74.

Anderson, J. M. 1968 Comments on the "Analysis of Group Composition." In Man the Hunter. Ed. R. B. Lee and I. DeVore. Chicago: Aldine.

Annals of Agriculture. 1796 London.

Arendt, Hannah 1959 The Human Condition, Chicago: University of Chicago Press.

Arensberg, Conrad M. 1963 Europe and Its Cultures. Anthropological Quarterly. 36:75–99.

1967 Theoretical Contributions of Industrial and Development Studies. Applied Anthropology in America. Ed. E. M. Eddy and W. L. Partridge. Pp. 49–78. New York: Columbia University Press.

Arensberg, Conrad M., Solomon Barkin, W. Ellison Chalmers, Harold L. Wilensky, James C. Worthy, Barbara D. Dennis. eds. 1957 Research in Industrial Human Relations: A Critical Appraisal. New York: Harper.

Arnoff, Joel and William D. Crano 1975 A reexamination of the Cross-cultural Principles of Task Segregation and Sex Role Differentiation in the Family. American Sociological Review 40 (Feb.):12–20.

Arthur, Harris 1978 Preface. In Native Americans and Energy Development. Ed. Joseph G. Jorgensen, Richard O. Clemmer, Ronald L. Little, Nancy J. Owens, Lynn A. Robbins. Cambridge Mass.: Anthropology Resource Center.

Atkinson, Frank 1974 Industrial Archaeology of Northeast England. 2 vols. London: David and Charles.

Bacon, Elizabeth 1958 Obok: A Study of Social Structure in Eurasia. Viking Fund Publications in Anthropology 25. New York: Wenner-Gren Foundation.

Baffin Region Inuit Association 1980 Socio-Economic Impacts of the Nanisivik Mine on Northern Baffin Region Communities. A Report for Nanisivik Mine Ltd., the Government of the Northwest Territories, and the Government of Canada, Baffin Region, Canada.

Bahr, Donald 1964 Santa Rosa, Arizona. Manuscript in files of the Bureau of Ethnic Research. University of Arizona, Tucson.

Bailey, P. 1978 Leisure and Class in Victorian England. London: Routledge and Kegan Paul.

Balzer, Richard 1976 Clockwork. Garden City, N.Y.: Doubleday.

Bandura, Albert and Richard H. Walters 1964 Social Learning and Personality Development. New York: Holt, Rinehart and Winston.

Banks, J. A. 1954 A Study of Family Planning among the Victorian Middle Class. London: Routledge and Kegan Paul.

Banton, Michael 1970 Adaptation and Integration in the Social System of Temne Immigrants in Freetown. In Black Africa. Ed. John Middleton. London: Macmillan.

Barnett, Homer G. 1937 Culture element, Distribution, VII, Oregon Coast, Anthro. Records (Berkeley) 1(3):155–204. 1938 The Nature of the Potlatch. American Anthropologist, 40:349–58.

Barth, Fredrik 1961 Nomads of South Persia: The Basseri Tribe of the Khamseh Confederacy. Boston: Little, Brown.

Bartholomew, George A., Jr. and Joseph B. Birdsell 1953 Ecology and the protohominids. American Anthropologist, 55:481–98.

Bascom, William R. 1948 Ponapean Prestige Economy. Southwestern Journal of Anthropology. 4:211–21.

Baumhoff, M. 1963 Ecological Determinant of Aboriginal California Population Univ. of Calif. pub. in American Archaeology and Ethnology, 49:155–236.

Beals, Alan R. 1962 Gopalpur. New York: Holt, Rinehart and Winston. 1967 Culture in Process. New York: Holt, Rinehart and Winston.

Bellah, Robert N. 1964 Religious Evolution. American Sociological Review. 29(3):374–78.

Bencsik, J. 1969 Herding on the Northern Area of the Hortobagy since the end of the Eighteenth Century. Debrecen.

Benjamin, A. Cornelius 1937 An Introduction to the Philosophy of Science. New York: Macmillan.

Berger, Thomas 1977 The Report of the MacKenzie Valley Pipeline: Northern Frontier, Northern Homeland. 2 vols. Ottawa: Dept. of Indian and Northern Affairs.

Bergson, Henri 1944 Creative Evolution. New York: Modern Library.

Berreman, Gerald D. 1964 Aleut Reference Group Alienation, Mobility and Acculturation. American Anthropologist 66:231–50.

Berry, J. W. 1976 Acculturative Stress in North Canada: Ecological Cultural and Psychological Factors. In Circumpolar Health. Ed. R. J. Shephard and S. Itoh. Pp. 490–97. Toronto: University of Toronto Press.

Berthoud, G. 1967 Changements économiques et sociaux de la montagne: Vernamiège en Valais. Berne.

Best, Elsdon 1912 The Stone Implements of the Maori. Department of Maori Affairs Bulletin no. 4. Wellington. 1925a Maori Agriculture. Dept. of Maori Affairs Bulletin no. 9. Wellington. 1925b The Maori Canoe. Dept. of Maori Affairs Bulletin no. 7. Wellington.

Biesele, M. In Press. !Kung Folklore. Cambridge, Mass.: Harvard University Press.

Blauner, Robert 1964 Alienation and Freedom in American Industry. Chicago: University of Chicago Press.

Boas, Franz 1909 The Jesup North Pacific Expedition (5,Pt.2): The Kwakiutl of Vancouver Island. Memoirs of the American Museum of Natural History, 8(2).N.Y. 1916 The Development of Folk-Tales and Myths. The Scientific Monthly, Vol. 3, Pp. 335–343. 1921 Ethnology of the Kwakiutl. Bureau of American Ethnology, Annual Report no. 35 for 1913–14, parts 1 and 2. Washington, D.C.

1935 Kwakiutl culture as reflected in mythology. American Folklore Society Memoir 28, Wash., D.C.

Bodley, J. H. 1975 Victims of Progress. Menlo Park, Calif.: Cummings.

Bohannan, Paul and George Dalton, Eds. 1962 Markets in Africa. Evanston: Northwestern University Press.

1963 Social Anthropology. N.Y. Holt, Rinehart & Winston.

Bokonyi, S. 1971 The Development and History of Domestic Animals in Hungary: The Neolithic through the Middle Ages. American Anthropologist 73:640–74.

Boserup, Esther 1965 The Condition of Agricultural Growth. The Economics of Agrarian Change under Population Pressure. Chicago: Aldine.

Boserup, Esther 1970 Women's Role in Economic Development. London: Allen and Unwin

Bottomore, Tom 1971 Class Structure and Social Consciousness. In Aspects of History and Class Consciousness. Ed. I. Meszaros. Pp. 49–65. London: Routledge and Kegan Paul.

Bourdieu, P. 1963 The Attitude of the Algerian Peasant toward Time. *In* Mediterranean Countrymen. Ed. J. Pitt-Rivers. Paris.

Boyd, David J. 1981 Village Agriculture and Labor Migration: Interrelated Production Activities among the Ilakia Awa of Papua, New Guinea. American Ethnologist (1):74–93.

Braverman, Harry 1974 Labor and Monopoly Capital: The Degradation of Work in the Twentieth Century. New York: Monthly Review Press.

Brody, Hugh 1975 The People's Land: Eskimos and Whites in the Eastern Arctic. Aylesbury: Penguin.

Bronson, Bennet 1972 Farm Labor and the Evolution of Food Production. In Population Growth: Anthropological Perspecive. B. Spooner, Editor. Cambridge, Mass.: M.I.T. Press. Pp. 190–218.

Brower, C. D., P. J. Farrelly, and Lyman Anson 1942 Fifty Years below Zero. New York: Dodd, Mead.

Brown, E. E. P. 1957 Introduction to The Labour Movement in the Sudan, 1946–1955, by Saad ed din Fawzi. London: Oxford University Press.

Brown, Judith K. 1975 Iroquois Women. In Toward An Anthropology of Women. Ed. R. Reiter. New York: Monthly Review Press.

Brun, W. V. 1912 Die Wirtschaftsorganization der Maori auf Neuseeland. Leipzig.

Buchanan, R. A. 1972 Industrial Archaeology in Britain. Harmondsworth, Middlesex, England: Penguin.

1976 Industrial Archaeology: Retrospect and Prospect. Antiquity 44:281–287.

Bucher, Karl 1924 Arbeit and Rhythmus. 6th Edition. Leipzig.

Buitrón, Anibal 1947 Situación económica y social del Indio Otavaleno. América Indígena 7:45–62.

1949 Síntesis de investigaciones sociales en la parroquia de Pomasqui. Boletín de Informaciones de Estudios Sociales y Económicos 12 (Quito,) (46–47):65–78.

Buitrón, Anibal, and Barbara Salisbury Buitrón 1945 Indio, blancos y mestizos en Otavalo, Ecuador. Acta Americana. 3:190–216.

1947 Condiciones de vida y trabajo del campesino de la provincia de Pichincha. Quito: Instituto Nacional de Prevision, Departamento de Propaganda.

Burawoy, Michael 1979 The Anthropology of Industrial Work. Annual Review of Anthropology 8:231–66.

Cameron, Raymond D., and Kenneth P. Whitten 1979 Seasonal Movements and Sexual Segregation of Caribou Determined by Aerial Survey. Journal of Wildlife Management 43(3):626–33.

Campbell, J. L. 1881 Poenamo. London.

Carneiro, Robert L. 1970 A Theory of the Origin of the State, Science 169:733–38.

Carr, L., and J. E. Sterner 1952 Willow Run: A Study in Industry and Cultural Inadequacy. New York: Harper

Casanova, José 1980 The Modernization of Spain. Telos. 53:29–43.

Casteel, Richard 1975 The Relationship between Population Size and Carrying Capacity. In Prehistorical Cultural Adaptations in W. North America. D. Browman, W. Irving, W. Powers, Editors. The Hague: Mouton.

Çerný, Jaroslav 1973 A Community of Workmen at Thebes in the Ramesside Period. Cairo: Institut Français d'Archaeologic Orientale du Caire.

Chagnon, Napoleon A. 1977 Yanomamo: The Fierce People. New York: Holt, Rinehart and Winston

Chance, Norman A. 1965 Acculturation: Self-Identification and Personality Adjustment American Anthropologist 67:372–93.

Chapple, Eliot D. 1953 Applied Anthropology in Industry. In Anthropology Today. Ed. A. L. Kroeber. Pp. 819–31. Chicago: University of Chicago Press.

1981 Letter to the Editor. Anthropology Newsletter 22: Page 8.

Chayanov, A. V. 1966 The Theory of Peasant Economy. Ed. D. Thorner, B. Kerblay, and R. E. F. Smith. Homewood, Ill.: R. D. Irwin.

Childe, V. Gordon 1946 What Happened in History. New York: Penguin.

1951 Man Makes Himself. New York: Signet Press.

Cisneros Cisneros, Cesar 1948 Demografía y estadistica sobre el indio acuatoriano, Quito: Talleres Grafico Nacionales.

Clemens, W. A. and G. V. Wilby 1946 Fishes of the Pacific Coast of Canada. Fisheries Research Board of Canada (Ottawa).

Clough, S. B., and C. W. Cole 1946 Economic History of Europe. Boston: D. C. Heath & Co.

Cloward, Richard A., and Lloyd E. Ohlin 1960 Delinquency and Opportunity: A Theory of Delinquent Gangs. New York: Free Press.

Coe, M. D. and K. V. Flannery 1964 Mesoamerican Prehistory. Science 143:650–54.

Cohen, Albert K. 1955 Delinquent Boys: The Culture of the Gang. New York: Free Press.

Cohen, John 1949 Analysis of "psychological" fields. In Science News 13:145–58. Harmondworth: Penguin.

Cohen, Yehudi A. 1968 Man in Adaptation. Chicago: Aldine.

Cohn, Edward J. 1964 Social and Cultural Factors Affecting the Emergence of Innovations in Social Aspects of Economic Development. Economic and Social Studies Conference Board. Istanbul: Hachette.

Cole, Donald 1973 Bedouins of the Oil Fields. Natural History Magazine, Nov.:632–38.

Cole, J. 1969 Economic Alternatives in the Upper Nonsberg. Anthropological Quarterly 42:187–213.

Cole, John W. and Eric R. Wolf 1974 The Hidden Frontier: Ecology and Ethnicity in an Alpine Valley. New York: Academic Press.

Colenso, W. 1898 Maori-English Lexikon. Wellington.

Collier, John, Jr., and Anibal Buitrón 1949 The Awakening Valley. Chicago: University of Chicago Press.

Condominas, George, 1957 Chronique de Sar Luk, Village M Nong. Paris: Mercure de France.

Conklin, Harold C. 1968 An Ethno-ecological approach to Shifting Agriculture. In Man in Adaptation, Ed. Yehudi Cohen. Pp. 126–31. Chicago: Aldine.

Cottrell, Fred 1955 Energy and Society: The Relation between Energy, Social Change and Economic Development. New York: McGraw-Hill.

Cowan, J. 1910 Maoris of New Zealand. Melbourne: Whitcombe and Tombs, Ltd.

Cox, Oliver C. 1948 Caste, Class and Race. Garden City, New York: Doubleday.

Cruise, R. 1823 Journal of a Ten Months' Residence in New Zealand. London.

Dalton, George, editor 1971 Studies in Economic Anthropology. Anthropological Studies No. 7. Washington, D.C.: American Anthropological Association.

Damas, D. 1969 Characteristics of Central Eskimo Structure. *In* Contributions to Anthropology: Band Societies. Ed. D. Damas. Pp. 116–38. Ottawa: National Museums of Canada Bulletin 228.

Damon, Albert 1966 The Human Body in Equipment Design. Cambridge: Harvard University Press.

Editor 1975 Physiological Anthropology. New York: Oxford University Press.

Damon, Albert. 1963 Anthropometry. In Human Engineering Guide to Equipment Design. C. T. Morgan, Alphonse Chadanis and Wendell R. Garner ed. Pp. 485–570. New York: McGraw-Hill.

Davis, J. L., P. Valdenburg, and H. V. Reynolds 1980 Population Dynamics of Alaska's Western Caribou Herd. Proceedings of the Second International Reindeer/Caribou Symposium. Trondheim: Directorater for vilt ogferkannsfisk.

Davis, J. Merle 1946 The Economic and Social Setting. In Indians of the High Andes. Ed. Stanley W. Rycroft. Pp. 13–93. New York: Committee on Cooperation in Latin America.

Dedijer, J. 1916 La transhumance dans les pays dinariques. Annales de Geographie (Paris) 25:347–65.

DeVore, I., and M. J. Konner 1974 Infancy in Hunter-Gatherer Life: An Ethnological Perspective. Ethnology and Psychiatry. Ed. N. F. White. Pp. 113–41, Toronto: Univ. of Toronto Press.

Digby, Adrian 1949 Technique and the Time Factor in Relation to Economic Organization. Man 49:16–18.

Divale, W. T. 1974 Migration, External Warfare and Matrilocal Residence. Behavior Science Research 9:75–133.

1977 Living Floor Area and Marital Residence: A Replication. Behavior Science Research 12:109–15.

Dosman, Edgar J. 1975 The National Interest: The Politics of Northern Development, 1968–1975. Canada in Transition Series. Toronto: McClelland and Stewart.

Dozier, Edward P. 1966 Problem Drinking among American Indians: The role of Socio-Cultural Deprivation. Quarterly Journal of Studies on Alcohol. 27:72–87.

Driver, Harold E. 1939 Culture Element Distributions, 10: Northwest California. Anthropological Records. (Berkeley). 1(6):297–433.

1961 Indians of North America. Chicago: University of Chicago Press.

Drucker, Philip 1946 The Way to Industrial Peace. Part I. Harper's Magazine (Nov.): 385–95.

1950 Culture Element Distribution, 26: Northwest Coast. Anthropological Records (Berkeley), 9(3):157–294.

1951 The Northern and Central Nootkan Tribes. Bulletin of the Bureau of American Ethnology. Wash., D. C.

1955 Indians of the Northwest Coast. New York: McGraw-Hill.

1965 Cultures of the North Pacific Coast. San Francisco: Chandler.

Dubois, Cora A. 1936 The Wealth Concept as an Integrative Factor in Tolowa-Tututni Culture. In R. H. Lowie, Editor, Essays in Anthropology Presented to A. L. Kroeber. Berkeley: University of California Press.

Duff, Wilson 1952 The Upper Stalo Indians of the Fraser Valley. British Columbia. In Anthropology in British Columbia. British Columbia Provincial Museum, Memoir No. 1. Vancouver.

1964 The Indian History of British Columbia. British Columbia Provincial Museum Memoir No. 5. Vancouver.

Durkheim, Emile 1947 The Division of Labor in Society, Glencoe, Ill.: Free Press.

Dyson-Hudson, Neville 1962 Factors Inhibiting Change in an African Pastoral Society: The Karimojong of Northeastern Uganda. Transactions of the New York Academy of Sciences, Ser. 2, Vol. 24, No. 7. Pp. 771–801. New York.

1966 Karimojong Politics. Oxford: Clarendon Press.

Dyson-Hudson, R. and N. Dyson-Hudson 1972 Subsistence Herding in Uganda. Biology and Culture in Modern Perspective. Edited by J. G. Jorgensen, Pp. 357–66. San Francisco.

Edgerton, Robert B. 1971 The Individual in Cultural Adaptation. Berkeley and Los Angeles: University of California Press.

Eggan, F. 1966 The American Indian. Chicago: Aldine.

1968 Comments on Typology and Reconstruction. In Man the Hunter, Edited by Richard B. Lee and Irven Devore. Chicago: Aldine

Elkan, W. 1956 An African Labour Force. Kampala: East African Institute of Social Research.

Elmendorf, W. W. 1960 The Structure of Twana Culture. Washington State University Research Studies, Monograph Supplement No. 2. Pullman: Washington State University.

Ember, E. R. 1975 Residential Variation among Hunter-Gatherers. Behavior Science Research, 10:199–227.

Ember, C. R., and M. Ember 1972 The Conditions Favoring Multilocal Residence. Southwestern Journal of Anthropology 28:382–400.

1973 Cultural Anthropology, New York: Appleton-Crofts.

Ember, M. 1973 Matrilocal vs. Patrilocal Residence. American Antiquity, 38:177–82.

Ember, M., and C. R. Ember 1971 The Conditions Favoring Matrilocal Versus Patrilocal Residence. American Anthropologist 73:571–94.

Erasmus, Charles J. 1955 Work Patterns in a Mayo Village. American Anthropologist 57:322–33.

1977 In Search of the Common Good: Utopian Experiments Past and Future. N.Y.: Free Press.

Erdman, David 1956 Coleridge, Wordsworth and the Wedgwood Fund. Bulletin of the New York Public Library 60.

Espenshade, T. J. 1977. The Value and Cost of Children. Population Bulletin, vol. 32, no. 1. Population Reference Bureau, Washington, D. C.

Evans-Pritchard, E. E. 1940 The Nuer: A Description of the Modes of Livelihood and the Political Institutions of a Nilotic People. Oxford: Clarendon Press.

1949 The Sanusi of Cyrenaica. Oxford. Clarendon Press.

Fei Hsiao-t'ung and Chang Chih-i 1947 Earthbound China. A Study of Rural Economy in Yunnan. Chicago: University of Chicago Press.

Ferdon, Edwin N., Jr. 1945 A Mountain Colony in Ecuador. El Palacio 52:129–37.

Ferguson, Frances N. 1968 Navajo Drinking: Some Tentative Hypotheses. Human Organization 27:159–167.

Finkler, Earl L. 1979 Resource Inventory, Galbraith Lake. Barrow, Alaska: North Slope Borough Government.

Finney, Ben 1965 Polynesian Peasants and Proletarians. Polynesian Society Reprint Series no. 9. Wellington.

1967a Money Work, Fast Money and Prize Money: Aspects of the Tahitian Labor Commitment. Human Organization 26: 195–99.

1967b Race and Class in the Society Islands of French Polynesia. Proceedings of the 7th International Congress of Anthropological and Ethnological Sciences. Moscow.

Firth, Raymond 1959 Social Change in Tikopia. London: Allen and Unwin.

1966 Malay Fishermen. Hamden, Conn.: Archon Books.

1972a Anthropological Background to Work. *In* The Social Dimensions of Work. Ed. Clifton D. Bryant. Pp. 8–16. Englewood Cliffs, N.J.: Prentice-Hall.

1972b The Organization of Work Among the New Zealand Maori. Wellington, New Zealand: Shearer.

1981 Spiritual Aroma: Religion and Politics. American Anthropologist 83:582–601.

Fittkau, E. J. and H. Klinge 1973 On Biomass and Trophic Structure of the Central Amazon Rain Forest Ecosystem. Biotropica 5:1–14.

Flannery, K. V. 1965 The Ecology of Early Food Production in Mesopotamia Science, Vol. 127, Pp. 1247–55

Florney, Bertrand 1945 Voyages en Haut-Amazone. Rio de Janeiro: Atlantica.

Forde, C. D. 1947 The Anthropological Approach in Social Science. Advancement of Science 4:213–24.

1963 Habitat, Economy and Society. New York: Dutton.

Foster, George M. 1948 Empire's Children, the People of Tzintzuntsan. Pub. no. 6, Institute of Social Anthropology, Smithsonian Institution, Washington, D. C.

Foster, John 1821 An Essay on the Evils of Popular Ignorance. London.

Franklin, Albert B. 1943 Ecuador, Portrait of a People. Garden City, N.Y.: Doubleday.

Franklin, S. H. 1969 The European Peasantry: The Final Phase. London: Methuen.

Frantz, Charles 1981 Development without Communities: Social Fields, Networks and Action in the Mambila Grasslands of Nigeria. Human Organization 40(3):211–20.

Frantz, J. B., and J. E. Choate 1955 The American Cowboy: The Myth and the Reality. Norman: Oklahoma University Press.

Freed, Stanley A., and Ruth S. Freed 1981 Sacred Cows and Water Buffalo in India: The Uses of Ethnography. Current Anthropology 22:482–502.

Fribourg, A. 1910 La Transhumance en Espagne. Annales de Géographie. (Paris) 19:231–44.

Fried, Morton 1967 The Evolution of Political Society. New York: Random House.

Friedl, J. 1974 Kippel: A Changing Village in the Alps. New York: Holt, Rinehart and Winston.

Friedmann, Georges, Pierre Naville Avec le concours de Jean-René Tréanton. 1961 Traité de Sociologie du Travail. Paris: Armand Colin.

Fumoleau, René n.d. As Long as This Land Shall Last. Toronto: McClelland and Stewart.

Galaty, John G. 1982 Being "Masai": Being "People-of-Cattle": Ethnic Shifters in East Africa. American Ethnologist, 9:1–20.

Gale, F. 1974 Woman's Role in Aboriginal Society. Australian Aboriginal Studies, no. 36. Canberra: Australian National University Press.

Gamst, Frederick C. 1975a The Diesel-Electric Locomotive as a Work Environment: A Study in Applied Anthropology. Rice University Studies 61(2):37–78.

1975b Human Factors Analysis of the Diesel-Electric Locomotive Cab. *In* Special Issue on Human Factors in Civil Systems. Ed. D. H. Harris. Human Factors 17:149–56.

1975c Rethinking Leach's Structural Analysis of Color and Instructional Categories in Traffic Control Signals. American Ethnologist 2:271–96.

1977 An Integrating View of the Underlying Premises of an Industrial Ethnology in the United States and Canada. Anthropological Quarterly 50(1):1–8.

1980a The Hoghead: An Industrial Ethnology of the Locomotive Engineer. New York: Holt, Rinehart and Winston.

1980b Toward a Method of Industrial Ethnology. *In* The Cultural Context: Essays in Honor of Edward Norbeck. Ed. C.M.S. Drake. Rice University Studies 66(1):15–42.

1981 Considerations for an Anthropology of Work. Anthropology of Work Newsletter. Vol. 2, No. 1. Pp. 2–7.

Garcés, Victor Gabriel 1941 Cuestionario de la Oficina Internacional del Trabajo sobre la situación de la raza indigenas. Previsión Social, no. 8:12–44.

Gardner, Burleigh B., and David G. Moore 1952 Human Relations in Industry. Homewood, Ill.: Irwin.

Garfield, Viola E. 1945 A Research Problem in Northwest Indian Economics. American Anthropologist. 47:626–30.

Garfield, Viola E. 1951 The Tsimshian and Their Neighbors. American Ethnological Society Publication No. 18. New York: Augustin.

Gartman, David 1979 Origins of the Assembly Line and Capitalist Control of Work at Ford. In Case Studies in the Labor Process. Ed. Andrew Zimbalist. New York: Monthly Review Press.

Gasparro, Anthony F. 1978 Yukon-Porcupine Regional Planning Study. Fairbanks: The Institute of Social and Economic Research.

Glen, Evelyn N. and Roslyn L. Feldberg 1979 Proletarianizing Clerical Work: Technology and Organizational Control in the Office. In Case Studies in the Labor Process. Ed. by Andrew Zimbalist. New York: Monthly Review Press.

Goldschmidt, Walter R. 1965 Theory and Strategy in the Study of Cultural Adaptability. American Anthropologist 67:(2)402–8.

1966 Comparative Functionalism: An Essay in Anthropological Theory. Berkeley and Los Angeles: University of California Press.

1968 The Anthropological Study of Modern Society. In International Encyclopedia of the Social Sciences. Vol. 1:330–38. New York: Macmillan.

1969 Kambuya's Cattle. The Legacy of an African Herdsman. Berkeley and Los Angeles: University of California Press.

1971 Independence in Pastoral Social Systems. Anthropological Quarterly, Vol. 44:132–141.

Goldschmidt, Walter R. and Robert B. Edgerton 1961 A Picture Technique for the Study of Values. American Anthropologist. 63:26–47.

Goldschmidt, Walter R., Philip W. Porter, Symmes C. Oliver, Francis P. Conant, Edgar V. Winans and Robert B. Edgerton 1965 Variation and Adaptability of Culture: A Symposium. American Anthropologist. 67:(2):400–447.

Goodale, Jane C. 1971 Tiwi Wives. Seattle: University of Washington Press.

Goodenough, Ward 1963 Cooperation in Change. New York: Russell Sage Foundation.

Gough, Kathleen 1970 Women in Evolution. Boston: New England Free Press.

1975 The Origin of the Family. In Toward an Anthropology of Women. New York: Monthly Review Press.

Gould, Richard A. 1966 The Wealth Quest among the Tolowa Indians of Northwestern California. Proceedings of the American Philosophical Society. 110(1):67–89. Philadelphia.

Granatstein, J. L. 1976 A Fit of Absence of Mind: Canada's National Interest in the North to 1968. In The Arctic in Question. E. J. Dosman, Ed. Pp. 13–33. Toronto: Oxford University Press.

Gras, N. S. B. 1930 Industrial Evolution. Cambridge: Harvard University Press.

Graves, Theodore D. 1966 Alternative Models for the Study of Urban Migration. Human Organization 25:295–99.

1967a Acculturation, Access and Alcohol in a Tri-Ethnic Community. American Anthropologist. 69:306–21.

1967b Psychological Acculturation in a Tri-Ethnic Community. Southwestern Journal of Anthropology. 23:337–50.

1970 The Personal Adjustment of Navajo Indian Migrants to Denver, Colorado. American Anthropologist. 72:35–54.

Graves, Theodore D. and Minor VanArsdale 1966 Values, Expectations and Relocation: The Navajo Indian Migrant to Denver. Human Organization. 25:300–307.

Grazia, Sebastian de 1962 Of Time, Work and Leisure. Garden City, N.Y.: Doubleday Anchor.

Grey, Geoffrey 1853 Ko Nga Moteatea: Poems, Traditions and Chants of the Maoris. Wellington. M. F. Marks

Grinnell, George B. 1923 The Cheyenne Indians: Their History and Ways of Life. (2 vols) New Haven: Yale University Press.

Gulliver, P. H. 1955 The Family Herds: A Study of Two Pastoral Tribes in East Africa, The Jie and Turkana. London: Routledge and Kegan Paul.

Gunda, B. 1968 Significance of Ecological Factors in Herding. Acta Geographica Debreceniensis (Debrecen) 7:93–103.

1970 Organization sociale des pasteurs dans la grande plaine Hongroise. Ethnologia Europaea (Arnhem) 2–3:170–79.

Győrffy, I. 1941a The Chronicle of the Nagykunsag. Budapest.

1941b Gazdalkodas (Economy). In A magyarsag neprajza. Ed. I. Gyorffy and K. Viski, vol. 2 Pp. 5–225. Budapest.

Hall, Edward T. 1965 The Silent Language. Greenwich, Conn.: Fawcett.

Hallowell, A. Irving 1957 Impact of American Indians on American Culture. American Anthropologist 59:201–17.

1937 Temporal Orientation in Western Civilization and in a Preliterate Society. American Anthropologist 39:647–70.

1952 Ojibwa. International Congress of Americanists, Indian Tribes of Aboriginal America. Chicago: Univ. of Chicago Press.

Handbook on the Trust Territories of the Pacific Islands vol. 2, no. 29, Pp. 105–12.

1948 A Handbook for Use in Training and Administration. School of Naval Administration, Hoover Institute, Stanford University. Washington, D.C.: U.S. Department of the Navy.

Hanks, Lucien 1972 Rice and Man: Agricultural Ecology in Southeast Asia. Chicago: Aldine.

Harding, Charles F. 1955 The Social Anthropology of American Industry. American Anthropologist 57:1218–31.

Harris, Marvin 1966 The Cultural Ecology of India's Sacred Cattle. Current Anthropology 7:51–66.

1975 Culture, People, Nature. New York: Crowell.

1977 Determinants of Bovine, Sex, Age and Species Ratios in Kerala and All-India. Paper presented at the annual meeting of the American Anthropological Association, Houston, Texas.

Hart, C. W. M., and Arnold R. Pilling 1960 The Tiwi of North Australia. New York: Holt, Rinehart and Winston.

Haswell, M. R. 1953 Economics of Agriculture in a Savannah Village: Report on Three Years' Study in Genieri Village. London: Colonial Research Studies No. 8. H.M.S.O.

Health, Education and Welfare 1975 Work in America Cambridge: M.I.T. Press.

Heath, Dwight B. 1964 Prohibition and Post-Repeal Drinking Patterns among the Navajo. Quarterly Journal of Studies on Alcohol. 25:119–35.

Heidegger, Martin 1971 Poetry, Language, Thought. New York: Harper and Row.

Heilbroner, Robert L. 1970 The Economic Problem. Englewood Cliffs, N.J.: Prentice-Hall.

Herman, M. W. 1956 The Social Aspects of Huron Property. American Anthropologist, 58, 1044–58.

Herskovits, Melville J. 1937 Life in a Haitian Valley. New York: Columbia University Press.

1938 Dahomey: An Ancient West African Kingdom. New York: Augustin.

1940 The Economic Life of Primitive Peoples. New York: Knopf.

1952, 1965 Economic Anthropology. 1st and 2nd eds. New York: Knopf.

Hertzberg, H. T. E., ed. 1958 Annotated Bibliography of Applied Physical Anthropology in Human Engineering. Wright Air Development Center. Technical Report, no. 56–30. Wright-Patterson Air Force Base. Riverside, Ohio.

1979 Engineering Anthropology: Past, Present and Potential. In The Uses of Anthropology. Ed. Walter Goldschmidt. Pp. 184–204. Washington, D. C.: American Anthropological Association.

Hiatt, L. R. 1968 Ownership and Use of Land among the Australian Aborigines. In Man the Hunter. Eds. Richard B. Lee and Irven DeVore. Chicago: Aldine.

Hobart, Charles W. 1974 Employee Adjustment and Effectiveness: Arctic Oil Exploration of Gulf Oil Canada. Edmonton: Westreed Institute.

1975 An Evaluation of a Training Program. Unpublished report.

1976 Rotation Work Schedules in the Northwest Territories: A Study of Variations and Consequences. A Report to the Planning and Development Division. Yellowknife: Department of Economic Development and Tourism, Government of the Northwest Territories.

1982 Industrial Employment of Rural Indigenes: The Case of Canada. Human Organization 41(1):54–63.

n.d. Impact of Commuting Employment on Coppermine in the Northwest Territories. Unpublished paper, Dept. of Sociology, University of Alberta.

In Press Employment and Aftermath: Effects of Rotation Employment on a Small Inuit Community. Edmonton: Boreal Institute Occasional Publications.

Hobart, Charles W. and George Kupfer 1973 Inuit Employment by Gulf Oil Canada. Edmonton: Westreed Institute.

Hobsbawn, Eric J. 1964 Introduction to Pre-Capitalist Economic Formation by Karl Marx. Trans. Jack Cohen. New York: International Publishers.

1968 Industry and Empire: The Making of Modern English Society, 1750 to the Present Day. New York: Pantheon.

Hochstetter, F. von 1867 New Zealand. Stuttgart.

Hockett, Charles F. and Robert Ascher 1964 The Human Revolution. Current Anthropology 5(3):135–52.

Hoebel, E. Adamson 1960 The Cheyennes, Indians of the Great Plains. New York: Holt, Rinehart and Winston.

n.d. Cheyenne Field Notes. Unpublished.

Hoijer, Harry 1953 The Relation of Language to Culture. In Anthropology Today. Ed. A. L. Kroeber. Pp. 554–73. Chicago: University of Chicago Press.

Hole, Frank 1966 Investigating the Origins of Mesopotamian Civilization Science 153:605–11.

Homer 1960 The Iliad. New York: Bantam Books, Inc.

Honigmann, John J. 1949 Incentives to Work in a Canadian Indian Community. Human Organization 8(4):23–8.

Honigmann, John J., and Irma Honigmann 1968 Alcohol in a Canadian Northern Town. Paper presented at Institute for Research in Social Science, Chapel Hill: University of North Carolina.

Hoselitz, Bert F., ed. 1952 The Progress of Underdeveloped Areas. Chicago: University of Chicago Press.

Howell, F. C. 1965 Early Man. New York: Time-Life Books.

Hoyt, Elizabeth E. 1960 Voluntary Unemployment and Unemployability in Jamaica, with Special Reference to the Standard of Living. British Journal of Sociology 11(2):129–36.

Hudson, Kenneth 1976 Industrial Archaeology: A New Introduction. London: John Baker.

1979 World Industrial Archaeology. Cambridge: Cambridge University Press.

Humphries, Jane 1977 Class Struggle and the Persistence of the Working Class Family. Cambridge Journal of Economics 1:241–58.

Huntingford, G.W.B. 1950 Nandi Work and Culture. Colonial Research Studies 4. London: The Colonial Office.

1953 The Nandi of Kenya: Tribal Control in a Pastoral Society. London: Routledge and Kegan Paul.

Huskey, Lee 1980 The Coincidence of Rural Development and Major Resource Development. Paper presented at the American Association for the Advancement of Science—Alaska Section, Anchorage, Alaska.

IEAG (Instituto Ecuatoriano de Antropología e Geografía) 1953a Reclamaciones e Investigación Social Informes no 3. Instituto Nacional de Previsión. Departamento de Información. P. 164 ff. Quito.

International Labor Organization 1949 Conditions of Life and Work of Indigenous Populations of Latin American Countries. Fourth Conference of American States Members, Montevideo April, 1949, Report 2. Geneva: International Labour Office.

Jacobeit, W. 1961 Schafhaltung und Schafer in Zentraleurope bis zum Beginn des 20. Jahrhunderts: Berlin.

James, Bernard J. 1961 Socio-Psychological Dimensions of Ojibwa Acculturation. American Anthropologist 63: 721–46.

Janzen, Daniel 1973 Tropical Agroecosystems. Science. 182:1212–1219.

Jenness, Diamond 1932 The Indians of Canada. Bulletin No. 65, National Museum of Canada: Ottawa.

1967 Eskimo Administration: 2. Arctic Institute of North America Technical Paper no. 14. Montreal.

Jessor, Richard, Roderick S. Carmen, and Peter H. Grossman 1968 Expectations of Need Satisfaction and Drinking Patterns of College Students. Quarterly Journal of Studies on Alcohol 29:101–16.

Jessor, Richard, Theodore D. Graves, Robert C. Hanson, and Shirley Jessor 1968 Society, Personality and Deviant Behavior: A Study of a Tri-Ethnic Community. New York: Holt, Rinehart and Winston.

Johnson, Allen 1970 On The Use of Computers in Anthropological Fieldwork. Paper presented at the annual meeting of the American Anthropological Association, San Diego.

1975 The Allocation of Time in a Machiguenga Community. Ethnology 14:301–10.

1978 In Search of the Affluent Society. Human Nature 1(9):50–59.

Johnson, Martin 1947 Time, Knowledge and the Nebulae: An Introduction to the Meanings of Time in Physics, Astronomy and Philosophy, and the Relativities of Einstein and Milne. New York: Dover.

Jorgensen, Joseph G. 1978 Energy, Agriculture and Social Science in the American West. In Native Americans and Energy Development. Ed. Joseph G. Jorgensen,

Richard O. Clemmer, Ronald L. Little, Nancy J. Owens, Lynn A. Robbins. Pp. 3–16. Cambridge, Mass.: Anthropology Resource Center.

Justus, Roger, and Joanne Simonetta 1979 Major Resource Impact Evaluation. Prepared for the Cold Lake Band and the Indian and Inuit Affairs Program.

1980 Effects of Heavy Oil Sands Development on Native Indian Employment: Benefits, Burdens and Implications of Heavy Oil Sands Development for Native Indian Communities in Northern Alberta. Paper presented at the American Association for the Advancement of Science—Alaska Section, Anchorage, Alaska.

Kaberry, Phyllis M. 1939 Aboriginal Woman: Sacred and Profane. London: Routledge and Kegan Paul.

Keesing, Felix M. 1957 Social Anthropology and Industry: Some Explanatory Workpapers. Stanford, Calif.: Dept. of Anthropology, Stanford University.

1966 Cultural Anthropology. New York: Holt, Rinehart and Winston.

Kelly, Maria Patricia Fernandez 1981 The Sexual Division of Labor, Development and Women's Status. Current Anthropology 22:414–19.

Kemnitzer, L. S., and John Spier 1975 Class and Integration of Labor in the Railroad Operating Crafts: An Ethnographic Example. Paper given at the American Association for the Advancement of Science Symposium on the Mode of Production, New York.

Kendrew, W. G. and D. Kerr 1955 The Climate of British Columbia and the Yukon Territory. Ottawa: The Queen's Printer.

Kenyatta, Jomo 1938 Facing Mount Kenya. London: Oxford University Press.

King, P. H. M. 1947–1948 Task Perception and Inter-personal Relations in Industrial Training: The Development of a Training Program in the Hosiery Trade. Human Relations. 1:121–30, 373–412.

Klausner, Samuel, Edward Foulks and Mark Moore 1980 Social Change and the Alcohol Problem on the Alaska North Slope. Philadelphia: Center for Research on the Acts of Man.

Kleinfeld, Judith, Jack Kruse, and Robert Travis 1981 Different Paths of Inupiat Men and Women in the Wage Economy: The North Slope Experience. Fairbanks: Institute of Social and Economic Research.

Kluckhohn, Clyde 1962 Culture and Behavior. New York: Free Press.

Kluckhohn, Florence 1953 Dominant and Variant Value Orientation. In Personality in Nature, Society and Culture. Ed. by Clyde Kluckhohn, H. A. Murray and D. M. Schneider. New York: Knopf.

Kopczynska-Jaworska, B. 1963 La vie pastoral dans les Carpates. Études Rurales, École Pratique des Hautes Études, 6-me section: Sciences Économiques et Sociales. Paris. 9:80–89.

Kraft, Philip 1979 The Industrialization of Computer Programming: From Programming to 'Software Production.' In Case Studies on the Labor Process. Ed. by Andrew Zimbalist. New York: Monthly Review Press.

Kroeber, Alfred L. 1925 Handbook of the Indians of California. Bureau of American Ethnology. Bulletin No. 78. Washington, D. C.

1939 Cultural and Natural Areas of Native North America. Berkeley: University of California Publications in American Archaeology and Ethnology. Vol. 38.

1955 The Nature of the Land-Holding Group. Ethnohistory. 2:303–314.

Kroeber, Alfred L. and S. A. Barrett 1960 Fishing among the Indians of Northwestern California. Anthropological Records (Berkeley). 21(1).

Kruse, Jack 1982 Subsistence and the North Slope Inupiat Eskimo. An Analysis of the Effects of Energy Development. Fairbanks. Institute of Social and Economic Research.

Kruse, Jack, Judith Kleinfeld and Robert Travis 1981 Subsistence and the North Slope Inupiat Eskimo. An Analysis of the Effects of Energy Development. Fairbanks: Institute of Social and Economic Research.

1982 Energy Development on Alaska's North Slope: Effects on the Inupiat Population. Human Organization. 41(2):97–106.

Kruse, Jack, Judith Kleinfeld, Robert Travis and Linda Leask 1981 Energy Development and the North Slope Impact: A Quantitative Analysis of Social and Economic Change. Fairbanks: Institute of Social and Economic Research.

Kubler, George 1947 The Quechua in the Colonial World. In Handbook of South American Indians. Ed. Julian H. Steward, Smithsonian Institution, Bureau of American Ethnology, Bulletin 143, Washington, D.C. Vol. 2:331–410.

Kuper, Hilda 1963 The Swazi, A South African Kingdom. New York: Holt, Rinehart and Winston.

Kupfer, George and Charles W. Hobart 1978 Impact of Oil Exploration Work on an Inuit Community. Arctic Anthropology. 15:58–67.

Kusterer, Ken 1978 Know-How on the Job: The Important Working Knowledge of Unskilled Workers. Boulder, Colorado: Westview Press.

Laslett, Peter, Ed. 1972 Household and Family in Past Time. Cambridge: Cambridge University Press.

Lattimore, Owen 1962 Inner Asian Frontiers of China. Boston: Beacon.

Leacock, Eleanor 1969 The Montagnais-Naskapi Band. Contribution to Anthropology: Band Societies, Ed. D. Damas, Pp. 1–17. Ottawa: National Museums of Canada Bulletin 228.

1978 Women's Status in Egalitarian Society: Implications for Evolution. Current Anthropology. 19(2):247–55.

Lee, Richard B. 1968 What do Hunters do for a Living, or, How to Make Out on Scarce Resources. In Man the Hunter, Ed. Richard B. Lee and Irven DeVore. Chicago: Aldine.

1969 !Kung Bushman Subsistence: An Input-Output Analysis. In Environment and Cultural Behavior: Ecological Studies in Cultural Anthropology, Ed. A. P. Vayda. Garden City: Natural History Press. Pp. 47–79.

1972a The Intensification of Social Life Among the !Kung Bushmen. In Population Growth: Anthropological Perspectives. Ed. Brian Spooner. Cambridge, Mass.: M.I.T. Press. Pp. 343–350.

1972b The !Kung Bushmen of Botswana. In Hunters and Gatherers Today. Ed. M. G. Bichiere. New York: Holt, Rinehart and Winston. Pp. 327–67.

1973 Mongongo: The Ethnography of a Major Wild Food Resource. Ecology of Food and Nutrition. 1:1–15.

1976 !Kung Spatial Organization: An Ecological and Historical Perspective. In Kalahari Hunter-Gatherers: Studies of the !Kung San and their Neighbors. Ed. Richard B. Lee and Irven DeVore. Cambridge, Mass.: Harvard University Press. Pp. 73–97.

1980 The !Kung San. Cambridge: Cambridge University Press.

Lee, Richard B., and Irven DeVore 1968 Man The Hunter. Chicago: Aldine.

Lees, Susan, and D. Bates 1974 The Origins of Specialized Nomadic Pastoralism: A Systemic Model. American Antiquity. 39:187–93.

Leeds, Anthony 1965 Reindeer Herding and Chukchi Social Institutions. In Man, Culture and Animals: The Role of Animals in Human Ecological Adjustments. Ed. A. Leeds and A. P. Vayda. Pp. 87–128. American Association for the Advancement of Science Publication No. 78. Wasington, D. C.

1980 A Resolution on the Conception and Naming of the Society. The Society for Urban Anthropology Newsletter. Vol. 10:5–6.

LeGoff, Jacques 1980 Time, Work and Culture in the Middle Ages. Chicago: Univ. of Chicago Press.

Leon, Luis A. 1952 Historia y extinción del cocaismo en el Ecuador. America Indígena 12:7–32.

Lerner, D., and R. Robinson 1960 Swords into Plowshares, the Turkish Army as a Modernizing Force. World Politics 13:19–44.

Leroy, Oliver 1926 L'Activité économique primitive d'après M. Charles Gide Paris.

Lewis, I. M. 1961 A Pastoral Democracy. London: Oxford University Press.

Lewis, Oscar 1951 Life in a Mexican Village: Tepoztlan Restudied. Urbana: University of Illinois Press.

Lindner, Steffan B. 1970 The Harried Leisure Class. New York: Columbia University Press.

Little, Kenneth 1957 The Role of Voluntary Associations in West African Urbanization. American Anthropologist 59:579–94.

Litwak, Eugene 1960 Occupational Mobility and Extended Family Cohesion. American Sociological Review 25:9–21.

Loudon, J. B. 1979 Workers, Lords and Masters: The Organization of Labour on South African Farms. In Social Anthropology of Work. Ed. Sandra Wallman. Pp. 87–134. New York: Academic Press.

Lucas, R. Minetown, Milltown, Railtown. Toronto: University of Toronto Press.

McArthur, Norma 1963 Contemporary Polynesian Emigration from Samoa and the Cook Islands. Journal of the Polynesian Society 63:336–39.

Macarov, David 1980 Work and Welfare. Beverly Hills, Calif.: Sage.

McBeath, Gerald 1981 North Slope Borough Government and Policy Making. Fairbanks: Institute of Social and Economic Research.

McCracken, Robert D. 1968 Urban Migration and the Changing Structure of Navajo Social Relations. Ph.D. dissertation, University of Colorado.

MacNeish, Richard S. 1964 Ancient Mesoamerican Civilization. Science 143:531–33.

MacIlwraith, Thomas F. 1948 The Bella Coola Indians. Toronto: University of Toronto Press.

McSwain, Romola 1965 The Role of Wives in the Urban Adjustment of Navajo Migrant Families to Denver, Colorado. Master's thesis, University of Hawaii.

Malinowski, Bronislaw 1922 Argonauts of the Western Pacific. London: Routledge.

1925 Labour and Primitive Economics. Reprinted from Nature 26 (December 1925):12 London: Routledge.

1935 Coral Gardens and Their Magic. 2 Vols. London: Allen and Unwin.

1965 Soil-Tilling and Agricultural Rites in the Trobriand Islands. Bloomington: Indiana University Press.

Maquet, J. J. 1961 The Premise of Inequality in Rwanda. London: Oxford University Press.

Marc, Gabriel 1964 Comptes Économiques de la Polynesie Française 1960–1961–1962. Institut National de la Statistique et des Éstudes Économiques. Paris.

Marks, S. A. 1976 Large Mammals and a Brave People: Subsistence Hunters in Zambia. Seattle: University of Washington Press.

Marshall, John 1956 The Hunters (Film). Somerville, Mass.: Center for Documentary Anthropology.

Marshall, Leonore 1976 The !Kung of Nyae Nyae. Cambridge: Harvard Univesity Press.

Marx, Karl 1933 Capital. London: Everyman.

1971 The Grundrisse. ed. David McClelland. New York: Harper.

Mauss, Marcel 1967 The Gift. New York: Norton.

McArthur, M. 1960 Food Consumption and Dietary Levels of Groups of Aborigines Living on Naturally Occurring Foods. *In* Anthropology and Nutrition. Ed. C. Mountford. Pp. 90–135. Records of the Australian-American Scientific Expedition to Arnhem Land, vol 2. Melbourne: Melbourne University Press.

Mead, Margaret 1953 Cultural Patterns and Technical Change. New York: UNESCO.

Meggitt, M. J. 1962 Desert People: A Study of the Walbiri Aborigines of Central Australia. Sydney.

Mehta, S. D. 1954 Professor Morris on Textile Labour Supply. Indian Economic Journal 1(3):333–40.

Merton, Robert K. 1957 Social Structure and Anomie. *In* Social Theory and Social Structure. Pp. 131–94. Glencoe: Free Press.

Michener, Bryan P. 1965 The Development and Scoring of a Test of Need Achievement for Navajo Indians. Navajo Urban Relocation Research Report No. 6. Tucson: University of Arizona Press.

Mills, C. Wright 1956 White Collar. New York: Oxford University Press.

Minge-Kalman, W. 1977 On the Theory and Measurement of Domestic Labor Intensity. American Ethnologist 4:273–84.

1978a Household Economy during the Peasant-to-Worker Transition in the Swiss Alps. Ethnology 17:183–96.

1978b The Industrial Revolution and the European Family: The Institutionalization of "Childhood" as a Market for Family Labor. Comparative Studies in Society and History. Vol. 20:454–67.

Minge-Klevana, W. 1980 Does Labor Time Decrease with Industrialization? Current Anthropology 21:279–98.

Misra, P. K. 1975 The Gadulia Lohars—Nomadism and Economic Activities. *In* Pastoralists and Nomads in South Asia. Ed. Lawrence Saadia Leshnik and Gunther-Dietz Sontheimer. Wiesbaden: Otto Harrassowitz.

Moomaw, Ira W. 1946 Agriculture. *In* Indians of the High Andes. Ed. Stanley W. Rycroft. Pp. 157–216: New York: Committee on Cooperation in Latin America.

Moore, Wilbert E. 1951 Industrialization and Labor. Ithaca, N.Y.: Cornell University Press.

1963 Man, Time and Society, New York: Wiley

Moore, Wilbert E., and Arnold S. Feldman 1960 Labor Commitment and Social Change in Developing Areas. New York: Social Science Research Council.

Morant, G. M. 1948 Applied Physical Anthropology in Great Britain in Recent Years. American Journal of Physical Anthropology 6:329–39.

Morehouse, Thomas, Robert A. Childers, and Linda Leask 1978 Fish and Wildlife Protection in the Planning and Construction of the Trans-Alaska Oil Pipeline. Washington, D.C.: U.S. Fish and Wildlife Services OBS-78-70.

Morehouse, Thomas, and Linda Leask 1980 Alaska's North Slope Borough: Oil, Money and Eskimo Self-Government. Polar Record: 8:19–29.

Mowat, Farley 1959 The Desperate People. Toronto: Little, Brown.

Mumford, Lewis 1934 Technics and Civilization. New York: Harcourt, Brace.

Murdock, George P. 1937 Comparative Data on the Division of Labor by Sex. Social Forces 15:551–53.

1949 Social Structure. New York: Macmillan.

1960 Ethnographic Bibliography of North America. New Haven: Conn.: Human Relations Area Files Press.

1967 Ethnographic Atlas, A Summary. Ethnology 6:109–236.

Murdock, George P., and C. Provost 1973 Measurement of Cultural Complexity. Ethnology 12:379–92.

Murphy, R. F., and J. H. Steward 1956 Tappers and Trappers. Economic Development and Culture Change 4 (July):335–53.

Murra, John 1947 The Historic Tribes of Ecuador. *In* Handbook of South American Indians, ed. Julian H. Steward, vol. 2. Pp. 785–821. Smithsonian Institution, Bureau of American Ethnology, Bulletin 143. Washington, D.C.

Murray, Colin 1979 The Work of Men, Women and the Ancestors: Social Reproduction in the Periphery of Southern Africa. *In* Social Anthropology of Work, ed. Sandra Wallman. New York: Academic Press.

Musil, Alois 1928 The Manners and Customs of the Twala Bedouins. Oriental Explorations & Studies 6. N.Y.: Amer. Geographical Society.

Myers, C. A. 1958 Labor Problems in the Industrialization of India. Cambridge: Harvard University Press.

Nagy-Czirok L. 1959 Pasztorelet a Kiskunsagon (Pastoral Life in the Kiskunsag). Budapest.

Nash, June 1978 Field Notes, Research on the Impact of Industry on Community. Unpublished.

1979 We Eat the Mines and the Mines Eat Us: Dependency and Exploitation in Bolivian Tin Mines. New York: Columbia University Press.

1981 The Anthropology of Work. Anthropology of Work Newsletter, Vol. 2, No. 1. Pp. 2–7.

Naylor, Larry L. and Lawrence A. Gooding 1978 Alaska Native Hire on the Trans-Alaska Oil Pipeline Project. Alaska Review of Social and Economic Conditions 15 (1): Pp. 1–19

Neale, E. Vansittart 1845 Feasts and Fasts. London.

Neff, Walter S. 1977 Work and Human Behavior. Chicago: Aldine.

Netting, Robert 1969 Ecosystems in Process. In Contributions to Anthropology. Ed. D. Damas. Nat'l Museum of Canada Bull. 230:102–12. Ottawa.

1972 Of Men and Meadows: Strategies of Alpine Land Use. Anthropological Quarterly 45:132–44.

Ngata, A. T. 1892 Past and Future of the Maori. Weekly Press. (Christchurch) 33 (nos. 1448–50).

Niblack, Albert P. 1890 The Coast Indians of Southern Alaska and Northern British Columbia. Annual Report of the U.S. National Museum: 225–386.

Nichols, Peter C. 1979 Overview of Local Economic Development in the Athabasca Oil Sands Region since 1961. Edmonton: Alberta Oil Sands Environmental Research Program.

Nicolaisen, Johannes 1963 Ecology and Culture of the Pastoral Tuareg. Copenhagen: The National Museum of Copenhagen.

Nilsson, M. P. 1920 Primitive Time Reckoning. Lund: Gleerup.

Norbeck, Edward 1965 Changing Japan. New York: Holt, Rinehart and Winston.

Nordstom, Jean, James P. Boggs, Nancy Owens, and JoAnn Sootkis 1977 Social, Cultural and Economic Investigations: A Report to the Northern Cheyenne Tribes. The Northern Cheyenne Tribe and Energy Development in Southeastern Montana, Lame Deer, Montana: Northern Cheyenne Research Project.

Novak, V. 1960 Alpine Herding in Slovenia. Muveltseg Hagyomany (Debrecen) 1–2:97–110.

Oakley, Kenneth 1972 Skill as a Human Possession. In Human Evolution, edited by S. A. Washburn and P. Dolhinow, Chicago: University of Chicago Press.

OED 1971 The Compact Edition of the Oxford English Dictionary, vol. 2. New York: Oxford University Press.

Organization for Economic and Cooperative Development 1977 The Treatment of Family Units in OECD Member Countries under Tax and Transfer Systems. Washington, D.C.: OECD Publication Center.

Orlove, Benjamin 1975 Relations of Production in Industrial Capitalism: A Mine in Central Peru. Paper read at the Symposium on Modes of Production, American Association for the Advancement of Science, New York.

O'Toole, James, editor. 1974 Work and the Quality of Life: Resource Papers for Work in America. Cambridge, Mass.: MIT Press.

O'Toole, James, Elizabeth Hansot, William Herman, Neal Herrick, Elliot Liebow, Bruce Lusignan, Harold Richman, Harold Sheppard, Ben Stephansky, James Wright 1973 Work in America. Cambridge, Mass.: MIT Press.

Owen, R.C., J.J.F. Deetz and A.D. Fisher 1967 The North American Indians. New York: The Macmillan Company.

Owens, Nancy J. 1978 Can Tribes Control Energy Development? *In* Native American and Energy Development. Ed. Joseph G. Jorgensen, Richard D. Clemmer, Ronald L. Little, Nancy J. Owens, Lynn A. Robbins Pp. 49–62. Cambridge, Mass.: Anthropology Resource Center.

1979 The Effects of Reservation Bordertowns and Energy Exploitation on American Indian Economic Development. Research in Economic Anthropology 2:303–37.

Paine, R., 1971a Patrons and Brokers in the East Arctic. St. John's Institute of Social and Economic Research. St. Johns: Memorial University of Newfoundland.

1971b Animals as Capital, Comparisons Among Northern Nomadic Herders and Hunters. Anthropological Quarterly 44(3):157–71.

Parker, Seymour 1964 Ethnic Identity and Acculturation in Two Eskimo Villages. American Anthropologist 66:325–40.

Parkes, Don 1980 Comment on Minge-Klevana's Article. Current Anthropology 21:292–93.

Parkin, David 1979 The Categorization of Work: Cases from Coastal Kenya. *In* Social Anthropology of Work. Ed. S. Wallman. Pp. 317–36. New York: Academic Press.

Parsons, Elsie Clews 1945 Peguche, Canton of Otavalo, Province of Imbabura, Ecuador: A Study of Andean Indians. Chicago: University of Chicago Press.

Patterson, Thomas C. 1971 The Emergence of Food Production in Central Peru. *In* Prehistoric Agriculture. Ed. S. Stuever. Garden City, N.Y.: Natural History Press.

Peacock, James L., and Thomas A. Kirsch 1970 The Human Direction, An Evolutionary Approach to Social and Cultural Anthropology. New York: Appleton-Century-Crofts.

Pehrson, Robert N. 1966 The Social Organization of the Marri Baluch. Viking Fund Publ. in Anthropology 43. Ed. F. Barth. New York: Wenner-Gren.

Pellow, Deborah 1978 Work and Autonomy: Women in Accra. American Ethnologist 5:771–85.

Piddocke, Stuart 1965 The Potlatch System of the Southern Kwakiutl. Southwestern Journal of Anthropology. 21:244–64.

Pollock, M. A., ed. 1926 Working Days. London.

Polock, J. S. 1840 Manners and Customs of the New Zealanders. 2 Vols. London.

Pospisil, Leopold 1963 Kapauku Papuan Economy. Yale University Publications in Anthropology, no. 67. New Haven: Dept. of Anthropology, Yale University.

Prattis, Ian 1979 The Survival of Communities: A Theoretical Perspective. Current Anthropology 20:361–75.

Price, John A. 1975 U. S. and Canadian Indian Urban Ethnic Institutions. Urban Anthropology 4:35–52.

Provinse, John H. 1965 Letter to the Editor. Human Organization 24:185–87.

Psacharopoulos, G. 1973 Returns to Education: An International Comparison. San Francisco: Jossey-Bass.

Radcliffe-Brown, A. R. 1930 The Social Organization of Australian Tribes. Oceania 1:34–63.

1933 The Andaman Islanders. Cambridge: Cambridge University Press.

Rappaport, Roy A. 1968 Pigs for the Ancestors: Ritual in the Ecology of a New Guinea People. New Haven: Yale University Press.

Rasmussen, Knud 1929 The Intellectual Culture of the Iglulik Eskimos. Report of the 5th Thule Expedition, 1921–24, vol. 7, no. 1. Trans. W. Worster. Copenhagen: Gyldendal.

Ray, Verne 1938 Lower Chinook Ethnographic Notes. Univ. of Washington Pub. in Anthropology. 7(2):29–165. Seattle.

Redfield, Robert 1960 Peasant Society and Culture. Chicago: University of Chicago Press.

Reiter, R. 1975 Toward an Anthropology of Women. New York: Monthly Review Press.

Rendon, Gabino, Jr. 1968 Prediction of Adjustment Outcomes of Rural Migrants to the City. Ph.D. dissertation, University of Colorado.

Richards, A. I. 1932 Hunger and Work in Savage Society. London: Routledge.

1939 Land, Labor and Diet in Northern Rhodesia. Oxford: Oxford University Press.

Richards, Paul 1973 The Tropical Rain Forest. Scientific American. 229:58–68.

Richardson, F. L. W., Jr. 1955 Anthropology and Human Relations in Business and Industry. In Yearbook of Anthropology. Ed. W. L. Thomas, Jr. Pp. 397–419. New York: Wenner-Gren Foundation.

1979 Social Interaction and Industrial Productivity. In The Uses of Anthropology. Ed. Walter Goldschmidt. Pp. 79–99. Special Publication of the American Anthropological Association no. 11. Wash., D.C.: American Anthro. Assn.

Richardson, F. L. W., Jr., and Charles R. Walker 1948 Human Relations in an Expanding Company: A Study of the Manufacturing Departments in the Endicott Plant of IBM Corp. New Haven: Labor and Management Center, Yale University.

Rivera, Trinita 1949 Diet of a food-gathering people. In Indians of the Urban Northwest. Ed. Marian Smith. British Columbia Contributions to Anthropology 36. Vancouver.

Rivet, Paul 1903 Étude sur les indiens de la région de Riobamba. Journal de la Société des Américanistes de Paris I:58–80.

Rivière, P. 1972 The Forgotten Frontier: Ranchers of Northern Brazil. New York: Holt, Rinehart and Winston.

Robbins, Louise M. 1976 The Nature of "Applied" Physical Anthropology. In Do Applied Anthropologists Apply Anthropology? Ed. Michael V. Agrosino, Pp. 17–22. Southern Anthropological Society Proceedings, no. 10. Athens: University of Georgia Press.

Robbins, Lynn A. 1978 Energy Developments and the Navajo Nation. In Native Americans and Energy Development. Eds. Joseph G. Jorgensen, Richard D. Clemmer, Ronald L. Little, Nancy J. Owens, Lynn A. Robbins. Pp. 35–48. Cambridge, Mass.: Anthropology Resource Center.

Roberts, Lance 1977 Wage Employment and Its Consequences in Two Eastern Arctic Communities. Ph.D. diss., University of Alberta.

Robinson, R. 1963 The First Turkish Republic: A Case Study in National Development. Cambridge: Harvard University Press.

Rodríquez Sandoval, Leonidas 1949 Vida económico-social del indio libre de la sierra ecuatoriana. Universidad Católica de America, Estudios en Ciencias Sociales no. 32. Washington, D. C.: Catholic University of America Press.

Rollins, P. A. 1936. The Cowboy. New York: C. Scribner's Sons.

Rounsefell, George A. and George B. Kelez 1938 The Salmon Fisheries of Swiftsure Bank, Puget Sound, and Fraser river. Bureau of Fisheries Bulletin No. 27. Washington, D.C.

Rubio Orbe, Gonzalo 1953 Aculturaciones de indígenas de los Andes. America Indigena 13:187–222.

Ruffing, Lorraine 1978 Navajo Mineral Development. The Indian Historian 11(2):23–41.

Saenz, Moises 1933 Sobre el indio ecuatoriano y su incorporación al medio nacional. Publicaciones de la Secretaria de Educación Publica. Mexico City.

Sahlins, Marshall 1965 The Sociology of Primitive Exchange, Association of Social Anthropologist Monograph no. 1. Pp. 139–236. London: Tavistock.

1970 Production, Distribution and Power in a Primitive Society. *In* Cultures of the Pacific. Ed. Thomas G. Harding and Ben J. Wallace. Pp. 78–84. New York: Free Press.

1972 Stone Age Economics. Chicago: Aldine-Atherton.

Salz, Beate R. 1955 The Human Element in Industrialization. American Anthropological Association Memoir no. 85. vol. 57, no. 6, part 2, December, Pp. 94–114. Washington, D.C.: American Anthropological Association

Salzman, Philip, Ed. 1971 Comparative Studies of Nomadism and Pastoralism. Anthro. Quart. 44(3):104–210.

Sande, Theodore Anton 1976 Industrial Archaeology: A New Look at the American Heritage. Brattleboro, Vt.: Stephen Greene Press.

Santiana, Antonio 1949 Los Indio Mojanda: etnografia y folklore. Filosofia y Letras Quito 12(4–5):238–74.

Saraydar, S. and I. Shimada 1971 A Quantitative Comparison of Efficiency Between a Stone Axe and a Steel Axe, American Antiquity 36:216–17.

Schuyler, Robert L. 1974 Review of Industrial Archaeology in Britain by R. A. Buchanan. Historical Archaeology 8:115–16.

Searle-Chatterjee, Mary 1979 The Polluted Identity of Work: A Study of Benares Sweepers. In Social Anthropology of Work. Ed. Sandra Wallman. Pp. 269–86. New York: Academic Press.

Serrano Moscoso, Eduardo 1946 A State of the Laws of Ecuador in Matters Affecting Business in Its Various Aspects and Activities. Washington, D. C.: Inter-American Development Commission.

Service, E. R. 1962 Primitive Social Organization: An Evolutionary Perspective. New York: Random House.

1966 The Hunters. Englewood Cliffs, N.J.: Prentice-Hall.

Shand, A. 1893 Moriori Grinding Song. Journal of Polynesian Society 1:82–83.

Shortland, E. 1856 Tradition and Superstitions of the New Zealanders. London.

Silver, Harry R. 1981 Carving up the Profits: Apprenticeship and Structural Flexibility in a Contemporary African Craft Market. American Ethnologist 8(1):41–52.

Simoons, Frederick J. 1979 Questions in the Sacred-Cow Controversy. Current Anthropology 20:467–94.

Slocum, Sally 1975 Woman the Gatherer. *In* Toward an Anthropology of Women. Ed. R. Reiter. New York: Monthly Review Press.

Smith, Adam 1937 An Inquiry into the Causes of the Wealth of Nations. New York: Collier.

Smith, M. Estellie 1977 Those Who Live from the Sea: A Study in Maritime Anthropology. New York: West.

Smith, S. P. 1899 The Tohunga Maori: A Sketch. Transaction and Proceedings of the New Zealand Institute 253–70.

Snyder, Peter Z. 1968 Social Assimilation and Adjustment of Navajo Migrants to Denver. Ph.D. diss., University of Colorado.

Sonnenfeld, Joseph 1957 Changes in Subsistence among the Barrow Eskimo. Ph.D. diss., Johns Hopkins University.

Sorenson, Richard 1972 Socio-Ecological Change Among the Fore of New Guinea. Current Anthropology. 13:349–83.

Sorenson, Richard and P. E. Kenmore 1974 Proto-Agricultural Movement in Eastern Highlands of New Guinea. Current Anthropology 15:67–72.

Spencer, Paul 1965 The Samburu, A Study of Geontocracy in a Nomadic Tribe. Berkeley and Los Angeles: University of California Press.

Stack, J. W. 1906 Kaipohia. Christchurch: Whitcombe and Tombs.

Staley, Eugene 1952 Creating an Industrial Civilization: A Report on the Corning Conference. New York: Harper.

Statistiques de la Suisse 1974 Berne.

Stavenhagen, R. 1975 Social Classes in Agrarian Societies. New York: Anchor.

Stevenson, D. S. 1968 Problems of Eskimo Relocation for Industrial Employment. Ottawa: Northern Science Research Group, Department of Indian Affairs and Northern Development, Government of Canada.

Steward, Julian H. 1950 Area Research: Theory and Practice. Social Science Research Council Bulletin, no. 63. New York.

1955 Theory of Culture Change. Urbana: University of Illinois Press.

1967 The Great Basin Shoshonean Indians. In The North American Indians, A Sourcebook. Ed. Roger C. Owen, James J. F. Deetz, and Anthony D. Fisher. Pp. 241–58. New York: Macmillan.

1968 Causal Factors and Processes in the Evolution of Pre-Farming Societies. In Man the Hunter. Ed. Richard B. Lee and Irven DeVore. Chicago: Aldine.

Stewart, Omer C. 1964 Questions Regarding American Criminality. Human Organization 23:61–66.

Strathern, Andrew 1982 The Division of Labor and Processes of Social Change in Mount Hagen. American Ethnologist 9:307–19.

Strickon, A. 1965 The Euro-American Ranching Complex. In Man, Culture and Animals: The Role of Animals in Human Ecological Adjustments. Ed. A. Leeds and A. P. Vayda. Pp. 229–258. American Association for the Advancement of Science Publication no. 78. Washington, D.C.

Suttles, Wayne 1960 Affinal ties, subsistence and prestige among the Coast Salish. American Anthropologist, 62:296–305.

1962 Variation in habitat and culture in the northwest coast. Akten des 34 Internationalen Amerikanistenkongresses, Wein, 1960:522–37.

Suttles, Wayne 1968 Coping with Abundance. In Man the Hunter. Ed. Richard B. Lee and Irven DeVore. Pp. 56–68. Chicago: Aldine.

Swan, James G. 1870 The Indians of Cape Flattery. Smithsonian Contributions to Knowledge No. 16. Washington, D.C.

Sweet, L. E. 1965 Camel Pastoralism in North Arabia and the Minimal Camping Unit. In Man, Culture and Animals. The Role of Animals in Human Ecological Adjustments. Ed. A. Leeds and A. P. Vayda. Pp. 129–52. American Association for the Advancement of Science Publication no. 78. Washington, D. C.

Swett, Daniel H. 1963 Characteristics of the Male Indian Arrest Population in San Francisco. Paper presented at the annual meeting of the Southwestern Anthropological Association: University of California, Riverside.

Szabadfalvi, J. 1970 Extensive Animals Husbandry in Hungary. Debrecen.

Szilágyi, M. 1968 Sheep Farming in Nagykunsag at the End of the Eighteenth Century. (Budapest) Ethnographia 79:350–65.

Tálasi, I. 1936 Herding in the Kiskunsag. Budapest.

Taylor, Herbert C. Aboriginal Populations of the lower northwest coast. Pacific Northwest Quarterly, 54:158–65.

Taylor, T. John 1958 Archaeology of the Coal Trade. Proceedings Archaeological Institute of Great Britain and Ireland. Newcastle Upon Tyne: Graham.

Tenenti, A. 1957 Il senso della morte e l'amore dellas vite nel rinascimento. Milan.

Testart, Alain 1982 The Significance of Food Storage among Hunter-Gathers. Current Anthropology 23:523–37.

Thomas, R. Brooke 1975 The Ecology of Work. *In* Physiological Anthropology. Ed. A. Damon. Pp. 59–79. New York: Oxford University Press.

Thompson, E. P. 1964 Review of Man, Time and Society by W. E. Moore Peace News, 26 June 1964.

1967 Time, Work-Discipline and Industrial Capitalism. Past and Present, No. 38: 56–97.

1978 The Poverty of Theory. New York: Monthly Review Press.

Thomson, A. S. 1859 Story of New Zealand. 2 Vols. London.

Thorns, D. C. 1971 Work and Its Definitions. The Sociological Review, new series 19:543–55.

Tilgher, Adriano 1931 Work: What It Has Meant to Men through the Ages. Trans. D. C. Fisher. London: Harrap.

Törö, L. 1968a Division of Labor and Pastoral Organization in Cattle Herding Communities of Hortobagy. Ethnographia (Budapest) 29:396–406.

1968b Order of Grazing in the Hortobagy. Müveltség és Hagyomány: (Debrecen) 10:265–278.

Travis, Robert 1981 Myths about Problem Drinking and Social Problems in Barrow, Alaska. Fairbanks: Institute of Social and Economic Research.

Treide, Dietrich 1965 Die Organisierung des indianischen Lachsfangs in westlichen Nordamerika. Veröffentlichungen des Museums für Völkerkunde (Leipzig), 14.

Truc, Pierre-Jean 1959 Le Taravana. Journal de la Société des Océanistes 15:227–36.

Turnbull, Colin 1968 Comments on Primate Behavior and the Evolution of Aggression. *In* Man the Hunter, Ed. Richard B. Lee and Irven Devore. Chicago: Aldine.

Udy, Stanley H., Jr. 1959 Organization of Work. New Haven: HRAF Press.

1970 Work in Traditional and Modern Society. Englewood Cliffs, N.J.: Prentice-Hall.

Underhill, Ruth M. 1948 Ceremonial Patterns in the Greater Southwest. American Ethnological Society, Monograph 12. New York.

Useem, John, Gordon Macgregor, and Ruth Hill Useem 1943 Wartime Employment and Cultural Adjustment of the Rosebud Sioux. Applied Anthropology 2(2):1–9.

Usher, Peter 1971 The Community. The Bankslanders: Economy and Ecology of a Frontier Trapping Community, volume 3. Ottawa: Northern Science Research Group, Department of Indian Affairs and Northern Development, Government of Canada.

Von Stone, James W. 1962 Point Hope: An Eskimo Village in Transition. Seattle: University of Washington Press.

Vayda, Andrew P. 1961 A Re-examination of Northwest Coast Economic Systems. New York Academy of Sciences Series 2. 23:618–24.

Vincze, L. 1973 Marginal Pastoralims. Paper presented at the annual meeting of the Central States Anthropological Society, St. Louis.

1974 Organization of Work in Herding Teams of the Great Hungarian Plain. Ethnology, Vol. 13, No. 2, Pp. 159–69.

Vogel, Robert M. 1969 On the Real Meaning of Industrial Archaeology. Historical Archaeology 3:87–94.

Vries, E. de, and J. M. Echavarria, eds. 1963 Social Aspects of Economic Development in Latin America. Paris: UNESCO.

Waddell, Jack O. 1969 Papago Indians at Work. Anthropological Papers of the University of Arizona, no. 12. Pp. 86–98. Tucson: University of Arizona Press.

Wadel, Cato 1979 The Hidden Work of Everyday Life. In Social Anthropology of Work. Ed. Sandra Wallman. Pp. 365–84. New York: Academic Press.

Walker, C., and R. Guest 1952 The Man on the Assembly Line. Cambridge: Harvard University Press

Wallace, A. 1951 Some Psychological Determinants of Culture Change in an Iroquoian Community. Bureau of American Ethnology, bull. no. 149. Pp. 55–76. Washington, D.C.

Ward, F. E. 1958 The Cowboy at Work. New York: Hasting House.

Warner, W. Lloyd, and J. O. Low 1947 The Social System of the Modern Factory. New Haven: Yale University Press.

Washburn, Sherwood L. 1975 Tools and Human Evolution. In Scientific Technology and Social Change, Readings from Scientific American. Pp. 11–23. San Francisco: W. H. Freeman.

Watkins, Mel, ed. 1977 Dene Nation: The Colony Within. Toronto: University of Toronto Press.

Webb, E. J., D. T. Campbell, R. D. Schwartz, and L. Sechrest 1966 Unobtrusive Measures: Nonrestrictive Research in the Social Sciences. Chicago: Rand McNally.

Weinberg, D. 1965 Models of Southern Kwakiutl Social Organization: General Systems. Yearbook of Society for General Systems Research 10:169–81.

1975 Peasant Wisdom: Cultural Adaptation in a Swiss Village. Berkeley and Los Angeles: University of California Press.

Weiss, R. S., and R. L. Kahn 1960 Definitions of Work and Occupations. Social Problems 18: 142–51.

Weppner, Robert S. 1968 The Economic Absorption of Navajo Indian Migrants to Denver, Colorado. Ph.D. diss. University of Colorado.

West, James 1945 Plainville, U.S.A. New York: Coumbia University Press.

White, B. 1976 Production and Reproduction in a Javanese Village. Ph.D. diss. Columbia University.

White, John 1887–90 Ancient History of the Maori. 6 vols. Wellington.

White, Leslie 1959 The Evolution of Culture. New York: McGraw-Hill.

Whiting, B., and J. Whiting 1974 Children of Six Cultures. Cambridge: Harvard University Press.

Whittacker, James O. 1962 Alcohol and the Standing Rock Sioux Tribe: The Pattern of Drinking. Quarterly Journal of Studies on Alcohol 23:468–79.

Whorf, Benjamin L. 1941 The Relation of Habitual Thought and Behavior to Language. In Language, Culture and Personality: Essays in Memory of Edward Sapir. Eds. Leslie Spier, Irving Hallowell, and Russell Newman. Pp. 75–93. Menasha, Wisconsin. University of Wisconsin Press.

Wiegandt, E. 1975 The Politics of Control: Power and Wealth in a Swiss Alpine Village. Paper presented at Symposium on the Comparative Study of Contemporary Switzerland, University of Geneva.

Williams, B. J. 1968 The Birhor of India and Some Comments on Band Organization. In Man the Hunter. Ed. Richard B. Lee and Irven DeVore. Chicago: Aldine.

Williams, H. W. 1917 Maori Dictionary. 5th Ed. Wellington: M. F. Marks.

Williams, W. L. 1913 Kumara Lore. Journal of the Polynesian Society 22: 36–41.

Williamson, Robert G. 1974 Eskimos Underground: Socio-Cultural Change in the Canadian Central Arctic. Uppsala: Institutionen for Allman och Jamforande Etnograft vid Uppsala Universited.

Williamson, Robert G., and Terrence W. Foster n.d. Eskimo Relocation in Canada. Ottawa: Social Research Division, Department of Indian and Northern Affairs. Government of Canada.

Willner, Ann Ruth 1961 Problems of Management and Authority in a Transitional Society: A Case Study of a Javanese Factory. Human Organization 21(1)133–41.

Wilson, J. A. 1894 Sketches of Ancient Maori Life and History. Auckland.

Wittfogel, Karl A. 1957 Oriental Despotism: A Comparative Study of Total Power. New Haven: Yale University Press.

Wolf, Eric 1966 Peasants. Englewood Cliffs, N. J.: Prentice-Hall.

Wolfbein, Seymour 1971 Work in American Society. Glenville, Ill.: Scott, Foresman.

Woodburn, J. 1964 The Social Organization of the Hadza, Unpublished Ph.D. dissertation, Cambridge University.

Wordsworth, William 1805 The Prelude. London.

Wright, T. 1868 The Great Unwashed. London.

Wynn, Margaret 1972 Family Policy: A Study of the Economic Cost of Rearing Children and Their Social and Political Consequences. Harmondsworth. Middlesex, England: Penguin.

Yinger, J. Milton Toward a Field Theory of Behavior: Personality and Social Structure. New York: McGraw-Hill.

Young, R.B. 1943 British Columbia Pilot, II: Ottawa: Queen's Printer.

Zambrano, Miguel Angel 1951 Las Comunidades indígenas en el Acuador y su posible estructuración cooperatisvista. Primer Seminario Regional de Asuntos Sociales, Mayo 27 a 10 de Junio de 1950. Pp. 175–202. Quito: Ministerio de Previsión Social y Trabajo.

Ziegler, Suzanne 1967 An Urban Dilemma: The Case of Tyler Begay. Unpublished manuscript.

Zimbalist, Andrew 1979 Technology and the Labor Process in the Printing Industry. *In* Case Studies on the Labor Process. Ed. Andrew Zimbalist. New York: Monthly Review Press.

Index

Nuer, 125; Division of work, The
Machiguenga, 225–26
Shamans: And the antelope drive, The
Cheyennes, 90–92; And work, 5–6
Sharing among hunters and gatherers,
67
Shifts in roles and expectations, 29–30
Shortages and slavery, The Tolowa, 111
Shoshonean rabbit drives, 8
Significance of data, Navajo Indians in
Denver, 279
Silent Trade, 12
Simple and complex work, The Maori,
187–88
Size of farm, Le Levron, Switzerland,
358
Skilled hunters and hangers-on, 113
Slash-and-burn cultivation, 157
Slaves, Northwest American Coast
Indians, 107–09
Small game hunting, The !Kung San,
78–79
Smith, Estellie, definition of subsistence
work, 20
Snares, description of, The !Kung San,
72
Snaring, The !Kung San, 71–72
Social: Adjustment, Inuit and Indian
workers, 250–53; Control, among
pastoralists, 140–41; Interaction and
time reckoning, 200–01; Life and job
demands, Papagos, 308; Organization
and surplus food, Northwest
American Coast, 109; Organization,
Alaska's North Slope, 320–21;
Problems, Alaska's North Slope,
329–31; Science and the study of
work, 40; Science on alienation in the
workplace, 55
Socialization process: Papagos on farms,
307; Pastoralists, 138
Sodalities, Ajo Indian village, 291
Sources of data, Canadian Indigenes
study, 247
Spain and the transition to modernity,
43–44
Spatial distribution of Papago kinship
units, 297
Special treatment for Papagos, Ajo, 293
Specialization: And the growth of
markets, 22–23; Limits in non-market
societies, 21–23; Of ethnic groups in
the ancient world, 47–48
Staffing organizations, new nations,
336–37
Stalking and killing, The !Kung San,
81–83

Standards of workmanship, Javanese
factory and village, 341
Starvation: Among the Kwakiutl, 98;
And sorcery, 98
Status: And work, Javanese villages,
345; Of women, horticultural
societies, 158
Steady farm jobs and Papago village
activities, 300
Steenbok snaring, The !Kung San, 72
Stimuli in Maori communal work,
192–96
Stone maul, Cheyenne women's tool,
87
Storage containers among Northwest
Coast Indians, 104
Store-bought food, Canadian Northwest,
258
Store operators, relations with Papagos,
310
Stratification: Among Papagos, Ajo
village, 291; And the division of
mental and manual work, 46–47
Strengths of value systems, 232–33
Stress among families, Northwest
Canada, 252–53
Structural determinants, Hungarian
pastoralists, 151–53
Study: Of time regimes, 205–06; Of
work by social scientists, 39–40; Of
work during 1930–1960 in North
America, 56
Subdivision of labor, The Mayo, 178
Subjugation of agriculturalists by
pastoralists, 117
Subsistence: Activities, North Slope
natives, 326–29; And food storage,
20; And social obligations, 21; Work,
characteristics, 20; Work, Tenía, 169
Supervision: And discipline, Javanese
factory, 337–38; New work role in
Java, 338–40
Surplus food converted into prestige,
Salish, 109
Survey questionnaires, North Slope
study, 319–20
Suttles, Wayne: Coping with abundance,
110–11; Indians of the Northwest
American Coast, 95–113; Northwest
American coast study data, 101–102
Swidden method of clearing fields, 157
Swiss Alps, nuclear family as a unit of
study, 357–58
Symbiotic relationship with animals,
pastoralists, 117–18
Számadó: Bojtar work group, 153–54;
Hungarian herding leaders, 146–48

Related Titles from SUNY Press

FOR WE ARE SOLD, I AND MY PEOPLE: Women and Industry in Mexico's Frontier. María Patricia Fernández-Kelly.

WOMEN, MEN, AND THE INTERNATIONAL DIVISION OF LABOR. June Nash and María Patricia Fernández-Kelly, editors.

THE REDIVISION OF LABOR: Women and Economic Choice in Four Guatemala Communities. Laurel H. Bossen.

WORK AND LIFECOURSE IN JAPAN. David W. Plath, editor.

CLASSIFICATION IN SOCIAL RESEARCH. Ramakrishna Mukherjee.

METHODOLOGY FOR THE HUMAN SCIENCES: Systems of Inquiry. Donald Polkinghorne.

UNDERSTANDING HUMAN ACTION: Social Explanation of the Vision of Social Science. Michael A. Simon.